Education
of Learners
with Severe Handicaps

Education
of Learners
with Severe Handicaps
Exemplary Service Strategies

Edited by

Robert H. Horner, Ph.D.
Division of Special Education and Rehabilitation
University of Oregon

Luanna H. Meyer, Ph.D.
Division of Special Education and Rehabilitation
Syracuse University

and

H.D. Bud Fredericks, Ph.D.
Research Professor
Teaching Research Division
Oregon State System of Higher Education

·P·A·U·L·H·
BROOKES
PUBLISHING CO.

Baltimore • London

Paul H. Brookes Publishing Co.
Post Office Box 10624
Baltimore, MD 21285-0624

Typeset by Brushwood Graphics Studio, Baltimore, Maryland.
Manufactured in the United States of America by
The Maple Press Company, York, Pennsylvania.

Library of Congress Cataloging in Publication Data
Main entry under title:

Education of learners with severe handicaps.

  Includes bibliographies and index.
  1. Handicapped children—Education—United States—Addresses,
essays, lectures. 2. Handicapped—Education—United States—
Addresses, essays, lectures. 3. Community and school—United
States—Addresses, essays, lectures. I. Horner, Robert H. II. Meyer,
Luanna H. III. Fredericks, H. D. Bud.
LC4031.E39   1986   371.9′0973   85-6710
ISBN 0-933716-51-6

Contents

Contributors

Jacki Anderson, Ph.D.
Department of Special Education
612 Font Boulevard
San Francisco State University
San Francisco, CA 94132

William Ashe, M.Ed.
Director, Adult Development Disabilities
Washington County Mental Health
  Services
326 North Main Street
Barre, VT 05641

Patricia Dobbe Beebe, M.S.
Program Consultant
Vocational Education Alternatives
445 Lakeview Boulevard
Albert Lea, MN 56007

G. Thomas Bellamy, Ph.D.
Division of Special Education and
  Rehabilitation
Room 135, College of Education
University of Oregon
Eugene, OR 97403

Holly A. Benson, M.Ed.
Department of Special Education
Bureau of Child Research
The University of Kansas
Lawrence, KS 66045

Kathy Doering, B.A.
Department of Special Education
612 Font Boulevard
San Francisco State University
San Francisco, CA 94132

Anne M. Donnellan, Ph.D.
Wisconsin Center for Educational
  Research
1025 West Johnson, #570
Madison, WI 53706

Ian M. Evans, Ph.D.
Psychology Department
SUNY-Binghamton
Binghamton, NY 13901

H.D. Bud Fredericks, Ph.D.
Research Professor
Teaching Research Division
Oregon State System of Higher Education
345 North Monmouth Avenue
Monmouth, OR 97361

Susan G. Friedman, Ph.D.
Department of Special Education
University of Colorado at Boulder
Boulder, CO 80309

Robert Gaylord-Ross, Ph.D.
Department of Special Education
1600 Holloway Avenue
San Francisco State University
San Francisco, CA 94132

Kathy Gee, M.A.
Department of Special Education
612 Font Boulevard
San Francisco State University
San Francisco, CA 94132

Lori Goetz, Ph.D.
Department of Special Education
612 Font Boulevard
San Francisco State University
San Francisco, CA 94132

Doug Guess, Ed.D.
Special Education
East Haworth Hall
University of Kansas
Lawrence, KS 66045

Ann Halvorsen, Ed.D.
California Research Institute
612 Font Boulevard
San Francisco State University
San Francisco, CA 94132

Edwin Helmstetter, Ph.D.
Special Education
377 E. Haworth Hall
University of Kansas
Lawrence, KS 66045

Alan M. Hofmeister, Ph.D.
Developmental Center for Handicapped
  Persons, UMC–68
Utah State University
Logan, UT 84322

Robert H. Horner, Ph.D.
Division of Special Education and
  Rehabilitation
Room 135, College of Education
University of Oregon
Eugene, OR 97403

Pam Hunt, M.A.
Department of Special Education
1600 Holloway Avenue
San Francisco State University
San Francisco, CA 94132

Orv C. Karan, Ph.D.
Director of Training and Clinical Services
Research and Training Center
Waisman Center on Mental Retardation
  and Human Development
1500 Highland Avenue
Madison, WI 53705-2280

William J. Keogh, Ph.D.
Center for Developmental Disabilities
College of Education and Social Services
University of Vermont
489C Waterman Building
Burlington, VT 05405

John J. McDonnell, Ph.D.
Department of Special Education
Room 215, Milton Bennion Hall
University of Utah
Salt Lake City, UT 84112

Luanna H. Meyer, Ph.D.
Division of Special Education and
  Rehabilitation
805 South Crouse Avenue
Syracuse University
Syracuse, NY 13210

Richard S. Neel, Ph.D.
Child Development and Mental
  Retardation Center
Experimental Education Unit, WJ-10
University of Washington
Seattle, WA 98193

Samuel L. Odom, Ph.D.
Developmental Training Center
Indiana University
2853 East 10th Street
Bloomington, IN 47405

Joe Reichle, Ph.D.
Department of Communication
  Disorders
University of Minnesota
115 Shevlin Hall
164 Pillsbury Drive, S.E.
Minneapolis, MN 55455

Wayne Sailor, Ph.D.
Department of Special Education
612 Font Boulevard
San Francisco State University
San Francisco, CA 94132

Keith Storey, Ph.D.
Department of Special Education
1600 Holloway Avenue
San Francisco State University
San Francisco, CA 94132

Phillip S. Strain, Ph.D.
Early Childhood Research Institute
Western Psychiatric Institute and Clinic
3811 O'Hara Street
Pittsburgh, PA 15213

Kathleen Stremel-Campbell
Teaching Research Division
Todd Hall
345 Monmouth Avenue North
Western Oregon State College
Monmouth, OR 97361

Ann P. Turnbull, Ed.D.
Department of Special Education
Bureau of Child Research
The University of Kansas
Lawrence, KS 66045

R. Timm Vogelsberg, Ph.D.
Center for Developmental Disabilities
499C Waterman
University of Vermont
Burlington, VT 05405

Wes Williams, Ph.D.
Center for Developmental Disabilities
499C Waterman
University of Vermont
Burlington, VT 05405

Foreword: Then and Now

Until recently, large numbers of people with severe intellectual disabilities did not exist in society. In fact, most of these individuals died before the age of 10 or soon thereafter. After World War II, several phenomena seem noteworthy. Specifically, there were comprehensive and significant advances in the sciences and technologies devoted to preserving and maintaining life, dramatic increases in birth rates and concomitant decreases in infant mortality rates resulted in substantial population increases, and America became a middle-class society of emerging affluence. These phenomena resulted in dramatic increases both in the number of severely intellectually disabled people born and in their life expectancies. Thus, for the first time, large numbers of people in all income strata were confronted with arranging for services for their children with severe disabilities throughout their ever-extending lives.

In examining services offered over the past four decades, four salient trends are particularly relevant.

First, institutions for retarded individuals proliferated. Indeed, at one point, almost 300,000 American citizens were confined to such facilities. After allowing reasonable chance for success, it soon became apparent that institutional models and the attitudes and values upon which they were based were inherently unacceptable. Thus, institutions are being depopulated and very soon will be reduced to a historical footnote. Why? Because it is now known that those individuals who were formerly placed in these cultural aberrations can function quite well in a wide array of small, more cost-efficient, higher quality, and normalizing community living environments.

Second, the locus of education was confined to segregated schools. Only a brief time ago, almost all students with severe disabilities were required to receive their education in segregated schools. It is now evident that when students complete segregated school programs, their most probable life options are also segregated. This educationally, economically, and ethically unbearable tracking system is now being rejected by almost all. Thus, more and more people who are severely intellectually disabled are being afforded their inherent right to a decent education in the schools of their brothers, sisters, friends, and neighbors.

Third, when most adults with severe intellectual disabilities were allowed to work, they were confined to sheltered workshops, enclaves, and "activity centers." In most places, the only postschool option available is lifelong placement in segregated "day programs." Fortunately, communities all over North America are now establishing integrated vocational options.

Fourth, people with severe intellectual disabilities were referred to demeaningly and depersonally as subjects, wards, cases, retardates, beds, chairs, autistics, mongoloids, and Does, as in Baby Jane, not as in Bambi. Attitudes pertaining to the humanity, the sexuality, and the individuality of people with disabilities are evolving affirmatively. Now they are related to as citizens, individuals, workers, learners, brothers, friends, and neighbors who have the right and the need to grow and to experience the dignity of risk in rich and varied environments. This belated and critically necessary emphasis on personhood rather than on syndrome, object, and disease has engendered exciting new expectations, values, goals, pressures, and opportunities.

In sum, the ideology of the segregationist dominated almost all cultural views and service models since the 1940s. Indeed, more money, more facilities, more staff, and more cultural support have been given to this ideology than to any of its predecessors in all of history.

During the late 1960s, it started to become obvious to many that large segregated service systems were untenable. That is, when required to function within segregated environments, people with severe intellectual disabilities could not achieve in reasonable accordance with capacities and could not even begin the quest for the personal freedoms and dignities that most others enjoy. Is it acceptable for someone to live in an institution, attend a segregated school until age 21, be confined to an activity center until age 65, and then be transferred to the retarded wing of a nursing home until death? Does it really matter if one attends a chronological age–appropriate regular school close to home that is naturally proportioned until age 21, but then is confined to a segregated "day program" until death?

The lowest intellectually functioning people in society are in need of sensitive, compassionate, instructive, and otherwise individually meaningful interactions with nondisabled people in every aspect of their lives; that is, 24 hours a day, 7 days a week, 365 days a year, for as long as they are alive. The segregationists did their best, but they have not done the job. They had their day, now they must step aside.

Soon, the parents, scholars, and practitioners of the year 2025 will be looking back and examining our work. Let them be able to say that the evolutionary fad known as segregation was scrutinized and abandoned. Specifically, let them say that institutions, handicapped schools, sheltered workshops, enclaves, activity centers, and nursing homes were terminated. Concomitantly, let them say that the number of integrated environments in which citizens with severe intellectual disabilities live, work, and play increased dramatically; that general functioning in this increased array of environments was enhanced; that options were created that allowed freedom of opportunity; that arrangements were made for meaningful choice-making; and that significant contributions were made toward the development of human dignity. They must not be able to say that today's integrationists participated in any way in the maintenance or justification of the lockup or the lockout.

The content and spirit of this book are clear reflections of changes from segregated to integrated thought and practice. The pressure is now on integrationists to help arrange for these deserving and challenging people to achieve, to grow, and to become as much as they possibly can. Every effort must be made to structure society in such ways as to allow the absorption of people with the most severe intellectual disabilities into every enhancing aspect of integrated community life.

Lou Brown, Ph.D.
University of Wisconsin-Madison

Preface

Educators and other service providers are receiving a consistent message that the outcomes and procedures of educational settings should reflect the basic values underlying normalization and integration. The educational objectives for learners with severe handicaps should be age appropriate, community referenced, and designed for maximal participation in integrated environments. The overall goal of these objectives is the achievement of as much independence for the learner as possibie. Each person graduating from school programs should have access to employment, community living, and social acceptance with persons in each environment. Procedures used to achieve these objectives should utilize criterion-referenced instruction conducted in educational settings that are least restrictive and avoid a ''saturation'' of persons with handicaps.

There is an overwhelming consensus that these basic values are both just and long overdue. Why, then, in many parts of the country, are there frequent and obvious discrepancies between services for persons with disabilities and these values? In the editors' view, discrepancies occur not only because of a disagreement over values, but because of difficulties encountered when translating these values into practice. *It sounds good, but how does it work?* This is a fundamental question that frames the role of an applied science in society. Whether the principles of normalization and integration are good ones is not an empirical question. An evolving public consciousness regarding the equal treatment of all persons has generated these principles. The role of empiricism must now be designing the technology that makes such principles work.

This book is directed toward those teachers, administrators, parents, and service providers who accept the values of normalization and integration necessary for effective education, and are looking for a technology that is consistent with these values. The objective of the book is to provide empirically validated examples of innovative pieces of this technology. The book is not intended as a comprehensive methods text that describes such topics as basic training procedures, behavior management, and IEP development. The focus is on new and innovative service strategies that are effective, and yet consistent with prevailing values.

The first section of the book is made up of five chapters describing exemplary service delivery strategies. In Chapter 1, Beebe and Karan discuss one model for vocational programming in urban environments, and, in Chapter 2, Vogelsberg, Ashe, and Williams describe an alternative system for employing disabled adults in rural settings. These two chapters share the emphasis on the critical and dignifying role of "work" in adult life, and the need for a variety of strategies for procuring and maintaining meaningful work options. Strain and Odom in Chapter 3 focus on the needs of young children with severe disabilities, and provide an overview of recent developments in the technology of instruction from their center at the University of Pittsburgh. Of particular note in their chapter is the use of advanced technology to meet educational objectives. Chapter 4, authored by Donnellan and Neel, emphasizes the integration of "service values" with service technology. This chapter illustrates programming for autistic and other students with severe handicaps, and the authors describe validated curricular components consistent with a set of "quality indicators" that can be used in evaluation of current education programs. The first section of the book ends with a description by Benson and Turnbull in Chapter 5 of their family systems theory approach for individualizing parent involvement in education. The critical role of families in the design and implementation of education is given a new perspective in this chapter, and one successful approach for maximizing functional family involvement is presented.

The second section of the book addresses recent advances in curriculum development for social skills, communication, and integrated instruction. In Chapter 6, Gaylord-Ross, Stremel-Campbell, and Storey define procedures for building functional social skills, and emphasize the dramatic role of social skills across several domains of community functioning. One of these domains is language. Reichle and Keogh in Chapter 7 expand on the importance of language, and deal directly with the outdated myth of the "prelanguage child." They present validated instructional options for building functional communication skills with children for whom language training was, in the past, frequently not made available. Chapter 8 provides the first comprehensive discussion of the Individualized Curriculum Sequencing Model. Guess and Helmstetter describe the importance of sequencing instruction around "skill clusters" rather than conventional massed practice of isolated skills. This important addition to the technology of instruction has dramatic implications for the way classroom and community instruction is organized.

The third and final section of the book introduces four recent advances in instructional procedures having immediate utility for teachers. In Chapter 9, Sailor, Halvorsen, Anderson, Goetz, Gee, Doering, and Hunt begin the section with a review of the procedures they are using in California to train in community settings. Many authors have advocated that more instruction should occur in the "natural" environment, yet all too often logistical and procedural barriers prevent effective community instruction. This chapter discusses both the advantages of community-based instruction, and strategies for making it happen. Horner, McDonnell, and Bellamy in Chapter 10 address the critical issue of training generalized skills, and provide specific guidelines for when and how to use inclass "simulations" to achieve functional responding across the normal range of community situations that a student will encounter. Chapter 11 by Meyer and Evans identifies the realities of implementing community-based instruction for learners with severe behavior problems. This difficult area affects all aspects of education and service to people with severe disabilities, and the existence of excess behavior is often seen as an obstacle to the implementation of principles. Meyer and Evans offer a minimally intrusive, yet effective, set of guidelines for dealing with behavior problems.

Chapter 12, the concluding chapter for this section and the book, looks into current and future applications of high technology in special education. Hofmeister and Friedman extend the earlier comments of Strain and Odom in emphasizing the important role of computer technology in special education. The task of building and using instructional procedures that expand access for persons with disabilities and result in valued outcomes clearly holds many opportunities for computer applications.

While these chapters illustrate the effective implementation of certain aspects of current recommendations, they are offered only as a beginning statement of growing instructional sophistication. It is hoped that this volume will encourage further research, development, and most important, the application of instructional procedures and service systems that return people with severe disabilities to the mainstream of life. At present, educators and other service providers have a set of values that in many ways outstrips their technology. The chapters in this book indicate, however, that current technological advances are being shaped by service values. Together, the chapters also emphasize the need for further technological development at many levels and in the various life domains. Translating research into practice ultimately is far more than a dissemination task, but must begin when an instructional innovation is conceptualized and be a consideration integral to each step in development and validation. The authors of the chapters provide models for expanding the vision and expectations of technology to evaluation, service planning, and implementation of comprehensive service models. While the challenge is an ambitious one involving drastic changes in the opportunities available to persons with disabilities, the editors believe that the necessary tools are now available to reach this long overdue goal.

Education
of Learners
with Severe Handicaps

EXEMPLARY SERVICE DELIVERY MODELS

Chapter 1

A Methodology for a Community-Based Vocational Program for Adults

Patricia Dobbe Beebe and Orv C. Karan

THE NEED FOR COMMUNITY-BASED INTEGRATED VOCATIONAL OPTIONS

Until quite recently, vocational services for individuals with mental retardation and other developmental handicaps were mainly provided within segregated sheltered settings. Conventional wisdom guided these services and sustained the misconception that competitive employment could only be considered after one acquired certain prerequisite skills. Presumably, as individuals demonstrated their competence, they advanced, that is, "flowed" (Bellamy, Rhodes, Bourbeau, & Mank, 1982), through a continuum of sheltered settings on their way to competitive employment. Those with the more severe handicaps were usually placed at the bottom levels of the continuum (Bellamy et al., 1982), where less than 3% ever advanced to the highest level (e.g., sheltered workshops) let alone into competitive employment (U.S. Department of Labor, 1979).

The "flow through" model, although still the standard of vocational services in this country, was never seriously challenged until well into the mid 1970s when national outcome data began illustrating the inherent limitations of this approach (Greenleigh Associates, Inc., 1975; Whitehead, 1979). Shortly

This work was supported in part by the Research and Training Center Grant No. G008300148 from the National Institute of Handicapped Research, Department of Education, Washington, DC 20202.

thereafter, several innovative demonstration projects (Moss, 1980; Rusch & Mithaug, 1980; Schneider, Rusch, Henderson, & Geske, 1982; Wehman, 1981) were starting to yield impressive outcomes, circumventing the flow through model completely and proceeding directly to training and placement at the site of employment. By achieving successful nonsheltered placement with individuals whose only prior vocational experiences were derived within sheltered environments, these demonstrations provided convincing evidence that one's lack of productivity could be more a function of the program than of the individual.

These and other more recent innovative programs continue to demonstrate that many individuals can benefit from employment services provided directly in the community. Furthermore, the benefits to society are frequently observable through indicators such as increased social skills by the participants, more individualized program options, and reduced program costs (Hill & Wehman, 1983). The natural interaction opportunities inherent in community-based vocational programs enable individuals both handicapped and nonhandicapped to learn from each other.

One of the major assumptions of this chapter is that severely handicapped persons can be competent in a wide variety of nonsheltered jobs, particularly when they can exercise choices based on their individual preferences. All too often, a person's choice is limited to the positions available within the current vocational system (Wolfensberger, 1972). In most cases, it is simply not possible to offer a wide array of vocational choices in a segregated setting, whereas the opportunities and choices that exist in the community are practically endless.

INTRODUCTION TO A COMMUNITY-BASED PROGRAM

The major purpose of this chapter is to present the Vocational Education Alternatives (VEA) model. VEA, a private nonprofit vocational services agency in Wisconsin, is committed to the employment of adults with significant handicaps within integrated community settings. This chapter focuses on VEA's methodology. The intent is to share the strategies that have evolved from VEA's 4 years of experience.

Both general and specific strategies are elucidated; generic resources are identified, methods for accessing these resources for persons with moderate to severe handicaps are discussed, and alternatives that enable full participation when such resources are insufficient are explained. Within this latter category, strategies for promoting job development, job adaptations, job training, and job retention are outlined. Additionally, administrative techniques that have proven effective in the operation of a community-integrated program are illustrated. Included in this discussion are such topics as staff performance evaluations, intake processes, overall program strategies, and the gathering of relevant data.

VEA's Principles and Guidelines

Individuals who work are valued members of society (Turkel, 1972). People are expected to work; it is considered "normal" to work. Participating in normal experiences such as relevant, age-appropriate, meaningful work not only increases the likelihood that individuals will be perceived in a positive and accepting manner (Nisbet, 1983), but has been shown to also contribute to improvements in their social adaptive functioning (Schroeder & Henes, 1978). Through nonsheltered employment, persons with handicaps can interact with nonhandicapped persons, begin to acquire the financial means to become self-sufficient, and share in the dignity that regular work can provide (Riccio & Price, 1984).

Since its inception, VEA has been philosophically committed to the belief that there are many handicapped individuals now being served in sheltered, segregated vocational environments who could benefit from community-based services if only given the opportunities. VEA's mission has been to provide these opportunities along with the training and support required to make for good matches between people and their jobs. The processes by which VEA attempts to fulfill its mission are based on the following basic principles.

All programs must be individualized and must consider individual preferences and offer options.

There must be a commitment to ongoing support and instruction.

All clients must participate in experiences that are community integrated.

There must be a meaningful variety of integrated work and pay options.

All services must make total use of community resources and experiences.

There must be ongoing program and individual assessment to enable program improvement.

VEA has operationalized these basic principles through the following programmatic guidelines:

Individuals should work as many hours as their health permits and as they desire.

Individuals should receive monetary compensation, or a wage commensurate with their productivity. Furthermore, these wages should be constantly monitored and upgraded when possible.

Individuals should work in settings that are located in the normal workplace, and with regular integration with nonhandicapped individuals.

Individuals who are placed on jobs should have opportunities for career advancement, job change, and further job training or retraining.

Individuals should have access to other appropriate community services (i.e., recreation, residential, and transportation).

Individuals should receive the support that they require to enable them to successfully participate in community-based vocational programs. This support must include instruction that leads to the growth and development of vocational skills.

Individuals should have access to appropriate case management services that guarantee access to community resources and experiences.

Individuals should have the benefit of services that operate efficiently.

The VEA Model

Organization   VEA is typical of most local, private, nonprofit corporations. The board of directors is composed of parents, consumers, professionals in the vocational field, elected officials, and representatives from the business community. The paid employees include an executive director, support staff who perform routine clerical and bookkeeping functions, and direct service staff who coordinate the agency's education, training, and employment functions.

The qualifications and responsibilities of the direct service staff differ and are based on the needs of the people for whom they provide service. The employment coordinator develops and secures jobs for people who require a week or less of training, whereas the training coordinator only works with individuals who require a week or more of training (in some cases even indefinite onsite support and supervision). The education coordinator secures vocational education training experiences for people in the community, working primarily with the vocational technical schools (in some states, these may be identified as community, technical, or junior colleges).

Administration   The central goal of administration is to help the employees achieve the stated purpose of the organization. To this end, VEA's administration attempts to support its employees and enhance their professional growth through staff training and development. Employee evaluations are crucial in determining the extent to which staff help the organization achieve its goals.

Typically, employee evaluations consist of a comparison between job descriptions and the execution of duties. However, in order to establish minimal safeguards within specific areas, performance standards are also established. These contain person-specific, long- and short-term goals; completion dates for these goals; placement quotas; and most importantly, retention rate goals. These goals are individually negotiated through discussion and mutual agreement.

Because the program is community-based, it is important to assess each employee's relationships in the community. In order to accomplish this, feedback is formally requested from various community members. A feedback process has been established whereby knowledgeable individuals are randomly selected, contacted, and asked a series of standardized questions. In this way, relevant information is obtained from employers, professionals (including case managers, parents, and teachers), co-workers, and consumers. No fewer than five individuals in each category are contacted for feedback. These data, along with the results of the performance standards and job descriptions, are then summarized. Specifically stated for each employee are his or her major accomplishments, problems, remediation dates, and correction goals.

Budget The process of developing the budget for a community-based program is unique as compared to that of a facility-based program. Salaries and costs associated with staff positions, such as fringe benefits and payroll taxes, make up the largest portion of the budget. Different budget categories are established for various anticipated expenses such as office supplies, printing and publications, telephone, postage, rent, equipment rental and maintenance, travel, conferences, and training.

It is possible to estimate a percentage of most of these categorical costs per staff person. However, one unique budget category is "the assistance to individuals" line item. This category ensures that there are funds available for assisting clients in using generic resources in the community (e.g., transportation services).

Use of Mainstreamed (Generic) Services The use of mainstreamed vocational services is a major step toward the achievement of full community integration for handicapped persons, and, therefore, the coordination of these is a key component of the VEA model. Operating under the assumption that mainstreamed services are, in many cases, appropriate for a given individual and, with minimal modifications, can adequately serve people who are moderately to severely handicapped, VEA developed strategies to help people gain access to such services.

Persons who are nonhandicapped use many vocational systems in the pursuit of their vocational/educational goals. Unnecessary duplication can be reduced by using or slightly modifying these resources for persons with handicapping conditions. By so doing, one can thereby alleviate some of the strain on systems that were created specifically to serve only handicapped persons.

Basically, seven major vocational systems exist that offer a myriad of program combinations. The state vocational rehabilitation agency is one system. At the local levels, the community boards with their state and municipal funding mechanisms comprise the second system, while the rehabilitation facilities and/or day activity centers are the third system. These three systems have historically provided the major vocational services to adults who are handicapped. In many cases, these services are segregated in nature, provided primarily within rehabilitation facilities.

Vocational Education Alternatives has concentrated on obtaining access to the other four systems. These four systems are: 1) the state job service or state-run employment agency; 2) what was previously called the Comprehensive Employment and Training Act and is now known as the Jobs Training Partnership Act, and locally as the Private Industry Council (PIC); 3) the community colleges (which are also referred to by other names such as vocational technical schools, technical colleges, etc.); and 4) the public school vocational education program.

VEA's role has been to encourage and assist these four systems to serve individuals who previously have not been able to fully benefit from them. For example, one of VEA's goals was to stimulate greater use of resources available through the Jobs Training Partnership Act. Among some of the strategies that proved successful in achieving this goal were providing technical assistance to program administrators and operators, offering enrollment assistance to individuals who could benefit from some of the services, and capturing appropriate funds to supplement current resources.

The assessment of these four existing community systems is an important step in analyzing the availability of vocational services that currently exist within the community. Once this has been completed, a detailed plan is developed that enumerates what this mainstreamed system can provide with assistance. Formal written working agreements detailing the understanding between the agencies (e.g., what the staff of each agency will do, who supervises the staff, who is responsible for fiscal components, etc.) are recommended. These should then be reviewed on an annual basis or as needed to clarify, change, or reaffirm working relationships.

One form of assistance is to assign staff to work on the premises. This is the strategy that VEA has used at both the technical school and the job service office. At the state job service office, designated VEA staff members have access to all the job listings and can use these for people on their caseload. This is an excellent resource since the job service office often gets listings from certain employers that do not go into the newspaper classified ads nor are relayed through any of the typical personnel networks.

One of the long-term benefits that sometimes comes from using generic resources is that the system gradually assumes an increasing responsibility for serving people who were previously unserved or underserved. For example, when VEA initially began placing people in classes at the local technical college, a VEA staff member modified the curriculum, helped individuals register for classes, secured financial aid, helped individuals purchase books, located and hired turors and attendants, and so forth. However, after demonstrating some of the ways to effectively serve developmentally handicapped students, the school's administrators and staff began assuming many of these responsibilities.

Parent and Advocate Participation   Participation of the family and significant others is a partial solution to the notorious fragmentation of the adult services system (Karan & Berger, 1986). The importance of parental involvement in the vocational processes of their children is often underestimated by the professional community (Arnold, 1985). In the past, it was assumed that only trained professionals had the expertise to determine what was the appropriate vocational and/or educational route for their client. In recent years, it has become more obvious to an increasing number of professionals that parents can be invaluable sources of information as well as instructors in the home.

Parents are their children's first teachers and they are involved in not only the instruction of different skills and activities, but also have a substantial impact influencing the values and attitudes that their children have toward work. In addition, parents spend more time than professionals with their children, have an opportunity to be with their children in a wider variety of places engaging in a wider variety of activities, and, therefore, have a great deal of relevant information to share. Parents also have historic information as to what skills their children possess as well as their interests, aptitudes, and abilities. As children's primary caregivers, parents have more of a vested interest in the long-term issues affecting their children than the majority of professionals. Once children reach adulthood, their parents play a

> major and ever-critical role in facilitating the advantageous aspects of competitive employment. By helping to overcome transportation problems, working out SSI limitations, and providing strong moral support to their son or daughter in the job placement, parents can make a competitive placement successful or completely block it. (Wehman, 1981, p. 7)

Parent training is a strategy that has been very effective in assisting parents who want their children to have access to vocational systems to become vocational advocates. VEA designed a parent training manual that provides both the information and the philosophical background that parents need to become effective advocates.

Advocacy training is another method that facilitates access to mainstreamed systems. In order to accomplish systems change, programs need access to information that can promote better awareness for those who may affect another's vocational outcome. For example, professionals, employers, and parents need to be informed about mainstreamed vocational systems, their value for vocational services, and the employment experiences of persons who are moderately or severely handicapped.

Gaining access to service systems that have not typically been available to people with handicaps may require considerable levels of advocacy. In all cases, it is much better to use "friendly" advocacy at the beginning. This could mean making phone calls on behalf of the person, convening meetings, speaking to others on his or her behalf, helping the individual and significant others understand the system, and helping to secure needed resources or programs. In some cases, however, in order to ensure that a service will be obtained, persuasive advocacy, which may later turn into adversarial advocacy, may become necessary.

Barriers to community-based vocational programs may exist for numerous reasons. Advocacy represents a means to help individuals overcome some of these barriers. But, in all cases requiring advocacy, VEA provides both the advocate and the individual (assuming that the person is not a self-advocate) with accurate information, administrative support, and resources throughout the process.

Direct Service/Intake   The intake process for those who desire entry into the VEA program was designed for the purposes of: 1) gathering diagnostic and demographic information, 2) determining the scope of the applicant's needs, and 3) identifying subsequent person/staff expectations and roles.

Although there are no admission criteria based on an individual's developmental level, there are three reasons why a person may not be eligible for service. These are: 1) there may be no openings (i.e., there may be a waiting list for services), 2) the person may not be handicapped as defined by the funding sources, and 3) the person may not meet the residency requirements. However, given that an individual has a desire to pursue a vocational goal, is considered handicapped, is a county resident, and that an opening is available, the person will be eligible for services.

If the person is capable of referring him- or herself to the program, it is preferable that this be done. However, if the person is unable to do this, the referral can originate from a variety of other sources, including but not limited to a teacher, an advocate, a case manager, the intake person within the agency, and so forth.

The intake process covers such basic issues as general demographic information, information about how the person lives, financial status, how he or she travels, what some of his or her special needs may be, medical information, employment history, and information about educational background. References may be appropriate at this stage depending on where the person is in the employment process. Additional experiences that may enable further understanding are noted and relevant records may be requested. A time-limited release of information form, restricted only to vocational information, is signed.

Since VEA's focus is on the provision of high quality, cost-effective vocational services, if the person's major employment barrier is due to nonvocational needs, a referral to an appropriate agency will be initiated. One major nonvocational service that VEA does provide, however, is mobility training that has proven to have a direct relationship to one's participation and success within the vocational program.

Assessment   Within the VEA model, assessment is specifically adapted to the needs of moderately and severely handicapped individuals in community work settings. Therefore, assessment is based on the actual work situation, and data are obtained while the person is in that environment. These data are used to provide feedback to the individual, the professional, and the employer about the quality of the individual's work.

Although such an assessment takes time, it can easily be justified because it provides direction for modifying environments and for developing individualized training sequences and strategies. Such an assessment facilitates a person-environment match (Karan & Schalock, 1983).

Job Development Process Job procurement and analysis are important program components. In all cases, an attempt is made to locate a job that meets an individual's personal and social preferences.

The job development process for community employment must also consider the level of supervision that the individual will require both in looking for a job in the first place and retaining it once it has been secured. Some individuals may require minimal assistance in securing a job (a week or less) and simply need to learn how to use available resources (e.g., phonebooks, employer contacts, the job service and their job orders, personal networks, etc.) to then locate a job on their own with perhaps only partial or even no supervision. For those whose needs require a week or more of training, considerably more assistance and individualized employer contacts will be required to secure a job.

Throughout the entire job development process, routine access to labor market trends and forecasts is important. The state employment office as well as other business groups frequently gather such data. Such trends and forecasts provide useful information about new potential employers as well as directions for realistic job development. For example, if a person desires work in an area within which no jobs are currently available, the person may be guided to other jobs within the same general occupational cluster that are available.

In an effort to promote visibility and a positive image among potential employers, VEA developed and routinely distributes descriptive brochures. The brochure contains information specifically for the employer and includes:

A listing of jobs within which people who are moderately to severely handicapped have been placed
Testimonials from satisfied employers
A listing of services provided to employers and descriptions of how VEA will
work with employers

Job Matching In every case, VEA attempts to match the person's skills with those required on the job as well as within the broader environment within which the job is located. This process begins with a thorough job and environmental analysis in which critical skills required both to perform the tasks (such as "placing small amounts of degreaser into the bucket") and to become integrated within the setting (such as "knowing how to express choices in the lunch room") are identified. Successfully matching one's skills with those required on the job is a crucial component of job retention.

Once placed on the job, there are many details still to consider other than just the job tasks themselves. For many, the job may be their first integrated community placement, and they may have never experienced natural community rewards nor felt their consequences. The job developers must therefore be concerned about additional parameters surrounding the job. The flow of work; the availability of restaurants, shopping, and recreation surrounding the job site; methods of transportation; environmental accessibility; and the psychosocial climate of the setting are just a few examples of these parameters.

Adaptations Frequently, successful job matches require adaptations. It may be necessary to either use or create special materials and devices to achieve fuller job participation for the individual. To compensate for one's physical disability, for example, a mechanical device of some sort may be required to help the person perform the task. Or, an augmentative communication system may help facilitate interaction opportunities between a nonverbal worker and his or her co-workers.

The actual job task sequence as well as the rules associated with that task may also need to be modified. For example, an individual may have difficulty solving problems related to a particular job, or could have difficulty completing an entire task. Such problems, if not corrected, could prevent the person from becoming an independent worker and would probably force the job trainer to spend a considerable amount of time simply correcting problems. With a little ingenuity, combined with employer flexibility, many of these problems can be corrected quite easily. For example, if the person has cleaning responsibilities but cannot discriminate when certain areas need cleaning, one solution would be to simply clean the entire area daily. Or, if a person cannot count, the portion of the task requiring counting could be assigned to a co-worker.

Providing assistance or supervision is another form of job adaptation. This may be necessary because the person needs intensive supervision in maintaining appropriate job behaviors, increasing stamina, or learning skills that will increase his or her job independence. This could require breaking the required skills into more basic sets of subskills (i.e., conducting a task analysis and teaching these), or it may involve direct instruction (through modeling, role playing, feedback, etc.) in job related areas to improve one's acceptability within the work environment (e.g., using vending machines, taking breaks with fellow co-workers, using the elevator, etc).

The physical environment itself may also need to be modified in order to achieve full job participation. This may include special devices that eliminate barriers and make the environment more accessible for employment (e.g., door stops, door handle adaptations, table height adjustments, etc). The trainer may also need to spend time orienting the new worker to the building and to the physical work area.

One may also need to adapt the social and attitudinal environment. This, of course, is much more difficult to address directly; nevertheless, its importance should not be minimized. Some strategies may include general inservice training or making oneself available to answer individual questions as they arise. It may also include being present to interact with the new worker, and through this form of modeling, subtly influence co-workers' attitudes. It may also be necessary to advocate on the person's behalf by describing his or her assets in other community residential, recreational, and leisure settings.

Job Training Once a job has been secured, there are a variety of strategies that may be needed to ensure the person's success on the job and that provide him or her with continued support within that environment. The extent of this involvement depends on the person's training needs. VEA categorizes these as being either minimal, moderate, or intensive.

Minimal Training If one requires "minimal training," this usually means he or she can successfully perform many components of the job independently. Less intensive training activities are usually required. Thus, the person may only need transportation assistance, or his or her employer and co-workers may need a brief inservice pertaining to some aspect of his or her handicap. Actual job intervention may be limited to only occasional spot checks for quality.

Moderate Training If "moderate training" is required, ongoing (often daily) staff involvement may be necessary for 4–6 weeks with a follow-up period lasting from 1 to 6 months. This level of training requires that a staff member meets with the employer prior to placing the person and completely learns the job. This same staff member is then the one who conducts training on that job site. Once the trainer has procured the job and learned the task, a job analysis is conducted. This analysis, an example of which is illustrated in Table 1, provides the trainer with a systematic method for assessing individuals in relation to: 1) the components of the job that they are able to perform independently, 2) job areas requiring assistance, and 3) additional areas of concern. This analysis provides feedback to the trainer on the types of quality checks and possible prescriptions for correction and refinement that may be required.

Intensive Training Some workers, because of their disabilities and/or handicaps, need "intensive training" or unlimited ongoing support to maintain their jobs within integrated community employment settings. As with moderate training, the trainer meets with the employer, learns the job completely, and conducts a job analysis prior to placing the person. The job analysis is used as a training tool and source of data to indicate when to begin systematic fading (Gold, 1980). However, since it is expected that the worker will require supervision for an indefinite period, the trainer also spends considerable time fitting into the work environment, and, along with the new worker, attempts to become an accepted team within that setting. The trainer strives to make the employer and co-workers feel comfortable with the profile created by two people, and is committed to contributing whatever supervision, training, support, and so on, that may be required to sustain the person's placement. VEA's "intensive training" exemplifies the concept of "supported employment" (Will, 1984) in practice.

Paraprofessionals As might be expected, the labor demands that are frequently a necessary part of community vocational placement can be intensive. VEA has had good success employing paraprofessionals for meeting these demands. Such individuals are currently available through a variety of sources.

Table 1. Job analysis

Date: _____

Name: _____

Trainer: _____

Skills required	Skills inventory + = acceptable performance − = adaptation	Adaptations/comments
1. Obtains bucket		
2. Places small amount degreaser into bucket	-see adaptation	Andy and Lori use 2 capfuls (cap of bottle)
3. Fills with water and obtains sponge	-see adaptation	Lori fills bucket to line inside of bucket, can push bucket on floor to work area
4. Squeezes sponge (until damp)		
Wall cleaning		
5. Back of toilet(s)	-see adaptation	Uses picture sequence book as a guide
6. Side walls		
7. Door(s) inside/outside		
8. Wall by mirror/sink		
9. Wall by towel		
10. Wall by towel holder		

Students are certainly one source, but with students, one must balance their advantages with their disadvantages. The advantages are that they have some professional training and commitment, but the major disadvantage is that they are short-term.

A second source of paraprofessionals are community members from the typical labor pool. Employees selected from this group represent a more stable work force than do students; however, more time must be committed for their training.

A third source of paraprofessionals are graduates from the local technical college. Recently, the Madison Area Technical College implemented a new program leading to a degree as a Community Developmental Disabilities Associate (Karan & Berger, 1986). Although there are now very few associate degree programs that offer this specific form of training (Karan & Gardner, 1984), certainly the demand for such programs is expected to grow as more community living, employment, and recreation opportunities become available for more people who are severely handicapped.

Sharing Information on the Job Site With the exception of the intensive training situations in which a staff member is usually present, there are many other placements in which trainers are not present all the time. For this reason, various mechanisms must be established for sharing important information on the job site when the trainer is not present. For example, it may be appropriate to leave information that clearly specifies the types of assistance that the person needs in order to successfully perform work assignments. It could cover the assistance that she or he requires in the bathroom, breakroom, cafeteria, or with communication, transportation, and/or the availability of community resources. Additionally, a listing of procedures for lunch, departures, or emergencies should be available as should be information on the person's behavioral characteristics and learning styles. The intent in all cases is to leave information for people at the job site (employers, co-workers, or paraprofessionals) that is accessible, easy to understand, relevant, and useful.

There are many different ways to share information at the job site. Tables 2 and 3 illustrate two formats that VEA uses to provide direction to paraprofessionals on routine assignments as well as other important information both for them and the person's co-workers.

Job Retention   There are many factors that influence job retention. Some of these include:

The success of the job match
The level of integration (social and physical)

Table 2.   Information left for others at job site

Individual information

Name: _____

Address: _____

Phone **#**: _____

Emergency contact: _____

Transportation: _____

Schedule

Arrival: _____

Work: _____

Break: _____

Work: _____

Lunch: _____

Transition information

Modifications

Medical information

Table 3. Sample format for keeping information at job site

UW HOSPITAL			
Supervisor: _____ Date: _____			
	Yes	No	Comments
Starts work quickly (before 9:00)			
Stays on task (pays attention to job)			
Finishes all work before leaving			
Completes good quality work			
Work schedule: 8:45–11:30 9:30–9:45	Work break (15 minutes)		

The availability of adaptive technology
The interests, aptitudes, and preferences of the individual
The level of pay
The level of training provided
The individual's inherent abilities
The commitment of the employer
The opportunities for interaction with nonhandicapped peers
The support of family and significant others

These and other critical factors related to job retention must be monitored and integrated into the total program evaluation. To increase the likelihood of one's job retention, there should also be a routine monitoring of service quality issues such as:

Is the rate of pay appropriate? Is a better paying job needed?
Is a more demanding job needed? Are the demands of a particular job in accord with the person's abilities?
Is the person working an appropriate number of hours per week?
How does the vocational plan fit in with other aspects of the person's life?
What other services are needed?
For those who are waiting for jobs or between jobs, how well is the agency meeting the needs of these individuals?

Considerable effort needs to be placed on intervening when necessary to minimize obstacles that mitigate one's job's retention. Maintaining people on jobs requires a commitment to continuous organized training; and when the formal training is completed, discontinuation of that training must be accomplished in a planned and systematic method. In addition, there will be occasions, even after training has been completed, when retraining will be needed.

Among other reasons, retraining may be necessary because the individual's job skills have changed, or because a new job component has been introduced, or because the person may be experiencing difficulty in social interactions that can adversely influence his or her retention if not satisfactorily remedied.

Outcomes from the VEA Model

Descriptive Data Regarding Population Served The people VEA has served are scattered throughout the community, working on a variety of different schedules. A striking feature of the VEA model has always been the diversity of its clientele. They represent all ranges of ability, physical mobility, learning styles, and methods of communication. Some individuals are very motivated and persistent, others are uncertain and dependent, and still others have histories of emotional instability, depressive disorders, and antisocial behavior.

A Program Analysis of Service Systems (PASS) evaluation (Wolfensberger & Glenn, 1975) completed on VEA in 1981 showed that the common characteristics of VEA's clients were: 1) the presence of a developmental disability, 2) a poor or nonexistent work history, and 3) an uncertain likelihood of getting or keeping decent jobs of their choices. This pattern continued throughout the history of the model both in its Madison and Milwaukee offices.

The population has typically represented three groups. One group consists of a significant number of people who have been involved in a variety of vocational and residential services, but who have failed in these systems. For them, VEA has been an alternative to the existing options.

A second, but smaller group, represents people who require modest amounts of support. For these individuals, VEA serves as a coordinator, backup, and case manager. The value of this assistance is crucial, for without it, the person could end up in a more costly program if he or she is in a crisis.

A third group, and the largest of the three, includes people who are moderately to severely handicapped whose needs for services are moderate to intensive. Many of these individuals are referred directly through the school system. Some received excellent and appropriate community-based instruction while in school and were well prepared for nonsheltered integrated employment (Brown et al., in press). Others, however, were considered as too low functioning for anything other than a sheltered segregated vocational placement.

Program Data VEA routinely gathers data that provide feedback about its overall effectiveness. These data are obtained from consumer satisfaction surveys, job placement and retention records, and employee evaluations.

VEA has found consumer feedback to be particularly valuable in contributing to program improvement. Consumer satisfaction surveys are sent out annually to all people who used VEA services in that year. For example, in 1982 in Madison, 265 people used the services and all were sent surveys along with a cover letter offering assistance in completing the survey and a self-addressed stamped envelope.

The survey instruments are designed to be easy to use, and respondents answer questions by checking off the items from a series of choices. Of 265 surveys sent out in 1982, 217 (or 82%) were returned.

The satisfaction survey distributed to Milwaukee consumers in 1984 is depicted in Table 4. The questions in that survey represented issues of concern during that program year. As issues change, new ones can be addressed on subsequent surveys.

Program achievements are evaluated monthly by reviewing current job placement and retention data. The job retention survey represented in Table 5 has proven helpful in logging pertinent parameters about the job (i.e., type, hours, wages, benefits, etc., and one's tenure on the job at the end of 60 days, 6 months, and 1 year).

It is particularly important to systematically monitor wages and benefits for at least two good reasons. For one, since many of the initial placements will be entry level positions, the minimum wages and infrequent benefits for such positions are at best barely subsistent. For some individuals, doing work that is meaningful, and that offers reasonable compensation, may mean placement in more than one competitive job. To not recognize and accept this as an integral aspect of community vocational placement is not consistent with society's acceptance of career advancement and changes for its working force. Obviously, individuals get bored even in competitive placements and may desire changes.

A second reason for monitoring wages and benefits is to demonstrate that nonsheltered employment is a worthwhile effort because the individual contributes resources back into the tax base and gross national product.

The systematic and routine evaluation of retention data yields the "bottom line" for assessing the success of VEA's job procurement and placement strategies. Of the 102 competitive placements that VEA made in 1983 (see Table 6), 85% were working after 60 days, 81% were on the job at 6 months, and 73% were on the job at 1 year. When grouped into job clusters, these placements were in the following categories: sales (1%), professional (1%), clerical (10%), craft (3%), operative machine tending (6%), service (64%), and labor (14%). This pattern was consistent with the county's overall labor market profile and illustrates that people who are handicapped were demonstrating the same employment profile as the rest of the community.

Another program area that receives careful scrutiny is the outcome data on people attending the technical college. VEA has historically viewed technical education as an integral aspect of its community-based programming. Appropriate vocational skill training can play a significant role in breaking through the cycle of entry level positions because if a person can enhance his or or her job skills through training, he or she can frequently attain higher paying jobs with benefits. It should be noted that, to date, the technical college's role has been most effective with persons who are mildly handicapped. However, the

Table 4. Vocational Education Alternatives (VEA) Milwaukee consumer satisfaction survey (1984)

1. Why did you seek the services of Vocational Education Alternatives? (Check all those that apply.)
    _____ for assistance in finding competitive employment
    _____ for assistance in attending the Milwaukee Area Technical College
    _____ for job trainers who provide ongoing assistance to you at your job site
    _____ for skills training in how to keep a job after it has been obtained
    _____ for assistance in transition to community work environments after graduating from high school
    _____ for assistance in cases of possible employment discrimination
    _____ for unpaid work experience (volunteer jobs) for gaining career exploration and/or work experience
    _____ for transportation assistance
    _____ for tutoring
    _____ for career awareness and exploration classes
    _____ for job-seeking skills classes
    _____ for parent support including advocacy training

2. Who referred you to VEA?
    _____ self
    _____ parent
    _____ friend
    _____ teacher
    _____ social worker
    _____ group home staff
    _____ Other—list:_____

3. Who were the primary staff people you worked with at VEA?
    _____ Pat Dobbe Beebe, Executive Director
    _____ Alice Kothbauer, Program Director
    _____ Dean Kresl, Employment Coordinator
    _____ Kay Metoxen, Employment Coordinator
    _____ Venessa Nelson, Training Coordinator
    _____ Linda Pearson, Employment Coordinator
    _____ Barbara Wenger, Education Coordinator

4. How long were you on the waiting list before beginning the program?
    _____ 1 week or less   _____ 6 months or less
    _____ 1 month or less   _____ 1 year or less
    _____ 3 months or less   _____ Over 1 year

5. Did you understand how long it would take and why?
    _____ Yes
    _____ No

6. Was the wait too long for you?
    _____ Yes
    _____ No

(continued)

Table 4. *(continued)*

7. After beginning the program, how long did you have to wait before receiving services?

    ____ 1 week or less   ____ 6 months or less
    ____ 1 month or less   ____ 1 year or less
    ____ 3 months or less   ____ Over 1 year

8. Did you understand how long it would take and why?

    ____ Yes
    ____ No

9. Was the wait too long for you?

    ____ Yes
    ____ No

10. What program(s) did you receive? (Check all those services that apply.)

    ____ VEA staff helped me find competitive employment
    ____ assistance with attending Milwaukee Area Technical College
    ____ job "coaching" to train me at my job site
    ____ skills training in how to keep a job after it has been obtained
    ____ assistance in transition to community work environments after graduating from high school
    ____ unpaid work experience (volunteer jobs) for gaining career exploration and/or work experience
    ____ transportation assistance
    ____ tutoring
    ____ career awareness and exploration classes
    ____ job-seeking skills classes
    ____ parent support including advocacy training
    ____ access to Division of Vocational Rehabilitation (DVR)

11. How would you rate the quality of those services?

    ____ adequate
    ____ more could have been done
    ____ not adequate

12. Are you still employed?

    ____ Yes
    ____ No

13. How long were you employed?

    ____ 2 months or less   ____ 1 year or less
    ____ 6 months or less   ____ More than 1 year

14. Did you like your job?

    ____ Yes
    ____ No

15. Are you receiving follow-up services?

    ____ Yes
    ____ No

16. If no, would you want such services?

    ____ Yes
    ____ No

Table 4. *(continued)*

17. How would you rate the quality of those follow-up services?

       _____ adequate
       _____ more could have been done
       _____ not adequate

18. If VEA assisted you with vocational training at MATC, have you received a certificate or diploma?

       _____ Yes
       _____ No

19. How long did you attend MATC?

       _____ 1 semester or less
       _____ 1 year or less
       _____ Over 1 year

20. Are you still attending?

       _____ Yes
       _____ No

21. Have you found a job as a result of your training at MATC?

       _____ Yes
       _____ No

22. Were you able to reach your VEA case worker when you needed to?

       _____ Yes
       _____ No

23. In general, how would you rate the quality of services you received at VEA?

       _____ excellent   _____ fair
       _____ good   _____ poor

24. Signature (optional): _____

25. Additional comments:

Madison Area Technical College is planning individualized functional adult education offerings for individuals who are moderately to severely handicapped.

Table 7 is a listing of the areas of instruction in which trainees enrolled during 1983. One question of continuing concern is, of course, "Do persons obtain employment after completing their coursework?". During the last two semesters at the Madison Area Technical College, VEA clients who attended classes often found jobs in their area of training as indicated by the following list:

(2) Cooking (Industrial Foods)
(2) Child Care Services

Table 5. Information maintained to evaluate job retention

JOB RETENTION SURVEY
Vocational Education Alternatives (VEA)

Person employed	Placed by	Employer	Type of job	Hours	Date placed	Wage	Benefits	30 Day	60 Day	6 Months	Yearly	Employment ending date

Table 6. Occupations of individuals placed during 1983

Page	Assembly	Pillow producer
Messenger	Cleaning person	Security guard
General clerk	Clerk	Research person
Delivery person	Attendant	Phone person
Janitor	Delivery	Building maintenance
Carpenter's helper	Maid	helper
Maintenance mechanic I	Stock person	Prep cook
Companion	Housekeeper	Housekeeper/companion
Salesperson/cashier	Repair and maintenance	Assistant manager
Laborer	person	Secretary
Clerical employee	Busperson	Lawn care employee
Glassblower	Key punch operator	File clerk
Lawn and garden care	Salad bar attendant	Temporary housekeeping
employee	Maintenance assistant to	Groundskeeper
Typist	mechanic	Clerical assistant
Maintenance person	Childcare employee	Patient escort
Assembly person	Clerical	Sorting licenses
Cashier/baker	Data entry operator	Carpenter
Operations assistant	Usher	Counter help
Kitchen helper	Packer	Attendant/housekeeper
Food service employee	Loader	Receptionist
Dishwasher	Ironing employee	Paper route
Laborer	Companion/housekeeper	Insulation installer
Counter help		

Table 7. Areas in which Vocational Education Individuals enrolled during 1983

Adaptive Physical	Intro. Drama	Cosmetology
Education	Communications Skills I	Auto for Consumers
How to Program a	Intro. to Data Processing	Wood Refinishing
Computer	Photography	Basic Microwave
Electronics I	Beverage Merchandising	Auto Body II
Liberal Studies	Principles of Word	Typing Refresher
Development Reading	Processing	Word Processing
Ceramics II	Disc Brakes	Recreation Resource
Auto Electrical Systems	Data Processing:	Operation
Computer Operations	Programming	Social Service Associate
Machine Tool	Horticulture	Dietetic Technician
Food Prep Assistant	Welding	Bakery
Marketing	Account Clerk	Commercial Art
Clerk-Typist	Electronics	Small Engine Repair
Data Processing	Interior Design	Bartender's Awareness
Auto Servicing	Operations	Homemaker Home
First Responder CPR	Printing	Health Aide
Drawing	Secondary Child Care	Child Care Services
Food Service Worker		

(1) Printing
(1) Homemaker Home Health Aide
(1) Auto Mechanics
(1) Electronics

VEA used a variety of approaches in making it possible for its clients to attend the technical college. Among these were:

Assisting with enrollment
Helping to secure financial aid
Assisting the person by meeting with him or her and his or her instructor to improve communication and to help plan course modifications and resources for the instructor
Arranging for tutors, either paid or volunteer, to assist the person during or after classes
Physically and fiscally assisting with the purchase of textbooks and adaptive equipment
Coordinating services with other appropriate community resources
Conducting both formal and informal career awareness and exploration classes and/or sessions
Arranging for transportation
Making referrals to VEA staff for assistance with job development and placement at the appropriate time
Where feasible, modifying the methods of instruction to fit the learning styles of the individual (e.g., a person might not benefit from lecture/notetaking but learns well in "hands on" lab experiences)
Arranging to have textbooks recorded on tape

Cost Benefit Data In 1982, VEA in Madison placed 73 people into competitive jobs. Those 73 people earned a total of $109,000. In 1983, VEA in Madison placed 102 people into competitive community jobs. The amount of wages earned by this group was $115,535. These were wages earned during the calendar year and do not include wages earned as individuals retained jobs into subsequent years. As individuals earn wages, they often become decreasingly dependent on assistance programs and simultaneously generate revenue through the payment of their local, state, and federal taxes (Wehman et al., 1982).

Another area of cost savings is reflected in the differences in program costs between facility-based versus community-based vocational programs. The average annual cost per client for a facility-based vocational program in the state of Wisconsin in 1983 was $5,000. The average annual cost for VEA per individual was approximately $800.[1] In arriving at these costs, the total

[1]Based on 1982 dollars, the cost per person data from other community-based vocational programs around the country varied from $6,000 to $9,750 (Riccio & Price, 1984). However, cost comparisons must be made cautiously since costs vary depending on the level of services and since different methodologies were used in estimating the costs for these other programs.

operating budget of the agency was considered. This figure was then divided by the total number of people served in that year resulting in an average annual cost per client. Or stated another way, in 1983, VEA in Madison provided services to 276 people with a total operating budget of $232,799, for a cost per person of $843. In 1982, VEA in Madison provided services to 265 people with a total operating budget of $190,545, for a cost per person of $719. These costs represent the average costs for persons ranging from those who were mildly to severely handicapped.

Although the data for only those who were moderately to severely handicapped could not be isolated, their need for more intensive staff involvement and other program resources would obviously result in greater program costs than those reflected in the average cost data above. The placement of a person who is moderately to severely handicapped in an individualized, integrated job in the community may require a variety of categorical resources, particularly if the individual needs continuous onsite supervision in order to maintain meaningful work and acceptable performance over time. This will be costly, perhaps even more costly than traditional facility-based programs.

However, based on the programmatic data that are available, it appears that a community vocational program is less costly than one that is facility based. There are basically four reasons for VEA's better cost effectiveness. First, the program does not have any facility expenses. Staff operate out of a central location that resembles an employment office. Since all the employment, education, and training sites are located in the community, office space needs are limited to those for clerical/reception, staff work space, counseling, and a conference room. Second, there are no costs associated with production such as vehicles, loading dock areas, work floors, special ventilating systems, or subcontract procurement staff. Third, since VEA's stated intent is to focus only on vocational programs, there are no overhead costs due to special education teachers, home economics instructors, choir directors, and so forth. The only staff are individuals working with the person, finding him or her jobs in the community, and providing support as needed. Finally, much of the cost is absorbed by business, the private sector, and generic vocational systems. Included in this are such things as the employment or training sites, a particular class (e.g., welding, printing, baking, etc.) at the technical school, job leads secured from the job service office, and so forth. These savings substantially contribute to the overall cost effectiveness of the VEA model.

Pay Options The issue of pay options appears to be one of growing concern and controversy. Two divergent opinions and a variety of spinoffs from each of these two viewpoints dominate current thinking. Some believe that pay at a competitive rate must be waived in order to enable immediate placement of people into jobs in the community (Brown et al., 1984). Proponents of this position argue that waiting until direct pay has been secured may mean the person will be placed in a segregated environment.

Meanwhile, Bellamy and his colleagues (Bellamy et al., 1984) assert that placing a person in a community job for no pay is exploitation. Furthermore, they maintain that federal wage and hour guidelines are being compromised since these guidelines clearly do not consider working without pay to be an acceptable practice.

VEA determined that the placement of people into unpaid jobs was a temporary solution to a long-standing problem, but to continue this as an acceptable practice in adult vocational services may be a mistake. Thus, although unpaid placements may serve a function in the process related to career awareness, exploration, preparation, and general work experience objectives, such placements must be goal directed, time limited, and carefully monitored.

SUMMARY AND CONCLUSIONS

Many individuals who are moderately and severely handicapped will continue to enter segregated sheltered vocational programs simply because no other options exist. Ironically, in spite of the field's strong commitment to individualized programs and community-based services, the majority of adults today who are moderately to severely handicapped receive their vocational services in segregated adult day programs that are recognized as offering limited opportunities (Bellamy, Sheehan, Horner, & Boles, 1980).

Creating more normalized vocational opportunities will require comprehensive policy changes to resolve many of the thorny issues that continue as obstacles (Bellamy et al., 1980). The problems of wages, disincentives, competitive placement into the community, and the inherent problems of the "flow through" continuum are some of the critical issues that must be addressed (Bellamy et al., 1982). Such problems are especially complicated by ineffective program strategies as well as the inherent difficulty of attempting to operate programs within unsupportive policies, rules, regulations, and resources that now exist. The resulting conflicts create tensions that affect service delivery. Yet, once these issues are resolved, enhanced service options may then be possible.

The VEA model, although still in the process of development, scrutiny, and refinement, has demonstrated that it is possible to provide an array of vocational services to adults who are moderately and severely disabled in the community. What continually remains is the need for others to continue the commitment to achieving the goal of community-based vocational programming for more people who are severely handicapped. Hopefully, this chapter will have provided some direction toward this goal.

REFERENCES

Arnold, M. (1985). Parent training and advocacy. In M. G. Fifield & B. C. Smith (Eds.), *Personnel training for serving adults with developmental disabilities* (pp. 99–116). Logan: Utah State University Developmental Center for Handicapped Persons.

Bellamy, G. T., Rhodes, L. E., Bourbeau, P. E., & Mank, D. M. (1982, April). *Mental retardation services in sheltered workshops and day activity programs: Consumer outcomes and policy alternatives.* Paper presented at the National Working Conference on Vocational Services and Employment Opportunities, Madison, WI.

Bellamy, G. T., Rhodes, L. E., Wilcox, B., Albin, J., Mank, D. M., Boles, S. M., Horner, R. H., Collins, M., & Turner, J. (1984). Quality and equality in employment services for adults with severe disabilities. *Journal of the Association for the Severely Handicapped, 9*(4), 270–277.

Bellamy, G. T., Sheehan, M. R., Horner, R. H., & Boles, S. M. (1980). Community programs for severely handicapped adults: An analysis of vocational opportunities. *Journal of The Association for the Severely Handicapped, 5*(4), 307–324.

Brown, L., Shiraga, B., Ford, A., Nisbet, J., Van Deventer, P., Sweet, M., York, J., & Loomis, R. (in press). Teaching severely handicapped students to perform meaningful work in nonsheltered vocational environments. In R. Morris & B. Blatt (Eds.), *Perspectives in special education: State of the art.* Glenview, IL: Scott Foresman Company.

Brown, L., Shiraga, B., York, J., Kessler, K., Strohm, B., Rogan, P., Sweet, M., Zanella, K., Van Deventer, P., & Loomis, R. (1984). Integrated work opportunities for adults with severe handicaps: The extended training option. *Journal of The Association for the Severely Handicapped, 9*(4), 262–269.

Gold, M. W. (1980). *Did I say that?* Champaign, IL: Research Press.

Greenleigh Associates, Inc. (1975). *The role of the sheltered workshop in the rehabilitation of the severely handicapped.* Report to the Department of Health, Education, and Welfare, Rehabilitation Services Administration. New York, NY.

Hill, M., & Wehman, P. (1983). Cost benefit analysis of placing moderately and severely handicapped individuals into competitive employment. *The Journal of the Association for the Severely Handicapped, 8,* 30–38.

Karan, O. C., & Berger, C. (1986). Training demands of the future. In W. Kiernan & J. Stark (Eds.), *Pathways to employment for adults with developmental disabilities.* Baltimore: Paul H. Brookes Publishing Co.

Karan, O. C., & Gardner, W. I. (1984). Planning community services using the Title XIX waiver as a catalyst for change. *Mental Retardation, 22*(5), 240–247.

Karan, O. C., & Schalock, R. (1983). Assessing vocational and community living skills: An ecological model. In O. C. Karan & W. I. Gardner (Eds.), *Habilitation practices with developmentally disabled persons presenting emotional and behavioral disorders* (pp. 121–173). Madison: Research and Training Center in Mental Retardation, University of Wisconsin-Madison.

Moss, J. (1980). *Post secondary vocational education for mentally retarded adults.* Reston, VA: Eric Clearinghouse on Handicapped and Gifted Children.

Nisbet, J. (1983). *The differences in interaction and behavior in sheltered and nonsheltered work environments.* Unpublished doctoral dissertation, Department of Studies in Behavioral Disabilities, University of Wisconsin-Madison, Madison.

Riccio, J. A., & Price, M. L. (1984). *A transitional employment strategy for the mentally retarded: The final stets implementation report.* New York: Manpower Demonstration Research Corporation.

Rusch, F., & Mithaug, D. (1980). *Vocational training for mentally retarded adults: A behavior analytic approach.* Champaign, IL: Research Press.

Schneider, K., Rusch, F., Henderson, R., & Geske, T. (1982). *Competitive employment for mentally retarded persons: Costs versus benefits.* Unpublished manuscript, University of Illinois at Urbana-Champaign.

Schroeder, S. R., & Henes, C. (1978). Assessment of progress of institutionalized and deinstitutionalized retarded adults: A Match-controlled comparison. *Mental Retardation, 16*(2), 147–149.

Turkel, S. (1972). *Working.* New York: Pantheon Press.

U.S. Department of Labor. (1977). *Sheltered workshop study: Vol. I. Working Survey.* Washington, DC: Author.

U.S. Department of Labor. (1979). *Study of handicapped clients in sheltered workshops, Vol. 2.* Washington, DC: Author.

Wehman, P. (1981). *Competitive employment: New horizons for severely disabled individuals.* Baltimore: Paul H. Brookes Publishing Co.

Wehman, P., Hill, M., Goodall, P., Cleveland, P., Brooke, V., & Pentecost, J. H. (1982). Job placement and follow up of moderately and severely handicapped individuals after three years. *The Journal of The Association for the Severely Handicapped, 7*(2), 5–16.

Whitehead, C. (1979). Sheltered workshops in the decade ahead: Work and wages or welfare. In G. T. Bellamy, G. O'Connor, & O. C. Karan (Eds.), *Vocational rehabilitation of severely handicapped persons: Contemporary service strategies* (pp. 71–84). Baltimore: University Park Press.

Will, M. (1984). *OSERS programming for the transition of youth with disabilities: Bridges from school to working life.* Position paper. Office of Special Education and Rehabilitation Services. Washington, DC: Department of Education.

Wolfensberger, W. (1972). *The principle of normalization in human services.* Downsview, Ontario, Canada: National Institute on Mental Retardation.

Wolfensberger, W., & Glenn, L. (1975). *Program analysis of service systems: A method for the quantitative evaluation of human services (3rd ed.). Volume 2: Field manual.* Toronto: National Institute on Mental Retardation.

Chapter 2

Community-Based Service Delivery in Rural Vermont
Issues and Recommendations

R. Timm Vogelsberg, William Ashe, and Wes Williams

In recent years, impressive results have been achieved regarding the complex community survival skills that individuals with severe handicaps can acquire when provided with well-designed, longitudinal, and systematic training programs. Studies report that individuals with severe handicaps have been taught to perform the skills necessary to produce at a "normal" rate in work settings (Bellamy, Horner, & Inman, 1979), obtain and maintain competitive employment (Goodall, Wehman, & Cleveland, 1983; Wehman, 1981; Wehman & Hill, 1979), shop and plan menus (Nietupski, Certo, Pumpian, & Belmore, 1976), move about the community (Certo, Schwartz, & Brown, 1975; Vogelsberg & Rusch, 1979), recreate (Wehman, 1980), use money

The writing of this chapter would have been impossible without the cooperation and support of the Vermont Department of Mental Health, Division of Vocational Rehabilitation, Agency of Human Services, and the Federal Department of Education, Office of Special Education and Rehabilitative Services.

Individuals who deserve recognition for their efforts are numerous and must include at least: Wayne Fox, Ron Melzer, Richard Hill, Sr. Elizabeth Candon, Richard Surles, Dave Burrus, Susan Hasazi, Roger Strauss, Mike Moeykens, Rich Hutchins, Tim Flynn, Dave Boyer, Patty Morgan, Debby Patterson, Robyn Schenck, Peggy Spaulding, Bob Phillips, Kathie Goodblood, Rick Wheeler, Sue Paquette, Shirley Dudley, and Ann King.

(Certo & Swetlik, 1976), use the telephone (Nietupski & Williams, 1974), socialize (Schutz, Williams, Iverson, & Duncan, 1984), learn family life and sex education skills (Hamre-Nietupski, Ford, & Williams, 1977), solve functional math problems (Williams, Coyne, Johnson, Scheuerman, Swetlik, & York, 1976), and read (Snell, 1978).

Unfortunately, the application of this systematic training technology is not widespread. National surveys (Appleby, 1978; Greenleigh & Associates, 1975; Stanfield, 1976; Whitehead, 1977) and surveys conducted in Vermont (Hasazi & Gordon, 1983; Vogelsberg, Williams, & Friedl, 1980) indicate that individuals with handicaps leaving public school and institutional services have substantial unmet needs. These needs include at least the following:

Lack of skills to participate in community vocational, independent living, and/or recreational opportunities

Lack of appropriate community-based adult services (existing services are often inappropriate and have long waiting lists)

Lack of interagency cooperation and planning between special education, vocational education, vocational rehabilitation, mental health, and other agencies

Lack of community-based support work opportunities

Lack of a system to develop employment opportunities (opportunities that exist are frequently oriented toward individuals with mild handicaps and have no provision for long-term follow-up)

Lack of sufficient residential settings that truly lead to less dependent living

Lack of a comprehensive service coordination system that develops, implements, and monitors a total service plan to assure that all individual needs are met

Since the implementation of Public Law 94-142, students with handicaps have received special educational services at both the elementary and secondary levels. Recently, an increasing number of students have been entering and aging out of secondary level public school services. Unfortunately, secondary public school and adult service delivery systems have been poorly prepared to serve the individual who is severely handicapped.

A rising concern of parents and professionals who deal with these individuals is service delivery after public school. Although the Rehabilitation Act of 1973 was designed to assist students with handicaps in the transition from school to employment, the outcomes of this act for individuals who are severely handicapped have been less than satisfactory (Urban Institute, 1975). The President's Committee on Employment of the Handicapped estimated that the unemployment rate among all workers who are handicapped is between 50% and 80% (U.S. Commission on Civil Rights, 1973). Parents throughout the country report that after graduating or leaving school, their sons or daughters spend a large amount of their time watching television, have little interaction with peers, and rarely participate in community activities (Stanfield, 1976; Will, 1984).

Individuals with severe handicaps who do receive postsecondary services are often placed in sheltered workshops where they receive little or no training for "real" jobs, and earn an average of $25 per month or $0.79 per hour (Whitehead, 1977). Others attend day activity or day treatment programs designed for individuals who supposedly have no potential for sheltered or competitive employment. The majority of day programs focus on teaching skills of daily living in segregated environments with limited opportunities for practice in real homes, supermarkets, parks, or places of employment. This deplorable situation continues despite the abundant literature that demonstrates that individuals with severe handicaps can learn skills necessary to live, recreate, and work in the community with an impressive degree of independence (Brolin, 1984; *Equal to the Task,* 1981; Gruenewald, 1969; Manpower Demonstration Research Corporation, 1980; Rudrud, Ziarnik, Bernstein, & Ferrara, 1984; Schutz, Vogelsberg, & Rusch, 1980; Vogelsberg, Williams, & Ashe, 1981; Vogelsberg, Williams, & Bellamy, 1982; Wehman et al., 1982).

Many factors exist that limit the availability of vocational services to individuals with severe handicaps. These factors have frequently been delineated in the literature (e.g., Bellamy, Sheehan, Horner, & Boles, 1980; Revell & Wehman, 1979; Urban Institute, 1975; Vandergoot & Worrall, 1979; Wehman & Hill, 1979) and include at least the following variables:

Vocational rehabilitation counselors are typically expected to carry full responsibility for serving all eligible individuals. It is infrequent that they can specialize in serving the individuals with severe handicaps when their caseload is usually 150–200 clients. Although recent mandates target the most severely disabled individual, these individuals must still be considered employable through existing limited resource capabilities and programs.

Many counselors have training of a general nature to meet the varied demands of a field caseload that is comprised of a wide variety of disabilities. They seldom receive the intensive training necessary to work with individuals who are severely handicapped.

Often there are no agencies in the community with whom vocational rehabilitation counselors can contract for the intensive evaluation, job development, placement, on-the-job training, and follow-up services that will be necessary to effectively place and maintain these individuals.

In the past, societal expectations for individuals with severe handicaps have not included employment beyond menial, sheltered, nonproductive activities (Gold, 1973; Wolfensberger, 1983). Although a wealth of literature indicates that these individuals are employable (e.g., Bellamy, 1976; Karan, Wehman, Renzaglia, & Schutz, 1976), service providers, parents, and business and industry still frequently predict that these individuals have no potential for employment.

There are few programs that provide supported employment opportunities to the individual who is severely handicapped. Indeed, many states are just at the initial stages of recognizing this concept.

Those programs that do provide competitive employment services for individuals who are severely handicapped have less long-term costs but greater short-term costs ($7,000 per year versus $5,000 per year) that are difficult for states to accept when budgets run on a yearly basis.

These factors indicate that there is a need to develop, implement, and evaluate innovative models for providing vocational and independent living services. This chapter describes one vocational model for employing people with severe disabilities who live in rural settings. The model was developed in Vermont between 1980 and 1982 and has been implemented in three programs. The issues surrounding employment in rural settings are discussed, the processes for model development in rural Vermont are described, and the service outcomes that have accrued thus far are presented.

RURAL SERVICE DELIVERY

Characteristics

Most people believe that living in a rural environment is synonymous with a higher quality of life (Coward, DeWeaver, Schmidt, & Jackson, 1983). This romanticized view is characterized by a wide range of stereotypes depicting rural existence as more relaxed, less complex, and highly agrarian (Coward et al., 1983; Nachtigal, 1982; Sher, 1977). This slow, easy pace of life is thought to be devoid of many city problems. Urban America has been represented as more technologically advanced and, consequently, the urban experience has been utilized when designing strategies for working with rural social issues (Buttram & Carlson, 1983; Coward et al., 1983; Rosenfeld & Sher, 1977; Sher & Tompkins, 1977). Current literature, however, suggests that many rural stereotypes are inaccurate, which raises questions about the efficacy of duplicating an urban model in a rural setting. Unfortunately, "[e]mpirical verification of any 'differences' remains, for the most part, a goal to be achieved" (Coward et al., 1983, p. 3).

From the references above, it is known that rural communities tend to have a larger proportion of very young and elderly persons, a consistently lower level of educational attainment, and higher rates of poverty. The previously assumed emphasis on agriculture no longer appears accurate. The National Rural Center (1981) indicated that nearly 7 out of every 10 rural workers were employed in service, manufacturing, or retail trade. Specific characteristics about education. health, and human services in rural communities include: fewer services, less accessible services, narrower program scope and funcion, poorly financed services due to smaller tax revenue, lower salaries for professionals, and large geographic areas that are sparsely populated and sometimes contain difficult terrain (Bowe, 1983; The Challenge of Rural Rehabilitation, 1983).

Suggestions for improving service delivery in rural areas as well as enriching the qualities of service providers in these rural areas indicate ". . . rural practitioners need a broader mixture of knowledge and skills because of the fewer service options available in their communities" (Coward et al., 1983, p. 16). Of the multiple suggestions (Coward et al., 1983; Ginsberg, 1976; Nooe, 1981), the most important appear to concentrate on building the service system as a component of the community and starting with direct service rather than upper level administration. The problems in the recruitment, retention, peer support, remuneration, and excessive caseloads that have been noted by Bachrach (1981) are areas of difficulty within rural settings that can be overcome with assistance from local leaders. Rural areas are less supportive of isolated service delivery, and effective services must be coordinated and identified as components of the community to have any expectation of long-term success.

Although there are numerous examples of the difference between rural and urban settings, the service delivery model and the instructional technology required are similar. The application of the technology may have to be adapted to fit the setting, but the technology is the same. An interesting point about the development of services is the continual reference to the fact that each geographic area is different, and methods that work in one location will not work in another. The only way to overcome this assumption is through repeated examples of high quality services in different geographic locations.

SERVICE DELIVERY IN VERMONT

Characteristics

Service delivery in Vermont is hampered by mountainous terrain, weather, transportation problems, a widely distributed sparse population, and poverty. Vermont is a relatively small rural state consisting largely of mountains and river valleys. These physiographic features create transportation problems in good weather, a limited commodity in Vermont where winters begin early, end late, and are notorious for cold weather, heavy snowfalls, and icy roads. In addition to the typical web of one-lane and two-lane country roads, there are only two major four-lane highways. Public transportation outside the major population centers is virtually nonexistent. Vermont's population of 518,000 (estimate based on 1980 census figures) is widely dispersed throughout 252 townships and 14 counties. Burlington, the state's largest city, has a population of less than 38,000. There are no large urban ghettos; however, there are many rural pockets of extreme poverty and isolation. Ten of Vermont's 14 counties are designated poverty areas by the U.S. Office of Economic Opportunity.

Special Education Service Delivery

The vast majority of Vermont's learners with mild handicaps receive their education within the regular education program (mainstreamed), with support provided by consulting teachers, resource room teachers, speech and language therapists, and other related services personnel. Children with sight and hearing impairments, cerebral palsy, or other physical disabilities also receive special education services within the regular education program by appropriate regional specialists serving several school districts.

The majority of Vermont's individuals with moderate and severe handicaps receive special education in regional programs located within or adjacent to the more densely populated areas of each region. These regional programs vary in size from one to six classrooms and are located in integrated public schools. In sparsely populated regions, a single class may serve students with moderate and severe handicaps across the entire age span (ages 3–21). Approximately 40 students with severe handicaps are served in regular classrooms in their home school districts with special education support.

Secondary level special education services for students with severe handicaps are underdeveloped and vary widely from program to program. A few programs provide extensive community-based independent living and vocational training and transition planning. However, the majority of programs provide little community-based training and transition planning and lack a model for delivering comprehensive services that meet the individual needs of all learners. Service delivery in general is hampered by lack of a well-defined model that facilitates employment of graduates and transitions students from public school to adult services. Recent data compiled by Hasazi and Gordon (1983) indicates that 15% of recent graduates from special education programs in Vermont have full-time jobs, 33% are in part-time employment, and 52% are either under- or unserved. These data represent the less handicapped individual, and the figures are markedly lower for those individuals who are severely handicapped.

Postsecondary Services

Postsecondary services for individuals with severe handicaps are generally provided by regional mental health centers located in population centers of the state. Surveys completed by the Center for Developmental Disabilities (Vogelsberg, Williams, & Friedl, 1980) indicated that Vermont's ability to provide community services to individuals who are severely handicapped approximates the national norm, and that the same unmet needs exist in Vermont. In relation to vocational needs, the needs in Vermont are also similar to those delineated by Greenleigh & Associates (1975) and Whitehead (1977). That is, vocational services are typically underdeveloped or nonexistent, sheltered workshop programs have long waiting lists, and the resources and systems necessary for providing intensive training, maintenance, and follow-up activities to place these individuals are also underdeveloped or nonexistent.

The capability of rural states to provide effective vocational services to this population is far below that of urban states (Leland & Schneider, 1982). The sparse population and limited resources have had both positive and negative effects upon the development of services in Vermont. One positive aspect is the lack of a strong sheltered workshop orientation in the state— Vermont did not (and does not) have adequate resources to develop a sheltered workshop model of service delivery. As a result, traditional difficulties usually encountered when changing sheltered employment to community employment have not occurred. Another positive aspect is the integration within public school programs. Over 95% of Vermont's school-age learners with severe handicaps are served in integrated programs. Vermont's commitment to providing special education services in integrated community schools is very positive and is beginning to spread to adult service settings as well.

Development of Vocational Service Model

Vermont has been initiating activities to improve vocational services to individuals who are severely handicapped since 1979 (Vogelsberg, Williams, & Friedl, 1980). During 1984, the Secretary of the Agency of Human Services sponsored a Vocational Policy Statement that included the development of competitive and supported employment programs. These programs are excellent beginnings; however, only a limited number of individuals who are severely handicapped are currently benefitting. The continual improvement and expansion of services is essential.

The development of a vocational service model consisted of many steps over a 5-year period and the process is ongoing. Initial steps in developing the model involved reviewing "best practices" in service delivery, documenting Vermont needs, developing a model that all involved agencies could support, and pilot testing model components. Essentially, it was an educational process where all involved parties received and shared information in the process of development. Some of the steps included review of available literature, needs assessment, meetings at the state and regional level, written reports and presentations, written proposals for development of a vocational service model, written proposal for a state plan, state funding of one component of the vocational service model, and replication of select programs of the model. Each component of this process has been described in detail elsewhere (Hill et al., 1980; Vogelsberg, Strauss, Keefe, & Brier, 1980; Vogelsberg & Williams, 1980; Vogelsberg, Williams, & Ashe, 1981; Vogelsberg, Williams, & Friedl, 1980; Williams, Friedl, & Vogelsberg, 1979a; Williams, Friedl, & Vogelsberg, 1979b; Williams, Friedl, & Vogelsberg, 1980a; Williams, Friedl, & Vogelsberg, 1980b; Williams, Vogelsberg, & Friedl, 1979). Among the most critical steps in building a vocational model that would meet with state support was the construction of a statewide vocational services task force.

State Mental Retardation and Vocational Rehabilitation Task Force

The state mental retardation and vocational rehabilitation task force was developed to delineate the elements necessary for a comprehensive vocational service model. The task force was made up of members from the State Planning Office, Division of Vocational Rehabilitation, CETA, Department of Mental Health, Department of Special Education at the University of Vermont, and the Center for Developmental Disabilities. This group was convened to examine the following six major areas:

1. Competitive and structured employment
2. Vocational assessment and training that leads to employment
3. Coordinated vocational training with community living to address all needs
4. Developmental training for those individuals who have programming needs that supercede vocational training (i.e., life support)
5. Interagency cooperation among the agencies represented on the task force
6. Transition from public school to adult services

The task force report delineated two major forms of service elements: 1) process, and 2) direct service elements. Process elements (case management, training-based evaluation, and employment development) were seen as those elements of a comprehensive model that guarantee that individuals receiving services are monitored, continually evaluated, and provided with the best opportunity for movement from one type of service to another.

Direct service elements were those elements of service that individuals actually received (competitive employment, transitional employment, supervised employment, extended sheltered employment, and developmental services). These elements were organized by service and curriculum area and were not seen as prerequisites to each other or as a continuum of services where an individual had to progress through all components to reach employment. The ideal format included an individual's capability to receive developmental services (such as social, recreation, independent living) in addition to ongoing vocational service (such as supervised employment or competitive employment). Some components were built into the system to guarantee that the present service difficulties were not replicated.

Final statements concerning the model included notation by multiple agencies that they were in total support of the model but lacked financial resources for implementation. The following recommendations were made by the task force:

Develop a pilot study of the process elements.
Identify a better system of evaluation of the present individuals in the system (which direct service elements are necessary).

Fund a pilot program that is also responsible to produce the process for replication.

Initiate job development coordination between the various agencies responsible for the identification of the jobs.

EMPLOYMENT PROGRAM DEVELOPMENT

The task force report was presented to the Secretary's Council on Employment of the Severely Disabled, and the council requested an operational plan including budgets, personnel descriptions, and project implementation guidelines. A detailed report was developed (Vogelsberg, Williams, & Fox, 1981) and presented that would provide comprehensive services within one geographic location for approximately 90 individuals. From the operational plan, discussions were initiated about funding capabilities and geographic locations for an initial program. The total budget for the comprehensive model was extensive and the state could not support this effort and asked for revised plans that developed detailed cost information about each element of the model. Once this was accomplished, determination of a priority element was initiated and competitive employment was defined as the most important and least evident within the existing system.

An establishment grant of vocational rehabilitation funds with mental health matching funds was prepared, submitted, and eventually funded in central Vermont (Barre). The data from this pilot program provided enough descriptive data to establish two other programs and plan for a fourth program (one of the programs is federally funded, the rest are establishment grants).

Effect upon Day Services in Pilot Location

The pilot program (Project Transition I) was initiated in April of 1980 through a Vocational Rehabilitation Establishment Grant to accomplish the following objectives:

Movement of a day program that had a recreation or custodial orientation from Riverton, Vermont (a small, remote, rural location) into Barre, Vermont (a much larger area of 9,800 people) so that the program would be located in *physical proximity* to community activities

Development of a vocational orientation for the day program

Replacement of the name "Riverton Activities Center" with "Central Vermont Employment Industries"

Development of the training and employment pilot program that would provide competitive employment to at least 12 individuals each year (these individuals had to be classified severely disabled and mentally retarded and considered unemployable by the existing vocational rehabilitation system)

The first competitive employment program was modeled after the work of Wehman (1981) and Rusch and Mithaug (1980). The major differences were that the program was in a rural area 50 miles from the nearest university support system and was designed to use a place and train approach rather than a train first and then place approach. This decision was made due to the expected lack of similar positions within the rural settings. Although traditional service occupations did exist, they usually included multiple additional responsibilities and a wide variety of approaches. Positions were identified and trainees were evaluated and placed directly into the position with an on-the-job trainer.

Full-time positions on the program consisted of a job training coordinator, job developer, and an on-the-job trainer. Secretarial and office support were provided by the mental health agency. The job training coordinator was responsible for case management, development of a total service plan, coordination and implementation of training, and continual monitoring and evaluation of trainees as well as program staff. The job developer was responsible for all "business" aspects. Major responsibilities included the identification of positions, analysis of these positions using a specific job skill inventory, communication and follow-up with employers after training staff had faded out, and identification of needed retraining or potential advancement for each individual. The on-the-job trainer was responsible for carrying out any necessary teaching to assure that an individual could do the job, assure that the total job requirements were met each day (even if the job trainer had to complete these requirements), develop co-worker support, teach the supervisors how to interact with the individual, and monitor progress and intervene wherever necessary to help the employee succeed.

To accurately describe the changes that occurred in the first competitive employment program, both the day program and the competitive employment program need to be discussed. Establishment grant funds were awarded for the relocation of an entire day program of approximately 50 people, and the development of a competitive employment program for 12 individuals to establish a movement pattern out of the day program. The actual day program staff were not supplemented in any way by the extra funds. The expectation was that the competitive employment program would establish employment placement, identify appropriate training curriculum, and initiate a vocational emphasis in the existing program. The day program went through three distinct phases and each phase consisted of specific program orientations.

Phase I (1979):   Recreation, arts and crafts
Phase II (1980):   Competitive employment
                   recreation, arts and crafts
Phase III (1981–1984):   Competitive employment
                   food service vocational training
                   supervised work crews in the community
                   subcontract assembly in facility
                   functional academics
                   independent living skill development

Phase I (1979)   Prior to the establishment grant, the day program had a recreation and custodial orientation and was located in an old schoool house 12 miles north of any community services or sources of employment. Staff were employed to make sure that participants' needs were being met. There were no individuals in the program who were classified as severely or profoundly mentally retarded.

Phase II (1980)   Once the establishment grant was funded, the name of the program was changed to Central Vermont Employment Industries, and the specific program for competitive employment was named Project Transition I. The entire day program was moved into a downtown location in Barre, Vermont, and existing staff began to receive inservice training on the development of community-based vocationally oriented services. Those individuals not receiving on-the-job training and placement services remained within the facility and continued to perform the same "traditional" day activity tasks. Essentially, the program had progressed from isolated day services to a competitive employment program within a day program that now had appropriate physical proximity to community activities.

Phase III (1981–1984)   As the competitive program continued to provide placement for individuals and demonstrate that employment was a viable and reasonable alternative, the remainder of the day program began to develop an improved orientation to work. The first individuals with severe handicaps from the state institution were accepted into the program during this phase. The program now consisted of the following emphases: competitive employment, food service vocational training, supervised community work crews, subcontract work within the facility, independent living, and functional academics. Although there is a continual need for development, the movement has been extremely positive.

Each transition program is small and provides competitive employment placement services to approximately one person a month. At this point, three projects have initiated placement services. Figure 1 provides an indication of geographic locations and Table 1 provides population figures for the cities and counties where the programs are located (or projected to be located). The third program site had such a small population base that two regional mental health agencies provided the matching funds to initiate the program. The programs are training and employment programs and have been named Transition Projects (i.e., Transitions I, II, III, and in the near future, IV).

To develop training and employment programs within regional mental health agencies that had existing day programs, there were some important guidelines that had to be met. These guidelines included at least the following:

1. Separate budgets from the day program
2. Specific staff responsibilities that excluded any day program or facility-based activities
3. Separate advisory and support boards

STATE COUNTY OUTLINE MAP

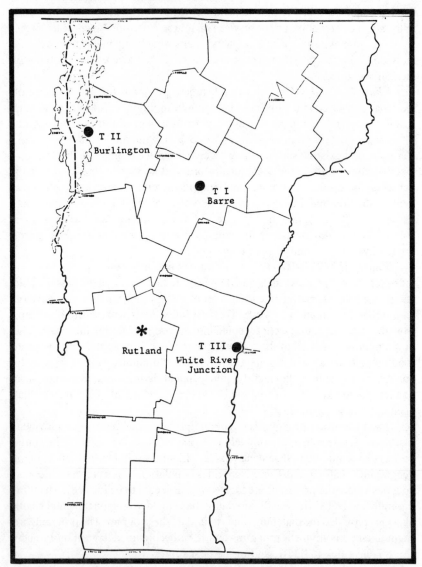

Figure 1. Location of transition projects in Vermont (Rutland Project expected in 1985).

4. Written interagency agreements with public schools, regional mental health agencies, sheltered workshops, vocational rehabilitation, and any private services that become involved
5. Guarantee of qualified consultation

Table 1. Population figures by program, county, and city (1980 census figures; Vermont's total population is 511,299)

Project	County	Population	City	Population
Transition I	Washington	52,391	Barre	9,835
Transition II	Chittenden	115,598	Burlington	37,727
Transition III	Windsor	50,874	White River	2,379
Transition IV[a]	Rutland	58,332	Rutland	18,427

[a]Projected site 1985.

6. Consistent data collection requirements across all sites
7. Specific placement and disability expectations
8. Staff development, training, and incentives to become a member of a model program

COMPETITIVE EMPLOYMENT PROGRAM DESCRIPTION

The competitive employment program initiated services with individuals classified as moderately mentally retarded and gradually provided services to individuals who were more severely handicapped. This was a constant area of conflicting expectations from the funding agencies. According to one agency (Vocational Rehabilitation), any individual considered severely disabled was acceptable for placement, *and* success was judged by the number of placements, *not* the severity of the handicap. The second funding agency (Mental Health) had a strong orientation to provide employment for the individual who was labeled severely and profoundly mentally retarded as a demonstration of the competence of these individuals. After multiple discussions between funding agency project officers, the project attempted to appease both agencies by placing some individuals considered severely mentally retarded as well as placing a larger number of individuals who were also considered mentally retarded but more likely to fit into the classification of moderate mental retardation. Approximately one out of five individuals placed were actually classified severely mentally retarded.

There are three major components in the programs: business, support, and trainee service. Each of these are presented in Table 2, with a brief discussion provided below.

The business component was handled by the job developer and included developing financial incentives, social incentives, employer commitments, specific jobs, a job skill inventory, a business task force on employability, and follow-up services with the employer to ensure continued success.

A multi-agency advisory board was developed to ensure maximum involvement of all appropriate agencies. Members of this board included individuals from the Department of Transportation, Department of Mental Health, Division of Vocational Rehabilitation, Employment Security Offices, Job

Table 2. Major components of the programs

Business	Support services	Trainee services
Generic job development	Advisory board	Initial intake
Public relations	Community advocacy	Parent or guardian support
Financial incentives	services	Agency support
Employer commitment	Department of	Service coordination
Specific job development	Transportation	Financial disincentives
Job skill inventory	Community mental health	Individual skill inventory
	Department of Employment	Vocational assessment and
	and Security	curriculum guide
	Division of Vocational	Transportation options
	Rehabilitation	
	Public school special	
	education	
	Business task force	

Job skill inventory and individual skill summary MATCH

Job sample assessment (OJT or Inhouse)

On-the-job training
Placement
Follow-up

Services, Adult Basic Education, Public Schools, and Residential Program Managers. Each member was invited to participate in monthly meetings to assist in the removal of specific barriers to community involvement. The advisory board has been extremely helpful in the ongoing success of the programs, especially during the first year of development. In one instance, a public transportation route was actually altered to assist in placement activities.

Trainee Services

Trainee services included initial intake, parent and guardian support, case management, financial incentives and disincentives, trainee evaluations, agency support, parental support, and transportation. Figure 2 provides a detailed flowchart of trainee services through the four major stages: referral, evaluation and job development, on-the-job training/placement, and follow-up. Each trainee entering the program would pass through these stages in preparation for placement and as placement occurred. Training was conducted on direct and indirect work skills. Direct work skills were defined as those necessary to carry out the actual job (e.g., operating a pricing gun), while indirect work skills (referred to frequently as social/vocational survival skills) consisted of any skill necessary to ensure continued job success. Indirect skills included the skills to get up in the morning, travel to work, and interact socially

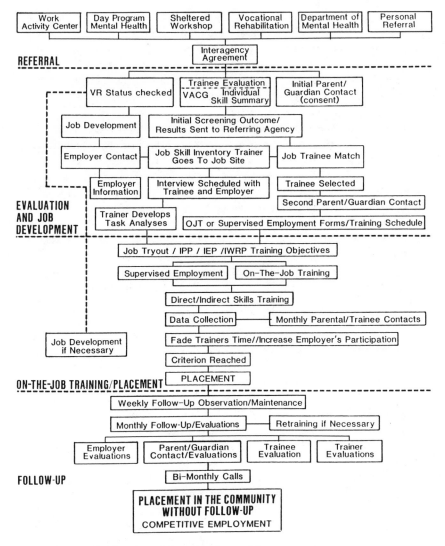

Figure 2. Detailed flowchart of the major phases of the programs.

while on the job. Frequently, it also became necessary for program staff to intervene within home settings after work hours to ensure that the trainee would be capable of attending work on the following day.

A complex case management system for the programs has been developed and is being revised presently (Vogelsberg, Spaulding, Patterson, Schenck, & Phillips, 1984). Selected aspects relating to the four major areas are described below.

Referral   Although the programs were initiated in the mental health programs, they accepted referrals from multiple agencies. They were developed to provide competitive employment training to all individuals. A series of working interagency agreements with multiple agencies assisted in the referral process. As with most adult service options, there were many more referrals than there were services available and each program had an active waiting list of individuals desiring services.

Evaluation and Job Development   Two separate forms of trainee evaluation were utilized: a program-produced instrument referred to as the Individual Skill Summary, and the Vocational Assessment and Curriculum Guide (VACG) (Rusch, Schutz, Mithaug, Stewart, & Mar, 1982). Traditional assessment information was collected and monitored through the vocational rehabilitation agencies. All individuals who were accepted as active trainees were accepted as vocational rehabilitation "clients" when the programs agreed to provide the intensive on-the-job training, placement, and follow-up services necessary to ensure a successful placement.

Job development was performed initially by the job developer and then by the on-the-job trainer who performed a detailed job skill inventory. Once a job was identified, carefully analyzed, and the employer was willing to hire, a complex process to identify the best trainee for placement and to work out the multiple details of parental support, agency support, and transportation began. The job skill inventory and the individual skill summary are informal instruments that have similar components so the job skill requirements and the individual skill capabilities can be matched to determine the best candidate for the position. Table 3 lists the components of the job skill inventory (modeled after Belmore & Brown, 1976) and the individual skill summary. This process has proven useful by identifying areas that will need intensive training immediately, identifying valuable skills for trainees who did not get the job, and identifying potential areas for job restructuring.

Although this process was developed to ensure that the job was filled with the best candidate, the actual outcome was frequently decided by the support from parents, agencies, or employers and the ability to develop a sufficient transportation plan for the individual. Many jobs were passed on to other agencies involved in placement due to transportation problems and parent vacillation. Parents were frequently initially supportive but undecided when the actual decision to provide a job placement occurred.

Frequently, the disadvantages of a community placement were enough to discourage potential workers. Parents often found themselves in the position of having to decide between a secure 9 A.M.–3 P.M. day program with transportation provided and a part-time position in the community where the hours were varied, requiring that parents would have to assist in transportation and community involvement. The potential of lost social security benefits and loss of a place in the day program (should the job fail) were also disincentives for the

Table 3. Job trainee match process to determine the best candidate for the job (II, III, IV, and V are matched)

Job skill inventory	Individual skill summary
I. Job components	I. History/skill summary
A. Job routine	A. Mobility
B. Indirect work skills	B. Sensory
C. Performance criteria	C. Communication
D. Machine use	D. Medical
E. Work environment(s)	E. Medication
F. Job considerations	F. History
G. Application process	G. Interests
H. Relation to public transportation	H. Physical exam
I. Time-off/benefits	I. Psychological information
J. Health and safety	J. Potential
II. Physical requirements—————————	II. Physical capabilities
A. Standing/walking	A. Standing/walking
B. Sitting	B. Sitting
C. Bending	C. Bending
D. Lifting	D. Lifting
E. Carrying	E. Carrying
F. Climbing	F. Climbing
G. Eye-hand coordination	G. Eye-hand coordination
H. Foot-hand coordination	H. Foot-hand coordination
I. Simultaneous movement	I. Simultaneous movement
J. Fine motor	J. Fine motor
K. Fine discriminations	K. Fine discriminations
III. Functional academics————————III.	Functional academic skills
A. Math requirements	A. Math skills
B. Money	B. Money
C. Time	C. Time
D. Telephone	D. Telephone
E. Home management	E. Home management
1. Money	1. Money
2. Meals	2. Meals
IV. Communication—————————IV.	Communication
A. Follows directions	A. Follows directions
B. Verbal expressive language	B. Verbal expressive language
C. Social interaction	C. Social interaction
D. Reading skills	D. Reading skills
E. Writing skills	E. Writing skills
V. Personal hygiene–grooming——————V.	Personal hygiene–grooming
A. Personal appearance	A. Personal appearance
B. Average worker dress	B. Dress/clothing
VI. Job specific vocabulary	VI. Other considerations
VII. Nature of supervision	

parent. Given these factors, it was not unusual to have to contact 8–10 trainees and their parents to find one person interested in a position.

On-the-Job Training/Placement Once an individual agreed to accept a position, a series of training exercises began. If the situation was ideal, an employer would allow an on-the-site job sample to determine priority teaching objectives. What usually happened was that the program was given a 3- or 4-day period to get someone on the job. The usual agreement between the program and the employer was that the trainee would receive full wages and the program would guarantee that the job would be completed to the employer's satisfaction. Frequently, this meant that the on-the-job trainer had to initially complete the job and/or work longer hours to ensure that all job requirements were met. Another assurance that the program staff frequently offered was an agreement that if things didn't work out to the employer's satisfaction within a 2-week tryout period, then the worker would move on to another position. Of the 70 placements that have occurred since 1980, not one employer has requested that a worker be removed or not continued after the 2-week tryout period.

To ensure that program staff and other agency personnel were communicating appropriately about training efforts, a definition of each stage of on-the-job training and placement was developed and refined so that everyone would understand when a trainee was in placement, follow-up, or retraining. Although the definitions at times appear artificial (i.e., a trainee may be in follow-up and still be receiving training for up to 20% of the time on the job), these definitions assisted in the standardization of communication between programs and adult service agencies. Table 4 provides an example of the variables and the definitions that were utilized. The entire process for on-the-job training and placement was a series of stages where the trainee and the employer were gradually learning the responsibilities of a new position and the requirements for maintaining that position.

Follow-Up Many of the trainees who were placed into community positions are still in a follow-up phase and will remain in this phase as long as the program can afford to provide it. An important point in successful placements was the long-term follow-up. It was difficult to convince a service system that services to maintain individuals in the community had a high priority. The usual expectation of existing adult services was that if an individual can work in the community, he or she should not require any other services—he or she must lose his or her position before the service system will attend to his or her training needs. There was no existing mechanism that was followed to ensure that community placements remained successful. The concept of supported work (Revell, Wehman, & Arnold, 1983; Wehman & Kregel, 1983; Will, 1984) was still a new concept to the ongoing service system.

Table 4. Phases in on-the-job (OJT) training cycle of the transition programs

Phase in training	Salary	Trainer behavior	Trainee behavior	Supervisor behavior
OJT tryout (2-week period)	Subsidy or paid	Teach job routine for 14 days	Acquire job routine	Observe and identify priority objectives
OJT	Subsidy or paid	Training and observation for 20%–100% of position	Demonstrate 95% correct work routine for 3 consecutive days	Observe, evaluate, and assist in supervision
Placement	Paid	Same	Same	Same
Follow-up/maintenance	Paid	Training and observation for 0%–20% of position	Continues 95% correct work routine	Usual supervision with training and reinforcement
Competitive employment	Paid	None	Independent work	Usual supervision
Retraining	Paid	Retraining necessary for more than 20% of position	Must reach 95% correct work routine 3 consecutive days	Usual supervision, monthly contacts with trainer and job developer

(return to follow-up upon reaching criterion)

Success of Competitive Employment Programs

It was extremely difficult to evaluate the success of earlier employment programs due to the lack of sufficient data bases and changing evaluation systems within agencies (Rowitz, 1984). Placements were considered successful if an individual had been on the job 2 weeks, 1 month, or 3 months depending upon the agency collecting the data. The Office of Vocational Rehabilitation successfully closed cases if an individual entered into activities other than competitive employment. The majority of the data available was not long-term data (it did not describe success over a long term).

Hunt (1982) described the long-term impact of vocational rehabilitation services in terms of severity of disability through a careful examination of the Rehabilitative Services Administration and Social Security Administration's (SSA) data bank. While this examination restricts the population to SSA recipients within the vocational rehabilitation system, it does provide severity of disability and long-term success information about competitive employment. Over a period of 36 months, the percentage of individuals who were still on the job was 41.5% for those classified as severely disabled, and 59.5% for all disabled individuals receiving services. Data from the transition programs that have been operating more than 1 year yielded the following success percentages. Project Transition in Barre had a 50% success rate after a 46-month period; Project Transition II in Burlington had a 68% success rate after a 29-month period. Those individuals who have been placed by Project Transition III remain on the job but the project is new and only six placements have been made as of this date (a total of 70 placements have occurred). These data compare favorably with the existing rehabilitation data. A further important point is that those individuals served by the competitive employment programs are more severely handicapped and, although IQ scores have proven to be of little use as indicators of job success, the range of IQ scores of individuals provided with employment has ranged from 10 to 70.

The majority of the positions have been service occupations (63%), but there have been multiple nontraditional positions as well. The best paying job has been a $19,000 a year position as a night custodian, while the most technically demanding position has been an Assembler II position at a large electronics plant. Thirty-four percent of the positions are full-time with full benefits; the rest are part-time with limited benefits. Salaries by hour have ranged from minimum wage up to $9.58 an hour ($4.32 average in Barre and $5.85 average in Burlington) or monthly salaries from $27 to $1,540. The average monthly take-home pay is $345 in Barre (Transition I) and $455 in Burlington (Transition II).

As mentioned earlier, these programs are similar to programs developed in Illinois and Virginia. They are intensive training programs in applied settings that verify skill acquisition and maintenance in the actual environment where they will be expected. As each program in Vermont was developed, technical assistance was provided to ensure that the same levels of quality and intensity were followed. Although many rural settings within Vermont consider themselves to be different, the fact that three projects have been developed in three geographic areas has begun to provide political support for future projects. Once the existing advocates and service providers accept the fact that these projects are successful and cost effective, movement toward more replication will begin. Each replication has added powerful data to the quality of these programs.

More complete data, as well as descriptions of the programs and the individuals placed, are available elsewhere (Vogelsberg, 1984; Vogelsberg, in press). The important fact about the programs has been their success in serving individuals typically considered unemployable, and the ability to build replication sites.

Cost Effectiveness   A major evaluation concern when the programs were first conceived was their level of cost effectiveness. There are many complex formulas that have been hypothesized to identify cost of service and the effectiveness of those costs (Schalock & Harper, 1982, 1983). The employment programs in Vermont have adopted a very simple formula for comparison. Regular adult day services in Vermont cost $5,000 per year. Alternative employment options are compared against this standard. If the competitive employment programs can find jobs for individuals who would otherwise remain in a day program, the 1-year costs will be $6,500 to $7,255 per placement. Multiple authors have identified the lack of movement from adult day services as a critical difficulty (Bellamy et al., 1980; Whitehead, 1977). Therefore, it is relatively safe to assume that individuals in adult day service will require $5,000 per year for the remainder of their lives. The individual who is provided with competitive employment training and follow-up services will cost the service system $7,255 for the first year and substantially less each following year (approximately $500 per year). Considering these figures, the 3-year cost for competitive employment would be $8,255, while the 3-year day program cost would be $15,000. Each year of competitive employment follow-up would add $500 to the figure while each year of adult day service would add $5,000 to the figure.

A simple table comparing the two transition programs, their costs, and the salaries of individuals in work activity or sheltered employment further details the difference and the savings. Table 5 provides these comparative data as of March of 1984 for the two programs that have been in existence more than 1 year. Although these data have proven extremely positive, it is critical to note that the money saved does not return to the existing service agencies. Explaining to social service personnel that their extra 1-year costs are saving society as a whole large amounts of money has not impressed staff in either the Vocational Rehabilitation or Mental Health Agencies of Vermont (they are still responsible for the extra costs).

Table 5. Cost-effectiveness of the transition programs as compared to traditional day/work activity programs

Program	Months of program	Number of trainees placed	Total cost of program	Cost per trainee		Training time	Salary per hour
				1-Year total (1-day cost)	3-Year total (1-day cost)		
Transition I Barre, VT	47	44	$253,856	$6,511 ($26.04)	$8,011 ($10.68)	2–3 months intensive training	$3.10–$4.62
Transition II Burlington, VT	25	25	$173,161	$7,215 ($28.86)	$8,715 ($11.62)	2–6 months intensive training	$3.35–$9.90
Traditional day/ work activity program	—	—	—	$5,000 ($20.00)	$15,000 ($20.00)	Continual	$ .00–$ .79

Not all individuals who are severely handicapped will be able to acquire and maintain independent employment in the community. However, there are numerous programs within the United States that demonstrate that a much larger percentage of individuals can work in community settings given adequate training, support, and long-term follow-up services. For those individuals who may not achieve independence in community work, there are multiple forms of supported or supervised employment that have not yet been adequately developed or tested.

PROBLEMS AND SOLUTIONS

The four replication programs have experienced five similar problems: 1) deficits in the service system; 2) employer, community, and parent expectations; 3) transportation; 4) financial incentives and disincentives; and 5) maintenance and follow-up issues. Note that of the five problems, only the last concerns actual trainee behavior.

Service System

Within the service system itself, the following difficulties have become apparent:

Lack of state, regional, and local agency coordination and cooperation
Multiple definitions utilized by various agencies (e.g., severely disabled, severely handicapped, etc.) that all have different interpretations
Multiple administrative requirements that are frequently different by agency
Multiple case managers (residential, vocational, day program, public school, and mental health case managers), none of whom had or expected responsibility to develop a total service plan
Competition for community positions among the various agencies involved in job development for individuals with handicaps
Lack of comprehensive vocational services
Lack of knowledge about available community services

Each of these areas of difficulty has been dealt with cautiously and politically. Final resolution of many of these problems came about through the development of written interagency agreements at the local, regional, and state levels. In many cases, once the programs were accepted as a component of the service system, the cooperation of the various agencies began to improve. It is extremely difficult to coordinate services between multiple agencies that have multiple and varied expectations about the same program.

Employer, Community, and Parent Expectations

Initially, it may appear that the three types of expectations (employer, community, and parent) comprise three separate sets of potential limitations. In actual practice, the difficulties encountered with employer, community, and parent expectations were very similar.

Too much support, not enough support, or inconsistent support for trainees
Inappropriate residential placements within the community that lack appropriate support to deal with varied work hours
Attitudinal barriers that included lack of belief by community, employers, and parents that an individual with significant handicaps can be successful in a community position
Vacillation between support, lack of support, expectations, and descriptions of responsibilities for the position

Many community education and advocacy activities were initiated in an effort to overcome some of these difficulties. Frequently, a parent of a successfully placed individual would speak to parent groups and provide detailed information about the placement process and the effects that it had on home life resulting in increased independence.

Transportation

Rural mass transportation leaves much to be desired. Those options that do exist are sparse and only operate on certain days at certain hours. Many different approaches were taken to deal with transportation issues. Frequently, a job placement would have to begin with artificial support (taxi, parents drive, etc.) and then during the training period other idiosyncratic solutions would be identified. Car pools became a partial solution to some transportation difficulties. The most common solution to transportation problems was to find a position within walking distance of the trainee's home. In a small rural community where group homes and ICF/MR settings may be within walking distance of a town, this is not an unmanageable solution.

Financial Incentives and Disincentives

Although there are a variety of salary subsidies available, there is a frequent change in employer evaluations once full salary is expected. When employers must pay full salary, their evaluations become more critical and accurate for training purposes. The safest approach appears to be to begin the position at entry level wages and guarantee that the job will be completed. This avoids many of the potential difficulties with providing employers with financial assistance to hire an individual with handicaps. It is interesting to note that project staff assisted in the paperwork for targeted jobs tax credit for many employers, but only a few employers actually applied for the tax credit when taxes were due.

The other financial difficulty has to do with the loss of social security benefits. Parents, protective of financial security, were often supportive of placement efforts until they were provided with information about the potential loss of benefits. Many service providers do not know that a person can earn up to $630 a month without losing Medicaid. The social security benefits were guaranteed while continued financial income from a community position was contingent upon the working capability of the trainee. The solutions to these difficulties included avoiding salary subsidy, attempting to place individuals in positions that had sufficient benefit packages, placing individuals in part-time positions, and advocating for changes in the social security system. Parents were informed of potential loss of benefits from the very beginning, and salaries versus benefits were carefully explained.

Maintenance and Follow-Up

The major difficulties with maintenance and follow-up of services for persons working in the community involved the service system itself, and the lack of expertise to deal with problems once they developed. Some of the more immediate difficulties that were presented included:

Lack of service capability for follow-up and retraining

Lack of alternate transportation options once one approach was unsuccessful or had to be changed

Employee, employer, and supervisor turnover (carefully developed support systems for trainees frequently had to be reestablished or established with new co-workers)

Position responsibility changes (seasonal variations in work expectations frequently necessitated retraining)

Residential situations changed (all support, scheduling, etc., that had been established in one residential setting would have to be reestablished within a new setting)

Budgetary difficulties (for some trainees this was the first time they had money on a regular basis and they had no skills or trainers to teach them budgeting or money management skills)

Employer failure to communicate (often employers were uncomfortable identifying difficulties that trainees were experiencing that would eventually cost them their jobs)

Social behavior changes (given new independence and confidence in themselves, trainees frequently developed new inappropriate social behavior)

The solution to these difficulties was to provide consistent employer, parent, and trainee follow-up. The long-term solution is the preparation of better trained, better paid professionals and paraprofessionals to work in the social services, and increased acceptance (improved expectations) of community members. The need for long-term follow-up has been recognized and is finally beginning to receive some attention (Will, 1984).

SUMMARY

The competitive employment programs in Vermont were initiated to improve the quality and variety of employment services available to individuals with severe handicaps in the state of Vermont. They are small programs, require limited financial resources, and have assisted in the development of competitive employment opportunities for approximately 12–15 individuals each year in each location. While this is not a large number, over time the numbers add up and the programs have become strongly established as contributing members of the service system. At a recent state conference on services to individuals with severe handicaps, many state regions without a program for competitive employment asked what they could do to facilitate the development of such a program in their region. The question indicates an acceptance of the program philosophy.

It is not easy to work within a fragmented service system where multiple agencies have varied administrative as well as applied expectations for their services; however, it is possible to develop coordinated and cooperative services for the benefit of the individual receiving services. Many different processes were initiated that were unsuccessful, but those activities that facilitated communication and cooperation included the following:

Quarterly and final reports in a format agreed upon by all invovled agencies
Information and dissemination activities that were approved by all agencies
Staff development and training that included staff from each agency involved
  with the programs
Consultation agreements with various involved agencies that consisted of
  shared reports
Agreed upon evaluation activities (all agencies had to agree to the most
  functional outcome measures for the trainees involved)
Formal process of resolution of disagreements that would result in written
  statements
Written financial agreements that explicitly explained which agency was
  responsible for what expenses, and a simplified bill and payment process
Written development, initial implementation, and full implementation guidelines that were agreed upon by all agencies involved with the programs
Agreement by the agencies to support the initial objectives of the projects, even
  in the face of crisis situations in other areas
Agreement of interaction patterns with other agencies or services that might
  include similar functions within the same geographic area

The frequent reason given for lack of improvement of quality of services is lack of resources and inadequate staff to trainee ratios. These are obvious and difficult problems within the existing adult system, but they are not insurmountable. Careful analysis of the service design, development of large group instruction for some individuals while others receive more intensive instruction, and effective utilization of parents and volunteers can frequently alter the service design and staff ratios. One staff member may become a full-time on-the-job trainer and begin the gradual process of identifying a position; analyzing that position; coordinating service agencies; gaining acceptance of a position for that individual; and providing intensive on-the-job training, follow-up, and long-term maintenance on the job. It is a slow process that does not begin to exhibit strength until after the second or third year of effort, but it is an effective process that will provide individuals with severe handicaps with the least restrictive community setting possible. The technology exists, the resources are scarce but (with coordinated effort) possible, and it is the best approach to develop quality services.

Eventually, community employment will become an expected service, communities and states will mandate such services, and the 1980s will be seen as the early stage of community acceptance of individuals with severe handicaps in the workplace.

REFERENCES

Appleby, J. A. (1978). *Training programs and placement services*. Salt Lake City, UT: Olympic Publishing Company.

Bachrach, L. L. (1981). *Human services in rural areas: An analytical review*. Rockville, MD: Project Share, A National Clearinghouse for Improving the Management of Human Services.

Bellamy, G. T. (1976). *Habilitation of severely and profoundly retarded adults: Reports from the Specialized Training Program*. Eugene, OR: Specialized Training Program.

Bellamy, G. T., Horner, R. H., & Inman, D. P. (1979). *Vocational habilitation of severely retarded adults: A direct service technology*. Baltimore: University Park Press.

Bellamy, G. T., Sheehan, M. R., Horner, R. H., & Boles, S. M. (1980). Community programs for severely handicapped adults: An analysis. *Journal of The Association for the Severely Handicapped, 5*, 307–324.

Belmore, K., & Brown, L. (1976). A job skill inventory strategy for use in a public school vocational training program for severely handicapped potential workers. In L. Brown, N. Certo, K. Belmore, & T. Crowner (Eds.), *Madison's alternative for zero exclusion: Papers and programs related to public school services for secondary age severely handicapped students* (pp. 143–219). Madison, WI: Madison Metropolitan School District.

Bowe, F. (1983). *Demography and disability: A chartbook for rehabilitation*. Fayettville: University of Arkansas, Arkansas Rehabilitation Services.

Brolin, D. E. (1984). Meeting the lifelong career development needs of students with handicaps: A community college model. *Career Development for Exceptional Individuals, 7*, 12–21.

Buttram, J. L., & Carlson, R. V. (1983, November). *Effective school research: Will it play in the country?* Paper presented at the American Education Research Association, Montreal, Canada.

Certo, N., Schwartz, R., & Brown, L. (1975). Community transportation: Teaching severely handicapped students to ride a public bus system. In L. Brown, T. Crowner, W. Williams, & R. York (Eds.), *Madison's alternative for zero exculsion: A book of readings: Volume V* (pp. 104–194). Madison, WI: Madison Public Schools.

Certo, N., & Swetlik, B. (1976). Making purchases: A functional money-use program for severely handicapped students. In L. Brown, N. Certo, K. Belmore, & T. Crowner (Eds.), *Madison's alternative for zero exclusion: Papers and programs related to public school services for secondary age severely handicapped students: Volume II, Part I* (pp. 271–344). Madison, WI: Madison Public Schools.

Coward, R. T., DeWeaver, K. L., Schmidt, F. E., & Jackson, R. W. (1983). Distinctive features of rural environments: A frame of reference for mental health practice. *International Journal of Mental Health, 12*(1–2), 3–24.

Equal to the task: 1981 DuPont survey of employment of the handicapped (1982). Wilmington, DE: E. I. DuPont DeNemours & Company.

Ginsberg, L. H. (Ed.). (1976). *Social work in rural communities. A book of readings*. New York: Council on Social Work Education.

Gold, M. (1973). Research on the vocational habilitation of the retarded: The present, the future. In N. Ellis (Ed.), *International review of research in mental retardation: Volume 6*. New York: Academic Press.

Goodall, P. A., Wehman, P., & Cleveland, P. (1983). Job placement for mentally retarded individuals. *Education and Training of the Mentally Retarded, 4*, 271–278.

Greenleigh & Associates. (1975). *The role of the sheltered workshop in the rehabilitation of the severely handicapped*. Report to the Department of Health, Education, and Welfare, Rehabilitation Services Administration, New York, NY.

Gruenewald, K. (1969). A rural county in Sweden: Malmohos county. In R. B. Kugel & W. Wolfensberger (Eds.), *Changing patterns in residential services for the mentally retarded*. Washingotn, DC: President's Committee on Mental Retardation.

Hamre-Nietupski, S., Ford, A., & Williams, W. (1977). Implementation of selected sex education and social skills programs with severely handicapped students. *Education and Training of the Mentally Retarded, 12*, 364–372.

Hasazi, S. B., & Gordon, L. R. (1983). *Factors associated with the employment status of handicapped youth*. Unpublished manuscript, Vermont State Department of Education, Montpelier.

Hill, R., Lagor, R., Moore, T., Hanzl, Z., Burrus, D., Williams, W., & Vogelsberg, R. T. (1980). Report to the Secretary of Human Services on mental retardation and vocational rehabilitaion. Burlington, VT: *Center for Developmental Disabilities Monograph Series, 1*, 1–35.

Hunt, A. S. (1982). *The long term impact of vocational rehabilitation services by severity of disability* (Information Memorandum RSA-IM-83-06). Washington, DC: Department of Education, Rehabilitative Services Administration.

Karan, O. C., Wehman, P., Renzaglia, A., & Schutz, R. (1976). *Habilitation practices with the severely developmentally disabled*. Madison, WI: Rehabilitation Research and Training Center, University of Wisconsin.

Leland, M., & Schneider, M. J. (1982). *Rural rehabilitation: A state of the art*. Fayetteville: Arkansas Rehabilitation Research and Training Center.

Manpower Demonstration Research Corporation. (1980). *Findings and recommendations from the national supported work demonstration*. New York: Author.

Nachtigal, P. (Ed.). (1982). *Rural education: In search of a better way*. Boulder, CO: Westview Press.

National Rural Center. (1981). *Rural poverty*. Washington, DC: Author.

Nietupski, R., Certo, N., Pumpian, I., & Belmore, K. (1976). Supermarket shopping:

Teaching severely handicapped students to generate a shopping list and make purchases functionally linked with meal preparation. In L. Brown, N. Certo, K. Belmore, & T. Crowner (Eds.), *Madison's alternative for zero exclusion: Papers and programs related to public school services for secondary age severely handicapped students: Volume VI, Part 1* (pp. 220–270). Madison, WI: Madison Public Schools.

Nietupski, J., & Williams, W. (1974). Teaching severely handicapped students to use the telephone to initiate selected recreational activities and to respond appropriately to telephone requests to engage in selected recreational activities. In L. Brown, W. Williams, & T. Crowner (Eds.), *A collection of papers and programs related to public school services for severely handicapped students: Volume 4* (pp. 507–560). Madison, WI: Madison Public Schools.

Nooe, R. M. (1981, December). *Clinical practice in rural settings: Curriculum implications*. Paper presented at the 26th Annual Program Meeting, Council on Social Work Education, Los Angeles, CA.

Revell, G. W., & Wehman, P. (1979). Vocational evaluation of severely and profoundly retarded adults. *Rehabilitation Literature, 39,* 1–8.

Revell, W. G., Wehman, P., & Arnold, S. (1983). *Supported work model of employment for mentally retarded persons: Implications for rehabilitative services*. Richmond: Virginia Department of Rehabilitative Services and Virginia Commonwealth University Rehabilitation Research and Training Center.

Rosenfeld, S. A., & Sher, J. P. (1977). The organization of rural schools: 1840–1970. In J. P. Sher (Ed.), *Education in rural America: A reassessment of conventional wisdom* (pp. 11–42). Boulder, CO: Westview Press.

Rowitz, L. (1984). The need for uniform data reporting in mental retardation. *Mental Retardation, 22,* 1–3.

Rudrud, E. H., Ziarnik, J. P., Bernstein, G. S., & Ferrara, J. M. (1984). *Proactive vocational habilitation*. Baltimore: Paul H. Brookes Publishing Co.

Rusch, F. R., & Mithaug, D. E. (1980). *Vocational training for mentally retarded adults: A behavior analytic approach*. Champaign, IL: Research Press.

Rusch, F. R., Schutz, R. P., Mithaug, D. E., Stewart, J. E., & Mar, D. K. (1982). *VACG: The vocational assessment and curriculum guide*. Seattle, WA: Exceptional Education.

Schalock, R. L., & Harper, R. S. (1982). Skill acquisition and client movement indices: Implementing cost-effective analysis in rehabilitation programs. *Evaluation and Program Planning, 5,* 223–231.

Schalock, R. L., & Harper, R. S. (1983). Untying some Gordian knots in program evaluation. *Journal of Rehabilitation Administration, 7,* 12–19.

Schutz, R. P., Vogelsberg, R. T, & Rusch, F. R. (1980). A behavioral approach to integrating individuals into the community. In L. Heal & A. Novak (Eds.), *Integration of developmentally disabled individuals into the community* (pp. 107–119). Baltimore: Paul H. Brookes Publishing Co.

Schutz, R. P., Williams, W., Iverson, G. S., & Duncan, D. (1984). Social integration of severely handicapped students. In N. Certo, N. Haring, & R. York (Eds.), *Public school integration of severely handicapped students: Rational issues and progressive alternatives* (pp. 15–42). Baltimore: Paul H. Brookes Publishing Co.

Sher, J. P. (1977). *Education in rural America: A reassessment of conventional wisdom*. Boulder, CO: Westview Press.

Sher, J. P., & Tompkins, R. B. (1977). Economy, efficiency, and equality: The myths of rural school and district consolidation. In J. P. Sher (Ed.), *Education in rural America: A reassessment of conventional wisdom* (pp. 43–80). Boulder, CO: Westview Press.

Snell, M. E. (1978). Functional reading. In M. E. Snell (Ed.), *Systematic instruction of the moderately and severely handicapped* (pp. 324–386). Columbus, OH: Charles E. Merrill Publishing Co.

Stanfield, J. S. (1976). Graduation: What happens to the retarded child when he grows up? In R. M. Anderson & J. G. Greer (Eds.), *Educating the severely and profoundly retarded*. Baltimore: University Park Press.

The Challenge of Rural Rehabilitation. (1983). *Rehab Brief: Bringing research into effective focus, 6*(9), 1–4.

Urban Institute. (1975). *Report of the comprehensive service needs study*. Washington, DC: U.S. Government Printing Office.

U.S. Bureau of the Census. (1983). *Labor force status and other characteristics of persons with a work disability: 1982* (Series P-23, No. 127). Washington, DC: U.S. Government Printing Office.

U.S. Commission on Civil Rights. (1973). *Accommodating the spectrum of individual abilities* (Clearinghouse Publication 81). Washington, DC.

Vandergoot, D., & Worrall, J. D. (1979). *Placement in rehabilitation: A career development perspective*. Baltimore: University Park Press.

Vogelsberg, R. T. (1984). Competitive employment programs for individuals with mental retardation in rural areas. In P. Wehman (Ed.), *Proceedings from the National Symposium on Employment of Citizens with Mental Retardation* (pp. 25–53). Richmond, VA: Rehabilitation Institute.

Vogelsberg, R. T. (in press). The employment training projects in Vermont. In F. R. Rusch (Ed.), *Competitive employment: Service delivery models, methods, and issues*. Baltimore: Paul H. Brookes Publishing Co.

Vogelsberg, R. T, & Rusch, F. R. (1979). Training severely handicapped students to cross partially controlled intersections. *AAESPH Review, 4*, 264–273.

Vogelsberg, R. T, Spaulding, P., Patterson, D., Schenck, R., & Phillips, R. (1984). Project Transition: Competitive employment case management system. *Center for Developmental Disabilities Monograph Series, 4*, 1–127.

Vogelsberg, R. T., Strauss, R., Keefe, S., & Brier, E. (1980). *Washington County Mental Health Inc. operational plan for the Vermont Mental Retardation and Vocational Rehabilitation Plan*. Barre, VT: Washington County Mental Health.

Vogelsberg, R. T, & Williams, W. W. (1980). *Towards comprehensive services for developmentally disabled individuals: Independent living and competitive employment*. Burlington, VT: Center for Developmental Disabilities.

Vogelsberg, R. T., Williams, W. W., & Ashe, W. (1981). Improving vocational services through interagency cooperation. In C. L. Hansen (Ed.), *Severely handicapped persons in the community* (pp.169–202). Seattle, WA: Program Development Assistance System.

Vogelsberg, R. T, Williams, W. W., & Bellamy, G. T. (1982). Preparation for independent living. In B. Wilcox & G. T. Bellamy, *Design of high school programs for severely handicapped students* (pp. 153–173). Baltimore: Paul H. Brookes Publishing Co.

Vogelsberg, R. T., Williams, W. W., & Fox, W. L. (1981). Comprehensive vocational services operational plan. *Center for Developmental Disabilities Monograph Series, 2*(3), 1–43.

Vogelsberg, R. T., Williams, W., & Friedl, M. (1980). Facilitating systems change for the severely handicapped: Secondary and adult services. *Journal of The Association for the Severely Handicapped, 5*, 73–85.

Wehman, P. (1980). *Recreational programming for developmentally disabled persons*. Baltimore: University Park Press.

Wehman, P. (1981). *Competitive employment: New horizons for severely disabled individuals*. Baltimore: Paul H. Brookes Publishing Co.

Wehman, P., & Hill, J. W. (1979). *Vocational training and placement of severely disabled persons: Project Employability: Volume I—1979*. Richmond: Virginia Commonwealth University.

Wehman, P., Hill, M., Goodall, P. A., Cleveland, P., Barrett, N., Brooke, V., Pentecost, J., & Bruff, B. (1982). Job placement and follow-up of moderately and severely handicapped individuals: An update after three years. In P. Wehman & M. Hill (Eds.), *Vocational training and placement of severely disabled persons* (pp.1–23). Richmond: Virginia Commonwealth University.

Wehman, P., &Kregel, J. (1983). *The supported work model: Toward job placement and retention of severely handicapped individuals*. Richmond: Rehabilitation Research and Training Center, Virginia Commonwealth University.

Whitehead, C. W. (1977). *Sheltered workshop study: A nationwide report on sheltered workshops and their employment of handicapped individuals*. Washington, DC: U.S. Department of Labor.

Will, M. (1984). *Bridges from school to working life. Programs for the Handicapped* (ISSN 0565-2804), Washington, DC: Clearinghouse on the Handicapped.

Williams, W., Coyne, P., Johnson, F., Scheuerman, N., Swetlik, B., & York, R. (1976). Skill sequences and curriculum development: Application of a rudimentary developmental math skill sequence in the instruction and evaluation of severely handicapped students. In N. Haring & L. Brown (Eds.), *Teaching the severely handicapped* (Vol. 2, pp. 234–279). New York: Grune & Stratton.

Williams, W., Friedl, M., & Vogelsberg, R. T. (1979a). *A secondary level special education survey of a rural state: Implications for service*. Burlington, VT: Center for Developmental Disabilities.

Williams, W., Friedl, M., & Vogelsberg, R. T. (1979b). *Characteristics of facilities providing prevocational and vocational services to the adult developmentally disabled in a small rural state*. Burlington, VT: Center for Developmental Disabilities.

Williams, W., Friedl, M., & Vogelsberg, R. T. (1980a). Adult developmental disabilities service provider training needs in a rural state. *Career Development for Exceptional Individuals, 3*(1), 53–60.

Williams, W., Friedl, M., & Vogelsberg, R. T. (1980b). *Training needs of vocational rehabilitation counselors: A survey to improve services to the severely developmentally disabled*. Burlington, VT: Center for Developmental Disabilities.

Williams, W. W., Vogelsberg, R. T., & Friedl, M. (1979). Prevocational and vocational services for severely disabled adults: A review and model description. *Center for Developmental Disabilities Monograph Series, 1*(5), 1–40.

Wolfensberger, W. (1983). Social role valorization: A proposed new term for the principle of normalization. *Mental Retardation, 21*, 234–239.

Chapter 3

Innovations in the Education of Preschool Children with Severe Handicaps

Phillip S. Strain and Samuel L. Odom

Early intervention for preschoolers has become one of the most active arenas for research and program development with severely handicapped persons. In preparing to write a chapter summarizing some of the new developments in this area, the authors were forced to focus on a limited number of topics from a much larger and exciting array of innovations. After considerable rumination and debate, the authors elected to describe recent developments in four areas: 1) parents as direct intervention agents, 2) peer-mediated instruction, 3) special education technology, and 4) program evaluation. For each area, the authors review the existing literature, describe relevant clinical applications, and offer some speculation on problems and potentials for the future.

PARENTS AS DIRECT INTERVENTION AGENTS

For many years, most early intervention programs have operated with a "more is better" philosophy when it comes to involving parents in their severely handicapped child's education. Indeed, there are a host of compelling reasons that promote this view:

Preparation of this chapter was supported by Contract No. 300-82-0368 (Early Childhood Research Institute) from the Department of Education, and by Grant No. MH 37110-01A1 from the National Institute of Mental Health to the University of Pittsburgh. However, the opinions expressed herein do not necessarily reflect the position or policy of the U.S. Department of Education or the National Institute of Mental Health, and no official endorsement should be inferred.

1. Federal law (Public Law 94-142, proposed version of the Education of the Handicapped Act Amendments of 1983) clearly stipulates parental involvement.
2. Grant preparation guidelines for early intervention programs under the U.S. Department of Education, Handicapped Children's Early Education Program auspices require extensive parent involvement.
3. Disabilities of severely handicapped individuals often dictate cross-setting, extensive, long-term training, training that for logistical reasons often falls on parents.
4. By gaining teaching competencies, parents may ameliorate or avoid feelings of depression, anxiety, incompetence, and guilt.
5. Growing evidence indicates that *extensive* involvement of parents as teachers greatly improves children's long-term outcomes.

The critical role of parents as educators for their severely handicapped children is evidenced by research efforts. For instance, in a long-term follow-up study of autistic children who were exposed to a behavior therapy program, Lovaas, Koegel, Simmons, and Long (1973) found that treatment gains were maintained *only* in homes where parents continued to implement training procedures. More recent outcome data presented by Lovaas (1982) indicated that 50% of the young autistic children who were exposed to an intensive, parent-implemented (or parent surrogate-implemented) intervention were behaviorally indistinguishable from normally developing classmates in the early elementary grades.

Short-term outcome data on a similar group of preschool-age autistic children are provided by Strain (1984). After participation in an intervention program that required parents to attend center-based training 9 hours each week and to conduct daily home programs, all the preschool-age autistic children functioned within normal intellectual limits and were behaviorally indistinguishable from normally developing, mainstream class peers.

Several characteristics of the above-mentioned studies require attention. First, each involved children labeled as autistic. Yet, that diagnosis for preschool-age children is hardly applied in a uniform fashion. From a *behavioral* description of the participants, it is clear that they: 1) performed in the moderate to severe degree of retardation prior to treatment, 2) engaged in frequent periods of self-stimulation, 3) had limited language and social skills, and 4) seldom imitated appropriate behaviors.

In addition to target child similarities, parent training interventions had many procedural features in common. For example, each project emphasized parents' skill building, as opposed to efforts aimed at either enhancing parents' general knowledge of handicapping conditions or improving parents' psychological adjustment to a handicapped family member. Moreover, one can find great overlap in the actual skills taught to parents. Specifically, parents were taught a wide array of behavioral teaching tactics including: shaping, differential attention, providing discrete trial instruction, collecting and graphing observational data, and implementing various behavior reduction programs. Many similarities also exist with respect to how parents were trained. Written instruction was minimized as was lecture/discussion formats. Instead, parents were provided with appropriate teaching models, offered practice opportunities, and given feedback on their performance. Essentially, a competency-based approach to parent training was used in each of the above-referenced treatment programs.

Another striking similarity between cited programs was the intensity of parent involvement. In each program, the parents were involved *daily*, and they often provided several hours of intervention (especially at the beginning of their child's treatment).

To summarize briefly, there are many forces that have brought about a strong professional emphasis on parents as instructional agents for young children with severe handicaps. The major questions around parental involvement in child treatment no longer center on the whys or hows, but rather draw attention toward an examination of: 1) the match between parental needs and program services, and 2) the recruitment and continued involvement of "high-risk" families.

Parental Needs and Program Services

Like most human services endeavors, the development of parent training programs preceded any careful analysis of the consumers' expressed needs for specific services. As researchers have begun to focus their attention on parents' priorities, the discontinuity between parent training goals and consumers' needs has become clear. For example, Sparling, Lowman, Lewis, and Bartel (1978) asked parents to describe various areas of knowledge pertaining to their handicapped child's development. Parents expressed a greater need for information on promoting physical health, identifying community resources, and coping with family stress than information on promoting learning and development. In effect, there may be many instances where parental needs and child needs actively conflict, at least on a resource allocation basis (Cansler & Winton, 1983). For example, many parents-in-training also must function competently as spouses, employees, parents of nonhandicapped children, and children themselves. There are, undoubtedly, times when parents must choose to be "good" spouses rather than "good" teachers for their handicapped children. For instance, the teacher-mother may be unable to conduct the clothes-dressing or hand-washing program for her child because she is behind schedule for dinner preparation. A singular focus on parents' roles as trainers may at best be shortsighted and at worst clinically irresponsible. Consider, for example, that divorce rates in families with severely handicapped children have been reported to be three times the average for families with nonhandicapped children, and the suicide rate in these families is nearly twice the national average (Love, 1973).

Other evidence (e.g., Winton & Turnbull, 1981) suggests that preschool programs must provide certain *preconditions* to ensure successful parent training. In their survey of 31 mothers, Winton and Turnbull found that the following factors, in order of importance, were influential in the selection and evaluation of preschool programs: 1) logistical concerns such as provision of day care, convenience, and cost of program; 2) professional's involvement in the child's education so that parents could have a break from this responsibility; 3) the presence of a satisfying parent-professional relationship; 4) presence of parent involvement activities such as opportunities for parent groups, parent training, and parent counseling; and 5) concerns about the impact of the child's peer group on the parents.

It is also apparent that most intensive parent training programs are predicated on an outdated view of American family life. As described by Foster, Berger, and McLean (1981), an examination of early intervention programs leads to the conclusion that

> . . . mothers are the primary caretakers for their children, that caring for children is the major or sole employment of most mothers, that children are raised by their two biological parents, and that fathers show their concern for their children through participation in organizational efforts such as fund raising, meeting with legislators, and so forth. (p. 58)

Parent training components that support and seem grounded in these "Beaver Cleaver Family" views include: 1) an exclusive focus on mothers as trainers, 2) a demand for training during regular working hours, and 3) a token involvement of fathers in child treatment.

Changes in the structure of American families and new information about the needs and priorities of parent training consumers obviously require careful professional attention and a modification of training programs. A danger exists that changes will be cosmetic only. That is, there is a clear temptation to rush toward fathers' support groups, volunteer baby sitter services, evening workshops, and the like, without examining the more fundamental economic and societal influences that impinge upon attempts at parent training.

Particularly with parents of children with severe handicaps, it is important to recognize that learning how to better teach and manage their youngsters is but one of a multitude of concerns. Often, and quite reasonably, parents are overwhelmed by: 1) their child's physical illness, 2) prospects for economic hardship, 3) a realization of life-long dependence by their child, and 4) uncertainties about how the family will cope psychologically.

Recruiting and Maintaining "High-Risk" Parents

Among professionals involved in parent training, there is a well-established folklore regarding difficult families. Often referred to as "high risk," these families typically represent some combination of the following characteristics: 1) low-income status, 2) low educational level, 3) single parent household, and

4) denial of child's disability. In fact, such families are "at risk" for not availing themselves of services, being undetectable to service providers, and dropping out of training programs.

Just how successful are current parent training efforts with high-risk families? The data available to answer this question are scattered, limited by handicapping condition, and imperfect. What can be stated with some confidence is that few efforts now exist that target high-risk families with severely handicapped children. Probably the efforts in the Milwaukee Project (Heber & Garber, 1975) represent the closest attempt to serve this parent population; however, the degree of child handicap in this project was relatively mild.

Most parent training programs, in fact, serve high-risk families on a random basis. Where enough families have participated, some interesting comparisons are available, most of which show that high-risk families have not been served adequately. For example, Wahler (1980) has shown that high-risk families, particularly those with minimal and largely negative extrafamilial social contacts, terminate treatment of their oppositional child after a few sessions. However, fathers' emotional support for mothers appears to attenuate early termination and training failures (Reisinger, Frangia, & Hoffman, 1976).

While the authors know of no systematic efficacy data, numerous programming techniques are often presented as vital elements in sustaining the involvement of high-risk families. A number of other authors have argued that child behavior change will serve as a potent reinforcer for parents' training efforts. Thus, it is commonplace for programs to target initially some child behavior that will be quickly altered (e.g., Gardner, 1976). It must be kept in mind, however, that available evidence suggests that even for simple child behavior problems, parents must persist in newly learned patterns of behavior before any child change is forthcoming. For example, Strain, Steele, Ellis, and Timm (1982) found that parents of oppositional preschoolers had to engage in differential reinforcement procedures for 2–3 weeks before satisfactory levels of child compliance were reached. In a replication of differential reinforcement training with parents of severely delayed preschoolers, Cordisco (1984) found that parents may not receive the "reinforcement" of improved child compliance for several months. While there is great intuitive appeal to the choice of easy-to-modify child behaviors as initial treatment targets, it does not seem as if one can rely on immediate child effects to maintain parents' involvement.

Another often used tactic for maintaining high-risk parents in training is to introduce various contingencies for involvement. Reputably successful contingencies include: continued child access to program services, financial reimbursement, continued access to ancillary services (e.g., baby sitting), and self-monitoring with self-reinforcement (Benassi & Benassi, 1973; Eyberg & Johnson, 1974; Kazdin, 1973). The authors emphasize that the data base in support of these contingencies is scant, and obvious logistical and ethical restraints will likely result in minimal improvement in the near future.

Still another set of procedures aimed at recruitment and maintenance of high-risk families involves what may be labeled as "consumerism." That is, parents monitor training, and even manage one another *and* professionals. The longest standing operation of this kind is the Regional Intervention Program (RIP) in Nashville, Tennessee. In this model, the parents not only provide treatment and training, but they constitute the majority voice in policy decisions at the program level. The effectiveness of such consumerism is best reflected by the fact that parents' income, education, and socioeconomic status (SES) are not related to child or parent outcomes at RIP (Strain, Young, & Horowitz, 1981).

In summary, a variety of approaches are available for helping to recruit and maintain high-risk families in training. As a group, these approaches focus primarily upon changing parents' behaviors; thus, they are professionally and politically safe. The authors fear that these approaches may foster a victim-blaming mentality, embodied in such often used parent descriptors as: "poorly motivated," "uncaring," and "in need of priority reordering." Unfortunately, such victim-blaming diverts attention away from more fundamental political solutions to problems produced when a severely handicapped child, poverty, and unemployment co-exist.

Conclusions

In the past decade, literally hundreds of projects have been established to help parents of young children with severe handicaps. Where intensive training opportunities have been provided, it appears that parents-as-educators come to play a very significant role in their children's behavioral development. In fact, there is some evidence, albeit scant, that significant improvement in some children with severe handicaps is dependent upon parents acquiring and using behavioral teaching tactics.

To a large measure, however, parents' priorities and concerns have not influenced the content or structure of parent training programs. The authors suspect this omission to be a fatal flaw, contributing greatly to the often observed lack of maintenance and generalization.

As parent training efforts become more consumer conscious (hopefully), it will also be important to acknowledge the social and economic forces that regrettably make certain families poor risks in existing service models. Simple technological sophistication in skill training is no substitute for a complex solution to the multiple needs of parents with severely handicapped children.

PEER-MEDIATED INSTRUCTION

One of the more recent service delivery innovations for severely handicapped preschool children is the utilization of classroom peers (disabled and non-disabled) as intervention agents. In peer-mediated interventions, a child or group of children are taught to engage in specific instructional behaviors that are designed to promote handicapped children's skill acquisition. With few exceptions, preschool peer interventions have been aimed at improving social interaction competencies.

Types of Peer-Mediated Instruction

Peer-mediated procedures vary widely in their degree of structure and the specific demands placed upon intervention agents. Three types of peer-mediated intervention have been identified: *proximity, prompt/reinforcement,* and *peer-initiation* (Odom & Strain, 1984b).

Proximity Interventions Proximity interventions occur when socially competent children are placed with the target children and are requested to: 1) play with the target children, 2) get the children to play with them, or 3) teach the target children to play. The socially competent peers are not given *direct* training for increasing the social interactions of the target children. Proximity interventions depend instead upon a natural transmission of social skills from one group of individuals to another through direct social interaction with more socially competent peers.

Several experiments have employed the proximity approach with autistic children. McHale (1983) grouped six autistic children with nonhandicapped children in daily play sessions for a 10-week period. Teachers instructed the nonhandicapped children to help the autistic children learn to play. Across the play sessions, the autistic children significantly increased their social interactions with nonhandicapped peers and decreased their levels of solitary play.

In the first experiment reported by Lord (1984), autistic children were grouped with the same-age or younger nonhandicapped children in dyadic play sessions. Using a within-subjects design in which subjects served as their own controls, little social interaction was seen when subjects were grouped with other autistic children during baseline/control sessions. When grouped with the nonhandicapped children who were instructed to help their autistic peers learn to play, the autistic children's social interchanges increased across sessions. Higher levels of social interaction occurred for the same-age groupings than for the younger-age groupings. Lord (1984) suggested that the same-age peers offered clearer social initiations than the younger peers and were better able to originate strategies for getting the subjects to respond. Lord (1984) replicated these findings in a second study with two autistic boys.

Prompt/Reinforcement A second type of peer-mediated intervention consists of training peers to *prompt and/or reinforce* the social behavior of target children. In these procedures, a prompt is an instruction (e.g., "Come play") to engage in some social behavior, and reinforcement is an event occurring after the behavior (e.g., "I like to play with you") that increases or maintains the frequency of the desired social behavior. Studies grouped under this classification may contain reinforcement alone or both prompt and reinforcement together.

A landmark study that gave impetus to much of the peer-mediation intervention research was conducted by Wahler (1967). The peer group of five preschool-age children was trained to give attention to five target children after the target children exhibited certain social behaviors; the peers were also taught to ignore other behaviors. Wahler demonstrated that peer attention could serve as a reinforcer for such behaviors as doll play, aggression, and cooperation. In a less frequently cited study, Weisen, Hartley, Richardson, and Roske (1967) trained severely mentally retarded children to be reinforcing agents to their peers. Through dispensing edible reinforcement to members of the peer group, these confederates increased the frequency of social interaction of their peers.

To increase the social play of two preschool handicapped children, Guralnick (1976) first used a modeling procedure with two nonhandicapped peers, resulting in few changes in social interaction. In a second phase of the study, the confederates (nonhandicapped peers) prompted and socially reinforced the social play of the subjects who had resultant gains in positive verbalizations and advanced levels of play with a more severely handicapped group of subjects. Young and Kerr (1979) had a mildly mentally retarded classmate prompt social interaction and deliver edible reinforcers to severely retarded subjects after interactions occurred; increases in positive social interaction resulted for both subjects.

Peer-Initiation Intervention In the peer-initiation approach, peers are instructed to direct social overtures to the target children. Such social initiations may include asking a child to play, giving a toy to a child, giving physical assistance, or suggesting a play idea.

Peer-initiation interventions were used by Strain, Shores, and Timm (1977) to promote the positive social behavior of six preschool-age behaviorally disordered boys. Two nonhandicapped boys, serving as confederates, were trained to direct social initiations to the subjects to increase the frequency of the subjects' social interactions. Each confederate was grouped with a triad of target children and intervened with each child, one at a time. Confederate initiations to subjects increased reliably during two intervention settings and were paralleled by increases in the positive social behavior of five of six subjects.

In a second study of this series, severely behaviorally disordered preschool children were once again recipients of social bids from a trained confederate (Strain, 1977). Observations of the children's performance were conducted during the four conditions of this withdrawal-of-treatment design study, as well as during a free-play generalization session that the peer trainer did not attend. Data on the three target children revealed that the peer trainer was successful in increasing the positive social behavior of all subjects. Generalization data for two of the subjects during intervention phases revealed that they also increased their social interactions during free play. Data on the third subject revealed no changes for the generalization sessions. The third subject was described as having displayed the fewest positive social behaviors during the first baseline. This differential outcome points to the magnitude of treatment effects as it relates to the entry level skills of the target children.

A more precise focus on the content of effective social initiations was reported by Hendrickson, Strain, Tremblay, and Shores (1982). In two experiments, these authors attempted to analyze the effects of specific social bids that had been identified in a naturalistic observation study as having the greatest likelihood of eliciting a subsequent positive social response (i.e., play organizers, shares, assists). (For a definition of these three behaviors, the reader is referred to Hendrickson et al., 1982.) In the first of the two experiments on the use of these tactics, a nonhandicapped 4-year-old girl was trained to emit these behaviors to three of her behaviorally handicapped peers. Preintervention training consists of explaining to the child the purpose of the intervention and the definition of the three behaviors. "Asking" and "helping" were the strategies emphasized during this training series. The peer trainer was also given ample practice in initiating these behaviors and in selecting materials to help her accomplish her goal. Direct prompting and reinforcement of the confederate was also provided during the sessions with target children. Prompting consisted of reminding the peer trainer to initiate if she did not do so within 15 seconds of her last interaction or initiation. Reinforcement consisted of providing the peer trainer with an edible reward at the end of each 5-minute intervention. Increases in the confederate's play organizer, share, and assistance social initiations lead to immediate and substantial increases in the three subjects' positive social behavior.

The second experiment in this series was a replication of the first, with more severely handicapped children as target subjects. The peer trainer in this study exhibited a variety of severe behavior problems. Procedures were identical to those used in the first study, and results were also similar. The use of play organizers, shares, and assists by the peer trainer resulted in dramatic increases in social interaction behaviors of the three target youngsters. As in a previous study by Young and Kerr (1979), the authors noted that the pretraining as well as direct prompting and praise provided to this peer trainer were more extensive than those provided to the normal trainer in the first experiment. Generalization data from this and from the first experiment revealed no clinically significant behavior change for any of the six target subjects. This supports the notion proposed by Guralnick (1976) and others that without formal and systematic structuring of the environment, generalization of social behaviors will not take place.

Curricular Innovations

As the peer-mediated intervention literature expands, and the more successful techniques are delineated, research needs to be translated into practical application. Curricular translations of peer-mediated intervention procedures for use by practitioners in the field have been developed and are approaching dissemination. The Social Competence Intervention Package for Preschool Youngsters (SCIPPY) by Day, Powell, and Stowitschek (1980) is one curricular procedure designed to assist psychologists or teachers in training peers as intervention agents for socially withdrawn children. Through a series of lessons employing role playing and some didactic instruction, peer confederates are taught ways to initiate specific social behaviors that are likely to elicit a response from a peer. Activity cards are provided to set an appropriate context for the interactions. An evaluation study with three withdrawn children and three confederates has documented the success of the procedures in promoting the specifically targeted confederate initiations and resulting responses from socially withdrawn children (Day, Powell, Dy-Lin, & Stowitschek, 1982).

A second curriculum that addresses social integration of handicapped and nonhandicapped children has also employed a peer-mediation strategy for promoting social interaction of withdrawn children. The Integrated Preschool Curriculum (IPC) (Odom et al., 1984) incorporates a direct instructional format for training peer confederates to direct social initiations to socially withdrawn peers. Scripted lessons that begin with didactic instruction and move to behavioral rehearsal are designed to teach confederates to promote the "good playing" (e.g., suggesting play ideas, shaing with a friend, etc.) of their handicapped peers. Peer-mediated procedures are expected to increase the responding behavior of handicapped children with limited social repertoires. Complimentary training procedures for the handicapped children provide direct instruction for social initiations. As with SCIPPY, a large number of play activities are described to set the context for interaction. Two recent studies have documented the effectiveness of the peer-mediated intervention (Odom, Stein, & Jenkins, 1983) and the IPC as a whole (Odom, Jenkins, Speltz, & DeKlyen, 1982) for improving the social behavior of handicapped preschool children.

While SCIPPY and the IPC concentrate on peer-mediated social skills training, the LEAP (Learning Experience . . . An Alternative Program for Preschoolers and Parents) curriculum model incorporates peer-based instruction for all developmental areas (Strain, 1984). Implemented in a mainstream preschool typically serving six normally developing and six autistic-like children, peer instruction takes three forms: 1) peers as participants in group-oriented contingencies, 2) peers as behavioral models, and 3) peers as direct agents of training. Each of these procedures is described below.

Group-oriented contingencies represent one of the most thoroughly researched procedures for managing children's behavior in classroom settings (Litow & Pumroy, 1975). Not only have these procedures been shown to be as effective as individually based contingencies, but they also have the advantages of being cost effective in terms of effort required to implement, likelihood of being used again, and potential positive side effects.

Of the various group-oriented strategies, interdependent reinforcement contingencies seem to be most efficient. As utilized by Gamble and Strain (1979), interdependent conditions are said to exist when all members of a group must perform to a minimum standard before any member of the group can achieve some positive consequence. Of course, the procedure makes for easy individualization in that performance standards and behaviors can be selected on a child-by-child basis.

Putting this information into practice, the following procedures are implemented in LEAP's classroom:

1. Normally functioning age-peers and handicapped children participate in a classroom behavior management program based on interdependent contingencies. For example, during a 15-minute group instructional period, each of the nonhandicapped children may have a behavioral goal of answering 100% of teacher questions correctly. During this same time period, one of the handicapped children may have the goal of remaining in the assigned seat for 80% of the time; another handicapped child may have the goal of looking at the teacher when spoken to on 80% of the opportunities; still another handicapped child may have the goal of not body-rocking more than 10% of the time interval. For any of the children to receive a positive consequence, each must meet his or her goal.

2. Prior to beginning each instructional period in which the group interdependent contingency is in effect (those situations in which children have the opportunity to influence each other's performance), the teacher announces each child's goal for that time period.

3. At the end of designated instructional periods, the teacher will announce each child's goal attainment, where appropriate. Then the handicapped children will be prompted to distribute reinforcers to class peers.

One of the more often voiced reasons supporting the integration of handicapped and nonhandicapped children is that the normally developing children will model appropriate behaviors for handicapped youngsters (Bricker, 1978; Guralnick, 1976). There is little doubt that normal peers indeed provide (at least on an informal basis) appropriate behavioral models. However, the mere availability of appropriate models in no way sets the occasion for handicapped children to *imitate* these behaviors. With autistic-like and severely mentally retarded children who display severe behavioral handicaps, this situation is further complicated by the general lack of observational learning skills exhibited by these youngsters. To utilize the influence of appropriate behavioral models, a number of preconditions are established at LEAP.

First, each of the handicapped children participate in a Peer-Imitation Training (PIT) program as outlined by Peck, Apolloni, Cooke, and Raver (1978). Briefly, in this procedure, a handicapped and a nonhandicapped child are paired together for training. The nonhandicapped child is trained initially by an accompanying teacher to model specific appropriate behaviors. The teacher then prompts the handicapped child to imitate the modeled behavior and subsequently reinforces correct responding. Daily PIT sessions typically include 20–30 opportunities for children to imitate appropriate behaviors. After behavioral criteria have been met, the teacher begins a response-dependent fading procedure in which the slow reduction of teacher prompts is tied to the subject's continued performance at a prespecified level. This response-dependent fading procedure has been validated with severely handicapped preschool children by Timm, Strain, and Eller (1979).

In addition to the PIT procedures, which are designed to develop basic prerequisite skills for imitating behavioral models, all daily group activities in LEAP (e.g., free play, work table time, snack time) are structured to enhance the likelihood of positive, appropriate behaviors being imitated by target children. Grouping, curricular, and instructional components are all arranged to facilitate the modeling of appropriate behavior.

Selecting specific children for groups and their physical placement within groups set the occasion for observing and imitating appropriate behaviors. Previous research has indicated that dyadic grouping may foster appropriate social responding (Strain & Kerr, 1979), so socially competent, non-handicapped children are "paired" with the autistic-like preschoolers during table time (i.e., fine motor) activities. In addition, some toys and play materials lend themselves more readily to cooperative use (Odom & Strain, 1984a; Strain & Kerr, 1979). Such "cooperative" toys are selected to focus the autistic-like children's attention upon a joint activity with their nonhandicapped peer, thus increasing the probability of imitating appropriate behavior.

In terms of curriculum planning issues, it is most important that modeled behaviors be those that the handicapped child already exhibits, but at an inconsistent or unacceptable level. For example, in a group work table setting, behaviors likely to be selected for imitation include: inseat behavior, requesting help, and functional object use.

The most consistent finding regarding the clinical implementation of the observational learning paradigm is that the model child's behavior must be reinforced by events that are also reinforcing to handicapped children (Strain & Hill, 1979; Strain & Kerr, 1979). Accordingly, teachers are encouraged to implement the following instructional procedures: 1) provide direct verbal and, when necessary, physical prompts for handicapped children to observe their peers (i.e., "John, watch Tim hammer."); 2) provide direct reinforcers, which are effective with *both* children, to the nonhandicapped child while specifying the desired behavior(s) (e.g., "Tim, I like the way you hit the peg with the hammer; you earned a piece of pretzel."); 3) provide direct verbal and, when necessary, physical prompts to the handicapped child to initiate imitative behavior (e.g., "John, use your hammer like Tim."); and 4) provide direct positive consequences to the handicapped child for approximations toward accurate imitation. These procedures are consistent with the instructional strategies found in PIT.

The successful use of young nonhandicapped age-peers as intervention agents for handicapped children with limited social repertoires requires attention to the following programmatic concerns: 1) selection of peer trainers, and 2) training of peer trainers. Each of these programming components, as employed in the LEAP model, is described below:

Selection of Peer Trainers An analysis of the literature that reports on the use of peers as training agents suggests a few distinct criteria for selection of peer helpers. The following criteria were used in this model program:

1. The student must attend school regularly to ensure uninterrupted training.
2. The student must display positive, unprompted social initiations toward peers during free play.
3. The student must respond positively to social initiations from peers.
4. The student must follow adult directions reliably.

Unlike many job descriptions, this one does not include minimum age (peer helpers as young as 36 months have been trained successfully), previous experience (only one had prior training as a peer helper), or specific education requirements (several peer helpers themselves have been enrolled in classes for behaviorally disordered or mentally retarded children; see Ragland, Kerr, & Strain, 1978). In prior training efforts, the authors have found that teacher nominations based upon the above-listed criteria provide a reliable and cost-effective selection procedure (Strain & Kerr, 1979).

Training of Peer Trainers Teaching a student to modify the isolate behavior of peers seems like a major undertaking. Yet, the previous studies have relied upon a rather simple training procedure that took place before any actual play sessions. The following two-part strategy is used at LEAP:

1. The child is given an explanation of the task such as, ''Try hard to get the others to play with you.''
2. ''Training to expect rejection'' is accomplished through a role play in which the adult ignores every other initiation by the peer helper, explains this behavior and, finally, encourages the peer helper: ''Keep trying, even when children don't play at first'' (Strain, Shores, & Timm, 1977).

These training steps are repeated in 20-minute daily sessions (usually four), until the peer helper can reliably make social bids to the occasionally reluctant adult.

Evaluations of participants (i.e., six autistic-like and 13 nonhandicapped children) in the LEAP project show that: 1) autistic-like participants achieved, on the average, a two-fold increase in their rate of growth across developmental domains during program participation; 2) autistic-like participants' rate of performance during intervention was *above* the program entry level rate of performance for nonhandicapped participants; 3) nonhandicapped participants averaged 2 months growth for each month in the program on developmental domains targeted for instruction; and 4) nonhandicapped participants averaged 1 month growth for each month in the program for developmental domains not targeted for instruction (Hoyson, Jamieson, & Strain, in press).

Conclusions

Peer-mediated instruction for social skill deficits, particularly the peer social initiation intervention, represents a rapidly expanding and useful technology for producing behavior change. If initial outcomes for target children are examined, it is clear that substantial behavior change is often achieved. Yet, like many interventions applied to groups of children with severe handicaps, data on the generalization of skills and their maintenance across time are disappointing.

If peer-mediated interventions are to become more widespread, it will be essential to examine some of the roadblocks to generalization and maintenance. The authors have three specific concerns in this regard. First, most social behavior generalization assessments have taken place in target youngsters' original developmentally segregated classrooms, and there is good reason to suspect that *typical* peer behavior in these settings operates to extinguish social interaction (Strain, 1983). Expecting social behavior generalization in these settings is logically similar to expecting telephone answering behavior in a setting without phones (Strain & Shores, 1983). Second, it seems likely that the typical, a priori method of target behavior selection has led to the teaching of socially trivial and occasionally inappropriate behaviors. Social behavior interventionists have seldom sought to define the functional social behaviors for a given setting prior to treatment. Third, and finally, most peer-mediated interventions have been applied for brief periods of time only. While 3–4 months may be adequate to demonstrate experimental control, such a time frame seems naively restricted if long-term gains are desired.

SPECIAL EDUCATION TECHNOLOGY

Few aspects of our lives have been left unaffected by the current wave of advanced technology. Advertisements herald the newest generation of the APPLE or IBM computer and explain how these instruments can make life less complicated. As the prices recede and the systems become more "friendly" to the user, availability and feasibility of using computers and related media become an everyday reality, with direct educational implications. In reference to special education, Stowitschek and Stowitschek (1984) noted that there are two factors that motivate educators to learn about the current technology: 1) genuine fascination or interest, or 2) fear of being left behind.

As a discipline, special education has not lagged behind in the current technological revolution. In the Stowitscheks' survey of resource room teachers in Washington, Utah, and North Dakota, they found that 90% of the respondents had access to a microcomputer, as compared to 66% of the regular education teachers surveyed (Stowitschek & Stowitschek, 1984). However, the use of current technology with young severely handicapped children may be less prevalent.

This section highlights a number of innovative technological practices that have been specifically developed or have potential application for young children with severe handicaps and their parents. These practices include: 1) the use of microcomputer and related technology for educational proramming; 2) the use of video, public media, and computer-based programs for delivering services to children and parents in the home and community; and 3) other technological innovations that serve an augmentative role for the communications skills of young children with severe handicaps or perform an administrative function.

Microcomputers and Education of Severely Handicapped Students

Microcomputers have the potential for serving a number of important purposes in education. They may present instruction to students, monitor students' performance, alter instruction based upon student responses, collect data on student performance for teacher use, provide feedback to students about their responses, and allow students to work at their own pace (Stallard, 1982). Presumably, the advantage of using a microcomputer rather than a teacher for the same purpose is that a computer will free the teacher for other instructional tasks, assuming that the student can perform independently at the computer.

Though there are potential advantages to using microcomputers in instruction, a number of disadvantages have also been noted. Much of the instructional software available for microcomputers is either inappropriate for severely handicapped individuals, is poorly designed, or has yet to be evaluated or validated with handicapped children (Budoff & Hutten, 1982; Hofmeister, 1982). Part of the reason for inadequate instructional design is that the computer programmers do not have an educational or instructional design background (Hannaford & Taber, 1982). Similarly, an adequate research base has yet to develop for addressing such critical design issues as sequencing instruction, timing and feedback, and differential learning rates.

A more critical issue for severely handicapped individuals is the mode in which computers typically present instructional stimuli and the accompanying response requirements. Most software presents instruction in a written mode that requires at least some reading skills. Similarly, the typical response mode requires some minimal typing skills. Such entry requirements exclude young severely handicapped individuals. Recognizing these disadvantages, a number of procedures employing microcomputer technology have been developed for use by or with young severely handicapped children.

Microcomputer-Videodisc Programs As noted above, a basic problem in designing technological procedures for young children with severe handicaps has been the mismatch between the technological requirements and the skills of the child. In the past, the learner has often been shaped to fit the demands of the microcomputer. With most young, severely handicapped children, the technology must be reshaped to fit the needs of the learner. In combining a videodisc technology with microcomputer processing, a first step has been taken that accomplishes this technological adaptation. For a comprehensive review of this technology, with a discussion of potential benefits and limitations for young children with severe handicaps, the reader is referred to Chapter 12 by Hofmeister and Friedman in this volume.

Contingency Intervention Training The work of Brinker and Lewis (1982b) provides another example of how technology may be shaped to the needs of the learner. Basing their work upon previous studies of Watson (1966) and Lewis and Goldberg (1969), Brinker and Lewis (1982c) built their instructional procedures around handicapped infants' need to recognize environmental contingencies (i.e., results that are produced by the infants' behavior) in their environment. Normally developing infants learn about cause and effect relationships by observing the changes that occur in their environment that are produced by their own actions (i.e., contingencies). Brinker and Lewis (1982c) proposed that handicapped infants are at a disadvantage because: 1) they may have motor disabilities that keep them from exploring their environment, and 2) parents have low expectations for the infants so they often do not wait for the infants to respond to environmental or social stimuli. As a result, handicapped infants may be delayed in becoming aware that they can have an effect upon their environment. Indeed, some severely and profoundly handicapped children may never learn that they can effect environmental changes (i.e., develop means-ends relationships in Piagetian terms).

To teach infants to recognize contingencies, Brinker and Lewis (1982b) first identified the voluntary motor responses that were within the infants' control, and developed mechanisms (e.g., switches, neck pads) that could be used to signal a microcomputer. They then programmed the computer to monitor and consequate discrete body movements (e.g., leg kick, arm wave) with auditory or visual stimuli. In this way, they differentially reinforced specific motor behaviors that taught the children that their behavior produced an interesting event in the environment. For example, an infant might move his or her right arm and receive a short visual array of colored lights. The computer, which could monitor up to 14 responses, was programmed to change the required motor behavior periodically, thus teaching the child that the contingencies, rather than the specific behaviors, were important. Also, the computer kept records of responses to the consequent events (i.e., reinforcers) and changed the form of reinforcement whenever the children began to habituate to it (e.g., grew tired of seeing the lights).

All interventions were conducted in the home using a portable micro-computer. In preliminary tests, four of five profoundly handicapped infants learned the contingencies, and the investigators detected two styles of learning. Some of the infants learned the contingencies after a few trials and generalized this "contingency awareness" to all other targeted body movements. Other infants initially exhibited generalized levels of arousal after reinforcement that eventually became specific to the single reinforced response. In addition to teaching children to identify and respond to the contingencies, Brinker and Lewis (1982a) noted increased rates of positive affect (e.g., laughing and smiling) by the infants, and positive attitudinal changes when parents realized that their children could learn. Though this intervention appears promising, it remains in the experimental stages. As of yet, no information about the infants' motor behavior or performance on cognitive tasks outside of the intervention task has been reported.

Corneal Reflection Monitoring Another example of using micro-computers for adapting technology to the skills of children with severe handi-caps is provided by investigations of the corneal reflection techniques for measuring visual gaze of severely involved children. This technique typically has been used when eye gaze is the only response available for identifying images or units on a communication board device. A small video camera attached to a pair of glasses detects the corneal reflection of an infrared light source. The information is processed through a microcomputer and analyzed with other information about the angle of the head and the images on the display to determine where the child is looking. The information is then used to identify which communication symbol the child has chosen (Finkle & O'Leary, 1980; Foulds, 1982).

Though the corneal reflection technique is not a teaching procedure, given the rapidly increasing sophistication of current technology, one could speculate on a future pedagogic direction for this device. Young normally developing children, as well as autistic and mentally retarded children, are poor scanners of visual arrays (Kail, 1979). They often attend to the perimeter of an array or nonsalient features, providing very little information about the visual stimulus. For example, in an expressive vocabulary task that requires children to label pictures of actions, a young autistic child might look at a child running through a field and visually fix upon a small flower that was in the background of the picture rather than the salient figure of the child. When the teacher asks what is in the picture, the child's response of flower may seem quite bizarre. Given the sensitivity with which gaze can be monitored (Foulds, 1982), and the sophisti-cation with which computers analyze child performance and provide reinforcement or feedback for a desired response, it seems likely that one could combine these two procedures to teach young handicapped children to be more efficient scanners of visual instructional material.

Logo A further example of computer technology that allows young severely handicapped children to learn to affect change in their environment is the Logo program (Weir, 1982). The central character of the program is a robotic turtle located on the floor that is remotely controlled by the computer or is visually represented on a computer screen. The program may be used simply to move the turtle to different locations on the floor or to design graphics on the terminal screen. Though the turtle is usually moved by typing instructions into the computer, simpler controls have been developed for young handicapped children. Goldenberg (1979) described a simplified set of controls that allowed a young autistic child to use, and indeed, to become engrossed in the Logo task. Though the Logo program appears appropriate for much of the handicapped preschool population, effective use for anything but recreation has yet to be described.

Biofeedback One frequently mentioned use of computers with severely handicapped children has been to provide physiological monitoring for biofeedback programs (Finkle, 1980; Goldenberg, 1979). In such programs, the involuntary muscles or neurologically involved parts of the body may be "reeducated" by providing visual or auditory feedback to the learner when a voluntary response occurs. For severely involved cerebral palsied children, the microcomputer may monitor the specific neurological or neuromuscular activity, analyze when a response has occurred, provide immediate feedback to the learner, and record the response occurrence. For biofeedback, the immediacy of the feedback is very important for assisting the learners to gain control of their bodies. Such procedures, though not often used with young severely handicapped children, could be effective.

Computer Feedback Though immediate feedback about learner responses has been emphasized as a strength of microcomputers (Bennett, 1982), Hofmeister and Thorkildson (1984) have raised questions about such beneficial qualities. They pointed out that there are little data to support the proported superiority of immediate feedback and cited studies in which delayed feedback produced results superior to immediate feedback.

It is quite possible that the timing of feedback to the learner would vary according to the task, type of learner, and correctness of the response. To be effective, biofeedback would require immediate feedback, at least during the early stages of training, whereas, feedback on a microcomputer-videodisc matching program could possibly require less immediate information about correctness. Similarly, certain learners, such as young severely handicapped children, may require more time than other learners (e.g., normally developing elementary-age children) to process the response that they have given before receiving feedback. Last, a maxim in behavioral psychology is that a reinforcer is most effective when it immediately follows a response (Sulzer-Azaroff & Mayer, 1977). However, it is possible that corrective feedback for an incorrect response may be more effective if there is a delay. In such a case, the delay itself could be an indicator that the response was incorrect and may cue the learner to examine alternative responses before the corrective feedback is given. All of these issues are open to empirical verification and the authors agree with Hofmeister and Thorkildson (1984) and Stowitschek and Stowitschek (1984) that this field is in great need of a solid research base from which to make decisions about instructional programming.

Computer-Based and Videotape Service Delivery in the Home

Severely handicapped infants and preschoolers in many states do not receive educational services until they reach school age. Special education technology and the public media have contributed a number of innovative procedures designed to assist parents in: 1) teaching their child at home, and 2) overcoming feelings of shock and grief after learning that their infant is handicapped.

Videotaped Programs for Parents Several projects have developed media packages for parents of severely handicapped infants. As one part of their "Home-Based Media Materials," the American Printing House for the Blind designed a slide cassette program for parents of multihandicapped blind infants (Moore, 1982). The program provided parents with information about building an educationally relevant environment for their child and suggested ways in which activities may be worked into the parents' daily routines.

To fill a service delivery gap for severely handicapped infants and toddlers in their area, Project Pre-Empt developed a series of films that could be aired on local television (Mauk, 1979). The films covered a number of topics such as early intervention and screening, teaching self-help and toileting, and behavior management. The purposes of the films were to provide information to the parents that would allow them to cope with their handicapped child and to create instructional opportunities in the child's everyday life.

In reaction to poor attendance at parent education meetings, Project HAND (Moseley, 1982) developed a series of videotaped vignettes that addressed a variety of sensitive issues concerning parents' reactions to the birth of severely handicapped infants, and the family's subsequent adaptations. The films, which assumed a soap opera format, differed from the two previously described programs in that they did not focus on parent teaching skills but rather on parents' attitudes or feelings about their children. Also, unlike the two previous programs, this project attempted to evaluate impact, documenting large increases in parent meeting attendance and positive parental responses toward the film series.

To teach parents to facilitate the development of their severely physically handicapped preschoolers, Project FEATT developed over 60 videotaped programs that described behavioral teaching strategies. In a well-controlled evaluation study, Holworth and Currie (1982) compared the televised parent training procedures to three other conditions in which a parent received an illustrated activity manual, the parent received the videotape presentation and the manual, or the parent was on a waiting list and received no instruction. Using the parents' interaction with their child in an instructional task as the dependent variable, the investigators found that both videotape only and curriculum manual conditions produced changes in parent behaviors superior to the control group, but none of the three were as effective as the videotape and curriculum manual combination. When supplemented with the curriculum manual, the videotaped presentations were very effective in teaching parents to be skilled teachers of their children.

Computer-Assisted Home-Based Programming In an effort to provide services to severely handicapped infants and their parents located in areas in which no service delivery model is available, the Computer-Assisted Program (CAP) has designed a format for developing an individualized battery of educational activities that parents can implement at home (Fewell & Sandall, 1984). A pool of activities designed to: 1) meet specific educational objectives of a child, and 2) be implementable within the child's daily routine, have been field-tested and are cross-referenced to specific assessment information. Professionals from the local educational agency conduct a standardized assessment of the child and enter the results into the computer. Based upon field-tested information, a variety of individualized activities are generated for the parents to conduct at home. Periodic monitoring allows the parent to change objectives as each child meets a pre-established criterion. Since the program is in its initial phase, data documenting the efficacy of this approach have not yet been reported.

Other Technological Innovations

Several other technological innovations have contributed to improvement in services for severely handicapped children in general. However, because of the large literature they have generated and their application to the whole age range of severely handicapped individuals, their contributions will be acknowledged briefly and readers will be referred to other more thorough reviews (Capozzi & Mineo, 1984; Harris & Vanderheiden, 1980).

Communications One of the major applications and contributions of current technology for severely physically handicapped individuals has been the development of alternative forms of communication. Communication apparatus such as the Xygo Board, the Lightbeam Headpointer (Vanderheiden, 1982), and infrared tracking of gaze responses to communication boards (Finckle & O'Leary, 1980) have provided a mode of communication for severely physically involved individuals. The use of such nonspeech communication systems as the Blissymbol System (Silverman, McNaughton, &

Kates, 1978) and NonSLIP (Carrier & Peak, 1975) have provided a syntax that nonverbal children may use. In addition, these nonspeech communication systems have begun to be linked with computer synthesis audio responses (see, e.g., the Semantically Accessible Language [Bennett, 1982]). Such innovations may reduce the complexity of learning these symbolic expressive language systems and expand the audience with whom the child can communicate.

One caution should be noted. The use of these communication innovations often requires some functional receptive language, such as basic vocabulary, simple direction-following, and so forth. Many young severely handicapped children will not have such prerequisite skills, and thus the impact of these innovations, at this point in time, would appear somewhat limited for this population.

Administration Computer management of child records is a second important technological innovation. The record keeping requirements of Public Law 94-142 and state monitoring agencies have produced major bookkeeping tasks for administrators and teachers. The use of microcomputers for storing and accessing child records, developing progress reports, and analyzing program effectiveness based upon child change data could potentially result in more effective and efficient administrative structures (Budoff & Hutten, 1982). Computer packages such as the CAMEO (Brown, 1982), which prepares individual educational programs, can save teachers a large amount of time. Such packages may have an indirect impact upon young children with severe handicaps because they free the teacher's time for more direct student instruction and instructional planning. Again, the reader is referred to Hofmeister and Friedman (Chapter 12, this volume) for a more thorough review of this topic.

Conclusions

A variety of technological and media innovations have direct relevance for the education of young severely handicapped children and their families. Computer technology is being shaped to match the entering skill levels of severely handicapped children, and media packages have been developed to provide services to children and families who would normally be left unserved. Though such innovations are exciting and bode well for the future use of technology with young severely handicapped children, they have yet to make a major impact upon early childhood special education. A sound research base is currently lacking (Stowitschek & Stowitschek, 1984), though there appear to be productive efforts to establish one (e.g., Brinker & Lewis, 1982c; Holworth & Currie, 1982; Thorkildson & Hofmeister, 1984). With continued empirically based efforts to evaluate computer and media packages, young severely handicapped children and their families may accrue substantial benefits in the future.

PROGRAM EVALUATION

Programs that provide educational services to young children with severe handicaps are often required to prove that their efforts have had a positive impact upon children and/or their families. They must monitor children's progress and provide evidence that their procedures, rather than other factors in the environment (e.g., services from other agencies, maturation, medication), produced the positive changes in the children's performance. Though this requirement is often explicitly stated by the funding agency (e.g., federal government, local education agency), project directors and classroom teachers are limited in their ability to comply because of the nature of the population of interest and the scarcity of appropriate tools and methods for conducting sound program evaluations. This section identifies methodological problems faced by program evaluators who attempt to measure efficacy of programs for young severely handicapped children, and describes innovative approaches used by individuals who have tackled this problem.

Definition of Terms

Unless stated otherwise, program evaluation will refer to the analysis of outcome variables used to determine an educational program's impact upon its clients. This form of program evaluation, also referred to as *summative* program evaluation (Scriven, 1974) and *efficacy research* (Strain, 1981), is designed to generate information that can be used for answering policy questions (e.g., Should funding for the program be continued? Should the program continue accepting severely handicapped children?). A second form of program evaluation, called *formative* evaluation, generates information for staff and program developers that can be used to revise or improve the program. Due to space constraints and other excellent papers on the topic (Hupp & Rogers-Warren, in press), the implication of formative evaluation for preschool programs serving severely handicapped children is not discussed here.

Traditional Evaluation: Problems for Children with Severe Handicaps

Severely handicapped preschool children are both a low incidence and highly diverse group of youngsters. These and other characteristics (e.g., deviation from normal developmental patterns) present a number of program evaluation problems that are unique to this population.

Program Evaluation Design   To demonstrate efficacy, programs must show that their procedures rather than other extraneous variables produced changes in a child's performance. Variables such as maturation, regression to the mean, mortality, or subject selection must be ruled out as being responsible for changes in children's performances. Traditionally, methodologies from experimental research have been used to control for these extraneous factors.

The classic work by Campbell and Stanley (1963), a standard against which all evaluation designs are evaluated, described several "true" experimental designs. These designs require random selection from the population of subjects at large, the formation of treatment and control (or comparison) groups, and random assignment to those groups. Prominent program evaluators have argued strongly for the adoption of true experimental designs in field-based evaluation research (Boruch, Cordray, Pion, & Leviton, 1980).

The problems of using "true" experimental designs for evaluating programs for severely handicapped preschool children are tremendous. Service delivery programs do not randomly select children that they serve, and ethical considerations preclude randomly assigning children to treatment and control (i.e., nontreatment) groups. Even if children could be randomly assigned to treatments, the number of severely handicapped children in most school districts is quite small, which would prevent "large N" statistical analyses.

Subject Population The skills and educational needs of children with severe handicaps are extremely varied. Such heterogeneity causes considerable problems when "true" experimental designs are used because the subject's characteristics must be comparable across treatment and control groups. Matching for handicapping condition will rarely be successful because of the idiosyncratic nature of the children's handicaps and, again, the relatively low incidence of this population. As Bricker and Sheehan (1981) questioned, how does one equate a "deaf-blind" multiply handicapped child with a severely mentally retarded child? Thus, the nature of the severe handicaps exhibited by some children would seemingly preclude the use of random assignment to treatment groups.

Assessments Psychometrically sound assessment instruments (i.e., instruments with adequate reliability and validity) tend to be norm-referenced developmental scales or tests that usually provide single global scores (e.g., IQ, Receptive Language Age). Such instruments do not give information about specific skills, cannot be administered repeatedly over a short time period, and may be affected by sensory or behavioral deficits of the child being tested (Ramey, Campbell, & Wasik, 1982). More importantly, these assessment instruments have been developed for and normed on a nonhandicapped population. Because a severely handicapped population will have a smaller range of correct responses on the tests than a nonhandicapped population, the test may be less sensitive to small changes in child behavior that, nevertheless, may be educationally significant.

When using norm-referenced assessments, an implicit assumption is made that severely handicapped children acquire developmental skills in the same order as nonhandicapped children; the validity of such an assumption is questionable (Garwood, 1982). For example, many young severely handicapped children sometimes exhibit "splinter" skills (i.e., isolated skills that are beyond their general developmental level). When such children are tested, and a ceiling is reached (e.g., child misses three in a row and the test is discontinued), it is possible that the child may still complete a number of isolated items at a higher developmental level. When subsequent posttests document the child's correct performance on those items, the correct scores are attributed to program impact, thus inflating the efficacy data from these tests. Because of the highly idiosyncratic nature of such a phenomenon, it is unlikely that random assignment or matching, even if it could occur, would control for such an extraneous variable.

A related assessment problem is the absence of psychometrically respectable instruments to measure outcomes that programs may judge as important. The parent training area provides a good example. Most programs for severely handicapped preschoolers include a parent component and, thus, would want to measure certain outcomes relating to their parent training goals. However, in a review of 27 early intervention programs for handicapped infants and families, Simeonsson, Cooper, and Scheiner (1982) concluded that measures of parent and family adjustment are limited. Indeed, the most commonly reported outcome measure for parent components of the 22 program evaluations reviewed by Odom and Fewell (1983) was documentation of parent participation, with a minority of the programs also including nonstandardized measures of parent knowledge or parent satisfaction.

Implementation   The success with which all program components are delivered to severely handicapped children will determine overall impact. Precise implementation may be difficult for programs serving young severely handicapped children in three ways. First, programs tend not to document the fidelity with which they implemented their full program. In a review of program evaluations involving young handicapped children, Odom and Fewell (1983) found that only one program provided implementation information for the complete model and related it to child performance. Second, because severely handicapped preschoolers tend to have a high frequency of medical problems that can cause absences, it is likely that they will receive the program, if it is fully implemented, for only a portion of the school year. Reporting child progress over a full year, without correcting for absences, may give an inaccurate, overly conservative measure of program efficacy. Third, though less of a problem in rural areas, urban areas often contain numerous agencies that provide a range of services for severely handicapped children and families. It is not uncommon for families to seek services from several such agencies at one time. For example, a parent may seek speech therapy from a speech and hearing center in addition to enrolling his or her child in a comprehensive early childhood special education program. Though the child may benefit when multiple agencies provide similar or supportive services, one could argue that the supporting agency was equally responsible for changes on the outcome measures.

Innovative Solutions to Complex Problems

Faced with the incredible range of problems described above, the "ostrich" approach is often adopted: stick your head in the sand and perhaps the problem will disappear. Such an approach is appealing, especially when staff see children in their program making important gains that they know would not have occurred if the child had not been enrolled in the program. However, given the latter-day "block grant" phenomena and the current climate of competition for funds among social agencies, the ostrich approach may be programmatically fatal. A number of innovative evaluation procedures have been developed to provide solutions for many of the problems noted above, and may be of interest to teachers, program directors, and evaluators who are concerned with demonstrations of program efficacy.

Assessment A frequently cited solution to the norm-referenced test dilemma with severely handicapped children has been to employ criterion-referenced assessments (White & Haring, 1978). Criterion-referenced assessments compare a child's performance against a mastery level on assessment tasks rather than against the performance of normally developing peers of similar chronological ages. Such assessments have the advantage of specifying behaviors that could be used as specific intervention targets and thus may present a more direct measure of program effect. However, to the extent that they are based upon normal developmental scales, are not standardized or normed upon a severely handicapped preschool population, and do not report reliability or validity, criterion-referenced tests are subject to many of the criticisms directed to norm-referenced measures.

Fortunately, a number of criterion-referenced measures, standardized with severely handicapped infants and preschool children, have recently appeared in the literaure. The Competence Assessment Profile Battery (Brooks-Gunn & Lewis, 1981) was designed to provide a profile of a child's performance across four domains (i.e., social, affective, perceptual-cognitive, and linguistic-communicative). The assessment has been standardized with over 100 handicapped infants and young children. A second assessment, used for identifying behavioral characteristics of handicapped infants and children, is the Carolina Record of Individual Behavior (Simeonsson, Huntington, & Short, 1982). This assessment also measures behaviors across a number of domains, and has been standardized with young multihandicapped children. A criterion-referenced test, standardized with older mildly to severely handicapped preschool children, is the Uniform Performance Assessment System (White, Edgar, & Haring, 1978). This assessment provides information on five domains (i.e., gross motor, preacademic, communication, social, and self-help), has accompanying software that computes the child's performance in relation to other items on the assessment (i.e., percent correct) and past performances, and has been used successfully to evaluate program efficacy for young severely handicapped children (Bricker & Dow, 1980). A fourth assessment that is becoming widely used is the Adaptive Performance Inventory (API) (Consortium on Adaptive Performance Evaluation, 1978). The API, standardized on a national sample of severely handicapped individuals, assesses the critical function of task items (i.e., the functional effect of a task rather than the process of completing it) and is adaptable for children with various sensory and motoric impairments.

An important consideration in selecting assessments is to ensure that they relate closely to the program objectives (Cooley & Lohnes, 1976; Strain, 1981). The assessments must test what the program is teaching. Criterion-referenced or curriculum-referenced (White & Haring, 1978) assessments have the advantage of specifying tasks that may directly relate to curricular content. They can provide an accurate measure of child progress resulting from the program's instructional procedures. However, such procedures could be criticized, perhaps unfairly, for "teaching to the test." A convincing counter to such an argument has been to use multiple outcome measures. For example, a program evaluation conducted by the Good Samaritan Diagnostic Prescriptive Program (Grove, 1981) used a curriculum-referenced assessment (i.e., Teaching Research Curriculum for Moderately and Severely Handicapped Children) to measure child progress on individual program objectives, and also the Student Progress Record (SPR), which is a criterion-referenced measure normed on a group of trainable mentally retarded children in Oregon. Significant child progress was demonstrated on content areas of the SPR that overlapped with the instructional procedures, but not on the content areas in which instruction had not been provided. This comparison provides convincing evidence of the program's impact upon the areas that were to be felt important for pupils (i.e., that related to the goals).

Analysis of Child Change Because control groups are not available for programs for severely handicapped children, evaluators have often relied on single group experimental designs. A variety of innovative data analysis procedures have been proposed to control for extraneous variables (i.e., maturation, regression to the mean) in evaluations of early intervention programs for severely handicapped children that do not have a control or comparison group. Without exception, these procedures seek to compare children's entering rates of development with their performance while in the program. Each procedure, along with accompanying mathematical formula, is described in Table 1. Brassell's (1977) procedure compared the developmental velocity or rate of development while children were in the program with the children's rates before they entered the program. To compute efficiency measures for early interventions, Bagnato and Neisworth (1980) analyzed the amount of progress made by children while in the program. Similarly, Simeonsson and Wiegerink (1975) compared the amount of progress made while children were enrolled in the program with that which would ideally be expected (i.e., based

Table 1. Methods of computing program impact with single groups

Authors	Procedure	Formula
Irwin and Wong (1974)	Age-compensated scores	Post DA $-$ [(Post CA $-$ Pre CA) $\times$ (Pre DA/Pre CA)]
Simeonsson and Wiegerink (1975)	Efficiency index	$\dfrac{\text{Post DA} - \text{Pre DA}}{\text{Ideal progress*}} \div \dfrac{\text{Pre DQ}}{100}$
Brassell (1977)	Changes in developmental velocities	$\dfrac{\text{Post DA} - \text{Pre DA}}{\text{Time in program}} - \dfrac{\text{Pre DA}}{\text{Pre CA}}$
Bagnato and Neisworth (1980)	Intervention efficiency index	$\dfrac{\text{Post DA} - \text{Pre DA}}{\text{Time in program}}$
Wolery (1983)	Proportional change index	$\dfrac{\text{Post DA} - \text{Pre DA}}{\text{Time in program}} \div \dfrac{\text{Pre DA}}{\text{Pre CA}}$
Bricker and Sheehan (1981); Tallmadge (1977)	Educationally significant gains	[Post DA $-$ Pre DA] $\div$ [(Pre Standard deviation + post standard deviation)] $\div$ 2
Simeonsson, Huntington, and Short (1982)	Goal attainment scaling	$50 + \dfrac{10\Sigma(w)(x)}{\sqrt{(1 - p)\,(\Sigma w^2) + p\,(\Sigma w)^2}}$

DA = Developmental age or age equivalency on dependent measure w = weight of subscale

CA = Chronological age x = outcome level value

Pre = Pretest or at entry to the program p = .30 (assumed intercorrelation of subscales)

Post = Posttest or when exiting from program Σ = sum of

DQ = DA divided by CA

*Ideal progress may be weighted according to DA, IQ, or handicapping condition

upon an estimate of ideal progress). In a more exact procedure for estimating ideal progress, Wolery (1983) computed the expected (i.e., ideal) progress without program impact using the developmental rate of the child before program entry. He then divided the rate of progress during intervention by the proportional measure of ideal progress to obtain a measure of the intervention's effects relative to pretest developmental rates. This procedure more closely controls for the varied entry levels and abilities of children. Using a slightly different formula to achieve essentially the same results, Irwin and Wong (1974) computed "age-compensated" scores by subtracting predicted posttest scores, based upon pretest rates of development, from actual posttest scores. Once a metric has been computed, such as the Proportional Change Index (PCI), inferential statistics may be used to determine the statistical significance of differences between rates of developmental gain while in the program and entry level rates.

Taking a slightly different approach, Bricker and Sheehan (1981) analyzed the "educational significance" of gains made by severely handicapped children in their program. By dividing gains made on the Uniform Performance Assessment System (UPAS) by the pooled standard deviation for pretest and posttest scores, gains were judged educationally significant if they exceeded .25% of the pooled standard deviation.

Because the diverse skills of handicapped children may preclude the use of a standard outcome measure for all children, the Goal Attainment Scaling approach (GAS), developed by Kiresuk and Lund (1976), has been suggested for evaluating outcomes of early intervention programs (Simeonsson, Huntington, & Short, 1982). Goals of individual children are scaled along a least (−2) to most (+2) favorable outcome continuum, and differential weights may be attached to different goals (e.g., social communication goals may be given a 5 weighting and motor goals may be given a 1 weighting for an autistic child). The teacher rates the goals before and at various times during the class treatment. Using the formula in Table 1, a standard score may be computed and used to compare children's goal attainment on differing individual objectives.

Of course, the methods in Table 1 may be criticized on several grounds. First, with the exception of GAS, the procedures rely on standardized assessments, and thus are subject to the criticisms mentioned above for such assessment instruments. Second, analyses of changes in rates of progress (i.e., all but Bricker & Dow, 1980, and Simeonsson, Huntington, & Short, 1982) assume that severely handicapped, and indeed normal children, develop linearly (i.e., make 1-month gains every month). Given the nature of the population, it is reasonable to assume that some young severely handicapped children may decelerate in their rate of development across time (i.e., advance at a slower rate as they grow older). Thus, at times, maintaining a current rate of progress could be an educationally significant outcome for severely or profoundly handicapped children. In addition, most of the analyses in Table 1 predict linear trends from only two data points (pretest and posttest), whereas three data points are commonly accepted as a minimum for predicting trends (Linn, 1981).

The practice of computing "educational significance" (e.g., Bricker & Sheehan, 1981) is an attempt to rely on criteria other than statistical significance for measuring and evaluating child gains. However, because the criterion is arbitrarily established (Tallmadge, 1977) rather than being based upon empirical measures of educational significance (e.g., child learns to communicate as a result of being in the program), the practice does little more than provide a more conservative statistical criteria for measuring program impact.

GAS offers the flexibility often needed when evaluating programs for young severely handicapped children. It allows children with different educational objectives to be compared on a common metric. Indeed, research using GAS with adults has documented moderate to high interrater reliability (Calsyn & Davidson, 1978), although reliability information for the use of GAS with severely handicapped children has not been reported. The critical weakness of GAS is validity. Because weights may often be assigned by subjective criteria (Wolery, 1983) and the scaling of the goal continua may vary across individuals who develop the GAS, treatment impact may be estimated inaccurately (Simeonsson, Huntington, & Short, 1982). However, content validity may be bolstered by using a group of professionals (e.g., the interdisciplinary team) to develop weightings and scaling levels for the goal continua. In addition, the GAS could be used in conjunction with a traditional standardized measure and the prediction formulae noted above (either the PCI or the age-compensated scores being the most useful) to provide evidence for concurrent validity.

Single-Subject Designs   The shortcomings of the data analysis procedures noted above may be overcome, in part, by the use of single-subject designs (Tawney & Gast, 1984). Through intra-individual comparisons and replications across subjects, program staff can keep close track of children's progress and simultaneously collect important information for evaluating program impact. A multiple probe design across individual educational objectives within domains (e.g., self-help) is one example of how single-subject designs may be used (Horner & Baer, 1978). In Figure 1, five objectives are listed for the self-help area. During baseline, probes were conducted three times, once during the beginning of the year assessment and twice before instruction begins. After instruction begins, probes would be conducted each week until a child reached criterion. At that time the child would move into a maintenance phase and instruction would begin on a second objective. Periodic probes, every 3 weeks, would measure maintenance of the completed objectives. Daily probes are preferable but often not practical for teachers with a relatively high student-teacher ratio. Graphs, as in Figure 1, could be kept for individual child objectives in each domain and would provide the teacher with

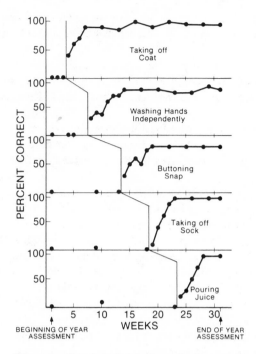

Figure 1. Hypothetical data illustrating the use of a multiple probe design for analysis of child progress on five self-help objectives.

immediate information about the child's performance across the year as well as document the functional relationship between children's objectives and instruction. Several Handicapped Children's Early Education Programs (HCEEP) Demonstration Projects have used single-subject designs to demonstrate convincingly the impact of their procedures with young severely handicapped children (Fredericks & Moore, 1978; Grove, 1981).

Social Validation A central concept in the current applied behavior analysis literature is social validation. It refers to the subjective evaluation of treatment effects by multiple expert judges or outcomes (Kazdin, 1977; Wolf, 1978). Interestingly, the concept has parallels in the program evaluation literature. The phrase "triangulation of program effects" often appears in discussions of program evaluation and refers to determination of program impact by examining a program from multiple independent perspectives (Cronbach, 1982). In an area fraught with methodological problems, social validation of program effectiveness may be a useful criterion by which to judge the worth of an early intervention program.

One method for determining social validation is to identify individuals who will be the "consumers" of the skills acquired by the severely handicapped children enrolled in the program and have them provide judgments (either directly or unobtrusively) about program outcomes. Parents, if they are not the focus of the program, are in a prime situation to judge improvements made by their children, and indeed, parent satisfaction measures are often used as outcome measures. The public school system is a consumer of early intervention programs in that the children, at the end of the program, may move to a placement within the public school system. The skills acquired by children in early intervention programs may enable them to move and function successfully in less restrictive class placements than otherwise would have occurred. Thus, the future educational placement may be a useful social validation outcome measure. For example, Bricker and Dow (1980) argued convincingly that the community placement of 46 of the 48 severely and profoundly handicapped infants in preschools was a positive outcome for their program.

Peers may also be the consumers of skills acquired by severely handicapped students. Thus, measures of social integration into peer groups of less handicapped or nonhandicapped youngsters may provide evidence for social validity of program efficacy. The community at large may also be consumers of children's newly acquired skills, and documentation of a child's independent functioning in a community (i.e., eating a hamburger at McDonald's without a tantrum; toileting in a public bathroom) by social agents outside of the school system (e.g., social worker from another agency, neighbor, another parent in the program) may provide evidence of social validity. Finally, a more traditional assessment of social validity may be conducted if time and equipment are available. Children's performances in the classroom at the beginning of the program and end of the program may be videotaped, and independent judges may rate differences in skill level. However, such a practice may not be feasible for most programs. As a last cautionary note, it should be added that social validity measures that provide evidence of socially and educationally significant results of programs are subject to the same threats to internal validity as the designs noted above. Their purpose in program evaluation is to provide important complementary information that allows program evaluators to make a more believable case for program efficacy.

Conclusions

Program evaluation as applied to interventions for young severely handicapped populations has been a topic for heated debate—a debate fueled by methodological saber-rattling and contributing little to the advancement of the field. Fortunately, the polemics surrounding control groups and the lack thereof have abated of late, and real progress has been made on assessment procedures, prediction designs, and single-case methodology.

Still, several problem areas require the most concerted efforts. For example, the instrumentation and procedures for monitoring the independent variable in early childhood programs are largely unexplored. Of course, no scientific replications are possible without a complete understanding of the interventions to be evaluated. Second, very little is known about the strategies necessary to reliably assess target behaviors that vary widely in their rate, duration, and intensity from day to day. For presumably more "stable" behaviors associated with cognitive performance, a few data points are probably safe; but what of the assessments of social skills, language production, and deviant behaviors? Essentially, there are no guidelines for selecting the number of data points sufficient for an accurate pre- or postintervention assessment. Finally, an erroneously applied assumption from normal child development still exists that a brief intervention experience will somehow "innoculate" severely handicapped children, and no or minimal intervention will be necessary in the future. Evidence for the operation of this assumption is the repeated incidence of follow-up assessment without follow-up treatment. The authors submit that follow-up assessment without follow-up treatment is a cruel hoax on the profession, on society, and on the children served.

SUMMARY

This chapter highlights four innovations in the education of severely handicapped preschool children: 1) parents as direct intervention agents, 2) peer-mediated instruction, 3) special education technology, and 4) program evaluation. Developments in each of these areas have added greatly to the quality of intervention afforded to clients. The volume and educational significance of these and other research and development activities bode well for young children with severe handicaps.

REFERENCES

Bagnato, S. J., & Neisworth, J. T. (1980). The Intervention Efficiency Index: An approach to preschool program accountability. *Exceptional Children, 46,* 264–269.

Benassi, V. A., & Benassi, B. (1973). An approach to teaching behavior modification principles to parents. *Rehabilitation Literature, 34,* 134–137.

Bennett, R. E. (1982). Application of microcomputer technology to special education. *Exceptional Children, 49,* 106–113.

Boruch, R. F., Cordray, D. S., Pion, G., & Leviton, L. (1980). *Digest of recommendations to the Congress and to the Department of Education.* Unpublished report to the United States Congress.

Brassell, W. R. (1977). Intervention with handicapped infants: Correlates of progress. *Mental Retardation, 15,* 18–22.

Bricker, D. (1978). A rationale for the integration of handicapped and nonhandicapped preschool children. In M. J. Guralnick (Ed.), *Early intervention and the integration of handicapped and nonhandicapped children* (pp. 3–26). Baltimore: University Park Press.

Bricker, D. D., & Dow, M. G. (1980). Early intervention with the young severely handicapped child. *Journal of The Association for the Severely Handicapped, 5,* 130–142.

Bricker, D., & Sheehan, R. (1981). Effectiveness of an early intervention program as indexed by measures of child change. *Journal of the Division for Early Childhood, 4,* 11–27.

Brinker, R. P., & Lewis, M. (1982a). Contingency intervention with the help of microcomputers. *Journal of Special Education Technology, 5,* 37–39.

Brinker, R. P., & Lewis, M. L. (1982b). Discovering the competent handicapped infant: A process approach to assessment and intervention. *Topics in Early Childhood Special Education, 2,* 1–16.

Brinker, R. P., & Lewis, M. (1982c). Making the world work with microcomputers: A learning prosthesis for handicapped infants. *Exceptional Children, 49,* 163–170.

Brooks-Gunn, J., & Lewis, M. (1981). Assessing young handicapped children: Issues and solutions. *Journal for the Division of Early Childhood, 2,* 84–95.

Brown, N. P. (1982). CAMEO: Computer-assisted management of educational objectives. *Exceptional Children, 49,* 151–153.

Budoff, M., & Hutten, L. R. (1982). Microcomputers in special education: Promises and pitfalls. *Exceptional Children, 49,* 123–128.

Calsyn, R. J., & Davidson, W. S. (1978). Do we really want a program evaluation strategy based solely on individual goals? A critique of Goal Attainment Scaling. *Community Mental Health Journal, 14,* 200–208.

Campbell, D. T., & Stanley, J. C. (1963). *Experimental and quasi-experimental designs for research on teaching.* Chicago: Rand McNally.

Cansler, D. P., & Winton, P. (1983). Parents and preschool mainstreaming. In J. Anderson & T. Black (Eds.), *Mainstreaming in early education* (pp. 65–83). Chapel Hill, NC: Technical Assistance Development System.

Capozzi, M., & Mineo, B. (1984). Nonspeech language and communication. In A. Holland (Ed.), *Language disorders in children: Recent advances* (pp. 173–209). San Diego: College-Hill Press.

Carrier, J. K., & Peak, T. (1975). *Program manual for Non-SLIP* (Non-Speech Language Initiation Program). Lawrence, KS: H & H Enterprises.

Consortium on Adaptive Performance Evaluation (CAPE). (1978). *Adaptive assessment for evaluation progress of severely/profoundly handicapped children functioning between birth and two years.* Annual report of field initiated research project, funded by the Bureau of Education for the Handicapped.

Cooley, W. W., & Lohnes, P. R. (1976). *Evaluation research in education.* New York: Irvington Publishers.

Cordisco, L. (1984, May). *Parent training: Programming for generalization.* Paper presented at the Association for Behavior Analysis Convention, Nashville, TN.

Cronbach, L. J. (1982). *Designing evaluations of educational and social programs.* San Francisco: Jossey-Bass.

Day, R., Powell, T., Dy-Lin, E., & Stowitschek, J. (1982). An evaluation of the effects of a social interaction training package on mentally handicapped preschool children. *Education and Training of the Mentally Retarded, 17,* 125–130.

Day, R., Powell, T., & Stowitschek, J. (1980). *SCIPPY: Social competence intervention package for preschool youngsters.* Nashville: Vanderbilt University.

Eyberg, S. M., & Johnson, S. M. (1974). Multiple assessment of behavior modification with families: Effects of contingency contracting and order of treated problems. *Journal of Consulting and Clinical Psychology, 42,* 594–606.

Fewell, R., & Sandall, S. (1984). *Computer-Assisted Program (CAP) Project.* Unpublished program description. Seattle: University of Washington.

Finkle, L. J. (1980). Teaching the severely/profoundly handicapped: The need for media in institutions. *Journal of Special Education Technology, 3,* 40–47.

Finkle, R., & O'Leary, J. P., Jr. (1980). The design of a line of gaze interface for communication and environment manipulation. *Proceedings of the International Conference on Rehabilitation Engineering, 1,* 96–97.

Foster, M., Berger, M., & McLean, M. (1981). Rethinking a good idea: A reassessment of parent involvement. *Topics in Early Childhood Special Education, 1,* 55–65.

Foulds, R. A. (1982). Applications of microcomputers in the education of the physically disabled child. *Exceptional Children, 49,* 155–162.

Fredericks, H. D., & Moore, W. G. (1978). *Data-based classroom for preschool handicapped children, Teaching Research Infant and Child Center.* Unpublished program evaluation report submitted to the Joint Dissemination and Review Panel, Washington, DC.

Gamble, A., & Strain, P. S. (1979). The effects of dependent and interdependent group contingencies on socially appropriate responses in classes for emotionally handicapped children. *Psychology in the Schools, 16,* 312–318.

Gardner, J. M. (1976). Training parents as behavior modifiers. In S. Yen & R. W. McIntire (Eds.), *Teaching behavior modification* (pp. 17–34). Kalamazoo, MI: Behaviordelia.

Garwood, S. G. (1982). (Mis)Use of developmental scales in program evaluation. *Topics in Early Childhood Special Education, 1,* 61–69.

Goldenberg, E. P. (1979). *Special technology for special children.* Baltimore: University Park Press.

Grove, D. N. (1981). *Good Samaritan Diagnostic-Prescriptive Classroom for Handicapped Preschool Children.* Unpublished program evaluation report submitted to the Joint Dissemination and Review Panel, Washington, DC.

Guralnick, M. (1976). The value of integrating handicapped and nonhandicapped preschool children. *American Journal of Orthopsychiatry, 46,* 236–245.

Hannaford, A. E., & Taber, F. M. (1982). Microcomputer software for the handicapped: Development and evaluation. *Exceptional Children, 49,* 137–142.

Harris, D., & Vanderheiden, G. (1980). Enhancing the development of communicative interaction. In R. Schiefelbusch (Ed.), *Nonspeech language and communication: Analysis and intervention* (pp. 227–259). Baltimore: University Park Press.

Heber, R., & Garber, H. (1975). The Milwaukee project: A study of the use of family intervention to prevent cultural-familial mental retardation. In B. Z. Friedlander, G. M. Sterritt, & G. E. Kirk (Eds.), *Exceptional infant: Assessment and intervention, 3* (pp. 399–433). New York: Brunner/Mazel.

Hendrickson, J. M., Strain, P. S., Tremblay, A., & Shores, R. E. (1982). Interactions of behaviorally handicapped children: Functional effects of peer social initiations. *Behavior Modification, 6,* 323–352.

Hofmeister, A. M. (1982). Microcomputers in perspective. *Exceptional Children, 49,* 115–121.

Hofmeister, A. M., & Thorkildson, R. (1984). Microcomputers in special education: Implications for instructional design. *Exceptional Education Quarterly, 4,* 1–8.

Holworth, T. E., & Currie, R. J. (1982). An evaluation of the efficacy of televised home instruction: Teaching parents to be trainers of their preschool handicapped children. *Journal for the Division for Early Childhood, 6,* 36–41.

Horner, R. D., & Baer, D. M. (1978). Multiple probe technique: A variation of the multiple baseline. *Journal of Applied Behavior Analysis, 11,* 189–196.

Hoyson, M., Jamieson, B., & Strain, P. S. (in press). Individualized group instruction of normally developing and autistic-like children: A description and evaluation of the LEAP curriculum model. *Journal of the Division for Early Childhood.*

Hupp, S. C., & Rogers-Warren, A. K. (in press). Evaluating educational processes in programs for severely handicapped preschoolers. In L. Bickman & D. Weatherford (Eds.), *Evaluating early intervention programs for young severely handicapped children and their families.* Baltimore: University Park Press.

Irwin, J., & Wong, S. (1974). Compensation for maturity in long-range intervention studies. *Acta Symbolica, 5,* 33–46.

Kail, R. (1979). *The development of memory in children.* San Francisco: W. H. Freeman & Company.

Kazdin, A. E. (1973). Issues in behavior modification with mentally retarded persons. *American Journal of Mental Deficiency, 78,* 134–140.

Kazdin, A. E. (1977). Assessing the clinical or applied importance of behavior-change through social validation. *Behavior Modification, 1,* 427–452.

Kiresuk, T. J., & Lund, S. H. (1976). Process and measurement using goal attainment scaling. In G. Glass (Ed.), *Evaluation studies review manual* (Vol. 1, pp. 383–399). Beverly Hills: Sage Publications.

Lewis, M., & Goldberg, S. (1969). Perceptual-cognitive development in infancy: A generalized expectancy model as a function of the mother-infant interaction. *Merrill-Palmer Quarterly, 15,* 81–100.

Linn, R. L. (1981). Measuring pretest–posttest performance changes. In R. Berk (Ed.), *Educational evaluation methodology: The state of the art.* Baltimore: Johns Hopkins University Press.

Litow, L., & Pumroy, D. K. (1975). A review of classroom group-oriented contingencies. *Journal of Applied Behavior Analysis, 8,* 342–347.

Lord, C. (1984). The development of peer relations in children with autism. In F. Morrison, C. Lord, & D. Keating (Eds.), *Applied developmental psychology* (Vol. 1). New York: Academic Press.

Lovaas, O. I. (1982, August). *The treatment of autistic children under 36 months of age.* Symposium presented at the Conference of the American Psychological Association, Washington, DC.

Lovaas, O. I., Koegel, R., Simmons, J. Q., & Long, J. S. (1973). Some generalization and follow-up measures on autistic children in behavior therapy. *Journal of Applied Behavior Analysis, 6,* 131–166.

Love, H. (1973). *The mentally retarded child and his family.* Springfield, IL: Charles C Thomas.

Mauk, W. C. (1979). Project Pre-Empt: A motion picture series helping parents of severely handicapped infants. *Journal of Special Education Technology, 2,* 73–76.

McHale, S. M. (1983). Social interactions of autistic and nonhandicapped children during free play. *American Journal of Orthopsychiatry, 53,* 81–91.

Moore, S. B. (1982). Student-use educational materials developed for the multi-handicapped visually impaired. *Journal of Special Education Technology, 5,* 26–30.

Moseley, P. F. (1982). Parenting and the handicapped. *Journal of Special Education Technology, 5,* 44–49.

Odom, S. L., Bender, M., Stein, M., Doran, L., Houden, P., McInnes, M., Gilbert, M., DeKlyen, M., Speltz, M., & Jenkins, J. (1984). *Integrated preschool curriculum.* Manuscript submitted for publication.

Odom, S. L., & Fewell, R. R. (1983). Program evaluation and early childhood special education: A meta-evaluation. *Educational Evaluation and Policy Analysis, 5,* 445–460.

Odom, S. L., Jenkins, J. R., Speltz, M. L., & DeKlyen, M. (1982). Promoting social integration of young children at risk for learning disabilities. *Learning Disabilities Quarterly, 5,* 379–387.

Odom, S. L., Stein, M., & Jenkins, J. R. (1983, May). *Peer-initiation and individual contingency interventions for promoting social interaction of handicapped preschool children.* Paper presented at the annual meeting of the Association for Behavior Analysis, Milwaukee, WI.

Odom, S., & Strain, P. S. (1984a): Classroom-based social skills instruction for severely handicapped preschool children. *Topics in Early Childhood Special Education, 4,* 97–116.

Odom, S. L., & Strain, P. S. (1984b). Peer-mediated approaches to promoting children's social interaction: A review. *American Journal of Orthopsychiatry, 54,* 544–557.

Peck, C. A., Apolloni, T., Cooke, T. P., & Raver, S. A. (1978). Teaching retarded preschoolers to imitate the free-play behavior of nonretarded classmates: Trained and generalized effects. *Journal of Special Education, 12,* 195–208.

Ragland, E. U., Kerr, M. M., & Strain, P. S. (1978). Effects of social initiations on the behavior of withdrawn autistic children. *Behavior Modification, 2,* 565–578.

Ramey, C. T., Campbell, F. A., & Wasik, B. H. (1982). Use of standardized tests to evaluate early childhood special education programs. *Topics in Early Childhood Special Education, 1,* 51–60.

Reisinger, J. J., Frangia, G. W., & Hoffman, E. G. (1976). Toddler management training: Generalization and marital status. *Journal of Therapy and Experimental Psychiatry, 7,* 335–340.

Scriven, M. (1974). Evaluation perspectives and procedures. In J. Popham (Ed.), *Evaluation in education: Current applications* (pp. 3–93). Berkeley, CA: McCutchan Publishing Corp.

Silverman, H., McNaughton, S., & Kates, B. (1978). *Handbook of Blissymbolics for instructors, users, parents, and administrators.* Toronto: Blissymbolics Communications Institute.

Simeonsson, R. J., Cooper, D. H., & Scheiner, A. P. (1982). A review and analysis of the effectiveness of early intervention programs. *Pediatrics, 69,* 635–641.

Simeonsson, R. J., Huntington, G. S., & Short, R. J. (1982). Individual differences and goals: An approach to the evaluation of child progress. *Topics in Early Childhood Special Education, 1,* 71–80.

Simeonsson, R. J., & Wiegerink, R. (1975). Accountability: A dilemma in infant intervention. *Exceptional Children, 45,* 474–481.

Sparling, J., Lowman, B., Lewis, I., & Bartel, B. (1978). What parents say about their information needs. *Progress report to ACYF* (Administration for Children, Youth, and Families).

Stallard, C. K. (1982). Computers and education for exceptional children: Emerging applications. *Exceptional Children, 49,* 102–104.

Stowitschek, J. J., & Stowitschek, C. E. (1984). Once more with feeling: The absence of research on teacher use of microcomputers. *Exceptional Education Quarterly, 4,* 23–39.

Strain, P. S. (1977). An experimental analysis of peer social initiations on the behavior of withdrawn preschool children: Some training and generalization effects. *Journal of Abnormal Child Psychology, 5,* 445–455.

Strain, P. S. (1981). Conceptual and methodological issues in efficacy research with behaviorally disordered children. *Journal of the Division for Early Childhood, 4,* 110–124.

Strain, P. S. (1983). Generalization of autistic children's social behavior change: Effects of developmentally integrated and segregated settings. *Analysis and Intervention in Developmental Disabilities, 3,* 23–34.

Strain, P. S. (1984). Social behavior patterns of nonhandicapped and nonhandicapped—developmentally disabled friend pairs in mainstream preschools. *Analysis and Intervention in Developmental Disabilities, 4,* 15–28.

Strain, P. S., & Hill, A. D. (1979). Social interaction. In P. Wehman (Ed.), *Recreation programming for developmentally disabled persons* (pp. 65–75). Baltimore: University Park Press.

Strain, P. S., & Kerr, M. M. (1979). Treatment issues in the remediation of preschool children's social isolation. *Education and Treatment of Children, 2,* 197–208.

Strain, P. S., Steele, P., Ellis, T., & Timm, M. A. (1982). Long-term effects of oppositional child treatment with mothers as therapists and therapist trainers. *Journal of Applied Behavior Analysis, 15,* 163–169.

Strain, P. S., & Shores, R. E. (1983). A reply to misguided mainstreaming. *Exceptional Children, 50,* 95–98.

Strain, P. S., Shores, R. E., & Kerr, M. M. (1976). An experimental analysis of "spillover" effects on social interaction among behaviorally handicapped preschool children. *Journal of Applied Behavior Analysis, 9,* 31–40.

Strain, P. S., Shores, R. E., & Timm, M. A. (1977). Effects of peer social initiations on the behavior of withdrawn preschool children. *Journal of Applied Behavior Analysis, 10,* 289–298.

Strain, P. S., Young, C. C., & Horowitz, J. (1981). An examination of child and family demographic variables related to generalized behavior change during oppositional child training. *Behavior Modification, 5,* 15–26.

Sulzer-Azaroff, B., & Mayer, G. R. (1977). *Applying behavior-analysis procedures with children and youth.* New York: Holt, Rinehart & Winston.

Tallmadge, G. (1977). *The joint dissemination review panel ideabook.* Washington, DC: U.S. Department of Health, Education, and Welfare.

Tawney, J. W., & Gast, D. L. (1984). *Single subject research in special education.* Columbus, OH: Charles E. Merrill Publishing Co.

Thorkildson, R., & Hofmeister, A. (1984). Interactive video authoring of instruction for the mentally handicapped. *Exceptional Education Quarterly, 4,* 57–73.

Timm, M. A., Strain, P. S., & Eller, P. H. (1979). Effects of systematic, response-dependent fading and thinning procedures on the maintenance of child-child interaction. *Journal of Applied Behavior Analysis, 12,* 308.

Vanderheiden, G. C. (1982). Lightbeam headpointer research. *Communication Outlook, 4,* 11.

Wahler, R. G. (1967). Child-child interactions in free field settings: Some experimental analyses. *Journal of Experimental Child Psychology, 5,* 278–293.

Wahler, R. G. (1980). The insular mother: Her problems in parent-child treament. *Journal of Applied Behavior Analysis, 13,* 207–219.

Watson, J. S. (1966). The development and generalization of "contingency awareness" in early infancy: Some hypotheses. *Merrill Palmer Quarterly, 12,* 123–135.

Weir, S. (1982). Logo: A learning environment for the severely handicapped. *Journal of Special Education Technology, 5,* 20–22.

Weisen, A. E., Hartley, G., Richardson, C., & Roske, A. (1967). The retarded child as a reinforcing agent. *Journal of Experimental Child Psychology, 5,* 109–113.

White, O. R., Edgar, E., & Haring, N. G. (1978). *Uniform Performance Assessment System, Birth–6 Year Level.* Seattle: University of Washington.

White, O. R., & Haring, N. G. (1978). Evaluating educational programs serving the severely and profoundly handicapped. In N. Haring & D. Bricker (Eds.), *Teaching the severely handicapped, Vol. III* (pp. 153–200). Seattle: American Association for the Education of the Severely/Profoundly Handicapped.

Winton, P. J., & Turnbull, A. P. (1981). Parent involvement as viewed by parents of handicapped children. *Topics in Early Childhood Special Education, 1,* 11–20.

Wolery, M. (1983). Proportional Change Index: An alternative for comparing child change data. *Exceptional Children, 50,* 167–170.

Wolf, M. M. (1978). Social validity: The case for subjective measurement or how applied behavior analysis is finding its heart. *Journal of Applied Behavior Analysis, 11,* 203–214.

Young, C. C., & Kerr, M. M. (1979). The effects of a retarded child's initiations on the behavior of severely retarded school-aged peers. *Education and Training of the Mentally Retarded, 14,* 185–190.

Chapter 4

New Directions in Educating Students with Autism

Anne M. Donnellan and Richard S. Neel

Until recently, students with autism were denied access to appropriate educational opportunities that would allow them to live productive and independent lives as adults (Sullivan, 1977; Warren, 1980). Consequently, there has historically been an educational information void about these learners. With the advent of federal and state mandates regarding free appropriate public education, however, some attention has been paid to educational issues that appear to be critical in producing more positive postschool outcomes for these students. This chapter addresses some of the recent developments in functional curricula, behavior management, social skill training, and educational technology for students with autism and similar severely handicapping conditions. Further research in these areas that may assist educators in planning individual educational programs is also discussed.

FUNCTIONAL CURRICULUM

During the last 10 years, the teaching of functional skills to students with moderate or severe developmental disabilities has become accepted as "best

Development of this chapter was partially supported by Grant No. 300-81-0355 to the University of Wisconsin-Madison in conjunction with the Madison Metropolitan School District by the Department of Education, Office of Special Education, Division of Innovation and Development, Washington, DC; by Grant No. NIE-K-81-009 to Wisconsin Center for Education Research by the National Institute of Education; and by the United States Department of Education Contract No. 300 800 842 (Special Needs Project: Model Education Program for Autistic Children and Youth), to the Experimental Education Unit, University of Washington.

Sandra L. Bailey, Ph.D., was to have been a co-author on this chapter. From her considerable experience and talent she contributed many ideas to the original outline. She died before the chapter was written. With gratitude, we dedicate it to her memory.

practice." There is a considerable body of literature that supports this concept (Alper, 1981; Brown, Nietupski, & Hamre-Nietupski, 1976; Halle, 1982). Brown et al. (1977) discussed what a functional curriculum for severely handicapped students should be:

> Severely handicapped students have the right to, and the need for, a longitudinal curriculum that prepares them to function as independently as possible . . . Components of curricula that do not contribute to the development of initial independent functioning skills should be left out . . . [Rather than] comparing severely handicapped students with younger age peers, it is often more beneficial to compare present repertoires with the skills necessary to function independently in a variety of environments. (pp. 8–9)

Brown, Branston et al. (1979) defined functional skills as those that are frequently required in the student's environments (home, school, and community), are longitudinal, and are age appropriate. Several other investigators have applied the same concepts to the education of students who have autism (Brown et al., 1976; Donnellan, 1980; Donnellan et al., 1980; Dunlap, Koegel, & Egel, 1979; Koegel, Rincover, & Egel, 1982; Neel & Billingsley, 1981; Neel, Billingsley, & Lambert, 1983). Donnellan (1980) suggested that the content include " . . . functional skills in community functioning, domestic living, recreation/leisure, vocational functioning, and social interactions with non-handicapped peers" (p. 65). Unfortunately, however, this goal of best practice rests on very little data (Freagon & Rotatori, 1982; Voeltz & Evans, 1983). It is impossible in a chapter of this size to cover extensively all the curricula available to the classroom teacher. The curricula chosen are ones that are functional in orientation, have some supporting data as to their educational effectiveness, and are familiar to the authors. The authors intend that their examples be treated as a representative sample of a larger body of available material.

Elements of a Functional Curriculum

A functional curriculum has several elements that distinguish it from other curricula. Each of the elements is discussed here as a separate entity. In practice, of course, they are combined into each educational program.

Environmental Assessment   The assessment process for functional programs consists of determining the functioning of a student in various environments. Environmental inventories are commonly used to collect and organize the data (Brown et al., 1976; Neel et al., 1983). Each inventory samples a wide variety of actual and potential environments. The community and home environments take precedence over school environments because they continue well beyond school age. The skills required of a student to function effectively in various home and community environments; the present level of functioning of the child; and environmental cues, consequences, and adaptations that are available to help the student perform are noted.

Most of the functional assessment devices rely heavily on the environments available to a student. These include both the environments that the student currently accesses as well as other environments that could be accessed in the student's community in the future. Thus, elementary school teachers must relate to middle school environments, high school teachers must inventory appropriate adult environments, and so forth. Functional assessments stress collecting information on the specific environments of each student. This allows for the individualization of instruction within each student's own environment so that the responses selected for instruction will be ones that are very likely to be functional for the student while she or he is learning them.

Utilizing Critical Effect in Instruction To generate a curriculum based upon ultimate functioning, one must first identify the critical effects that are necessary for successful, independent performance in important environments (White, 1980). A critical effect is the outcome or result to be achieved when selecting a behavior or group of behaviors to teach. Most critical effects can be achieved with more than one group of behaviors. For example, suppose a student who has autism is hungry and the desired effect is that he or she eat. The student has a variety of behaviors that she or he could use to communicate this desire. He or she could: 1) cry or scream until fed (Donnellan, Mirenda, Mesaros, & Fassbender, 1984); 2) pull another person to the refrigerator and point; 3) sign for drink; 4) ask for food; 5) go get the food; 6) go to a restaurant; or 7) go to the store, buy the food, go home, and prepare it. Each of these behaviors can produce the same effect, namely, a full stomach. Though some of these strategies are more desirable than others, the important point is that they all produce the same *effect*.

Many students with autism have difficulty initiating or terminating social interactions. Again, many forms are available to teach this effect, including gestures, signing, or speech. Speech can be understood by most people, and, therefore, would be first choice; gesture would be next, and maybe signing last. But, if in teaching any of these forms, the social interaction effect is lost, form has outweighed function. This could be the case if, for example, dozens of prompts were required to help the student say or sign, ''play ball.'' If teaching a simple gesture could communicate this social interaction request for the student, then it could be taught first. In other words, the instructional form selected must be the one that reliably produces a desired critical effect throughout instruction.

Another example of critical effect is the area of transportation. Many curricula include programs to teach transportation skills such as bus riding. What should be considered is not only how to teach a child who has autism to ride the bus, but also what effect riding a bus will produce. If the critical effect is getting to work, then there are a number of alternatives to bus riding (moving within walking distance of the work setting, riding a bike, taking a taxi, riding in a car pool, etc.). Furthermore, though bus riding has apparent face validity (many people would judge bus riding to be a "critical" skill), it may not have functional importance for a particular student. If work/school, recreational facilities, stores, services, and friends are within walking distance, then learning to ride a bus may be no more functional than learning to touch the color purple, at least for the forseeable future. A functional curriculum will include teaching tool skills only when they produce a desired critical effect in the natural environment. This focus on critical effect in normal settings is a major part of functional curricula.

Several skills that are not required in present environments may be needed in predictable future environments. Attention to these skills is also a major part of a functional curriculum. As mentioned earlier, assessment of future environments is a critical component of educational planning. A functional approach to curriculum, however, requires that a current critical effect for these skills is developed as they are instructed. Following the previous example, if there is no current need for bus riding, but if it is suspected that such a skill will be needed in the future, then a need for bus riding that will be valuable to the student should be developed while the skill is being taught. The development of critical effect during instruction is fundamental to functional instruction in natural environments.

Longitudinal Age-Appropriate Tasks It is difficult to justify the instruction of skills that will not be useful to the child in the future. Many students have spent countless hours learning the recreational/leisure skill "puts together three-piece puzzle"—an activity that will stigmatize anyone over 3 years old. Of course, it is also important to select instructional forms that are appropriate to the student's age. Instructional items should be carefully selected so that the form content can be shifted as the students get older, but the skill required to access that content will remain relatively the same. For example, you can teach a young student to turn on a TV or tape recorder to watch Sesame Street. As the student gets older, the content of the tapes can change to Michael Jackson or Bach, but the skill of using the machines maintains throughout the student's life. Other leisure examples are card playing, playing ball, and bike riding. The point is that the particular form selected and the skills taught to utilize those forms should be longitudinal and age appropriate.

Instruction in Natural Contexts A functional curriculum teaches students to respond to the skill requirements of the natural environment (e.g., the skills required to purchase food in a grocery store or a restaurant). To adapt to a variety of situations, students must increase their ability to perform required tasks with minimal levels of supervision, to communicate effectively across situations, and to follow the social rules and regulations of each environment. Students are taught to respond to the natural cues and consequences present across settings. Natural cues and consequences signal when to perform specific tasks, when a task should be completed or terminated, and when the requirements of the environment have changed (Falvey, Brown, Lyon, Baumgart, & Schroeder. 1980).

Instruction must be done in context, training skills when and where they will be used. In a functional program, the instruction setting becomes any setting that naturally requires the skill being taught. Many skills have existing contexts at school (e.g., toileting, eating). For other skills, a natural context must be created. For example, dressing and undressing are not skills usually required at school. By setting up gym or swimming programs where students need to change their clothes, a natural context is created for this instructional routine. It is impossible, however, to create a natural context in school for skills such as grocery shopping or eating in a restaurant. For these skills, instruction must be provided outside the classroom. This can be accomplished in several ways. First, activities can be scheduled in the community (stores, video arcades, parks, zoos, etc.). Some routines may be a part of the regular activities of the student's family. In these cases, family members can be trained to teach the student the targeted skills. A second way to teach routines outside the classroom is to help the student develop links with peers. Voeltz's (1984) Special Friends Program is one example. Strain (1983) also showed how the use of peer-mediated programming could increase the number and quality of peer interactions.

Routine Format The final component of functional curricula is reliance on routine or skill cluster formats of instruction (Holvoet, Mulligan, Schussler, Lacy, & Guess, 1982; Neel et al., 1983). A routine is a task analysis of the series of events that are necessary to produce the desired effect for the student in the natural environment. Each routine begins with a natural cue and ends with the realization of the critical effect. A dinner routine may begin with, "It's time to eat" (the natural cue), and end with the student eating at the table (the critical effect). Routines differ from other formats in that they mix skills across several more traditional domains into one instructional procedure. Often fine motor, gross motor, communication, self-help, and preacademic or academic skills are found in one routine. Routine formats more closely resemble the sequence required in the normal environments. Some preliminary studies have shown that students with autism acquire skills faster when a routine format is used (Holvoet et al., 1982). The implementation data on the IMPACT curriculum (Neel et al., 1983) indicate that routine formats can be used effectively to teach a wide range of desired functional skills (Neel et al., 1983). (Some additional data on routine formats are included in the discussion of the IMPACT curriculum below.)

Current Functional Curricula An ideal functional curriculum should, theoretically, include all the above characteristics. Several curriculum efforts have addressed different parts. Wehman (1979) and White (1980) each describe useful and appropriate models for functional skillstreaming and make precise suggestions for program design. They do not, however, provide adequate strategies for implementation. Many other models have been developed that include implementation strategies (Baumgart et al., 1982; Brown, Branston-McClean et al., 1979; Wilcox & Bellamy, 1982). Typically, these programs have been demonstrated but not systematically evaluated in public school classrooms. Other models do include a functional design, instructional strategies, and evaluation data (e.g., Brown, Holvoet, Guess, & Mulligan, 1980; Holvoet, Guess, Mulligan, & Brown, 1980; Mulligan, Guess, Holvoet, & Brown, 1980). Many of the curriculum steps, however, focus on isolated parts of a school program.

Several other curricula efforts have been developed that are more complete (Brown et al., 1980; Holvoet et al., 1980; Mulligan et al., 1980; Wehman, 1979). Most of them have only been tried with a specific group of students at this time. When these programs are extended to the whole range of students who have autism or other developmental disabilities, the acceptability will be increased. Other programs available are limited to a particular skill area (e.g., Wuerch & Voeltz, 1982). The collection of evaluation data on these efforts continues. The process of developing successful procedures and then collecting the necessary data to validate those procedures takes time. The next section of this chapter outlines one of these programs (The IMPACT program) and provides the implementation data from a 3-year study. There are several curricular efforts continuing. Many of them have provided seeds for this project in the past and are currently adding to curricular development. The IMPACT project is a benchmark example that represents a great deal of other work.

IMPACT CURRICULUM

The IMPACT curriculum includes the following components: an individualized, systematic method for targeting functional goals; an instructional technology for assessing and teaching skills; and an evaluation system that measures functional skill aquisition. Although the IMPACT curriculum was developed for use with students with autism, it has also been used successfully with those having other severe developmental disabilities.

Goal Setting

The IMPACT curriculum begins with an individualized process for targeting functional goals using environmental inventories. What makes such goal setting different from more traditional methods is that instructional targets are derived from the environment rather than from developmental milestones. The most logical means of determining functional goals is to evaluate how the student functions within specific environments.

Many students with disabilities such as autism display idiosyncratic forms of behavior. Merely determining how far these behaviors deviate from normal leads to nonfunctional instruction. Instead, what should be determined is how well the particular behavior achieves the desired effect for the student (i.e., how functional it is). The focus should be, first, on whether or not the pupil can act on his or her environment (functions), then, on the ways he or she accomplishes those behaviors (forms).

With a functional curriculum, instructional targets come directly from the environment. What the student does, how he or she does it, where and with whom the behaviors take place are identified. The purpose of the inventories is to identify each student's level of functioning in current environments and to focus educational programming on increasing the student's independent functioning in those environments. Skills that will allow the student to access new environments and activities, as well as prepare him or her for future environments, are targeted by the inventories. The inventories pinpoint the student's abilities and deficits within the specific contexts in which they occur.

Once the specific functions of the student have been identified, the particular forms that he or she uses are determined. For example, to target communication priorities, the functions that the student has are identified (e.g., asks for something, protests), then, how (i.e., the forms), where, and with whom the behavior occurs are determined (Donnellan, Mirenda, Mesaros, & Fassbender, 1984). Different students may display different functions in a variety of ways. They may cry, tantrum, point, reach, or use some sort of verbalization. Students may also use more than one way to express the same function (see discussion below). A student may ask for help by pointing to or taking an adult's hand to the place where assistance is needed, or by using some language system. The environmental inventories provide information about these differences between students.

Environmental Inventories Home and school environmental inventories have been developed as a part of the IMPACT project. The school inventory is to be completed by the student's teacher, and the home inventory is to be completed by the parents or primary caregivers. These environmental inventories measure the number and type of functions a student has in four areas: communication, transition, recreation/leisure, and self-help. The inventories also list which form(s) the student uses across environments. Any discrepancies between performance at home and school are noted. Finally, the inventories measure the degree of restriction for each student. This includes the number and types of environments that are currently accessed and the amount of supervision and/or assistance required in each setting.

Once the inventories are complete, parents and teachers select priority goals using the guidelines developed by the IMPACT staff and others (Baumgart et al., 1982; Brown, Branston-McClean et al., 1979; Guess et al., 1978). These guidelines include selecting behaviors that: 1) are currently functional, 2) can be used in multiple environments, 3) are longitudinal, 4) are age appropriate, 5) are universally understood, and 6) reliably produce the desired critical effect.

The IMPACT environmental inventories provide a process for developing IEPs that reflect the functional needs of each pupil in the environments that she or he accesses. They also allow the parents and teachers to identify additional environments (current and future) in which they want the student to learn to participate. By relying on the student's current level of performance in specific situations, a truly individualized IEP based upon the functional needs of each student is produced.

Teaching in Routines

How Routines Are Different   IMPACT uses routines as the instructional format. Since routines are skill sequences required to reach a critical effect, it is important that they are taught when and where they naturally occur. Routine teaching begins with a task analysis of the skill sequence. As with any task analysis, the skill sequence is broken down into individual steps. However, what makes the task analysis of a routine different from traditional task analyses is that it always begins with the natural cue and ends with a critical effect for the behavior. For example, a task analysis of eating at a fast food restaurant might end with cleaning up and throwing away the trash. However, for many students with autism, the critical effect of social responsibility has not been learned. Their routine would most likely end with the eating of the food. Thus, even though a usual eating task analysis would include cleaning up, an IMPACT routine would not. Social responsibility, and the rewards that accompany it, may need to be taught as a separate routine.

A natural cue is defined as whatever stimulus or stimuli in the environment that signals the beginning of a routine. This cue can be a natural environmental occurrence such as the alarm clock going off, or an arranged cue in which the teacher has structured the environment to elicit the behavior. If possible, artificial instructional cues are avoided. When they are introduced, they must be faded before instruction is complete. The skill sequence is considered mastered only when it is initiated in the presence of the natural cue or cues (see Falvey et al., 1980).

Programming   Communication/social skills are considered by IMPACT to be an integral component of the instructional process. These skills are a major deficit not only of persons with autism, but for all people with severe developmental disabilities. Evaluating the communicative ability of each student is a crucial part of programming. The student is evaluated in terms of the number of communicative functions and forms that she or he has. The goal of each program is to increase the student's ability to control and participate in his or her environment through communication. To realize this goal, programming must include teaching a communication behavior (form) that is effective in producing changes for the student (function) across several situations. Regardless of the form used, if the student's communicative intent increases control over the environment, then that communication is functional for him or her. Communication targets become part of routines, receiving instruction where and when the skill is naturally required. For instance, requesting help might become part of a lunch routine for a student who cannot open his or her lunch box. The primary function of other routines may be to teach communication/social skills. For example, the goal of one routine might be for the student to interact appropriately with the office staff of the school.

Evaluation

The final component of the IMPACT process is the evaluation system. It includes an instructional format and rules for making program changes. The ultimate goal of instruction in a functional curriculum is to make the student as independent and interactive as possible. To facilitate this, a nonhierarchial range of assistance is available and is individually determined for each child and task. Assistance could include: 1) full and partial physical assists, 2) physical prompting, 3) verbal/gesture prompts, and 4) verbal prompts. The instructional level is determined by the least intrusive level of assistance required to ensure that the individual student reaches the critical effect. After the student can reliably produce the desired result, the assistance is faded to less intrusive levels until the student can successfully perform the routine without instructional assistance. There are routines that may require some assistance indefinitely. For example, a student who has limited mobility skills as a result of physical handicaps may always need help in getting around from place to place. In these cases, a final performance is described and instruction ends when that level of performance is reached.

A set of decision rules has been developed for use with the curriculum. These rules define the types of correct and incorrect responses, and provide instructors with guidelines for making changes in levels of assistance. Specific instructions on how to collect data and measure progress are also included. These decision rules were developed based on the information collected during the demonstration year of the project and are subject to change as the data are analyzed.

Implementation Results

Analyses of the data collected by classroom teachers during the third year of the project were used to determine the validity of the IMPACT curriculum. The purpose of the final year of the project was to replicate the curriculum in a wide variety of public school settings. Although the data from the second year demonstration classrooms showed that students made impressive growth, it was desirable to demonstrate that the curriculum process could be adapted to fit a variety of settings.

The IMPACT curriculum was implemented in 12 classrooms in three states. Fifty-three students between the ages of 5 and 21 were included in the study. Thirty-seven of the students had diagnoses of autism or autistic-like behaviors. The remainder of the pupils had other severe developmental disabilities. Ten of the classrooms were in public schools and two were located in a university-based experimental school. Seven of the 12 classrooms were housed in integrated facilities. Table 1 summarizes the population used in the study and also shows the number and types of routines used in each setting.

Reliability Observational reliability checks were conducted once a month by a member of the project staff in four of the project classrooms: two at

Table 1. Population summary

Classroom #	Setting	Number of students	Age range	Routine types
1	Segregated	8	15–21	*Self-Help*: brush teeth, wash hands, toileting, dressing, snack/lunch preparation, at snack/lunch, snack/lunch clean-up. *Transition*: to/from; change activities.
2	Integrated	7	7–11	*Self-Help*: brush teeth, wash hands, dressing, snack/lunch preparation, snack/lunch clean-up, eat lunch/snack. *Transition*: to/from, change activities.
3	Integrated	5	12–17	*Self-Help*: wash hands, wash face, brush teeth, toileting, dressing, snack/lunch preparation, snack/lunch clean-up, eat lunch/snack, clean-up, workshop, wash/dry dishes, wash/dry laundry, fold/sort clothes/towels, make bed. *Transition*: to/from.
4	Integrated	9	7–12	*Self-Help*: toileting, wash hands, comb hair, dressing, snack/lunch clean-up, eat snack/lunch. *Transition*: to/from, change activities.
5	Integrated	1	18	*Self-Help*: toileting, wash hands, eat lunch/snack, snack/lunch clean-up, workshop, fold towels. *Transition*: to/from. *Recreation/Leisure*: play cards/board game.
6	Segregated	7	6–11	*Self-Help*: wash hands, brush teeth, dressing, snack/lunch clean-up, snack/lunch preparation, fold/sort clothes, toileting, comb hair, clean-up, sort/put away dishes/flatware. *Transition*: community mobility, to/from. *Recreation/Leisure*: toy play, tape recorder.
7	Segregated	7	7–16	*Self-Help*: lunch/snack preparation, prepare food, eat lunch/snack; snack/lunch clean-up, dressing, wash hands, toileting, brush teeth, comb hair, wash/dry dishes, load/unload dishwasher, wash/dry laundry, fold/sort clothes. *Transition*: to/from, change activities, community mobility. *Recreation/Leisure*: P.E. activities, play board game, play UNO card game.

8	Integrated	1	11	*Self-Help*: comb hair, clean-up, wash/dry laundry, fold/sort clothes/towels. *Transition*: to/from.
9	Integrated	4	6–12	*Self-Help*: wash face, shower/bathe, brush teeth, dressing, make snack/lunch, wash/dry dishes, snack/lunch clean-up, clean-up, wash/dry laundry, fold/sort clothes/towels, make bed. *Transition*: to/from. *Recreation/Leisure*: feed pet.
10	Integrated	2	12	*Self-Help*: snack/lunch clean-up. *Transition*: change activity.
11	Segregated	1	5	*Self-Help*: toileting, eat snack/lunch. *Transition*: to/from.
12	Segregated	1	7	*Self-Help*: toileting.

a university-based experimental school and two in the public schools. Percentage agreement scores (i.e., the percentage of agreement between raters), calculated by dividing the number of agreements by the number of agreements plus disagreements and multiplying by 100, ranged between 85% and 100% across all routines, with 100% agreement for the majority of routines.

Curriculum Effectiveness The effectiveness of the curriculum process was determined by how many students made progress toward independence on the routine steps that were instructed. Since the students started at many different levels between and within routines, each step was evaluated independently. Table 2 shows a tabulation of the net change of all the steps from their original level of required assistance. A total of 6,317 steps across 511 routines were tabulated. The total number of steps that were performed independently rose from 1,871 (29.6%) at the beginning of the year to 3,234 (51.2%) at the end. This is an increase of 1,363 steps (21.6%) after 9 months of instruction. As can be seen in Table 2, similar growth was recorded across all initial levels of assistance. Even those steps that required the most assistance initially showed substantial growth. Over 50% of the students moved one or more levels, and 23.5% of them advanced to a less intrusive level of assistance or to independence. One hundred fifty-five (2.4%) steps reverted back to a lower level following instruction.

The data presented above demonstrate the effectiveness of the IMPACT curriculum process. The usefulness of the model is also supported by the field-testing process that operated over the 3 years of its development. As a result of this continuous field testing, the manual has gone through a series of revisions based on feedback from teachers and parents. Anecdotally, the parents and teachers found the curriculum to work equally well with students who have severe handicapping conditions other than autism—an observation supported by the data.

BEHAVIOR MANAGEMENT

A second major area of concern in working with students with autism has been behavior management, as the behavior difficulties associated with the disorder are well known and well documented (see Koegel et al., 1982). A powerful technology for managing such behavior has been developed over the past 2 decades, with the result that both researchers and educators have available to them many effective procedures for decreasing or eliminating behavior in school and nonschool settings. In the past, that technology as applied to persons with autism has often been punitive and utilized with little or no reference to the communicative functions that such behaviors might serve for the individual. In a recent review of 97 autism-related articles in seven major journals from 1968 to 1982, Mesaros (1983) found that 40% of the articles dealt with strategies used to decrease behavior, and, of these, only three (or 11%) used nonpunitive interventions.

Table 2. IMPACT curriculum implementation results

		Final level						Row total
		FP 1	PA 2	PP 3	VG 4	V 5	I 6	
Count Row % Column %	FP 1	220 41.2 93.2	139 26.0 25.0	66 12.4 13.6	35 6.6 4.7	16 3.0 1.5	58 10.9 1.8	534 8.5
	PA 2	10 1.0 4.2	385 39.9 69.1	172 17.8 35.5	106 11.0 14.3	96 10.0 9.0	195 20.2 6.0	964 15.3
	PP 3	2 .3 .8	13 2.2 2.3	197 33.8 40.6	128 22.0 17.3	91 15.6 8.6	151 25.9 4.7	582 9.2
	VG 4	0 0 0	11 1.0 2.0	18 1.7 3.7	444 41.3 59.8	224 20.8 21.1	378 35.2 11.7	1075 17.0
	V 5	2 .2 .8	3 .2 .5	22 1.7 4.5	22 1.7 3.0	609 47.2 57.3	633 49.0 19.6	1291 20.4
	I 6	2 .1 .8	6 .3 1.1	10 .5 2.1	7 .4 .9	27 1.4 2.5	1819 97.2 56.2	1871 29.6
Column total		236 3.7	557 8.8	485 7.7	742 11.7	1063 16.8	3234 51.2	6317 100.0

Count = total steps in each cell.
Row % = percent of total steps starting at initial level of assistance, percent ending at final level of assistance.
Column % = percent of total steps ending at final level of assistance, percent starting at initial level of assistance.
Key: FP = full physical; PA = partial physical; PP = physical prompt; VG = verbal/gestural cue; V = verbal cue; I = independence.

Fortunately, several factors are contributing to a major change in attitude and technology related to the management of problem behavior associated with autism. For one, a number of investigators are beginning to address the function of behaviors that would earlier have been automatically targeted for reduction (Carr, 1985; Neel et al., 1983). Echolalia is a good case in point. Researchers operating from a pragmatics framework have suggested that only a small percentage of echolalic responses are nonfocused and nonfunctional (e.g., Fay, 1969; Paccia & Curcio, 1982; Prizant & Duchan, 1981; Shapiro, 1977). These authors, and others, suggest that the indiscriminate elimination of echolalic behavior through behavioral interventions is inappropriate since individuals with autism may rely on echolalia as a viable, if unusual, means of communication and interaction. Similarly, Carr (1977), Durand (1982), and Iwata, Dorsey, Slifer, Bauman, and Richman (1982) have looked at self-injurious behaviors (SIB) and found that even these extremely bizarre-appearing and highly dangerous behaviors can serve differential communicative functions for the individual client or student.

Given this accumulating data regarding the functions of behaviors, it may be less dangerous to assume that all behavior is communicative (Donnellan, 1984). In this regard, Watzalawick, Beavin, and Jackson (1967) have noted:

> No matter how one may try, one cannot not communicate. Activity or inactivity, words or silence, all have message value: they influence others and these others, in turn, cannot respond to these communications and are, thus, themselves communicating. It should be clearly understood that the mere absence of talking or of taking notice of each other is no exception to what has been asserted. (p. 49)

Several authors have offered strategies for determining and categorizing the potential communicative functions of problem behaviors as an aid in developing more appropriate and successful intervention strategies (Donnellan et al., 1984; Peck, Schuler, & Semmel, 1983). The suggestion is that by determining the function of the behavior, one is more likely to be able to change the "means" while maintaining the communicative value of the behavior to the individual. Such interventions, if successful, would obviously have considerable social validity (Wolf, 1978) as well as broad implications for communication and social interactions training for individuals with autism. As noted by Carr (1985), by utilizing information and concepts such as pragmatics generated outside of behavioral psychology, one can potentially develop behavior strategies to broaden the communicative repertoire of persons with autism beyond the narrow focus presently addressed. Instead of eliminating the behavior of "throwing the materials," an individual who is assessed to be bored can be taught to signal for a break.

Another factor contributing to changing attitudes and treatment strategies for dealing with the problem behaviors often associated with autism is the growing awareness of the need for and availability of nonaversive interventions for managing such behaviors. Professionals and advocates in education and psychology have long been concerned with the potential abuse of behavioral technology (Martin, 1979; Stuart, 1975). There have been many attempts to regulate the use of aversives that have met with limited success for a variety of reasons (see LaVigna & Donnellan, 1985, for a review of these issues). Some advocates such as The Association for Persons with Severe Handicaps call for the complete abolition of aversive interventions, while others continue to attempt to determine appropriate regulation, licensing, definition of competency, and so on relative to aversive interventions. The combined effect of legal and administrative regulation, the increased concern about ethical issues, and the procedural limitations of aversive techniques have combined to create a heightened interest in nonaversive strategies for behavioral intervention (LaVigna & Donnellan, 1985).

Fortunately, behavioral psychology and special education provide a wide variety of interventions that are nonpunitive, constructive (Goldiamond, 1974), and effective for managing even the most dangerous behaviors. Foremost among these is "programming," that is, the design and implementation of ecological manipulations, curriculum revisions, or other environmental changes to preclude the occurrence of the behavior and/or to teach more socially appropriate replacement behaviors (see Evans & Meyer, 1985; LaVigna & Donnellan, 1985, for a review). In addition to programming options, the literature is replete with examples of nonaversive and less or non-stigmatizing (Wolfensberger, 1972) behavioral interventions to deal with serious problems typically associated with autism. For example, Rotholtz and Luce (1984) eliminated self-stimulation in a person with autism by using a differential reinforcement of low rates (DRL) schedule. Touchette (1983) and Woods (1980) used stimulus control, that is, reinforced the problem behavior under strict stimulus conditions and then gradually faded out the stimulus to successfully control severe injurious behavior and property destruction. It is also clear that these interventions can be used successfully by teachers, parents, and others. Donnellan and LaVigna (in press) reported the use of a variety of nonaversive interventions by classroom personnel to manage the behaviors of students in an autism classroom. Throughout the school year, the staff never had to resort to punishment of any kind. Similarly, Donnellan, LaVigna, Zambito, and Thvedt (1985) reported the use of positive procedures to successfully deal with highly dangerous behaviors such as property destruction, aggression, self-injury, and hyperventilation in 16 children and adults with developmental disabilities, including autism, in community-based settings.

The combination of functional-pragmatic analysis of aberrant behavior, the use of positive programming, and nonpunitive behavioral procedures have combined to create a very optimistic attitude about the nonaversive management of behaviors typically associated with autism (Keller, 1985).

Research Needs

Though there is much to stimulate optimism in terms of new attitudes, strategies, and technology for working with students with autism, there is still much to be learned. Several areas in particular require further thought and study. This section briefly addresses some of the research issues currently receiving or requiring attention.

It is generally acknowledged that cognitive deficits interact with communication and social skills deficits and contribute to the severe communication/social disorders typically associated with autism (Hermelin, 1982; Prior, 1984; Rutter, 1982, 1985). Current research on remediating such deficits is encouraging. Schuler's work on the assessment of the relationship between cognitive abilities and communicative intents has become the framework for a variety of investigations (Peck & Schuler, 1983; Schuler & Goetz, 1981). Strain (1983) also reported successful attempts to use peers to teach social interaction, and noted that the students were able to generalize the skills they learned provided they were not placed in segregated facilities. McHale (1983) demonstrated the ability of peers to teach children with autism to play, and suggested that peers are better teachers of play than are adults. Donnellan and Kilman (in press) and Kilman (1981) report on successful strategies for integrating behavioral technology, developmental information regarding cognitive processing, and chronological age-appropriate content to assist students with autism in learning more appropriate social interaction skills. These and other studies make it clear that the social deficits of autism are not static and that these students are able to develop such skills even when they are well into adolescence and older. However, there is much left to be done to develop systematic strategies for teaching such skills and for teaching teachers how to use such strategies.

Similarly, there is much to be learned about teaching students with limited verbal ability to functionally use alternative and augmentative communication systems in school and nonschool settings (Yoder, 1980). Recent work using incidental teaching, shaping, and response delay is encouraging but this, too, is an area of education for students with autism that will require more work. However, as noted by Carr (1985) and others, this area is so vital to the ultimate functioning of these students that it is worthy of intensive attention from behavioral scientists and other educators.

Much of the successful technology for teaching students with autism involves the discrete-trial format (Donnellan-Walsh, Gossage, LaVigna, Schuler, & Traphagen, 1976; Koegel, Russo, & Rincover, 1977). Though this format has been shown to be an effective way to teach students with autism a wide variety of skills, as typically utilized it has some serious limitations for remediating social skills and for teaching students to initiate or respond to natural cues and consequences (Carr, 1985; Donnellan & Kilman, in press; Donnellan, Mesaros, & Anderson, 1984). Nonetheless, the discrete-trial format has been demonstrated to be a useful way to characterize the student-teacher interaction and can be readily taught to teachers, parents, and others (Donnellan, LaVigna, Schuler, & Woodward, 1982; Koegel, Glahn, & Nieminen, 1978; Koegel et al., 1977). One task for the future is to explore and expand this technology and others (cf. Donnellan, Mesaros, & Anderson, 1984 for a review) to teach these students to initiate, to respond to natural cues in complex stimulus environments, and to shift responses in the presence of familiar natural cues. For example, a student with autism recently learned to buy three items in a supermarket. The next week, despite successful practice in his classroom on the new item, when he went back to the store, he bought the items from his first week's list. Likewise, there is much research needed on techniques to assist these students to generalize if they are to use the skills they learn in their school years in novel adult environments (cf. Donnellan and Mirenda, 1983, for a review).

PROGRAM STANDARDS AND THE
CRITERION OF THE LEAST DANGEROUS ASSUMPTION

Teachers, researchers, and others concerned with educational ''best practices'' have begun to fill in some important information gaps regarding educational needs of students with autism. Many have called for programs that are referenced against Brown et al.'s (1976) ''criterion of ultimate functioning,'' and data are accumulating regarding critical educational dimensions that may contribute to a more independent and productive life-style for adults with autism. Unfortunately, however, the problem for educational practitioners is that the needs of these students are many and the information presently available for making a critical difference in postschool performance is still severely limited relative to need. Yet, daily, educators are required to make judgments concerning educational interventions, placements, materials, curriculum, and so on, and often with insufficient data. Moreover, educators and other advocates are increasingly being asked to testify in the legal arena to make qualitative judgments regarding one type of program over another. Under such circumstances, sincere disagreements can occur. Some would argue, for example, that the ultimate functioning of students with autism and other severely handicapping conditions is enhanced by the acquisition of developmentally relevant, albeit chronologically age-irrelevant, tasks. Others might argue that specialized settings designed for autistic students allow for maximal control over environmental stimuli and the intensive intervention required for skill acquisition and control of stereotypy, and that such specialized centers offer greater opportunity in terms of adult functioning. Certainly, some of the data presented in this volume could be used to clarify the issues raised by such a position. Unfortunately, however, what are needed are longitudinal outcome data, which, by definition, will not be readily forthcoming. In lieu of longitudinal data supporting one intervention or strategy over another, educators need interim standards on criteria for evaluating program options. One such standard is the criterion of least dangerous assumption (Donnellan, 1984):

> The criterion of the least dangerous assumption holds that, in the absence of conclusive data, educational decisions ought to be based on assumptions which, if incorrect, will have the least dangerous effect on the likelihood that students will be able to function independently as adults. (p. 142)

The proposal here is that the combination of the criteria of ultimate functioning and least dangerous assumption can assist in making critical evaluative decisions regarding program options. For example, in several federal court cases (*Campbell v. Talladega County Board of Education,* 1981; *Pennsylvania Association for Retarded Children v. Commonwealth,* 1971), the district court accepted certain minimum standards for programs for students with severe and profound handicaps based, in part, upon an evaluation format referenced against the criterion of ultimate functioning (see Donnellan et al., 1980 for a detailed description). That format included an evaluation of programs on at least the following nonmutually exclusive dimensions:

Chronologically age-appropriate functional curriculum
Functionality
Instructional settings
Interactions with nonhandicapped age peers and other nonhandicapped persons
Instructional arrangements and personnel resource allocation
"Dead time"
Minimal reliance upon instructional inference, the ability to generalize, transfer of training, and so forth
Individualized adaptations
Principle of partial participation
Instructional measurement strategies
Teaching techniques
Home/school proximity and cooperation
Coordinated and comprehensive nature of the educational program
Preparatory nature of the curriculum
Strategies utilized to generate and prioritize curricular content
Inservice training
Legal and ethical considerations in behavior change programs

The following section provides information on how one might combine the criteria of ultimate functioning and of the least dangerous assumption to evaluate a program along two of these dimensions: curriculum and settings.

Chronologically Age-Appropriate and Functional Curriculum

A student with a severe handicap such as autism is probably not capable of learning to perform all of the skills in the repertoires of nonhandicapped students. One could assume, therefore, that curriculum strategies such as IMPACT are unnecessary, since curricula need only be referenced against the abilities of the autistic students. Thus, adolescents who have conceptual skills similar to 2-year-olds would have a curriculum that stresses skills typically mastered between the ages of 2 and 3. One assumption behind such a strategy is that the students then will progress developmentally and acquire some of the conceptual abilities commonly found in 3-year-olds, such as "object permanence" and "means/ends relationships" (Inhelder & Piaget, 1969). This strategy further assumes that engaging in tasks that are markedly discordant with a person's chronological age will not contribute to further stigmatization and devaluation of a person with a severely handicapping condition. Obviously, these strategies are based on assumptions that are fairly dangerous because, if they are incorrect, the students will become adults who are unable to perform adult tasks and who are not valued by society.

Alternatively, if educators develop curriculum strategies that address chronologically age-appropriate functional skill development, they are making assumptions that, even if incorrect, will *not* add substantially to the problem of stigmatization and devaluation. Moreover, within the context of a chronologically age-appropriate curriculum development strategy, relevant developmental information can be incorporated in a variety of ways. One way is to use information about conceptual development to aid in the development of appropriate adaptations (see Baumgart et al., 1982, for a discussion of adaptations). For example, a student with poor object permanence can still be taught to make a meal. One adaptation of the materials would be to have a kitchen with an open pantry. A sequence adaptation might include building a motor pattern in the cooking routine to locate items that are out of sight. Likewise, a teacher might use information about means/ends deficits of a particular student in setting priorities for tasks to be learned in vocational settings. Thus, that student's vocational program might initially concentrate on tasks that have a clear beginning and ending and an obvious transformation of the materials. Such tasks might include emptying the wastebaskets and/or stacking the chairs in a meeting hall. These strategies are based on far less dangerous assumptions because, even if the student does not make the developmental progression, he or she will still be able to perform chronologically age-appropriate and functional tasks that are valued in adult environments.

Instructional Settings

As noted earlier, there are those who would argue that autistic students need the specialized learning environments, with specially trained staff, that can be best arranged in separate autism programs. Following intensive treatment, they can then go on to less intensive and less specialized settings for further education and training (e.g., Lettick, 1979). This kind of educational milieu for students with autism is very common in some parts of the United States and Canada.

Many who argue for it will provide evidence of the number of skills learned, behaviors managed, and so on, via this approach to support the need for separate autism centers on the continuum of least restrictive educational resources required for this population of learners. In part, this is because much of the earlier data on these students was generated in segregated clinic and school settings (cf. Handleman, 1979). Recently, however, much empirical work is taking place in integrated public school settings (e.g., Gaylord-Ross, Haring, Breen, & Pitts-Conway, 1984).

This rationale for separate settings for students with autism is based on highly dangerous assumptions given the documented learning characteristics of autism, the dismal outcome data for adults with autism, and the data available on successful, integrated programs such as those described in this chapter. At a minimum, it must be pointed out that these students have considerable difficulty in generalizing from one setting or set of stimuli to another (see Donnellan & Mirenda, 1983, for a review). To teach a set of behaviors under one set of stimulus conditions and assume that generalization will take place puts an unfair burden on the student. The more specialized the initial learning environment, the more dangerous the assumption that the behaviors will generalize to the complex, integrated environments in which students will ultimately need to function. If the assumptions are incorrect, that is, the behaviors do not generalize, then they must be retaught in the new environment or the person will only be able to function in specialized, segregated environments. Moreover, there are no data to support the need for specialized separate settings for people with autism. All recent evidence indicates that successful programming for students with autism need not be exclusively with other students with similar disabilities (see Donnellan, 1984; Mesaros, 1984 for a discussion of the issue of homogeneous grouping). Interestingly enough, the nature of the educational environments provided for the students with autism changes markedly in different areas of the United States. Separate settings are far more prevalent in the East. This fact is primarily a reflection of the pioneering role many easterners took in providing programming at a time when public school education was unavailable for these students (Donnellan, 1980).

Today, those who argue for the separate setting model are quick to point out that they serve the "severely autistic." Yet, there are states where virtually every student with autism is identified and is served in an integrated setting (Lansing & Schopler, 1978). Unless it can be found that severity is a function of geography, this argument will not support a segregated model. Others argue that segregated settings are necessary as the community schools are "not ready" for these students. Again, it is highly dangerous to assume that local public schools will ever be ready to accept students with very difficult learning and social problems unless they are helped to see that all handicapped students are their responsibility. Many school districts and state agencies are taking exactly such a stand regarding students with autism. And, fortunately, it has been shown that the specialized technologies helpful for teaching students with autism are not confined to specialized environments. Those technologies can be efficiently and effectively disseminated to classroom staff (Donnellan & LaVigna, in press; Koegel et al., 1977) and to state/provincial resource teams who can successfully provide inservice training to local school personnel (Donnellan, in press; Donnellan et al., 1982).

Clearly, the position that the disorder of autism requires a specialized, segregated educational setting is based on assumptions that are not supported by evidence. Even if it could be shown, however, that more skills could be taught or more behaviors shaped in such environments, such data would be insufficient to ''prove'' the validity of that position for at least the following reasons.

One, there is a legal (e.g., *Brown v. Board of Education of Topeka*, 1954) and societal presumption that it is in the public interest to have a diverse and integrated society (Galloway, 1979). This is not an empirical issue any more than the legal/societal presumption about the value of ''one person one vote.'' As citizens, persons with autism have the right to community presence and participation and do not have to earn that right. By extension, students with autism ought not to have to earn the right to opportunities for longitudinal interactions with their nonhandicapped peers. The burden of proof is not on the student but on the segregated setting that must prove that it provides a service that cannot be provided in a less restrictive integrated setting.

Two, the burden of proof will not be met by measuring only the number of tasks mastered by a student with autism in a particular setting. Given the criteria of ultimate functioning and least dangerous assumptions, notions of social and educational validity require that success be measured in a wide variety of ways (Kazdin, 1977; Voeltz & Evans, 1983). Educational researchers will have to assess choices about educational settings as well as materials, environments, and techniques in terms of their longitudinal impact on variables such as: 1) community attitudes about persons with handicaps, 2) the nature of generic services provided to students in their adult communities, 3) the status of students within their own families, and 4) the nature of domestic and employment options ultimately available to these students as adults in their own communities. The issue, then, is not number of tasks mastered, but number, kind, and quality of the environments ultimately available to the individual in adulthood.

Three, the least restrictive environment for persons with severe learning and social interaction problems such as those associated with autism ought to be based on a low-inference model (Brown et al., 1976). That is, educators ought to make no inferences that these students will generalize what they have learned from one set of conditions to another. These students need to be taught and to have their skills verified in the environments in which they ultimately have to use them. If, in fact, generalization of outcome skills does take place using such a strategy, their options will be increased. If not, the danger to ultimate functioning is minimized because at least students will be able to succeed in a variety of environments in which they were taught.

At least one adult service program has taken this notion of least restrictive environment and successfully redefined it for more than 50 adolescents and adults with autism, many of whom had never received appropriate education in childhood. In that program, very severely impaired clients learn to live, work, and recreate in nonsheltered, integrated environments (Gorski, 1983). The burden of proof was shifted from the client to the service provider. The program's definition of the least restrictive environment is presented here as it might well be useful to special educators serving students with severe handicaps such as autism:

> A continuum of services for persons with handicapping conditions means a progressive set of duties for those who work and advocate for them, designed to implement the goal of total independence. It does not mean a series of progressively less restrictive environments. Under this definition the person with handicapping conditions is helped to become independent in the community by first living there; and the rate of success for the provider of services can be measured in terms of the rapidity with which attendant staff can safely be removed from the client's home, work, travel and leisure environments. (Warren & Juhrs, 1984, pp. 1–2)

CONCLUSION

This chapter has reviewed some recent developments in curriculum, non-aversive behavior management, social skill development, and technology as these relate to educational programming for students with autism. Certainly, this review is not exhaustive, but is meant to highlight some current work and to point to needed demonstration effort and research. Many other areas of needed program development information have not been highlighted but are equally critical. These include issues in developing nonsheltered vocational options (Brown et al., 1983), individualized placement strategies (Mesaros, 1984), integration with nonhandicapped peers and others (Falvey, Grenot-Scheyer, & Luddy, in press), and individualized domestic living options (Hitzing, in press). An attempt was made to provide some guidance for educational decision-making until such information is available. With the data that are currently available, program options that address the criterion of ultimate functioning, that focus on critical effects for the student, that stress positive programming and nonaversive interventions, and that utilize functional curriculum in natural settings seem to be the most warranted. And, until more data are available, a focus on the criterion of the least dangerous assumption may make the critical difference in outcome for these learners.

REFERENCES

Alper, S. (1981). Utilizing community jobs in developing vocational curriculum for severely handicapped youth. *Education and Training of the Mentally Retarded, 16*(3), 217–221.

Baumgart, D., Brown, L., Pumpian, I., Nisbet, J., Ford, A., Sweet, M., Messina, R., & Schroeder, J. (1982). Principle of partial participation and individualized adaptations in educational programs for severely handicapped students. *Journal of The Association for the Severely Handicapped, 7*(2), 17–21.

Brown v. Board of Education, of Topeka, 347 U.S., 483 (1954).

Brown, F., Holvoet, J., Guess, D., & Mulligan, M. (1980). The individualized curriculum sequencing model (III): Small group instruction. *Journal of The Association for the Severely Handicapped, 5*(4), 352–367.

Brown, L., Branston, M. B., Hamre-Nietupski, S., Pumpian, I., Certo, N., & Gruenewald, L. (1979). A strategy for developing chronological age appropriate and functional curricular content for severely handicapped adolescents and young adults. *Journal of Special Education, 13,* 81–90.

Brown, L., Branston-McClean, M. B., Baumgart, D., Vincent, L., Falvey, M., & Schroeder, J. (1979). Utilizing the characteristics of a variety of current and subsequent least restrictive environments as factors in the development of curricular content for severely handicapped students. *AAESPH Review, 4*(4), 407–424.

Brown, L., Nietupski, J., & Hamre-Nietupski, S. (1976). The criterion of ultimate functioning and public school services for severely handicapped students. In L. Brown, N. Certo, & T. Crowner (Eds.), *Papers and programs related to public school services for secondary-age severely handicapped students* (Vol. VI, pp. 2–15). Madison: WI: Madison Metropolitan School District.

Brown, L., Shiraga, B., Ford, A., Nisbet, J., VanDeventer, P., Sweet, M., York, J., & Loomis, R. (1983). Teaching severely handicapped students to perform meaningful work in non-sheltered vocational environments. In L. Brown, J. Nisbet, A. Ford, M. Sweet, B. Shiraga, R. Loomis, & P. VanDeventer (Eds.), *Educational programs for severely handicapped students* (Vol. XIII, pp. 1–100). Madison, WI: Madison Metropolitan School District.

Brown, L., Wilcox, B., Sontag, E., Vincent, L., Dodd, W., & Gruenewald, L. (1977). Toward the realization of the least restrictive educational environments for severely handicapped students. *AAESPH Review, 2*(4), 195–201.

Campbell v. Talladega County Board of Education, 518 F. Supp. 47 (N.D. Ala. 1981).

Carr, E. G. (1977). The motivation of self-injurious behavior: A review of some hypotheses. *Psychological Bulletin, 84,* 800–816.

Carr, E. G. (1985). Behavioral approaches to language and communication. In E. Schopler & G. Mesibov (Eds.), *Current issues in autism: Vol. III. Communication problems in autism* (pp. 37–54). New York: Plenum Publishing Corp.

Donnellan, A. (1980). An educational perspective of autism: Implications for curriculum development and personnel development. In B. Wilcox & A. Thompson (Eds.), *Critical issues in educating autistic children and youth* (pp. 53–88). Washington, DC: U.S. Department of Education, Office of Special Education.

Donnellan, A. M. (1984). The criterion of the least dangerous assumption. *Behavioral Disorders, 9,* 141–150.

Donnellan, A. M. (in press). Personnel preparation and autism. In D. J. Cohen & A. M. Donnellan (Eds.), *Handbook of autism and disorders of atypical development.* New York: John Wiley & Sons.

Donnellan, A. M., Ford, A., Nisbet, J., Falvey, M., Pumpian, I., Baumgart, D., Schroeder, J., & Brown, L. (1980). A strategy for evaluating programs for students with autism and other handicapping conditions. In L. Brown, M. Falvey, I. Pumpian, D. Baumgart, J. Nisbet, A. Ford, J. Schroeder, & R. Loomis (Eds.), *Curricular strategies for teaching severely handicapped students functional skills in school and non-school environments* (Vol. X, pp. 206–272). Madison: University of Wisconsin-Madison and Madison Metropolitan School District.

Donnellan, A. M., & Kilman, B. (in press). Behavioral approaches to social skills development: Strengths, limitations and alternatives. In E. Schopler & G. B. Mesibov (Eds.), *Social behavior and autism*. New York: Plenum Publishing Corp.

Donnellan, A. M., & LaVigna, G. W. (in press.) Non-aversive control of socially-stigmatizing behaviors. *The Pointer*.

Donnellan, A., LaVigna, G. W., Schuler, A. L., & Woodward, P. E. (1982). A strategy for widespread dissemination of inservice training of classroom personnel. *Teacher Education and Special Education, 5*, 36–42.

Donnellan, A. M., LaVigna, G. W., Zambito, J., & Thvedt, J. (1985). A time limited intensive intervention program model to support community placement for persons with severe behavior problems. *Journal of The Association for Persons with Severe Handicaps, 10*(3).

Donnellan, A. M., & Mesaros, R. A. (in press). Strategies for developing individual placement options for students with autism. In D. J. Cohen & A. M. Donnellan (Eds.), *Handbook of autism and disorders of atypical development*. New York: John Wiley & Sons.

Donnellan, A. M., Mesaros, R. A., & Anderson, J. L. (1984). Teaching students with autism in natural environments: What educators need from researchers. *Journal of Special Education, 18*(4), 505–522.

Donnellan, A. M., & Mirenda, P. L. (1983). A model for analyzing instructional components to facilitate generalization for severely handicapped students. *Journal of Special Education, 17,* 317–331.

Donnellan, A. M., Mirenda, P. L., Mesaros, R. A., & Fassbender, L. L. (1984). A strategy for analyzing the communicative functions of aberrant behavior. *Journal of The Association for Persons with Severe Handicaps, 11,* 201–212.

Donnellan-Walsh, A., Gossage, L. D., LaVigna, G. W., Schuler, A. L., & Traphagen, J. (1976). *Teaching makes a difference*. Sacramento: California State Department of Education.

Dunlap, G., Koegel, R. L., & Egel, A. L. (1979). Autistic children in school. *Exceptional Children, 45,* 55–58.

Durand, V. M. (1982). Analysis and intervention of self-injurious behavior. *Journal of The Association for the Severely Handicapped, 7*(4), 44–53.

Evans, I. M., & Meyer, L. H. (1985). *An educative approach to behavior problems: A practical decision model for interventions with severely handicapped learners.* Baltimore: Paul H. Brookes Publishing Co.

Falvey, M., Brown, L., Lyon, S., Baumgart, D., & Schroeder, J. (1980). Strategies for using cues and correction procedures. In W. Sailor, B. Wilcox, & L. Brown (Eds.), *Methods of instruction for severely handicapped students* (pp. 109–133). Baltimore: Paul H. Brookes Publishing Co.

Falvey, M., Grenot-Scheyer, M., & Luddy, E. (in press). Developing and implementing integrated community referenced curriculum. In D. J. Cohen & A. M. Donnellan (Eds.), *Handbook of autism and disorders of atypical development*. New York: John Wiley & Sons.

Falvey, M., Luddy, E., & Grenot-Scheyer, M. (in press). Developing and implementing integrated community referenced curriculum. In D. J. Cohen & A. M. Donnellan (Eds.), *Handbook of autism and disorders of atypical development*. New York: John Wiley & Sons.

Fay, W. H. (1969). On the basis of autistic echolalia. *Journal of Communication Disorders, 2*, 38–47.

Freagon, S., & Rotatori, A. F. (1982). Comparing natural and artificial environments in training self-care skills to group home residents. *Journal of The Association for the Severely Handicapped, 7*(3), 73–86.

Galloway, C. (1979, March). *Toward a policy of community presence and participation*. Paper presented at the University of Southern California, Institute on Law and Mental Health, Sacramento.

Gaylord-Ross, R. J., Haring, N. G., Breen, C., & Pitts-Conway, V. (1984). The training and generalization of social interaction skills with autistic youth. *Journal of Applied Behavior Analysis, 17*, 229–248.

Goldiamond, I. (1974). Toward a constructional approach to social problems. *Behaviorism, 2*, 1–84.

Gorski, R. (1983). Blue collaring it in Rockville. *Disabled USA, 4*, 12–15.

Guess, D., Horner, R. D., Utley, B., Holovet, J., Maxon, D., Tucker, D., & Warren, S. (1978). A functional curriculum sequencing model for teaching the severely handicapped. *AAESPH Review, 3*(4), 202–215.

Halle, J. W. (1982). Teaching functional language to the handicapped: An integrative model of the natural environment teaching techniques. *Journal of The Association for the Severely Handicapped, 7*(4), 29–36.

Handleman, J. A. (1979). Generalization by autistic-type children of verbal responses across settings. *Journal of Applied Behavior Analysis, 12*, 273–282.

Hermelin, B. (1982). Thoughts and feelings. *Australia Autism Review, 1*, 10–19.

Hitzing, W. (in press). Community living alternatives for persons with autism and related severe behavior problems. In D. J. Cohen & A. M. Donnellan (Eds.), *Handbook of autism and disorders of atypical development*. New York: John Wiley & Sons.

Holvoet, J., Guess, D., Mulligan, M., & Brown, F. (1980). The individualized curriculum sequencing model (I): A teaching strategy for severely handicapped students. *Journal of The Association for the Severely Handicapped, 5*(4), 337–351.

Holvoet, J., Mulligan, M., Schussler, N., Lacy, J., & Guess, D. (1982). *The KICS model: Sequencing learning experiences for severely handicapped children and youth*. Lawrence: University of Kansas, Department of Special Education.

Inhelder, B., & Piaget, J. (1969). *Early growth of logic in the child*. New York: W. W. Norton & Co.

Iwata, B. A., Dorsey, M. F., Slifer, K. J., Bauman, K. E., & Richman, G. S. (1982). Toward a functional analysis of self-injury. *Analysis and Intervention in Developmental Disabilities, 2*, 3–20.

Kazdin, A. E. (1977). Assessing the clinical or applied significance of behavior change through social validation. *Behavior Modification, 1*, 427–452.

Keller, F. S. (1985). Preface. In G. W. LaVigna & A. M. Donnellan (Eds.), *Alternatives to punishment: Non-aversive strategies for solving behavior problems*. New York: Irvington Press.

Kilman, B. (1981, July). A social skills development for individuals with autism. In D. Park (Ed.), *Proceedings of the annual meeting and conference, National Society for Autistic Children* (pp. 318–327). Washington, DC: National Society for Autistic Children.

Koegel, R. L., Glahn, T. J., & Nieminen, G. S. (1978). Generalization of parent training results. *Journal of Applied Behavior Analysis, 11,* 95–110.

Koegel, R. L., Rincover, A., & Egel, A. L. (1982). *Educating and understanding autistic children.* San Diego: College-Hill Press.

Koegel, R. L., Russo, D. C., & Rincover, A. (1977). Assessing and training teachers in the generalized use of behavior modification with autistic children. *Journal of Applied Behavior Analysis, 10,* 197–205.

Lansing, M. D., & Schopler, E. (1978). Individualized education: A public school model. In M. Rutter & E. Schopler (Eds.), *Autism: A reappraisal of concepts and treatment* (pp. 439–452). New York: Plenum Publishing Corp.

LaVigna, G. W., & Donnellan, A. M. (1985). *Alternatives to punishment: Non-aversive strategies for solving behavior problems.* New York: Irvington Press.

Lettick, A. (1979). *Benhaven then and now.* New Haven, CT: Benhaven Press.

Martin, R. (1979). *Legal challenges in regulating behavior change.* Champaign, IL: Research Press.

McHale, S. M. (1983). The effects of repeated interaction on promoting play and communication between autistic and nonhandicapped children. *American Journal of Orthopsychiatry, 53,* 13–29.

Mesaros, R. A. (1983). *A review of the issues and literature regarding positive programming and contingency procedures for use with autistic children.* Unpublished manuscript, University of Wisconsin-Madison.

Mesaros, R. A. (1984). *Behavioral differences among autistic students in homogeneous and heterogeneous classroom grouping arrangements.* Unpublished doctoral dissertation, University of Wisconsin, Madison.

Mulligan, M., Guess, L., Holvoet, J., & Brown, F. (1980). The individualized curriculum sequencing model (I): Implication from research on massed, distributed, or spaced trial training. *Journal of The Association for the Severely Handicapped, 5*(4), 325–336.

Neel, R. S., & Billingsley, F. F. (1981). Instruction for autistic children: Some critical problems and possible solutions. In R. B. Rutherford & A. G. Prieto (Eds.), *Monograph in Behavior Disorders,* Arizona State University, Teacher Educators for Children with Behavioral Disorders and Council for Children with Behavior Disorders.

Neel, R. S., Billingsley, F. F., & Lambert, C. (1983). IMPACT: A functional curriculum for educating autistic youth in natural environments. In R. B. Rutherford, (Ed.), *Monograph in Behavioral Disorders,* Arizona State University, Teacher Educators for Children with Behavioral Disorders, and Council for Children with Behavior Disorders.

Paccia, J. M., & Curcio, F. (1982). Language processing and forms of immediate echolalia in autistic children. *Journal of Speech and Hearing Research, 25,* 42–47.

Peck, C. A., & Schuler, A. L. (1983). Classroom-based language intervention for children with autism: Theoretical and practical considerations for the speech and language specialist. *Seminars in Speech and Language, 4,* 93–103.

Peck, C. A., Schuler, A. L., & Semmel, M. I. (1983). *Developing social competence in autistic and severely handicapped children: A curriculum planning guide.* Santa Barbara: University of California Special Education Research Institute.

Pennsylvania Association for Retarded Children v. Commonwealth, 344 F. Supp. 1257 (E.D. Penn. 1971).

Prior, M. (1984). Developing concepts of childhood autism: The influence of experimental cognitive research. *Journal of Consulting and Clinical Psychology, 62,* 4–16.

Prizant, B. M., & Duchan, J. F. (1981). The functions of immediate echolalia in autistic children. *Journal of Speech and Hearing Disorders, 3,* 241–249.

Rotholtz, D. A., & Luce, S. C. (1984). The development of alternative reinforcement strategies for the reduction of self-stimulatory behavior in autistic youth. *Education and Treatment of Children. 6.* 363–377.

Rutter, M. (1982). Concepts of autism: A review of research. In S. I. Harrison & J. F. McDermott, Jr. (Eds.), *New directions in childhood psychopathology* (pp. 321–322). New York: International Universities Press, Inc.

Rutter, M. (1985). Commentary. In A. M. Donnellan (Ed.), *Classic readings in autism* (pp. 50–52). New York: Teacher's College Press.

Schuler, A. L., & Goetz, C. (1981). The assessment of severe language disabilities: Communicative and cognitive considerations. *Analysis and Interventions in Developmental Disabilities, 1*(3/4), 333–346.

Shapiro, T. (1977). The quest for a linguistic model to study the speech of autistic children. *Journal of the American Academy of Psychiatry, 16,* 608–619.

Strain, P. (1983). Generalization of autistic children's social behavior change: Effects of developmentally integrated and segregated settings. *Analysis and Intervention in Developmental Disabilities, 3*(1), 23–24.

Stuart, R. B. (1975). *Presidential address.* Paper presented at the 9th annual convention of the Association for the Advancement of Behavior Therapy, San Francisco, CA.

Sullivan, R. (1977). *National information and advocacy project for autistic and autistic-like persons* (HEW grant #54P-7120712-03). Washington, DC: National Society for Autistic Children.

Touchette, P. E. (1983, August). *Nonaversive amelioration of SIB by stimulus control transfer.* Paper presented at the annual convention of the American Psychological Association, Anaheim, CA.

Voeltz, L. M. (1984). Program and curriculum innovations to prepare children for integration. In N. Certo, N. Haring, & R. York (Eds.), *Public school integration of severely handicapped students: Rational issues and progressive alternatives* (pp. 155–183). Baltimore: Paul H. Brookes Publishing Co.

Voeltz, L. M., & Evans, I. M. (1983). Educational validity: Procedures to evaluate outcomes in programs for severely handicapped learners. *Journal of the Association for Persons with Severe Handicaps, 8,* 3–15.

Warren, F. (1980). Future directions in educational planning. In B. Wilcox & A. Thompson (Eds.), *Critical issues in educating autistic children and youth* (pp. 286–315). Washington, DC: U.S. Department of Education, Office of Special Education.

Warren, F., & Juhrs, P. (1984). Community philosophy—continuum of services. *Community News, 1*(1), 1–2.

Watzalawick, P., Beavin, J. H., & Jackson, D. D. (1967). *Pragmatics of human communication.* New York: W. W. Norton & Co.

Wehman, P. (1979). *Curriculum design for the severely and profoundly handicapped.* New York: Human Sciences Press.

White, O. (1980). Adaptive performance objectives: Form versus function. In W. Sailor, B. Wilcox, & L. Brown (Eds.), *Methods of instruction for severely handicapped students* (pp. 47–70). Baltimore: Paul H. Brookes Publishing Co.

Wilcox, B., & Bellamy, G. T. (1982). *Design of high school programs for severely handicapped students.* Baltimore: Paul H. Brookes Publishing Co.

Wolf, M. M. (1978). Social validity: The case for subjective measurement, or how applied behavior analysis is finding its heart. *Journal of Applied Behavior Analysis, 2,* 203–214.

Wolfensberger, W. (1972). *The principle of normalization in human services.* Toronto: National Institute on Mental Retardation.

Woods, T. S. (1980). Bringing autistic self-stimulatory behavior under S-Delta stimulus control. *British Columbia Journal of Special Education, 4,* 61–70.

Wuerch, B. B., & Voeltz, L. M. (1982). *Longitudinal leisure skills for severely handicapped learners: The Ho'onanea curriculum component.* Baltimore: Paul H. Brookes Publishing Co.

Yoder, D. (1980). Augmentative communication systems for severely speech handicapped children. In D. Bucher (Ed.), *Language development and intervention with the exceptional child* (pp. 24–38). San Francisco: Jossey-Bass.

Chapter 5

Approaching Families from an Individualized Perspective

Holly A. Benson and Ann P. Turnbull

Over the past 4 or 5 decades, attitudes regarding the role of parents in the care, education, and treatment of a family member who experiences a severe handicap have changed dramatically. Parents, who were once accused of being a major cause of their child's handicap, are now considered by many to be the essential and primary influence on development. Parents, who were once routinely advised and in some cases admonished to relinquish all responsibility for their handicapped child to an institution, are now applauded for maintaining their child at home. Parents, who were once expected to make the child experiencing a handicap the focal point of the family in committing themselves to multiple additional responsibilities, are increasingly being respected for establishing balanced family relationships and addressing the needs of all family members. What has caused these tremendous changes in philosophy guiding parental roles? How have these changes affected, and how do they continue to affect, parents and other family members? What is the current state of the art on family involvement and what are promising future directions? This chapter addresses these questions. Emphasis is placed on the concept of individualization for families. Just as individualization has increased program relevance for children and youth with severe handicaps, it has great promise in its application to families as well.

OVERVIEW OF HISTORY AND CURRENT POLICY

Prior to 1950, attitudes toward persons with severe handicaps and their parents were largely negative. Most parents were strongly encouraged and sometimes even pressured into institutionalizing their child (Gordon & Ullman, 1956). Professionals commonly justified their recommendations to institutionalize by elaborating on the negative impacts that the child could have upon the development of siblings and welfare of the parent's marriage. Moreover, families were led to believe that the child would be much better off and happier in an institution (Aldrich, 1947). Once the child was institutionalized, parents were oftentimes strongly urged to avoid any further involvement with their child on any level (Avis, 1978).

The movement toward a more optimistic and humanitarian view of retardation gained momentum in the 1950s. Efforts were largely directed by parents who banded together to demand improved services for their children with handicaps as well as for themselves (Katz, 1961). The National Association of Parents and Friends of Mentally Retarded Children (now known as the Association for Retarded Citizens/United States) was one of the first organizations that was effective in lobbying for the interests of persons with mental retardation. In 1954, this organization published the first Educational Bill of Rights for the Retarded Child setting forth the rights of children as well as the rights of their parents (Boggs, 1978).

Research conducted during the late 1950s and early 60s primarily focused on the impact of children with handicaps on their families and has been comprehensively reviewed by Wolfensberger (1970). Particular attention was given to the sequential "stages of adjustment" that were presumably experienced by family members in response to the birth of a child with handicaps. An outgrowth of the emphasis on stages of adjustment was counseling as the primary intervention mode for family members.

As activist groups were exerting pressure in judicial and legislative arenas, compensatory education programs for economically disadvantaged children were gathering force in effecting public policy and practice (Turnbull & Winton, 1984). In 1966, Public Law 89-794 (The Economic Opportunity Act Amendments of 1966) was passed authorizing the well-known national Project Head Start. This was particularly significant because it was the first legislation to reflect a policy of parent involvement (Wiegerink, Hocutt, Posante-Loro, & Bristol, 1980).

According to Zigler and Valentine (1979), parental involvement was considered to be essential to the success of the Head Start project. Two distinctly different perspectives supporting the perceived need for parent involvement were articulated by Valentine and Stark (1979). The first perspective arose out of what has been referred to as the cultural deficit model. From this perspective, parents were viewed as deficient in knowledge and skills related, and essential, to child-rearing (Foster, Berger, & McLean, 1981). The second perspective focused on politically based deficits in members of disadvantaged classes of people. Proponents of this rationale believed that differences in achievement and social success result from fewer opportunities for decision-making and less access to resources than those that are available to more advantaged classes of people.

One can speculate that the assumptions underlying the cultural deficit model and the increasing enthusiasm over the success of behavioral interventions accelerated the proliferation of parent training programs. This trend represented a significant and rapid shift in perspective from the 50s and early 60s to the 70s. Whereas in the 50s and early 60s the emphasis was placed on studying the ways in which a child with handicaps affected family adjustment and development, the emphasis of the 70s was on studying the ways in which the family (e.g., mother) affected the adjustment and development of the child.

Probably the most significant landmark events shaping current parent roles were the passage in 1975 of Public Law 94-142, The Education for All Handicapped Children Act and its implementation in 1977. This was the federal government's first formal response to advocacy for equal access to free and appropriate public education for *all* children, including those with severe handicaps. Furthermore, it enacted farreaching parent involvement requirements based primarily on the political perspective and secondarily on the cultural deficit model.

Public Law 94-142 establishes guidelines that educational agencies must observe in the areas of parental notification, consent, and decision-making. These guidelines provide parents with the authority to protect the rights of their children. It is important to recognize that, while parents may be granted the authority to protect the rights of their children, they are not required to do so by law (Strickland, 1983). Although parents have the legal option to accept or refuse their role as decision-maker, the encouragement of active parent involvement continues to be a priority of the academic community (Lillie & Place, 1982; Paul, 1981), parent advocates (Cutler, 1981; Goldberg & Goldberg, 1979), and federal granting agencies (e.g., Office of Special Education and Rehabilitation Services). Thus, the role expected of parents resulting from Public Law 94-142 is that of educational decision-maker.

The secondary role that parents are expected to assume is that of intervenor. The intervenor role is directly supported by the congressional testimony of Senator Harrison Williams (1975), one of the bill's major proponents.

> The individualized planning conference is also intended as a method of providing additional parent counseling and training so that the parent may bolster the educational process at home. This involvement is important to assure the educational services are meeting the child's needs and so both parents and child may be part of the process from which they're so often removed. . . . (126 Cong. Rec. S1950, daily ed., June 18, 1975)

Two of the Public Law 94-142 requirements are also related to the intervenor role. First, parent training is included in the definition of related services. Second, parents are designated as a target group for the Comprehensive System for Personnel Development (*Federal Register*, 1977) Thus, in enacting Public Law 94-142, Congress was operating under the presumption that parent involvement would increase the probability that the rights of students with handicaps would be assured (parent as decision-maker) and that the educational process would extend into the home (parent as intervenor). The primary beneficiary of both of these outcomes was to be the student. The next section (pp. 130–137) reviews the research on the degree to which parents have assumed these roles.

CURRENT RESEARCH ON PARENTS AS DECISION-MAKERS AND INTERVENORS

Parents as Decision-Makers

Public Law 94-142 defines two primary forums in which parents and educators interact to make educational decisions, that is, the IEP (individualized education program) conference and due process hearing. The IEP conference provides an opportunity for joint decisions concerning goals, objectives, evaluation procedures, related services, and placement. The due process hearing enables either parents or educators to contest formally the decisions made by the other party. Decisions made at IEP conferences are generally arrived at through consensus or negotiation, whereas the due process hearing is a more adversarial procedure involving conflict resolution (Turnbull & Strickland, 1981).

The earliest study of the decision-making role of parents in the IEP conference was conducted in the second year of Public Law 94-142 implementation (Goldstein, Strickland, Turnbull, & Curry, 1980). This study examined two variables associated with the IEP conference for elementary students with mild handicaps: 1) topics of discussion, and 2) frequency of contributions by persons in attendance. These variables were measured using an observational analysis that involved coding speakers and topics at brief time intervals. Parental contributions, most frequently on the topic of personal/family issues, accounted for less than 25% of the total conference contributions. The typical conference (36 minutes in length) involved the teacher (as primary speaker) describing an IEP that had been developed prior to the meeting without participation or input from the parents. Despite their passive involvement, the parents reported an extremely high level of satisfaction with their degree of decision-making on a follow-up questionnaire.

Although passive parental participation in IEP decision-making was clearly not the legislative intent, later studies have confirmed that many parents participate in this fashion (Goldstein, 1980; McKinney & Hocutt, 1982). The largest parent participation survey reported to date (Lynch & Stein, 1982) included a sample of 400 parents of special education students. Thirteen percent of the students were severely handicapped with the chronological ages ranging from 4 to 20 years. Nearly three-fourths of the families reported that they were "actively" involved in the development of their child's IEP; however, specific examples of their active involvement included expressing opinions and suggestions, working with and trusting the professionals, listening to and agreeing with the teacher's recommendations, and understanding what was happening. While only 47% of these parents indicated that they were actively involved by making suggestions during the meeting, 76% of all families reported that they were satisfied or very satisfied with their child's current special education program. No significant differences were found between parents of children with severe handicaps and parents of children with learning handicaps. A significant finding, however, was that parents of physically handicapped students and parents of 13- and 14-year-old students participated significantly less in IEP meetings than parents of students in other program and age categories. Another interesting finding was that parents of Caucasian children were significantly more aware of related services included on the IEP as compared to parents of children in other ethnic groups. These data are particularly enlightening in suggesting variations in parent participation according to type of handicap, family life cycle stage, and cultural background.

Parent preferences for educational decision-making are helpful in interpreting the nature of IEP meeting participation. One survey asked parents to specify their actual and desired level of participation in making nine different types of decisions (Lusthaus, Lusthaus, & Gibbs, 1981). The results of actual participation revealed that giving and receiving information was the most frequent role, followed respectively by having no role or decisional control. A majority of the parents indicated a desire to maintain the informational role in six of the nine decisional areas including discipline, class placement, evaluation, instructional grouping, transportation, and special resources; and a desire to have control over decisions pertaining to types of records maintained, medical services, and student transfers to other schools.

Other information on parent preferences indicates that all parents do not agree with the assumption implicit in the comments of key legislators and congressional witnesses that parents are interested in assuming a strong advocacy role (Turnbull, Turnbull, & Wheat, 1982). Many parents have reported a need for a break from educational responsibilities. Based on interviews with mothers of preschool children with mild and moderate handicaps, Winton and Turnbull (1981) reported a strong emphasis given by parents on the availability of competent teachers so that they can attend to other family concerns knowing that their child's educational needs are being addressed.

Some professionals argue that parents do not act on their rights for active educational decision-making because they are ill-informed regarding what rights they have. Documentation exists that parents do lack information on their legal rights pertaining to educational decision-making (Budoff, 1979; Mitchell,

1976; Rubin & Quinn-Curran, 1983; Strickland, 1983; Turnbull, Winton, Blacher, & Salkind, 1983; Yoshida, 1979). This situation is particularly true for minority families (Strickland, 1983). Ninety percent of the parents of preschoolers with mild and moderate handicaps responded in an interview study that they would like to have additional information on mainstreaming as an educational alternative (Turnbull, Winton, Blacher, & Salkind, 1983).

A common professional assumption is that parents need training in order to enhance their level of participation; however, it must be recognized that many parents are not interested in receiving training. Goldstein (1980) conducted observational analyses of the IEP conference participation of 45 parents of elementary students with learning disabilities and surveyed them concerning their interest in receiving training on a variety of topics (i.e., child development, assertiveness training, making teaching materials, legal rights and responsibilities, teaching reading and math, writing IEP goals and objectives, and educational activities for home). The least frequently desired topic for training was writing IEP goals and objectives. It is paradoxical that in the analyses of these IEP conferences, parents revealed a passive style of involvement in decision-making and a high level of conference satisfaction according to parental self-report. Thus, these parents participated at a passive level, they were satisfied with the passive style, and IEP training was not a priority.

Dissatisfaction with IEP development and implementation has been a catalyst for some parents to pursue a due process hearing (Strickland, 1982b, 1983). Due process hearings typically can be characterized as a legalistic and adversarial forum. This is likely attributable to the regulations (*Federal Register,* 1977) pertaining to hearings that allow for the presence of counsel, presentation of evidence, examination and cross-examination of witnesses, and subpoena of documents. In such hearings, parents divest themselves and school personnel of ultimate decision-making authority and place that authority in the hands of a third party.

The majority of hearings have focused on the issue of placement (Mitchell, 1976, National Association of State Directors of Special Education [NASDSE] 1978; Strickland, 1982a), with conflicting interpretations by parents and school personnel of the meaning of "appropriate" education. Whereas school personnel frequently interpret "appropriate" to mean the provision of an "adequate" program, parents interpret it to mean the "most appropriate" or "best possible" program. Two studies have indicated that due process hearings most frequently involve issues associated with appropriate education for learning disabled students (Mitchell, 1976; NASDSE, 1978).

Estimates of the cost to a family who enters a due process hearing range from $300 to $4,000 (NASDSE, 1978; Yoshida, 1979), covering items such as attorney's fees, payment of witnesses, independent evaluations, consultation with specialists, copying of records, and telephone calls. Because of the legal intricacies of hearings and the fact that the school's attorney is almost always present, parents have recognized that the absence of an attorney can place them at a considerable disadvantage (Strickland, 1982b). Further confirmation exists that parents who pursue hearings are primarily from middle and upper socio-economic status (Lay, 1977; NASDSE, 1978).

Has the due process hearing been an effective forum for making fair decisions? Strickland's (1982b) research of the perceptions of parents and school representatives regarding their relationship before, during, and after the due process hearing provides the most comprehensive answer to this question. Of the total population of parents surveyed, 46% had children with severe handicaps, while 64% had children who attended a special class on a full-time basis. Following the conclusion of the hearing, parents and school representatives reported significantly less confidence in the due process hearing as an effective means of settling disputes. It was also found that parents who tended to be dissatisfied with the hearing decision were also dissatisfied with its implementation. A disheartening finding was that 45% of the local hearing decisions were not implemented. A reason for lack of implementation in many states is that few educational agencies have any mechanism for monitoring implementation (Budoff, 1979; Strickland, 1982b). Hearing officers can determine that a given student with a handicap is not receiving an appropriate education; however, they have no authority to monitor the implementation of an improved program.

A synthesis of these data suggests that due process hearings are frequently less than satisfactory procedures from the parents' perspective. Two critical variables associated with the usage of due process hearings appear to be the parents socioeconomic status and the program category of the child.

Parents as Intervenors

As stated earlier, congressional testimony and specific Public Law 94-142 requirements underscore the importance of the interventionist role for parents. The basic rationale for the role is that children with handicaps will make more developmental progress when teachers and parents implement coordinated instructional programs. Other reasons cited include personnel shortages, prevention of behavior problems, continuity of parent responsibility versus the transiency of professionals, generalization and maintenance of effects, and the strength of parents as reinforcers (Altman & Mira, 1983). A review of the literature suggests that enthusiasm for the intervenor role has emanated more from professional sources (Baker, Heifetz, & Brightman, 1972; Shearer & Shearer, 1977) than from parent sources.

The intervenor role has primarily been actualized through the provision of training to parents in the areas of behavior management and direct instruction. Although the research in this area can be critiqued on several grounds (Buchman, 1983), it is a clearly established fact that parent training can be effective in increasing developmental and behavioral outcomes for children with handicaps. Comprehensive program models have been developed and applied to an increasing number of parents. Baker and his colleagues (Baker, 1984; Baker, Heifetz, & Murphy, 1980) have developed a group training format with a curriculum that focuses on the development of behavioral skills related to self-help, play, speech, and language. Outcome data based on measures of knowledge, teaching skill, and trainer evaluation of family progress indicate that approximately two-thirds of the families meet proficiency criteria by the end of training. The parent variable most predictive of lack of success was low socioeconomic status. Baker (1984) has made curriculum and instructional modifications to individualize for these families, including a decrease in the number of didactic presentations and an increase in experimental (e.g., role playing, videotapes, live demonstrations) ones.

It is important and necessary to document the gains parents make at the end of training; however, increases in skill do not ensure that parents will follow through on teaching their child at home. In one follow-up study (Baker et al., 1980) of 95 families, it was found that, 14 months after training, 16% of the families were carrying out formal teaching sessions for a new skill (i.e., setting aside time for planned sessions several times a week), and 22% had started a new behavior management program. Seventy-six percent of the families reported incidental teaching for at least one skill. It should be noted that a 14-month follow-up is considered rather long-term from the perspective of researchers; however, one can speculate that it is a short-term perspective for parents of children having severe handicaps. Since many of these parents will deal with the special needs of their sons and daughters over the full life cycle, it may be appropriate to consider maintenance over 5- and 10- year intervals.

According to the research, there are a number of factors that influence whether or not parents generalize the skills that they gain through parent training. Ambrose and Baker (1979) found that the primary obstacles to home interventions were major disruptive events (e.g., death in the family, divorce), lack of time, and daily interruptions. Other factors influencing generalization are marital discord (Reisinger, Frangia, & Hoffman, 1976), similarity of training and natural setting (Miller & Sloane, 1976), and social support (Wahler, 1980). These findings suggest that variables in the family ecology are determinants of the degree to which parents are successful in the intervention role. No study to date, however, has examined the impact of parent intervention from a family systems perspective.

Bijou (1984) underscores the difficulties that parents face in implementing new behavioral practices at home. He states:

> The mother, usually the one who volunteers for parent training, finds that she must not only reorient her own lifelong ways of thinking in order to apply behavioral child management techniques with conviction, but she must also persuade the members of the household to cooperate in attaining her goals. Getting the family to act in concert

on a child's behaviors can be a burdensome task: Some family members are unconcerned about the problem and prefer not be involved; some are skeptical about the approach; some believe that goals and techniques conflict with their cultural values and practices; and some are simply and realistically preoccupied with economic survival. If a parent can be taught to deal with such obstacles, at least in some measure, the chances of his or her continuing in the program would probably increase. (p. 24)

Thus, the trends of research indicate that: 1) parents can learn effective procedures to intervene with their children, 2) parent intervention generally results in child progress, 3) maintenance of formal teaching is questionable, and 4) maintenance of incidental teaching (e.g., social skills at movie theater) is more likely. Given these trends, a critical question is: Are parents interested in assuming the intervention role? Extensive data on parent interests, particularly data focused on the preferences of parents who have children with severe handicaps, are unavailable. There are data, however, suggesting that parents "at risk" for abuse, neglect, emotional disturbance, and developmental delay have a low interest in attending group parent education training (Rosenberg, Reppucci, & Linney, 1983). In their 1-year demonstration project, Rosenberg et al. (1983) anticipated serving 130 families. By the end of the demonstration year, 48 parents had been referred, and only 25 parents attended at least one group meeting. This 52% participation rate is comparable to, and even higher than, attendance rates in many other parent education projects focusing on disadvantaged populations (Chilman, 1973). Some of the reasons that parents have given for not participating in training programs have been: low socioeconomic status resulting in survival-oriented priorities (Bijou, 1984; Chilman, 1973), medical complications of children with disabilities (Altman, Haavik, & Cook, 1978), and a desire to defer responsibility for teaching the child to professionals (Baker, 1984).

Evaluation of the effectiveness of a parent (almost always the mother) as intervenor is considered an essential element of most parent training programs. What has not been addressed are some of the unintentional relational outcomes, such as the paradox stated by the father of a child with a sensory handicap (Winton, Turnbull, & Blacher, 1984):

> I believe that parents should love their handicapped children as they are and work with everything they've got to help them reach their highest potential. But there is a fine line involved in doing this, almost a paradox. To love them as they are might tempt parents to not encourage them to achieve their highest potential, but rather to be content. On the other hand, emphasizing reaching their highest potential could lead parents to dwell on what they can't do. The result could be that it is harder to love them as they are.

A consumer perspective sheds light on another possible unintended consequence—the perpetual patient perspective (Gliedman & Roth, 1980). Sondra Diamond (1981), a psychologist having a physical disability, shares her own childhood experience:

Something happens in a parent when relating to his disabled child: he forgets that they're a kid first. I used to think about that a lot when I was a kid. I would be off in a euphoric state, drawing or coloring or cutting out paper dolls, and as often as not the activity would be turned into an occupational therapy session. "You're not holding the scissors right," "Sit up straight so your curvature doesn't get worse." That era was ended when I finally let loose a long and exhaustive tirade. "I'm just a kid! You can't therapize me all the time! I get enough therapy in school every day! I don't think about my handicap all the time like you do!" (p. 30)

A final unintended consequence is the creation of stress for parents when they prefer not to be an interventionist, but believe that they are expected to function in this role. A mother of a child with a handicap, who is also an elementary teacher, stated:

I think you have to be removed as a parent from the situation . . . Living with a child like this and trying to train him is just about an impossibility. It's just the constant supervision of a child like this that really gets to you after a while . . . it's frightening enough without having to teach him too. (Turnbull & Winton, 1983, p. 65)

The time demands of parent training can also result in parent stress. Given the extensive needs of children with severe handicaps, the responsibilities and complexity of family life for all members, the demands of the workplace, and the complications of multiple problems (e.g., poverty, abuse, alcoholism) in many families, some of the practical questions that continually must be addressed are: Where do families get the time to assume the intervenor role? What activities do parents forego to devote increased time to home intervention? What are the implications for the child, as well as for all family members?

In summary, the role of parent as intervenor has distinct benefits and drawbacks. Its utility must be assessed in light of certain parental characteristics and circumstances as well as alternative modes for delivering program content.

Gap between Policy and Practice

An obvious gap exists between parent involvement policy and practice. The assumptions underlying parent involvement policies of Public Law 94-142 (parents are willing and able to assume active roles as decision-makers and interventionists) are valid for some parents but not for all. It is interesting to consider the dichotomy that exists between the Public Law 94-142 policy requirements for children and those for parents (Turnbull & Turnbull, 1982). The policies for children require that services be individualized according to the particular needs of each child; this same concept of individualization, however, is not applied to the parents or families of these children. The expectation that all parents will be active decision-makers and interventionists does not take into account the individual needs, capabilities, and interests of families with members who are handicapped.

The concept of individualization for families requires that the present theoretical basis for family involvement be reexamined. The assumptions underlying the models of the 60s and 70s must be carefully examined in terms of their continuing applicability for parents of children with handicaps today. It cannot be assumed that families in the 80s have the same needs, knowledge base, skills, interest, and time as did families 10 and 20 years ago.

Service providers must take into consideration competing time and responsibility demands, assess and account for diverse needs, and plan interventions that encourage family integration and well-being. Turnbull, Summers, and Brotherson (1983b) suggest that professionals consider the family systems theoretical perspective as a relevant guide to serving persons with severe handicaps and their families. The family systems perspective provides a synthesis and expansion of the two earlier models discussed in the historical overview section by focusing on the reciprocal and individualized needs of children with severe handicaps, their parents, and other family members within the naturally occurring ecology of family life.

FAMILY SYSTEMS THEORY AS A GUIDE TO INDIVIDUALIZATION

Family systems theory views the family from a systems perspective. From this perspective, the family is seen as a social system with unique characteristics and needs comprised of individual members who also have unique characteristics and needs. The basic belief is that all parts of the family are interrelated and that events affecting one member of the family inevitably affect all family members (Carter & McGoldrick, 1980; Hoffman, 1980; Minuchin, 1974). According to Goldenberg and Goldenberg (1980), family systems theorists approach intervention in a way that "aims beyond the treatment of individuals to the treatment of families, and beyond separately treating individuals who comprise the family to treating the family as a unitary group" (p. 105).

A conceptual framework organizing family systems theory is presented in Figure 1 (Turnbull, Summers, & Brotherson, 1983b; Turnbull, Summers, & Brotherson, 1986). This framework consists of three components—structure, function, and life cycle—that shape family interaction, the hub of the system. This section's analysis of the family system provides a discussion of concepts, a rationale for individualization, and suggestions of areas for intervention and evaluation.

Family Structure

Very simply put, family structure is a picture of how the family looks. The major components that comprise family structure are its membership characteristics, cultural style, and ideological style. A number of subcomponents comprise each of these major components, all of which interact in various ways to give the family its unique identity.

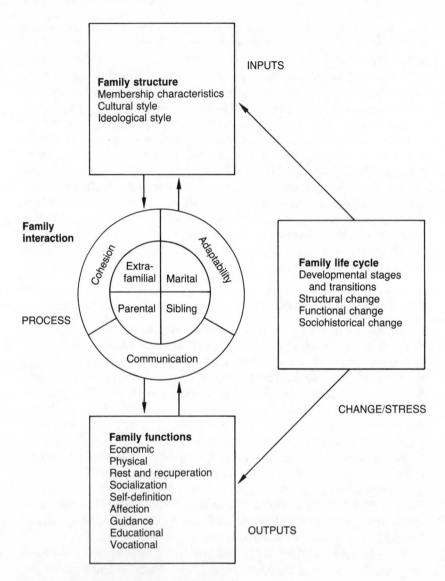

Figure 1. Family systems conceptual framework.

Membership Characteristics The *membership characteristics* of a family are formed by the size of the family, the characteristics of individual members, and the nature of the extrafamilial system. In the past, the term family was generally associated with a very specific type of arrangement—the nuclear family in which the mother remained at home to care for the children while the father worked. Today there are recognized many different types of families and there is evidence that the number of different types are actually on the increase (Glick & Norton, 1979; Skolnick & Skolnick, 1977). Several factors have been suggested as responsible for this increase including the high rate of divorce and remarriage, greater incidence of single-parent families, blended families, extended families, changing gender roles, low birth rate, and a greater number of women in the work force (Foster et al., 1981; Goldenberg & Goldenberg, 1980).

It is important that persons working with individuals experiencing handicaps recognize the heterogeneity of families in respect to membership characteristics. In many ways, membership characteristics can influence how the family relates to the member who is handicapped, which, in turn, influences the needs of the child and the family. For instance, the needs of a single-parent family of five will likely be very different from the needs of a two-parent family with only one child. Similarly, a family that has the support and guidance of relatives, friends, and neighbors will have needs very different from a family that is isolated and lacks extrafamilial resources (Wahler, 1980).

Membership characteristics also have implications for the person or persons who make educational decisions on behalf of the child. For example, a mother whose child was enrolled in an early intervention program was invited to come in for an interview and bring her family. She brought her grandmother, mother, and three children, one of whom had a handicap. Her grandmother (i.e., the child's great-grandmother) was the daily care provider for the child. In many programs, only the child's mother would have received an invitation to participate in conferences, when, in fact, the great-grandmother was a vital resource.

Cultural Style   In addition to the influence of different membership characteristics, families are also influenced by *cultural style*. Cultural style refers to the background or foundation of the family that shapes its current needs and ideologies. Four major components of cultural style are ethnicity, religion, socioeconomic status, and geographic location.

Ethnicity   Ethnicity is the unique flavor or personality of a family that has been handed down through generations. According to McGoldrick (1982):

> Ethnicity patterns our thinking, feelings, and behavior in both obvious and subtle ways. It plays a major role in determining what we eat, how we work, how we relax, how we celebrate holidays and rituals, and how we feel about life, death, and illness. (p. 4)

Without a doubt, ethnicity also plays a major role in determining how a family will relate to a member who is handicapped (e.g., deciding who makes decisions, placing emphasis on independence and achievement, highlighting a need for protection, and perceiving stigma).

Religion   Factors related to a family's religious or spiritual beliefs may also be important considerations when working with families with members experiencing handicaps. Research conducted in the early 1960s on the reactions of families of varying religious denominations to a disability indicates some significant differences between groups (Farber, 1959; Stubblefield, 1965; Zuk, Miller, Bartram, & Kling, 1961). For example, Zuk et al. (1961) found that Catholic mothers are generally more accepting of their children with handicaps than are nonCatholic mothers. Interestingly, the results of more recent studies have emphasized the importance of the family's religious interpretations of the handicap as contrasted with their denominative affiliation (Turnbull, Brotherson, & Summers, 1985). While it is not necessary for the service provider to understand or agree with the family's religious perspective, having a sense of what the perspective is can be helpful. In addition, information about the family's degree of emphasis on religion may, at times, be helpful in understanding the way in which the family interacts with the handicapped member as well as the way in which the family copes with stress. Furthermore, for many families with a strong religious perspective, professionals from religious organizations may be appropriate referral sources for counseling and social support.

Socioeconomic Status   A family's socioeconomic status is determined by the amount of money it makes, the level of education, and the kinds of jobs held. Socioeconomic status can have an enormous impact upon a family's perception of the world. Two distinctly different ways of viewing the world that researchers have found are related to socioeconomic status evolve around the issues of control and future orientation. According to Rubin (1976), many working class families feel that they have very little control over what happens to them; as a result, their ability to plan for the future is often severely limited. This perspective could partially account for the reluctance of parents at lower socioeconomic levels to function as decision-makers and interventionists. In contrast, middle- and upper-class families are frequently very future-oriented, motivated by a sense of control of their circumstances, self-determination, and desire to achieve. In their research on families with members having handicaps, Farber and Ryckman (1965) found results that support Rubin's (1976) work and that have implications for service providers. Farber and Ryckman (1965) found that families characteristically experience one of two kinds of stress associated with a child experiencing handicaps: the "tragic crisis" and the "role-organization crisis." Families who view the presence of a handicapping condition as a tragic crisis are generally in higher socioeconomic brackets and see the disability as a frustration of future aspirations for achievement and a happly life. The role-organization crisis usually occurs in families of lower socioeconomic status, with the stress centering around the problems of distributing the family's resources to cope with a lifelong burden of care.

Another important factor for service providers to consider is the family's relationship to the work force. In many families today, both parents are employed. It is important to take into consideration the time demands placed on families with dual careers when scheduling meetings or planning home inter-ventions. Outside employment can greatly influence the way that families prioritize their responsibilities, allocate their time, and use formal and informal support.

Geographic Location The last subcomponent of cultural style has to do with the geographic location in which the family lives. Families who choose to reside in rural areas may have different needs and support systems than families who reside in more populated, urban settings. Consequently, interventions designed to serve the needs of families in rural areas may need to be very different from those designed for urban families (Helge, 1984).

Ideological Style The third major component that comprises family structure is ideological style. A family's ideological style is based on its beliefs, values, and coping behaviors. The family's perspective of the world and how the perspective is actualized grows out of ideological style. Ideological style can include the family's child-rearing philosophy; attitudes toward the dis-ability, education, the concept of independence and the work ethic; and patterns for reacting to stress. Families vary greatly in their ideological styles. Some families value security and constancy while other families value adventure and change. Some families believe that it is important to establish a sense of routine and discipline while other families place greater emphasis on variety and spontaneity.

The resistance of some families in considering integrated placements for their child with handicaps may relate to their values for protection and security. Considered within a family systems perspective, these values may be recog-nized as culturally based and ones that are applied to every family member. Considered in isolation, service providers may draw narrow interpretations that the parents are ''overprotecting'' the child with the handicap because they are not committed to the developmental model.

Families are likely to need assistance in clarifying their values and examining them in light of their current and future effect on the member experiencing a handicap (e.g., if a family values security and constancy, what are the implications for the member having a handicap over the next 5, 10, and 20 years?). Educators also need to examine their own values and to be aware of situations in which their values are likely to conflict with those of the family. In such cases, value differences may need to be analyzed and discussed prior to attempting to define goals and objectives.

In addition to values and beliefs, coping patterns also comprise a family's ideological style. Coping patterns refer to the ways in which families deal with stress (McCubbin et al., 1980; Pearlin & Schooler, 1978). The recognition that a child has a handicap can cause varying degrees of stress in different families as well as in members within the same family. This experience of stress can be related to a number of factors including membership characteristics, cultural style, prior experience with stress, and the effectiveness of the coping strategies that the family has developed. Some families may rely on informal mechanisms within the family constellation to assist them in dealing with stress, while other families may elect to seek social or professional support from outside sources. By being sensitive to a family's coping style, service providers increase the probability that the assistance they offer will complement and not challenge the manner in which the family has learned to handle stress.

Family Interaction

Family interaction refers to the interplay that is constantly occurring among individual family members on a daily basis. The family systems framework developed by Turnbull, Summers, and Brotherson (1983b) identifies four major components of the interactional system: subsystems, cohesion, adaptability, and communication.

Subsystems Every family is comprised of a number of co-existing *subsystems*. It is through these subsystems that the family carries out its functions. The number, or even existence, of subsystems can vary significantly according to the family's membership characteristics. In the traditional nuclear family there are four distinct subsystems: 1) marital (husband/wife), 2) parental (child/parent), 3) sibling (child/child), and 4) extrafamilial (entire family's or individual members' interactions with others including neighbors, friends, work associates, and professionals). According to the family systems perspective, events affecting any of these subsystems inevitably reverberate through the family and affect all members. This has important implications for the manner in which service providers interact, or intervene, with families with members experiencing handicaps. Although the member having a handicap is typically considered the ''target'' of intervention, all other subsystems are also affected (Turnbull et al., 1983b):

> Consider the example of a mother who has agreed to work on a home training program in the area of feeding with her severely retarded child. Allowing her child to feed himself triples the time involved in each meal. While the mother is working with the child on feeding, her dinner conversation with her husband and other children is substantially limited. After the other family members finish dinner, the father cleans the kitchen and the siblings proceed to their homework all feeling that some of their needs have been overlooked. Meanwhile, the mother is feeling isolated from the rest of her family and frustrated over all the tasks to which she must attend before midnight. (p. 5)

Prior to recommending home intervention for a child, service providers and family members might conduct an ecological assessment of the likely benefits and drawbacks of the intervention from the perspective of individual (Turnbull, Brotherson, Summers, & Turnbull, in press) and subsystem (Skrtic, Summers, Brotherson, & Turnbull, 1984) interests. In some cases, the intervention might have potential benefit for the child's developmental progress but might pose potential harm for the parents' marriage. In such cases of competing equities, decisions need to be made concerning priorities and availability of other intervention resources.

Cohesion The degree of cohesion, adaptability, and communication in a family determines the way in which subsystems interact (Olson, Russell, & Sprenkle, 1980). *Cohesion* refers to the force that holds family members together. Too much cohesion can result in enmeshment—a situation in which the boundaries between subsystems are poorly differentiated and weak (Minuchin, 1974). Interactions among members in enmeshed subsystems are typically characterized by overconcern and involvement (e.g., a mother so intensely involved in the "handicap establishment" in supporting the needs of her child that she becomes alienated from her husband and peers). In such cases, members have difficulty developing a sense of individuality of self. In contrast, too little cohesion or disengagement can have equally detrimental effects. Disengaged families have very rigid boundaries between the subsystems, communication between members is severely impaired, and there is frequently very little family unity or loyalty (e.g., husbands and wives choosing not to share with each other the emotional reactions they feel when they learn that their child has a handicap). A healthy balance between the two extremes of enmeshment and disengagement characterizes well-functioning families.

When planning intervention strategies, it is important for service providers and families to consider the amount of cohesion between and within subsystems. Often, mothers are reinforced for establishing enmeshed relationships with the young child who has a handicap. Then they are later criticized when they have a difficult time letting go. Again, balance is the keystone of healthy relationships.

Adaptability The ability to conform to new or changed circumstances is referred to as the family's *adaptability* (Olson et al., 1980). As with cohesion, adaptability can be conceptualized along a continuum of lesser to greater degrees. At one end of the continuum are the rigid families that are unwilling or unable to change in response to new circumstances. At the other end of the continuum are the chaotic families that are characterized by fluctuating relationship rules, instability, and general lack of leadership (Turnbull et al., 1983b). Well-functioning families are those that are able to maintain a balance between change and stability (Olson, Sprenkle, & Russell, 1979). Families may be better able to adapt to change and stress at certain points in time than they are at others. Having a general sense of where the family is functioning along the continuum of adaptability can be useful information for service providers who are considering changes in the handicapped member's educational or habilitation program.

Communication The last major component of the interactional system is *communication*. A family must develop ways and means of establishing and maintaining clear communication channels if it is to function effectively. In a survey conducted in 1973, Beck and Jones found that poor communication was by far the major problem reported by couples seeking family counseling (Goldenberg & Goldenberg, 1980). Poor communication does not necessarily refer to lack of communication. Some families may communicate frequently but seldom touch on any meaningful or emotional issues. Other families may limit their communication to the exchange of highly emotional issues and seldom relate rationally. Families who function at optimal levels are able to communicate openly and effectively by consistently sending clear messages, listening with genuine intent and interest, and providing feedback in constructive and positive ways.

In order for service providers to communicate effectively with families, they must have an understanding of the family's communication style. In some cases, service providers may need to modify their own communication style in order to be optimally effective. For instance, service providers who value communication at a rational level may have to alter their approach when interacting with families whose communication is limited to the exchange of emotional issues only.

Family interaction patterns (i.e., cohesion, adaptability, and communication) are constantly changing in response to shifts in climate both within and outside of the family unit. It is, in fact, this ability to change that keeps families functioning in a healthy, well-balanced fashion. According to Green and Framo (1983), families who attempt to "maintain the interactional status quo even when a flexible change in its rules is essential for the development of its members or for adaption of new extrafamilial conditions become dysfunctional" (p. 4). It is essential that service providers assess the potential impact of their interactions and interventions on the entire family to ensure that they encourage, and not discourage, healthy interactions among family members.

Family Functioning

According to Goldenberg and Goldenberg (1980)

> [A] family is far more than a collection of individuals occupying a specific physical and psychological space together. Rather, it is a natural social system with properties all its own, one that has evolved a set of rules, roles, a power structure, forms of communication, and ways of negotiation and problem solving that allow various tasks to be performed effectively. (p. 3)

These tasks that the family performs are referred to as the functions, or outputs, of the family system. By carrying out its functions, the family shares the common goal of serving the collective and individual needs of its members. The family systems framework identifies nine specific functions that families typically perform (Turnbull, Summers, & Brotherson, 1983): economic, physical, rest and recuperation, socialization, self-definition, affection, guidance, educational, and vocational.

Families today differ tremendously in terms of the number and kinds of functions they perform. It is important to consider this heterogeneity in functional responsibilities in light of the heavy emphasis, as earlier reported, on the parental roles of decision-maker and interventionist. For example, education is but one of nine family functions, and it is the only function for which parents of children with severe handicaps have a legal claim to free and appropriate community services. Thus, some families may make a decision to delegate educational responsibilities to teachers so that they will have additional time to invest in responding to their child's needs in other functional areas (for which there are no services) or to their own needs, as well as the needs of other family members. The fact that parents are not involved as advocates or intervenors with educational programs does not in any way imply that they are not involved with their child in meeting needs in other functional areas (MacMillan & Turnbull, 1983); too frequently this fact is overlooked.

In considering the range of family functions, it is important for service providers to acknowledge that children and youth with severe handicaps may increase the consumptive demands on families across many functional areas (Birenbaum, 1971; Boggs, 1979; Bristol & Schopler, 1983; Dunlap & Hollingsworth, 1977; Gallagher, Cross, & Scharfman, 1981). There is evidence, however, that persons with severe handicaps may contribute significantly to the more intangible functions of affection, self-definition, and guidance (Turnbull, Brotherson, & Summers, 1985; Turnbull, Summers, & Brotherson, 1986). In recent interviews conducted by the authors, parents of children experiencing severe handicaps were asked: "What has been [child's name] biggest contribution to your family?" The following responses represent common themes:

Living proof that God exists, that he asks people to love and forgive one another
Helps me to feel and appreciate nice little things that will happen
For me, unreserved love
He has brought his mother and me closer together. He's taught us to respect others' feelings and share responsibility.

Through research and intervention programs, more emphasis needs to be placed on the positive contributions of members with severe handicaps to family well-being.

Service providers working with persons who are severely handicapped need to take into consideration the functional demands placed on the family. Any intervention will inevitably require some degree of time, energy, and emotional investment. For the family that is already feeling overburdened with the tasks that they must perform each day, one more task may be too much to ask. However, some families may welcome professional assistance in reexamining their priorities relative to the functional tasks in which they engage. Time management training or assistance in locating resources that would help relieve the burden of excess demands may be ways in which the professional might offer assistance.

Family Life Cycle

Becoming familiar with a family's unique structure, interactional patterns, and the functions it performs can be a valuable experience for service providers working with persons having severe handicaps. Service providers must realize, however, that "getting to know" the family is an ongoing process that follows the family as its needs and characteristics change over the course of its life cycle. Just as individuals pass through a series of developmental processes and milestones throughout the course of their lifetime, so, too, do families. Goldenberg and Goldenberg (1980) describe family life cycle as "successive patterns within the continuity of family living over the years of its existence—with members aging and passing through a succession of family roles" (p. 14).

It is important that service providers be aware of the life cycle events that may affect the families of the children they serve. First, this awareness may clarify the changing nature of the family's needs and characteristics over time. Second, it may heighten the service providers' sensitivity to the sources of stress that affect the family over the course of its life cycle (Turnbull, Summers, & Brotherson, 1986). From a family systems perspective, four different types of change that families characteristically experience throughout the course of the life cycle include: 1) developmental stages and transitions, 2) structural change, 3) functional change, and 4) sociohistorical change. Each of these types of change and their elements are discussed in sequence.

Developmental Stages   Developmental stages are the stages through which families typically pass. Each stage has a different set of tasks to which the family must learn to adapt in order to continue functioning effectively. The number and duration of stages, as well as the nature of the tasks involved at each stage will vary tremendously from family to family according to the family's structure. The following seven stages are included in the family systems framework: couple, childbearing, school age, adolescent, launching, post-parental family, and aging.

In order to move from one stage to another, families must experience transition. Transitions, although generally expected and experienced by most families, are frequently a major source of stress. Even greater sources of stress are the occurrence of transitions at unexpected times or no transitions whatsoever (Neugarten, 1976). Families with members who are severely handicapped must learn to adapt to schedules of transition that are very different from the ones that most families experience. For instance, parents of a teenage child who is severely handicapped may still be carrying out the tasks of feeding, dressing, and toileting while their peers are making plans for sending their children off to college and on to independent living. Dependency over the life cycle has major implications for all family members.

Structural Change   The following three types of change in family life cycle—structural, functional, and sociohistorical—are differentiated from developmental stages and transitions in an important way. Whereas developmental stages and transitions are considered to be normative changes (commonly occurring, standard), structural, functional, and sociohistorical change are considered to be nonnormative and precipitated by life events unrelated to passage through developmental stages (McCubbin et al., 1980). Some examples of structural changes are: institutionalization or deinstitutionalization of a member, death, remarriage, divorce, or the birth of a baby.

Structural change can often be accompanied by stress. The literature on family reactions to deinstitutionalization supports this view. According to Willer and Intagliata (1984), deinstitutionalization of a family member who is mentally handicapped is a major source of concern and stress for most families. Families may need assistance in dealing with the feelings of guilt, fear, and anxiety that arise when deinstitutionalization occurs.

Functional Change The second nonnormative change that a family may experience is functional change. Functional change results in a shift in the way in which a family carries out its various functions. These changes can be both gradual and rapid. In many families, children are expected to take on increasing responsibility for caring for themselves as they grow older, and for contributing to the needs of the household; however, this is not always true for families with severely handicapped members. Families with members experiencing severe handicaps may need assistance in learning to handle the chronicity of parenthood through interventions such as stress management, increasing social and formal support, and time management.

Sociohistorical Change The third kind of nonnormative change is sociohistorical change. Sociohistorical changes can be effected by cultural and political trends, the state of the economy, and formative events such as natural disasters and participation in activist movements. Such trends and events can have profound effects upon families, particularly when the event results in a structural or functional change in the family. An example of sociohistorical change is the expansion of the roles and expectations of parents of children with handicaps over the last several decades. It is not surprising that many parents have "jet lag" (Avis, 1978) from the rapidity of these changes. Service providers need to be sensitive to the fact that parents may not share their enthusiasm for the latest trend due to the stress generated from trying to keep pace with previous ones.

IMPLICATIONS FOR SERVICE DELIVERY

Depending upon how it is implemented, a family systems orientation can have a variety of service outcomes. The primary outcome should be to enhance the successful integration of children and youth with severe handicaps into their family unit. A great deal of attention has been directed toward strategies for successful school and community integration of persons with severe handicaps, yet family integration has been expected to occur automatically.

The outcome of parent involvement practices of the past has been to make the person with a severe handicap the focal point of the family. An unintended consequence has been that many family members denied their own needs in order to meet the needs of one member. Thus, the placement of the member with a severe handicap in the least restrictive environment of the home required the rest of the family to live in a highly restricted manner. A family systems orientation defines the consumer as the whole family and asserts that the child or adolescent with a severe handicap can best be served by an educational program that strengthens family integration.

Because a family systems orientation is so new in the field, model programs are currently at the point of initial implementation. The challenge of the next several years is to operationalize a family systems approach for assessing family needs, developing realistic and effective methods of intervention, and working together with families in a manner that is consistent with their style and preferences.

Such an approach necessitates that persons specifically trained to work with family systems, such as social workers, be considered as integral members of the interdisciplinary team along with occupational, physical, and speech therapists. Working together with other members of the interdisciplinary team, the social worker could ensure that the needs of individual family members were being met as well as the needs of the member who is handicapped.

In situations in which the services of a social worker are not available, the service provider must adopt a method for interacting and intervening with the family that is practical and effective. The method used to gather information about the family and how the information is utilized once gathered can vary greatly according to two factors: 1) the resources available to the service provider, including: interest, motivation, expertise, time, ability, and administrative support, and 2) the preferences of individual families and their resources. These two factors, because they are multifaceted, can combine in a variety of ways to determine assessment and intervention approaches.

There are many different ways that the task of gathering information about the family system and designing intervention strategies can be accomplished. Assuredly, the quality and quantity of information gathered or shared will vary according to the methods used and the manner in which the tasks are completed. For instance, the service provider may have a high level of interest but limited expertise and time in the day for working with families. This service provider might come into contact with a family that enjoys sharing information, but doesn't wish to be formally involved in assessments or intervention programs. In this situation, the service provider might discover that an informal approach to gathering information about the family is most appropriate. An informal approach in this case may be an after school/work visit to the family's home. While this type of assessment may not yield the kind of specific information that a more formal assessment might, it could nonetheless be a very valuable experience. Observing the family at home can reveal a great deal about what the family values, the family's life-style, the manner in which members relate with one another, and the functions that members are called on to perform. This kind of information can sensitize the "sensitive" service provider to the kinds of services that the family may be open to, or benefit from, in the future. It could also be helpful in determining what carry-over effects, if any, certain kinds of interventions with the member who is handicapped would have on other family members or the family unit as a whole. Additionally, this visit could provide the family and service provider with an opportunity to develop a rapport based on mutual respect and support. Oftentimes, the display of genuine concern and interest on the part of the service provider does much to dissolve the invisible barriers that sometimes exist between professionals and parents/families.

A situation very different from the one described above would be one in which the service provider has a high degree of interest, time, motivation, and expertise in working with families. This service provider encounters a family that is experiencing some degree of stress and is highly motivated to be involved in a program of intervention. In this case, both parties may elect to pursue a more formal approach. An example of a more formal approach to assessment is one that involves the administration of questionnaires and structured interviews with all members of the family over time. Interventions might involve weekly sessions with a facilitator, a redefinition of family roles, or participation in stress reduction workshops.

At the very minimum, service providers endeavoring to work with the families of the individuals whom they serve will want to have basic information regarding the structure of the family, the impact of the disability on family functions, the nature of family interactions, and their life cycle stage. Table 1, which is a modified version of a family assessment model developed by Power and Dell Orto (1980), provides examples of the basic kinds of information that a service provider utilizing a family systems approach may find useful. To be most effective, it is recommended that service providers make adaptations to suit individual program and family needs.

Unfortunately, there is no fixed recipe or formula regarding what will work in all situations with all families. No two families are alike, and what has worked in the past with one family will not necessarily work in the future with another. This is why an individualized approach to relating with families is so vital. Relating to families in an individualized way means that the service provider must set aside any inclination to pigeon-hole or categorize families based on preconceived notions of families or what their needs are. It is time to stop limiting families' options by offering only what is available, or only what service providers deem appropriate from their own perspective. It is time to start by asking what the family's perspective is, what the family's needs are, and whether or not members wish to collaboratively pursue possible solutions to any problems they may experience. There are some who may not wish or

Table 1. Assessment guide for a family systems approach

I. Family structure
    A. Who are the members of family?
    B. What are the ages and sexes of family members?
    C. What is the nature of disability and age of onset?
    D. What is the occupation of family members?
    E. What is the educational background of family members?
    F. What is the family's ethnic background?
    G. Does the family have a religious preference? Does it have theological interpretations of disability?
    H. Where does the family live and what is its access to professional services?
    I. How long has the family lived in the present location?
    J. Are relatives living nearby and available for assistance and support?
    K. Is family income sufficient to meet expenses?
    L. Does the family have medical coverage?
    M. Are there any serious family problems (e.g., poor health, alcoholism, drug addiction, abuse)?
    N. What are the general attitudes of significant others toward the disability?
    O. To what extent do family members have access to outside social and cultural experiences?
    P. What are the family's values?
    Q. When faced with disability-related stress, what coping strategies does the family use?
II. Impact of disability on family functions
    A. What is the impact of disability on the regular performance of duties within the home?
    B. What is the impact of disability on the regular performance of duties outside the home?
    C. Do family members identify any continued adjustment problems resulting from the disability?
    D. Does the disability create any financial restrictions?
    E. Does the disability create any restrictions on the family's desire to engage in recreational/leisure activities such as vacations or evenings out?
    F. Does the disability create any restrictions on the family's ability to locate in desired areas of the country?
    G. Does the disability create any restrictions on the family's ability to pursue careers or personal interests?
    H. Does the disability create any restrictions on family members' ability to spend time with other family members or friends?
    I. Who takes primary responsibility for caring for the member who has the disability?
    J. How are household responsibilities divided among family members?
    K. Does the member who has the disability contribute to family functions? If so, how?
III. Family interactions
    A. Do family members provide emotional support for each other? How is this given?
    B. What activities do family members share together?
    C. Who generally has the final say regarding decisions that affect the entire family?
    D. Are family members encouraged to have individual interests?

Table 1. *(continued)*

    E. Do all family members express their opinions readily or is someone the spokesperson for the family?

    F. Do individual schedules permit much time together at home as a family?

    G. Are family members free to express thoughts and feelings?

    H. Do family members openly discuss the disability?

    I. What is the nature of the relationship between siblings and the member who has the disability?

    J. What do family members understand about the nature and implications of the disability?

    K. Does the family have an established routine?

    L. How does the family react to expected and unexpected change?

IV. Life cycle

    A. Does the family relate to the person with a disability in an age-appropriate fashion?

    B. What are the family plans for the future concerning education, work, vacations, retirement?

    C. What is the family's perception of the future for the member who has the disability?

require services or direction. Those families who do wish to work together with service providers deserve to have the interaction style and methods employed fashioned to suit the existing family ecology.

In working with children with severe handicaps, emphasis is placed on teaching skills that are functional, and lead to greater integration with non-handicapped peers and a more normalized life-style in the least restrictive environment. All of these very important concepts apply equally to the families of individuals with handicaps. Family members also have special needs for training and interventions that are most functional for them, that allow them the time and energy to associate with their peers, and to engage in normalized activities that are not disability related. The goal of family integration for children and youth with severe handicaps will most successfully be accomplished when the individual needs of all members are respected within the context of the educational program.

IMPLICATIONS FOR RESEARCH

The family systems perspective generates a wealth of important research directions. Furthermore, the application of family systems theory has potential for addressing some of the critical problems that continue to flaw research efforts to examine the impact of a child with handicaps on the family. According to Turnbull, Summers, and Brotherson (1983a) some of these problems include: 1) the atheoretical nature of much of the family impact research; 2) the narrow focus on the mother-child dyad with relatively little regard for the effects on other family subsystems; 3) the paucity of studies dealing specifically with families that have members with severe handicaps; 4) the failure to examine the stresses experienced by families with handicapped members in light of the stresses typically experienced by families in general; 5) the lack of a taxonomy for identifying family "types" and guiding the selection of intervention strategies; 6) failure to address the differential aspects of family impact in light of life cycle stages and needs; and 7) the failure to specify and evaluate the outcome of family interventions.

A broad research agenda is necessary to examine the impact of a child with handicaps on the family unit as well as the impact of various intervention strategies. This requires that new theories and new methodologies be adopted by researchers that take into account factors such as changing family structures, the multiple functions that families must perform in addition to caring for the child with handicaps, the interrelation of family members, and the impact of the various life cycle stages that families with members who are handicapped experience. Some specific examples of research questions in the areas of family structure, function, and life cycle that warrant investigation include: 1) What are the structural characteristics of families who successfully adapt to the presence of a child with handicaps? 2) What is the relationship between structural characteristics and the adaptation within and across family subsystems? 3) How do different types of disabilities influence family functions and the family's ability to carry out its functions? 4) What are the most effective intervention strategies for providing assistance to families in carrying out their functions? 5) What coping strategies are employed by families who maintain successful adaptation over the full life cycle? 6) How might life cycle issues be influenced by variations in family structure and functioning?

REFERENCES

Aldrich, A. (1947). Preventive medicine and mongolism. *American Journal of Mental Deficiency, 52,* 127–129.
Altman, K., Haavik, S., & Cook, J. W. (1978). Punishment of self-injurious behaviour in natural settings using contingent aromatic ammonia. *Behaviour Research and Therapy, 16,* 85–96.
Altman, K., & Mira, M. (1983). Training parents of developmentally disabled children. In J. G. Matson & F. Andrasik (Eds.), *Treatment issues and innovations in mental retardation* (pp. 303–371). New York: Plenum Publishing Corp.
Ambrose, S. A., & Baker, B. L. (1979, September). *Training parents of developmentally disabled children: Follow-up outcome.* Paper presented at the 67th annual convention of the American Psychological Association, New York, NY.
Avis, D. W. (1978). Deinstitutionalization jet lag. In A. P. Turnbull & H. R. Turnbull (Eds.), *Parents speak out.* Columbus, OH: Charles E. Merrill Publishing Co.
Baker, B. L. (1984). Parents as teachers: Issues in training. In J. A. Mulick & S. M. Pueschel (Eds.), *Parent-professional partnerships in developmental disability services* (pp. 55–74). Cambridge, MA: The Ware Press.
Baker, B. L., Heifetz, L. J., & Brightman, A. J. (1972). *Parents as teachers.* Cambridge, MA: Behavioral Education Projects.

Baker, B. L., Heifetz, L. J., & Murphy, D. M. (1980). Behavioral training for parents of mentally retarded children: One-year follow-up. *American Journal of Mental Deficiency, 85*(1), 31–38.

Beck, D. F., & Jones, M. A. (1973). *Progress on family problems.* New York: Family Service Association of America.

Bijou, S. W. (1984). *Parent training research and implications for training parents of retarded children.* Unpublished manuscript, University of Arizona, Tucson.

Birenbaum, A. (1971). The mentally retarded child in the home and the family cycle. *Journal of Health and Social Behavior, 12,* 55–65.

Boggs, E. M. (1978). Who is putting whose head in the sand or in the clouds as the case may be? In A. P. Turnbull & H. R. Turnbull (Eds.), *Parents speak out* (pp. 50–68). Columbus, OH: Charles E. Merrill Publishing Co.

Boggs, E. M. (1979). Allocation of resources for family care. In R. H. Bruininks & G. C. Krantz (Eds.), *Family care of developmentally disabled members: Conference proceedings* (pp. 47–60). Minneapolis: University of Minnesota.

Bristol, M. M., & Schopler, E. (1983). Stress and coping in families of autistic adolescents. In E. Schopler & G. B. Mesibov (Eds.), *Autism in adolescents and adults* (pp. 251–276). New York: Plenum Publishing Corp.

Buchman, B. M. (1983). *A review of research methods and benefits of behavioral parent-training with handicapped children: A call for research.* Unpublished manuscript, Department of Human Development and Family Life, University of Kansas, Lawrence.

Budoff, M. (1979). Implementing due process safeguards: From the user's point of view. In Department of Health, Education, and Welfare, Office of Education. *Due process: Developing criteria for the evaluation of due process procedural safeguards provisions.* Philadelphia: Research for Better Schools, Inc.

Carter, E., & McGoldrick, M. (1980). The family life cycle and family therapy: An overview. In E. Carter & M. McGoldrick (Eds.), *The family life cycle: A framework for family therapy.* New York: Gardner Press.

Chilman, C. S. (1973). Programs for disadvantaged parents: Some major trends and related research. In H. N. Ricciuti & M. Caldwell (Eds.), *Review of child development research: Vol. 3* (pp. 403–465). Chicago: University of Chicago Press.

Cutler, B. C. (1981). *Unraveling the special education maze: An action guide for parents.* Champaign, IL: Research Press.

Diamond, S. (1981). Growing up with parents of a handicapped child: A handicapped persons's perspective. In J. L. Paul (Ed.), *Understanding and working with parents of children with special needs* (pp. 23–50). New York: Holt, Rinehart & Winston.

Dunlap, W. R., & Hollingsworth, J. S. (1977). How does a handicapped child affect the family? Implications for practitioners. *The Family Coordinator, 26,* 286–293.

Farber, B. (1959). Effects of a severely mentally retarded child on family integration. *Monographs of the Society for Research in Child Development (Serial No. 71).*

Farber, B., & Ryckman, D. B. (1965). Effects of severely mentally retarded children on family relationships. *Mental Retardation Abstracts, 2,* 1–17.

Federal Register. (1977, August). Washington, DC: U.S. Government Printing Office.

Foster, M., Berger, M., & McLean, M. (1981). Rethinking a good idea: A reassessment of parent involvement. *Topics in Early Childhood Special Education, 1*(3), 55–65.

Gallagher, J. J., Cross, A., & Scharfman, W. (1981). Parental adaptation to a young handicapped child: The father's role. *Journal of the Division for Early Childhood, 3,* 3–14.

Glick, P., & Norton, A. (1979). *The future of the American family in current population reports* (Special Studies Series p. 23, No. 78). Washington, DC: Government Printing Office.

Gliedman, J., & Roth, W. (1980). *The unexpected minority: Handicapped children in America.* New York: Harcourt Brace Jovanovich.

Goldberg, P., & Goldberg, M. (1979). PACER Center: Parents learn about special education laws. *Education Unlimited, 1*(4), 34–37.

Goldenberg, I., & Goldenberg, H. (1980). *Family therapy: An overview.* Monterey, CA: Brooks/Cole Publishing Co.

Goldstein, S. E. (1980). *The effects of two intervention strategies on parental participation in and satisfaction with the individualized education program conference.* Unpublished doctoral dissertation, University of North Carolina at Chapel Hill.

Goldstein, S., Strickland, B., Turnbull, A. P., & Curry, L. (1980). An observational analysis of the IEP conference. *Exceptional Children, 46*(4), 278–286.

Gordon, E. W., & Ullman, M. (1956). Reactions of parents to problems of mental retardation in children. *American Journal of Mental Deficiency, 61,* 158–163.

Green, R. J., & Framo, J. L. (Eds.). (1983). *Family therapy major contributions.* New York: International Universities Press Inc.

Helge, D. (1984). Models for serving rural students with low-incidence handicapping conditions. *Exceptional Children, 50*(4), 313–324.

Hoffman, L. (1980). The family life cycle and discontinuous change. In E. Carter & M. McGoldrick (Eds.), *The family life cycle: A framework for family therapy* (pp. 53–68). New York: Gardner Press.

Katz, A. H. (1961). *Parents of the handicapped: Self-organized parents' and relatives' groups for treatment of ill and handicapped children.* Springfield, IL: Charles C Thomas.

Lay, C. A. (1977). Due process in special education (Doctoral dissertation, Boston University). *Dissertation Abstracts International, 37,* 7687A.

Lillie, D. L., & Place, P. A. (1982). *Partners: A guide to working with schools for parents of children with special instructional needs.* Glenview, IL: Scott, Foresman and Co.

Lusthaus, C. S., Lusthaus, E. W., & Gibbs, H. (1981). Parents' role in the decision process. *Exceptional Children, 48*(3), 256–257.

Lynch, E. W., & Stein, R. (1982). Perspectives on parent participation in special education. *Exceptional Education Quarterly, 3*(2), 56–63.

MacMillan, D. L., & Turnbull, A. P. (1983). Parent involvement with special education: Respecting individual preferences. *Education and Training of the Mentally Retarded, 18*(1), 5–9.

McCubbin, H. I., Joy, C. B., Cauble, A. E., Comeau, J. K., Patterson, J. M., & Needle, R. H. (1980). Family stress and coping: A decade review. *Journal of Marriage and the Family, 42*(4), 855–871.

McGoldrick, M. (1982). Ethnicity and family therapy: An overview. In M. McGoldrick, J. K. Pearce, & J. Giordano (Eds.), *Ethnicity in family therapy* (pp. 3–30). New York: The Guilford Press.

McKinney, J. D., & Hocutt, A. M. (1982). Public school involvement of parents of learning-disabled children and average achievers. *Exceptional Education Quarterly, 3*(2), 64–73.

Miller, S. J., & Sloane, H. N., Jr. (1976). The generalization effects of parents training across stimulus settings. *Journal of Applied Behavioral Analysis, 9,* 355–370.

Minuchin, S. (1974). *Families and family therapy.* Cambridge, MA: Harvard University Press.

Mitchell, S. (1976). *Parental perceptions of their experiences with due process in special education: A preliminary report.* Cambridge, MA: Research Institute for Educational Problems (ERIC Document Reproduction No. Ed. 130 482).

National Association of State Directors of Special Education. (1978). *The implementation of due process in Massachusetts.* Washington, DC: Author.

Neugarten, B. (1976). Adaptations and the life cycle. *The Counseling Psychologist, 6*(1), 16–20.

Olson, D. H., Russell, C. S., & Sprenkle, D. H. (1980). Marital and family therapy: A decade review. *Journal of Marriage and the Family, 42*(4), 973–993.

Olson, D. H., Sprenkle, D. H., & Russell, C. (1979). Circumplex model of marital and family systems. I: Cohesion and adaptability dimesion, family types and clinical applications. *Family Process, 18,* 3–28.

Paul, J. L. (1981). *Understanding and working with parents of children with special needs.* New York: Holt, Rinehart & Winston.

Pearlin, L. I., & Schooler, C. (1978). The structure of coping. *Journal of Health and Social Behavior, 19,* 2–21.

Power, P., & Dell Orto, A. (Eds.). (1980). *Role of the family in the rehabilitation of the physically disabled.* Baltimore: University Park Press.

Reisinger, J. J., Frangia, G. W., & Hoffman, E. H. (1976). Toddler management training generalization and marital status. *Journal of Behavior Therapy and Experimental Psychiatry, 7,* 335–340.

Rosenberg, M. S., Reppucci, N. D., & Linney, J. A. (1983). Issues in the implementation of human service programs: Examples from a parent training project for high-risk families. *Analysis and Intervention in Developmental Disabilities, 3,* 215–225.

Rubin, L. B. (1976). *World of pain: Life in the working-class family.* New York: Basic Books, Inc.

Rubin, S., & Quinn-Curran, N. (1983). Lost then found: Parents journey through the community service maze. In M. Seligman (Ed.), *The family with a handicapped child: Understanding and treatment* (pp. 63–94). New York: Grune & Stratton.

Shearer, M. S., & Shearer, D. E. (1977). Parent involvement. In J. B. Jordan, A. H. Hayden, M. B. Karnes, & M. M. Wood (Eds.), *Early childhood education for exceptional children* (pp. 208–305). Reston, VA: Council for Exceptional Children.

Skolnick, A. S., & Skolnick, J. H. (Eds.). (1977). *Family in transition: Rethinking marriage, sexuality, child rearing, and family organization* (2nd ed.). Boston: Little, Brown & Co.

Skrtic, T. M., Summers, J. A., Brotherson, M. J., & Turnbull, A. P. (1984). Severely handicapped children and their brothers and sisters. In J. Blacher (Ed.), *Young severely handicapped children and their families: Research in review.* New York: Academic Press.

Strickland, B. (1982a). Parent participation, school accountability and due process. *Exceptional Education Quarterly, 3*(2), 41–49.

Strickland, B. (1982b). *Perceptions of parents and school representatives regarding their relationship before, during, and after the due process hearing.* Doctoral dissertation, University of North Carolina at Chapel Hill.

Strickland, B. (1983). Legal issues that affect parents. In M. Seligman (Ed.), *The family with a handicapped child: Understanding and treatment* (pp. 27–59). New York: Grune & Stratton.

Stubblefield, H. (1965). Religion, parents and mental retardation. *Mental Retardation, 3*(4), 8–11.

Turnbull, A. P., Brotherson, M. J., & Summers, J. A. (1985). The impact of deinstitutionalization on families: A family systems approach. In R. H. Bruininks & K. C. Lakin (Eds.), *Living and learning in the least restrictive environment* (pp. 115–140). Baltimore: Paul H. Brookes Publishing Co.

Turnbull, A. P., Brotherson, M. J., Summers, J. A., & Turnbull, H. R. (in press). Fathers of disabled children. In B. Robinson & R. Barret (Eds.), *Fatherhood*. Baltimore: University Park Press.

Turnbull, A. P., & Strickland, B. (1981). Parents and the educational system. In J. L. Paul (Ed.), *Understanding and working with parents of children with special needs* (pp. 231–263). New York: Holt, Rinehart & Winston.

Turnbull, A. P., Summers, J. A., & Brotherson, M. J. (1983a, September). *Family life cycle: Theoretical and empirical implications and future directions for families with mentally retarded members*. Paper presented at the NICHD Conference on Families with Retarded Children, Rougemont, NC.

Turnbull, A. P., Summers, J. A., & Brotherson, M. J. (1983b). *Working with families with disabled members: A family systems perspective*. Lawrence, KS: University of Kansas, Research and Training Center on Independent Living.

Turnbull, A. P., Summers, J. A., & Brotherson, M. J. (1986). Family life cycle: Theoretical and empirical implications and future directions for families with mentally retarded members. In J. J. Gallagher & P. Vietze (Eds.), *Families of handicapped persons: Current research, treatment, and policy issues*. Baltimore: Paul H. Brookes Publishing Co.

Turnbull, A. P., & Winton, P. J. (1983). A comparison of specialized and main-streamed preschools from the perspectives of parents of handicapped children. *Journal of Pediatric Psychology, 8*(1), 57–71.

Turnbull, A. P., & Winton, P. J. (1984). Parent involvement policy and practice: Current future and perspectives. In J. Blacher (Ed.), *Young severely handicapped children and their families: Research in review* (pp. 377–397). New York: Academic Press.

Turnbull, A. P., Winton, P. J., Blacher, J. B., & Salkind, N. (1983). Mainstreaming in the kindergarten classroom: Perspectives of parents of handicapped and non-handicapped children. *Journal of the Division of Early Childhood, 6*, 14–20.

Turnbull, H. R., & Turnbull, A. P. (1982). Parent involvement in the education of handicapped children: A critique. *Mental Retardation, 20*(3), 115–122.

Turnbull, H. R., Turnbull, A. P., & Wheat, M. (1982). Assumptions about parental participation: A legislative history. *Exceptional Education Quarterly, 3*(2), 1–8.

Valentine, J., & Stark, E. (1979). The social context of parent involvement in Head Start. In E. Zigler & J. Valentine (Eds.), *Project Head Start* (pp. 291–313). New York: The Free Press.

Wahler, R. G. (1980). The insular mother: Her problems in parent-child treatment. *Journal of Applied Behavior Analysis, 13*, 207–219.

Wiegerink, R., Hocutt, A., Posante-Loro, R., & Bristol, M. (1980). Parent involvement in early education programs for handicapped children. In J. J. Gallagher (Ed.), *New directions for exceptional children: Ecology of exceptional children* (pp. 67–85). San Francisco: Jossey-Bass.

Willer, B., & Intagliata, J. (1984). *Promises and realities for mentally retarded citizens: Life in the community*. Baltimore: University Park Press.

Williams, H. (1975). 126 Cong. Rec. S1950, daily ed., June 18, 1975.

Winton, P., & Turnbull, A. (1981). Parent involvement as viewed by parents of preschool handicapped children. *Topics in Early Childhood Special Education, 1*(3), 11–19.

Winton, P. J., Turnbull, A. P., & Blacher, J. (1984). *Selecting a preschool: A guide for parents of handicapped children*. Austin, TX: Pro-Ed.

Wolfensberger, W. (1970). Counseling the parents of the retarded. In A. A. Baumeister (Ed.), *Mental retardation: Appraisal, education, and rehabilitation* (pp. 329–400). Chicago: Aldine Publishing Co.

Yoshida, R. (1979). *Developing assistance linkages for parents of handicapped children*. Washington, DC: U.S. Department of Health, Education, and Welfare, Bureau of Education for the Handicapped.

Zigler, E., & Valentine, J. (Eds.). (1979). *Project Head Start: A legacy of the war on poverty*. New York: The Free Press.

Zuk, G. H., Miller, R. I., Bartram, J. B., & Kling, F. (1961). Maternal acceptance of retarded children: A questionnaire study of attitudes and religious background. *Child Development, 32,* 515–540.

CURRICULUM DEVELOPMENT

Chapter 6

Social Skill Training in Natural Contexts

Robert Gaylord-Ross, Kathleen Stremel-Campbell, and Keith Storey

Social skill training is directly related to recent educational developments for students with severe handicaps. Among the more important of these developments is the instruction that severely handicapped students are receiving in less restrictive, more integrated environments (Certo, Haring, & York, 1984). Classes for students with severe handicaps are more likely to be located on a public school site, and instruction is more likely to occur in natural, non-classroom settings. Rather than students receiving 6 hours of instruction in the special education classroom, they may spend 3 hours at other sites on the campus (e.g., cafeteria, typing class, gym), 1 hour off campus (restaurant, shopping, work site), and 2 hours in the special education classroom (cf. Gaylord-Ross & Pitts-Conway, 1984). The logic behind this out-of-class instruction is that because severely handicapped students generalize poorly from one setting to another, it is more efficient to key instruction to the criterion environment, that is, an actual work setting, a real restaurant. Furthermore, by locating special education classes on regular school campuses, the handicapped student can participate in the numerous program offerings at that site with his or her nonhandicapped peers.

The writing of this chapter was supported in part by Contract No. 300-82-0356 and Contract No. 300-81-0411 from the U.S. Department of Education, Office of Special Education Programs. The information and opinions expressed herein do not necessarily reflect the positions or policy of the department, and no official endorsement should be inferred.

In addition to learning a variety of vocational, leisure, and community skills at the regular school site, a further benefit of less restrictive education is that the severely handicapped student should become better socialized because of his or her frequent encounters with an array of nonhandicapped persons. At the regular school site, the student may have contact with a variety of non-handicapped peers (different ages, ethnic, and ability groups), teachers (different ages and areas of expertise), and community members (policemen, store owners, waitresses, etc.). This variety of social contact should better socialize the student to the varied patterns of social responding in a multicultural society. In contrast, special education programs that limit the student to 6 hours of instruction in an isolated classroom (and in a segregated site) are likely to limit the social development of their students because of the restricted range of social contacts offered in undifferentiated environments (cf. Gaylord-Ross & Peck, 1985).

In spite of the imminent logic of normalized educational programming, one matter cannot be overlooked. There is a clear body of research documentation reporting that the mere placement of severely handicapped students in proximity to nonhandicapped persons does not necessarily lead to the social development of the handicapped students (Fredericks et al., 1978; Gaylord-Ross, Haring, Breen, & Pitts-Conway, 1984). In fact, when severely handicapped students are left in proximity to nonhandicapped persons, they will tend *not* to have social interactions. In these contexts, the severely handicapped students are likely to drift off into isolated play or engage in self-stimulation; the nonhandicapped students are most likely to interact with other nonhandicapped persons. A social skill training program is a key factor in guaranteeing that the handicapped and nonhandicapped students interact, develop social skills, and develop positive relationships with each other (Haring, Breen, Pitts-Conway, Lee, & Gaylord-Ross, 1984; Voeltz, 1982).

The rationale of this chapter assumes that successful social integration is a two-step process. The first step is to physically integrate students in normalized settings. The second step is to implement social skill training programs in these natural contexts.

Social skills are the behaviors that enable two or more persons to have direct interactions with each other. The social behaviors may be verbal statements (e.g., "Hi"), and nonverbal behaviors like smiles, posturing, approaching others, and so forth. This chapter focuses on direct behavioral interactions rather than abstract aspects of social development such as interpersonal networks, leadership roles, and transactional negotiating strategies.

Social skill training includes instructional strategies that facilitate direct interactions between two or more people. The original social skill training work with persons with severe handicaps was conducted by Shores, W. Bricker, D. Bricker, Strain, Cooke, and Appolloni at George Peabody College in the 1960s. The thrust of this early work was to prompt and reinforce social exchanges between handicapped and nonhandicapped students. The training often consisted of evoking responses (like greetings) that already existed in the child's repertoire at a higher rate and under better stimulus control. The work at Peabody and elsewhere (cf. Guralnick, 1978) was usually conducted with preschoolers in university laboratory settings. The social skill training tended to be carried out in free-play, leisure contexts.

A major purpose of this chapter is to show how social skill training efforts have been greatly expanded to include:

1. Persons of varying *ages* and not just preschoolers
2. A number of *settings* such as vocational and community contexts as well as leisure contexts
3. Teaching *new response* repertoires in addition to prompting existing social behaviors

This chapter is organized around the different settings and domains where social skill training has occurred to date. The first area deals with social communication. Social communication, while not a setting, is a performance modality that cuts across all settings. The communication section of this chapter portrays the role that communication plays in social interaction and social skill training. The subsequent sections describe social skill training in leisure, social-sexual, community, and vocational settings. The importance of social skill training is evidenced by attempts to truly integrate persons with severe handicaps in a range of community-referenced settings. The physical placement of a person in an independent living residence or a competitive employment site does not guarantee the full social integration of the individual in those natural sites. Social skill training is a critical vehicle to promote social integration through facilitating interactions between co-workers, students, and neighbors.

THE RELATIONSHIP OF LANGUAGE
AND COMMUNICATION WITHIN SOCIAL SKILL TRAINING

A major emphasis within exemplary service programs is the systematic programming of communication skills, social skills, and other functional living skills within an interrelated sequence of training. This emphasis is based on a number of different perspectives, issues, and research, including: 1) the importance of the social aspects of language in normal development (Bates, Benigni, Bretherton, Camaioni, & Volterra, 1979; Bruner, 1975; Halliday, 1975); 2) the use of social functions within programs for children with handicaps (Mahoney, 1975; McLean & Synder-McLean, 1978); 3) the results of investigations involving young children with severe handicaps that have demonstrated increases in social skills when they are trained systematically in integrated settings (Guralnick, 1976; Peck, Apolloni, Cooke, & Rover, 1978); 4) the limited generalization results from isolated, skills-specific training within the area of language (Harris, 1975; Stokes & Baer, 1977) and across other domains (Wehman, Abramson, & Norman, 1977); and 5) the concept of educating persons with severe handicaps in the least restrictive environment (Brown, Nietupski, & Hamre-Nietupski, 1976). This section briefly reviews the relevant issues, research, and strategies used in training social skills, and discusses the aspects of language and communication that are critical for effective social skill training.

Training the Social Functions of Language
and Communication Behaviors within Social Skill Training

One of the primary uses of language within society is as a social behavior (Halliday, 1978). Once an individual has the ability to understand and use even the basic forms of the language system common to his or her social community, she or he has the potential to exert more control within that environment. Gottman, Gonso, and Rasmussen (1975) and LaGreca and Mesibou (1979) found that the ability of mildly handicapped children to use language effectively in initiating and maintaining interactions appeared to facilitate peer acceptance. There is no doubt that language can serve as a valuable tool in increasing an individual's social integration.

The presence and extent of an individual's communication system within social interactions is a key aspect of social skill training. While the overall function of communication is to exchange information (Sailor et al., 1980), more primary functions are the use of specific communication behaviors to mediate the behavior of others, to receive specific consequences, and to be mediated by the communication behavior of others. Voeltz (1984) outlines eight major social performance situations for social skill development. Seven of those performance situations could include the functional use of communication. In fact, the majority of skills listed within her model of social performance involve receptive and expressive communication skills. As Certo and Kohl (1984) point out, communication or "interpersonal interactions" are often conceptualized as forms of conversation. This conceptualization would seem to limit the extended use of communication skills within social skill development. Anytime a person purposefully attempts to mediate the behavior of another person, a communicative behavior has occurred. However, the other person has to consequate that specific communicative behavior in a certain way before it could be evaluated as a successful social exchange.

Social skill training for persons with severe handicaps can be augmented by three major strategies that are in part based upon research in early social communication development. First, training strategies must focus on both persons involved in the interpersonal interaction across an extended social context (leisure, shopping). Many educational programs are beginning to focus on social skill training, even though the student with handicaps is often the sole recipient of assessment and training (Schutz, Williams, Iverson, & Duncan, 1984). If the social interaction between two persons is to be successful, the roles of both partners of that interaction must be considered. Second, programs need to focus on the prelinguistic/prelanguage systems (Peck & Schuler, 1983) used by both the student and the partner. Third, the social functions that are expressed by prelanguage and language behavior need to be incorporated into assessments and social skill training (McLean & Synder-McLean, 1978; Prutting, 1982; Schuler & Goetz, 1981). The list of social functions (based on Dore, 1975) that were developed by Stremel-Campbell, Clark-Guida, and Johnson-Dorn (1984) is provided below:

1. Protest/rejection
2. Requesting continuation of an object/activity
3. Requesting object/action or choice
4. Repeating
5. Social (greeting, thank you)
6. Calling
7. Requesting attention to self
8. Requesting attention to a referent (object, activity, event)
9. Offer
10. Answer (yes/no, what is question)
11. Request permission
12. Comment
13. Request answer
14. Give unknown information

Weekly observations across different social contexts were collected over 3 years for 20 individuals (ages 3–21 years) with severe/profound handicaps. Only conventional prelanguage behaviors that could be reliably coded (touching an object/person, manipulating a person, extending objects, extending hand, pointing, gesturing) and language responses were recorded. An additional criterion required that the individual child/youth acknowledge the social partner by giving eye contact (however brief) or by orienting toward that person (for individuals with visual impairments) before a behavior was recorded as "communication." An initial analysis of the longitudinal data shows that the first functions to be expressed by both younger and older groups were: 1) protest/rejection, 2) requesting continuation of an object/activity, and 3) requesting object/action as a response and initiations. The younger preschool group demonstrated more functions of repeating (a gesture, sign, vocalization), greeting (including "bye"), and offering than did the older group. The individuals who began to use language (one-word signs, pictures, or speech) initially used language as a response while using the prelanguage acts concurrently as spontaneous initiations.

Training across Multiple Natural Settings and Social Contexts

Changes in the communicative behavior of individuals with more severe handicaps have the potential to affect social integration, particularly if the communication skills are trained in conjunction with other social behaviors and within natural settings. The integrated activities can be analyzed to determine the specific objectives, activities, and skills for the social interaction (Brown et al., 1979), as well as to determine the appropriate time for the social interaction and persons involved in the interaction (Schutz et al., 1984). Certo and Kohl (1984) have presented a hierarchy of social interactions that can be used to assist in the task analysis of social skills and to determine probable social functions and sequences of different social skills. Their four levels within the hierarchy include interpersonal interactions that: 1) must occur to continue or complete the activity; 2) occur in conjunction with task-related interactions; 3) are not essential to continue or complete the activity, yet can increase the social effectiveness of the activity; and 4) occur apart from any task-related interactions. The levels of interactions presented by Certo and Kohl (1984) as well as the social skill performance model proposed by Voeltz (1984) can be used as categories to conceptualize overall social communicative interactions within a social skill program. Training social-communicative behaviors within a social activity or routine occurring in the natural environment would seem to increase the potential for generalization to other, nontrained natural settings.

Strategies and Considerations in Interrelating Communication and Social Skills across Other Living Skills Programs

The following general and specific strategies and considerations for programming social-communication skills within social skill training are based, in part, upon the previous research discussed earlier and the models that were reviewed.

1. In order for more effective social skills to occur, the individual must have the means to communicate different social functions (greeting, requesting, calling, requesting answer, commenting); the partner must attend to the prelanguage behaviors that the individual may need to use to engage in different social functions; and the partner may need to use additional nonverbal cues that serve as discriminative stimuli for different social behaviors.

2. If an individual with severe handicaps is communicating by means of a language system (speech approximations or manual signs), it may be necessary to train the use of an additional communication system across the integrated environments. Often, a second system is defined to augment "speech." However, a more workable approach is to build *one or more* communication systems that augment the individual student's primary language system (Harris & Vanderheiden, 1980). Three points are important in the selection of an extended communication system:

a. The system must be effective in getting the message across to the other person in the most socially appropriate way.
b. The system must be efficient in that the interaction is maintained in a positive manner, based on the speed with which the message is transmitted.
c. The system may need to be adapted or modified so that it does not interfere physically with the overall social interaction.

3. Social skill programs should arrange the environment so that peers become important persons for social interactions. Often, the individual's educational experience includes only parents and teachers as the major reinforcing agents. It is critical for the person's current and future functioning that siblings, classmates, and other peers become significant partners in social interactions across all settings. Social skills need to be designed to train and motivate siblings, classmates/workmates, and other peers for interaction with the individual with severe handicaps. Integrated activities within the community (shopping, eating in a restaurant, swimming) should be used as a context for training appropriate social interactions between classmates/ housemates and other peers so that the dependence on authority figures decreases and prepares the student for ultimate functioning within the community.

4. For individuals with limited communication and imitation skills (or nonvocal language systems), social skill training may be necessary for the peer partner. The partners within the social interaction must have a ''shared system of communication'' in which the partner learns to use and receive additional prelanguage behaviors, learns manual signs, or learns the functions of a communication board. Some persons may understand speech and use signs or a communication board for an output mode. However, peer partners who are trained to use the individual's language system may require additional training to serve as a model and to learn to be more tolerant of the time it may take to transmit a message. Also, the person with severe handicaps is more likely to utilize the augmentative system (and not revert back to gestures, unintelligible speech, or vocalizations) if the peer shares the communication system. Knowing the manner in which the individual communicates sets the occasion for more effective social interactions to occur, but does not ensure that these interactions will occur. Often, additional training and arrangements of the environment are necessary. A number of features of the training should include:

a. Training or facilitating a proper physical and orientation position for communication
b. Training the peer to use specific cues to increase the individual's responding and initiating
c. Training the peer to make social bids (initiations) and to serve as a model and a reinforcing agent

d. Providing the peer with specific knowledge concerning what the person can communicate about

e. Providing cues and consequences to facilitate the interactions without interfering with the interactions

Thus, in order for the communication exchange to be successful, the focus of training may need to include the individual with handicaps, others in the integrated settings, and the organization of the activities within the integrated environment (Stainback, Stainback, Raschke, & Anderson, 1981).

5. Interactions that involve frequent reciprocal actions, cooperation (Rynders, Johnson, Johnson, & Schmidt, 1980), and activities that are mutually reinforcing will serve as the major activities in which social skills can be trained. For example, breakfast and dinner may be appropriate activities to increase communication skills with siblings or housemates (for older individuals). Task-related and other more social communicative skills may be trained while eating in a restaurant. However, lunch within a public school may not afford as many appropriate opportunities for the student to communicate at his or her level. This does not mean that opportunities and interactions with peers should not be encouraged. Rather, independent eating skills may be a priority IEP objective in which the person is *not* to request that others get his or her napkin, open his or her milk, or return his or her tray. If an individual's communication is limited to requests, protests, and simple comments about the here-and-now, his or her noncommunicative social skills may be the primary targets within that specific social skill activity. A number of features should include:

a. Allowing time for natural social interactions to occur

b. Using positive facial expressions in addition to giving positive feedback

c. Using polite forms of request ("Are you ready to order?", "Please give me the paper.", "Will you help me?")

d. Expanding the types of communication functions beyond "protesting" and "requesting" functions

e. Allowing time for the student to respond

f. Becoming more responsive to the use of the communication expressed by the individual with severe handicaps

g. Utilizing variations of environmental cues to facilitate the individual's initiations

THE LEISURE DOMAIN

The leisure domain has received by far the most attention in promoting social skill development. Typically, a teacher or a researcher works with a group of students in a recess or free-play setting. A training procedure is then instituted to enable the students to converse, play a game, or attend to each other (look, touch, etc.). Since nonleisure times at school are devoted to mastering particular educational tasks (e.g., self-care, vocational), they typically are not viewed as contexts where explicit social skill training may take place. The authors take exception to this view and provide examples of training in these contexts in subsequent sections of this chapter. First, procedures for instituting social skill training in leisure settings are examined.

There are many ways to define a social interaction. One way is to separate the phases of a social interaction into initiation, elaboration, and termination phases. The initiation phase involves two or more persons coming together and acknowledging each other with some type of greeting (a wave, "hello," handshake, etc.). After the brief initiation or greeting, the persons may immediately terminate the interaction with a "good-bye" or departing gesture. Such brief or transient interactions (Gaylord-Ross & Pitts-Conway, 1984) often occur when people do not have time to interact for longer durations. It is also possible to have an extended interaction after the initiation by elaborating the exchange with conversation, game playing, or idle posturing. Elaborated interactions may last a number of seconds or minutes and are consequently longer than transient interactions.

Much of the initial work in social skill training (e.g., Stokes, Baer, & Jackson, 1974) focused solely on teaching students with severe handicaps how to greet others. Greeting others is very useful because it takes the person from an isolated or a social state of affairs to one where there is a direct social interaction with another person (Gaylord-Ross & Holvoet, 1985). Yet, teaching only greeting behaviors is limited because the interaction lasts but a couple of seconds and the severely handicapped person is likely to return to isolate forms of behavior. Clearly, it is important to train the elaboration phase of social interactions so that longer, more meaningful exchanges may occur. The elaborations of nonhandicapped persons are often language based, that is, the interactions center around conversations. Since persons with severe handicaps are often limited conversationally, alternative vehicles to facilitate social exchanges must be explored. One alternative is to teach students to play a game or engage a leisure object that is low in verbal demands.

Gaylord-Ross, Haring, Breen, and Pitts-Conway (1984) developed a training program where a group of autistic youth was trained to approach nonhandicapped peers and elaborate an exchange by using a hand-held video game, a Walkman radio headphone, or a stick of chewing gum. The training procedure task analyzed three extended social sequences with each of these objects (see Table 1). The students were then taught to emit these sequences with a nonhandicapped peer in a separate training session. When the student learned to emit these social sequences, it was observed that his or her behavior generalized to untrained leisure exchanges. That is, the autistic students approached and played with their nonhandicapped, adolescent peers in a recess courtyard with no intervention from adults or other trainers. Interestingly, the

Table 1. Task analyses for social skills training (Gaylord-Ross, Haring, Breen, & Pitts-Conway, 1984)

Pacman

1. AS approaches NS.[a]
2. AS establishes one m proximity.
3. AS establishes a face-forward orientation.
4. AS says, "Hi."
5. AS waits for response.
6. AS says, "Want to play?"
7. AS waits for response. AS finds someone else if NS does not indicate willingness to play. AS then begins sequence at step 1 again.
8. AS turns on game.
9. AS hands game to NS.
10. AS watches NS play.
11. AS receives game from NS.
12. AS reads NS's score.
13. AS turns off game.
14. AS turns game on to reset score to zero.
15. AS plays game.
16. AS reads own score.
17. AS offers game to NS. If NS accepts, play continues in alternating fashion. When NS indicates that she or he is finished, AS takes game back.
18. AS says, "Bye."

Walkman

1. AS approaches MS.
2. AS establishes one m proximity.
3. AS establishes face-forward orientation with NS.
4. AS says, "Hi."
5. AS waits for response.
6. AS says (and writes), "Want to listen?"
7. AS shows radio to NS. If NS is not interested in interacting, AS approaches another student (step 1).
8. AS turns on radio.
9. AS adjusts volume to level 6.
10. AS hands headphones to NS.
11. AS puts on headphones.
12. AS selects rock and roll station.
13. AS remains in proximity to NS until termination of interaction by NS.
14. AS says, "Bye."

Gum

1. AS approaches NS.
2. AS establishes one m proximity.
3. AS establishes a face-forward orientation.
4. AS says "Hi" to NS.
5. AS waits for a response.
6. AS says (and writes[b]), "What are you doing?"
7. AS waits for a response.
8. AS says (and writes[b]), "Want some gum?" and shows pack of gum.
9. If NS says yes, AS hands pack of gum to NS.
10. NS hands pack back to AS.

Table 1. *(continued)*

11. AS selects a stick of gum and chews it until the end of the interaction.
12. AS remains in one m proximity to NS for at least 30 seconds or until the end of interaction.
13. AS says "Bye" when NS terminates the interaction.

Galaxian

1. AS approaches NS.
2. AS establishes one m proximity.
3. AS establishes face-forward orientation with NS.
4. AS says, "Hi."
5. AS waits for a response.
6. AS writes and says, "Want to play?"
7. AS shows message and game to NS.
8. If NS indicates no, AS goes to another student (step 1).
9. AS turns on game.
10. AS hands game to NS.
11. AS looks at game for 10 out of every 15 seconds NS is playing.
12. AS receives game from NS.
13. AS says NS's score.
14. AS turns off game.
15. AS turns on game.
16. AS depresses right directional dial with right hand.
17. AS repeatedly depresses fire button with left hand.
18. AS depresses left directional dial with right hand.
19. AS reads own score at end of game.
20. AS offers game to NS. Steps 11–20 continue if NS indicates interest in playing.
21. AS says, "Bye" when NS ends interaction.

[a]AS = student with autism, NS = nonhandicapped student.
[b]Applies only to AS, who would write on a notebook the words he or she was saying and display the notebook to the NS.

autistic students tended to approach familiar, nonhandicapped peers to play with the objects. They did not approach peers who were unfamiliar to them. This discrimination of familiar and unfamiliar peers was not trained, but was an important and desired effect. It would often be inappropriate and possibly dangerous for persons with severe handicaps to approach strangers to have extended social interactions. In most contexts, it is desirable to have handicapped persons approach familiar persons in familiar settings.

The program by Gaylord-Ross, Haring, Breen, and Pitts-Conway (1984) involved training the handicapped student in a set of social skills. It was found that the handicapped student would emit these behaviors and receive reciprocal responses from his or her nonhandicapped peers. It is also possible to reverse the direction of training. Strain (1981) has completed numerous studies where the nonhandicapped peer was trained to interact with handicapped students. The trained student was taught the applied behavior analytic skills of prompting and reinforcing a peer's behavior. A student may prompt an interaction through demonstrating, modeling, and verbally cueing responses. The peer can reinforce behaviors from the handicapped student with smiles, praise, and gestures. Thus, there is a substantial body of research showing how leisure interactions may be promoted through behavior analytic training packages (see Guralnick, 1978; Strain & Kerr, 1981) that focus on either the handicapped or nonhandicapped peer as the agent of change.

It is also possible to induce social interaction through less controlled training procedures. Handicapped and nonhandicapped pupils can be placed in student-centered contexts (Gaylord-Ross & Pitts-Conway, 1984) with little or no adult intervention. During recess, students may be placed in proximity to each other so that conversations or "hanging out" behaviors may occur. One must carefully observe to see whether such incidental, untrained interactions occur. The research literature indicates that such interactions are not likely to develop on their own. Yet, upon occasion, observed social interactions have been observed to develop when the teacher has engineered the environment so that familiar students are in proximity to each other. It is likely that persons receiving no previous social skill training will fail to interact when placed in student-centered contexts. Individuals who have undergone social skill training are more likely to emit new, untrained social responses as a function of informal peer modeling when they are in student-centered contexts. At present, this explanation of past research and the authors' anecdotal observations is speculative and in need of further experimental verification.

A more formal procedure for inducing social interaction is to establish a "special friends" program whereby pairs of handicapped and nonhandicapped students can form a buddy system to interact at leisure times (cf. Voeltz, 1981). The special friends could meet two to five times a week during a designated period of the school day. At that time they could play table games, ambulate around the campus, engage in an athletic or large motor activity, go to a restaurant or shopping center off-campus, and so forth. The special friends encounters are defined as leisure exchanges, and the nonhandicapped student is told that he or she is *not* there in the role of an instructor to teach the handicapped student. Undoubtedly, some informal instruction may occur as the handicapped student is taught, for example, how to play a table game.

Attempts to set up social skill programs in leisure settings should keep at least four points in mind. First, the leisure activities selected should be reinforcing to both the handicapped and nonhandicapped students. If the activity is not of interest to both persons, it is unlikely that continued, longer duration interactions will persist after training on a special program has ended. Second, social sequences that do not entail a substantial amount of language should be identified. Third, when interactions are centered around objects, it is helpful to select objects that are portable. Portable objects like hand-held video games permit the student to initiate and elaborate interaction in a large number of settings since the student can carry the object around. Fourth, it is important to program for the generalization of the leisure exchanges to other persons and settings. Social skill development will be limited if the student only interacts with a few people in a single setting. Therefore, identify the people and settings that increase the probability that social interactions will occur. Conduct training in some of these settings and observe whether generalization appears in the other, nontrained settings (cf. Horner, Sprague, & Wilcox, 1982). It is usually preferred that particular social behaviors generalize to familiar persons in designated settings (e.g., playground, assembly, church). Thus, effective social skill training should teach the learner both to use appropriate social skills in certain stimulus situations and to *not* use those skills in other, nontargeted situations.

THE SOCIAL-SEXUAL DOMAIN

Though social-sexual skills are an important aspect of an individual's life, they have received relatively little attention with regard to the lives of severely handicapped persons. Social-sexual skills become increasingly important as severely handicapped individuals are integrated into community activities and settings (Gordon, 1979; Hamre-Nietupski, Ford, Williams, & Gruenewald, 1978). As in other living skills areas, severely handicapped persons must be taught social-sexual skills in order to display appropriate behaviors. Social-sexual education is being increasingly seen as a right for all handicapped individuals (Perske, 1973; Wolfensberger, 1972), though it is still a sensitive issue for teachers, parents, administrators, and others. As Johnson (1975) has noted, " . . . this society is not yet very tolerant either of sexual expression or of the mentally retarded—let alone sexual expression of the mentally retarded" (p. 30). Community attitudes toward the sexuality of mentally retarded persons reflect community attitudes toward retarded persons in general. Johnson (1975) has identified three philosophies concerning sex education and counseling of special group members. These are: 1) eliminate sexuality, 2) tolerate (and perhaps accommodate) sexuality, and 3) cultivate sexuality. The authors support the third position and feel that social-sexual skills training is an important part of an appropriate education for severely handicapped persons.

Hamre-Nietupski and Ford (1981) and Hamre-Nietupski et al. (1978) have suggested that social-sexual skills training should have content areas that include bodily distinctions, self-care, family life, social interactions, social manners, reproduction, birth control, and venereal disease information (see Table 2). Hamre-Nietupski et al. (1978) used a model-test-teach design during instructional procedures. Direct or indirect verbal cues, modeling, and physical prompting were used to teach the specific skills. The content of their suggested curriculum is quite diverse. Its implementation is likely to be altered according to the level of functioning of the student, particularly with respect to the person's ability to imitate modeled behaviors.

Table 2. Content areas for sex education compiled from Hamre-Nietupski and Ford (1981); Hamre-Nietupski, Ford, Williams, and Gruenewald (1978); Hamre-Nietupski and Williams (1977)

I. Bodily distinctions skill content area:
  A. Body parts program—ability to discriminate and label body parts on others and self
  B. Sex distinctions program—ability to discriminate the sex of clothed unfamiliar people, classmates, teachers, and family
  C. Sex distinctions program—ability to discriminate the sex of unclothed representational figures
  D. Bodily changes related to growth program—ability to express own body growth and discriminate men-boys and women-girls
  E. Growth distinctions program—ability to discriminate between babies and grownups
  F. Growing Up Program—ability to discriminate between babies and grownups
II. Self-care skills content area:
  A. Grooming
  B. Dressing
  C. Domestic maintenance
  D. Cooking
III. Family life skills content area:
  A. Names of family members and family relationships program
  B. Family roles and responsibilities program
IV. Social interactions skills content area:
  A. Ability to initiate and receive verbal and physical social interactions that are appropriate to sex, age, and place
    1. Cooperative social interactions—teaching appropriate initiation, receiving, sustaining, and ending of a selected interaction with peers, adults, and young children
    2. Isolative social skills—activity at appropriate time and place, appropriate activity, sustaining and terminating activity
    3. Verbal interaction skills for making "small talk"
    4. Appropriate responses to inappropriate and appropriate verbal and physical interactions
V. Social manners skills content area:
  A. Dressing
  B. Walking
  C. Sitting
  D. General Posturing
VI. Reproduction, birth control, and venereal disease information content area:
  A. Reproduction
    1. Ability to verbally explain intercourse
    2. Ability to verbally explain conception
    3. Ability to verbally explain prenatal growth
    4. Ability to verbally explain birth
  B. Birth control
    1. General information
    2. General definition
    3. Reasons for using or not using birth control
  C. Venereal disease
    1. Information and checkups

The type of instructional device used in training is an important consideration for teachers. Vandervoort and McIlvenna (1979) suggest that graphically explicit materials be used in teaching sexual skills to nonhandicapped individuals. For instance, will the individual be able to better understand bodily distinctions with real bodies, pictures, or drawings of the body parts? Though explicit materials may be better for instructional purposes, local cultural standards must be considered in the selection of educational materials. Social-sexual skills should be community referenced in much the same way as vocational or leisure skills training. The instructor may want to consider what types of materials are used in local non–special education settings (i.e., schools, planned parenthood, social service organization) and either make use of their resources or stay within the general range of the types of materials that they are using. It may be appropriate to form an advisory committee of local community members (e.g., parents, social workers, health professionals) in developing and implementing the social-sexual skills curriculum. This would allow community input, bring in resource materials and persons, and increase the likelihood that the curriculum will be community referenced.

Many severely handicapped persons have inappropriate behaviors such as indiscriminate touching of others, public masturbation, or a lack of vocabulary in this area (Hamre-Nietupski & Ford, 1981). Through social-sexual skills training, individuals can learn appropriate behaviors that are necessary for community living, and inappropriate behaviors can be decreased. For example, it may be difficult to engage in community training with an individual who hugs strangers. However, if this person learns how to appropriately greet and interact with strangers, their chances of successfully functioning in, and being accepted by, the community have been greatly increased. As Hamre-Nietupski and Ford (1981) have stated, "sex education and related skills acquired should facilitate appropriate adult functioning in less restrictive school, home and community environments" (p. 192).

In teaching social-sexual skills, the teacher should use systematic instructional procedures such as task analysis, cue hierarchies, positive reinforcement, and so forth. Parents and significant others should be solicited for input and support. Murphy, Coleman, and Abel (1983) suggest that simple terms, repetition, individualized presentation, and natural visual aids be used in teaching social-sexual skills to handicapped persons.

THE COMMUNITY DOMAIN

The "community" includes a wide range of settings such as stores, restaurants, walkways, transportation vehicles, and so forth. The field of educating persons with severe handicaps has moved toward a functional skill model that emphasizes the teaching of community-referenced skills in order to prepare the individual to perform competently in this wide range of environments. Six important steps must be taken in order to ensure effective community-referenced, social skill training. First, an environmental inventory (Brown et al., 1979) should be conducted so that settings for community training are selected. Second, the skills necessary for successful performance should be identified. Third, these skills should be task analyzed so that the social and other behaviors in the sequence (e.g., Table 1) are delineated. Fourth, an instructional program should be written so that cues, reinforcers, and strategies for generalization and maintenance are described. Fifth, the program should be implemented. Sixth, the effectiveness of the instructional program should be evaluated with a data based monitoring system.

Often, the most effective way to teach severely handicapped individuals the social skills necessary for survival in the community is to train the student in the actual community settings where the skills are needed. Social skills taught in a classroom or institutional setting may not generalize successfully to the setting where the skills must ultimately be displayed (Bates, 1980; Renzaglia & Bates, 1983).

One way to teach social skills in the community is to choose a functional activity (i.e., leisure/recreational, vocational, or community living) and teach needed social skills in the context of the activity. For example, Storey, Bates, and Hanson (1984) assessed the skills needed by six adults labeled mentally retarded to purchase coffee in four community restaurants. One task analysis of 46 steps was developed for three sit-down restaurants. The task analysis was initially developed by the trainers going into the restaurants and purchasing coffee in order to determine what skills were needed. Second, two adults labeled profoundly retarded who were not part of the study were taken to the restaurants and taught how to purchase coffee. During this process, necessary changes in the task analysis were made. Finally, the disabled people involved as participants in the study were taught to use the restaurants. Ten steps of the task analysis involved social interactions in the restaurant. These social skills were taught in the context of the whole chain of behaviors involved in purchasing coffee using a teach-all chaining procedure. A system of least to greatest prompts (verbal instruction, gesture, physical prompt, and hand guidance) was used to teach the appropriate responses. Verbal feedback and contingent social approval were delivered in the form of smiles, social praise, and physical contact immediately following correct responses. Other naturally occurring potential reinforcers were also available during training. These included coffee, interactions with nonhandicapped people, time away from work, one-to-one trainer attention, and encouragement from the waitresses.

The results of the study indicated that each of the individuals showed an improvement in the percentage of steps performed independently over baseline through training. Both social and nonsocial skills learned successfully generalized to two nontrained sites with virtually identical task demands. There was limited generalization to the site with different task demands (i.e., the "fast food" restaurant). The individuals had a mean baseline rate of 28% of the social interaction steps correct during baseline. At the end of training they had improved to a mean of 77% correct, which was exactly the same percentage that nonhandicapped individuals scored on the task analysis when covertly observed. Table 3 shows the percentage of correct responses for the individuals across different aspects of the study.

Bradlyn et al. (1983) taught conversational skills to five mentally retarded adolescents using a group training format. The individuals were taught social skills involving conversational questions, self-disclosing statements, reinforcing/acknowledging comments, and high interest statements. Training consisted of instruction, modeling, behavior rehearsal, and feedback/reinforcement during 20-minute training sessions. Results indicated that the conversational behaviors generalized to novel nonhandicapped confederates. The individuals were also judged, using a social validation measure, to have improved in overall conversational competence.

Research has shown that individuals with severe handicaps can learn social skills that are needed in community settings. Though it may not always be the most efficient method in teaching social skills, it is usually desirable to teach the skills in the setting where they must ultimately be displayed. This has the advantage of allowing naturally occurring discriminative stimuli, reinforcers, and punishers to occur and makes the issue of generalization of less critical importance. That is, a method of sequential programming for generalization (Stokes & Baer, 1977) may be followed, so, as the targeted skills in a community environment are identified, they may be successively trained by special education staff. Whether programming for the general case (Horner et al., 1982) or for more limited sequential programming, social skills are most critical for displaying competence in a variety of community environments.

Table 3. Percentage of correct responses at "Motel Murphysboro" for baseline, training, maintenance, social baseline, nonsocial baseline, social training, and nonsocial training (Storey, Bates, & Hanson, 1984)

Name	Baseline X%	Training X%	Maintenance X%	Social baseline X%	Social training X%	Nonsocial baseline X%	Nonsocial training X%
Cynthia	54	88	80	48	91	57	86
Linda	52	87	90	10	62	63	97
Stuart	62	82	81	40	76	68	83
Pete	50	87	79	15	79	59	89
Patti	54	84	76	11	75	68	87
Maureen	54	89	83	25	79	62	92
Mean	54	86	81.5	28	77	62	88
Normative data		87			77		89
Elsie's	54.5	83.4	83.5				
Tippy's	57.3	87.3	81.7				
Hardee's	76.5	86.3	82.5				

THE VOCATIONAL DOMAIN

At first glance, one might think that social behaviors were not that important in work settings. Yet, past research has shown that when disabled persons fail in a job placement, it is likely to be because of the presence of socially inappropriate behaviors rather than the failure to perform job tasks (Greenspan & Shoultz, 1981; Greenspan, Shoultz, & Weir, 1981; Rusch & Schutz, 1981). Thus, one aspect of social skill training in vocational contexts is to implement effective behavior management programs that can reduce problem behaviors to a near-zero level. There is likely to be little tolerance for disruptive behaviors in competitive work settings. Often, persons displaying problem behaviors will never be selected for employment positions. Yet, when an employed worker or a student in community vocational training does display problem behaviors at the work site, professionals must be prepared to implement behavior management procedures like response cost, differential reinforcement, timeout, and so forth.

In addition to dealing with socially inappropriate acts, it is also important to program for the development of positive social skills in the workplace. At almost any workplace, it is important for co-workers to "get along" with each other. Getting along can mean not disrupting others, assisting others in job tasks, and socializing with others while working or during break times. Displaying all of these behaviors tends to lead the worker to be viewed positively by his co-workers and supervisors. It is particularly important for disabled persons to be perceived positively in work settings. This will overcome the initial negative perceptions that co-workers might have of disabled persons. It can also provide a support system of one or more individuals who can assist or reinforce the disabled worker. Such assistance may be critical in maintaining the placement of a disabled worker when he or she has lapses in performance or displays antisocial acts.

One way to enhance the perception of disabled persons in work settings is to promote positive leisure interactions during break times. This approach would draw upon the existing knowledge base of social skill training in the leisure domain. Breen, Haring, Pitts-Conway, and Gaylord-Ross (1985) trained a group of autistic students to emit conversational and related social behaviors with co-workers. The autistic youth completed job tasks at a nursing home off the school campus and at a restaurant on campus. The autistic students received training in social sequences with nonhandicapped students from the high school that they both attended. The autistic students acquired these social skills during training and generalized them to the adult co-workers in the nursing home and restaurant. Figure 1 shows the number of peers (exemplars) needed to produce generalization for each student. It also displays the extent of generalization of the social and related behaviors to the adult co-workers during break time. Two of the students learned to generalize the social behaviors to

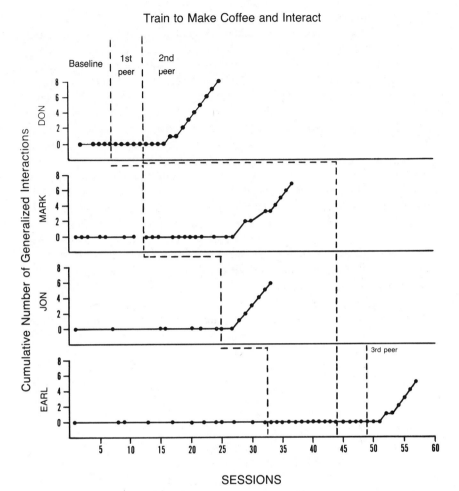

Figure 1. Number of generalized social interactions with co-workers as a function of peer social skill training (adapted from Breen, Haring, Pitts-Conway, & Gaylord-Ross, 1985).

co-workers after training with one peer. The other two students required training with two or three peers, respectively, before generalization of the social behaviors appeared during interactions with co-workers.

It is also possible to conduct social skill training while the person is working. In some positions, it would be unacceptable to socialize while working on task. In most jobs, though, there are intervals of time between or while working on task when workers may socialize. Haring, Roger, Lee, Breen, and Gaylord-Ross (1984) showed that it is possible for workers to socialize while completing the task. A group of moderately mentally retarded preadolescents were trained to do jobs in the school's cafeteria. The handicapped students worked alongside their nonhandicapped peers. Conversations among peers were audiotaped with microcassettes carried in the shirt pockets of the handicapped students. At separate training sessions, the handicapped students were trained to initiate conversations and to elaborate conversations while they worked stacking trays or handing out food. In training, students were also reinforced for expanding new topics of conversation so as to not only repeat the same trained conversations in a rote manner. The training program resulted in generalization to the work settings with a substantial increase in appropriate initiations and expansions by the handicapped students. While working, the handicapped students would start convesations with their nonhandicapped peer co-workers. In addition, they generated conversations about new topics in which they had not been previously trained. The generation of new topics and behaviors counters the common criticism of behavior analytic approaches to social skill training. When handicapped persons solely repeat social responses in which they were previously trained, it could be asserted that they were not truly ''social'' but were merely parroting stipulated, trained behaviors. The training in the Haring, Roger, Lee, Breen, and Gaylord-Ross (1984) study reinforced novel responses. Thus, the reinforcement of response generalization led to creative, unstipulated behaviors (cf. Stokes & Baer, 1977).

In addition to formal training at a work site, there are many incidental developments that can take place that will promote the development of social behavior. It is important for social service personnel to identify workers at a site who are supportive of disabled persons being trained or employed in non-sheltered settings. Those workers should be informally reinforced for their efforts in cultivating relationships with disabled persons. Second, there is undoubtedly a foreman or supervisor who has immediate authority over the employees. It is important for the social integration of the disabled worker that this person be supportive of the training or employment program. The goals and assumptions of vocational development for disabled persons should be clear to this individual. The foreman/director as a representative of the company should be positively reinforced both informally, and when appropriate, formally through certificates of appreciation, award ceremonies, and so on (see Gaylord-Ross, Forte, & Gaylord-Ross, 1983). The foreman/director is a role model for his or her employees and may set a positive tone for how the work site accepts and integrates its disabled workers into the social fabric of the setting. One indication of such social acceptance is the informal birthday and other parties that are held in workplaces. The parties are informally organized and may occur monthly for the birthday or other special event of the small group of 5–10 employees. When the disabled student (worker) is invited and participates in these informal yet important social gatherings, an event has transpired that can facilitate the social development of the handicapped person. As disabled persons become more visible at work sites, their nonhandicapped co-workers will undoubtedly reevaluate their view of the place for disabled persons in the work force (cf. Gaylord-Ross, Forte, Storey, Gaylord-Ross, & Jameson, 1984). Some employees will be initially disposed in a favorable manner toward handicapped persons. Other workers will undoubtedly develop more positive views of disabled persons as their contact with them increases. Some workers will gladly redefine their job as one that not only entails completing particular tasks at certain times, but one that also includes a human relations component of working with handicapped persons (Gaylord-Ross, Forte, & Gaylord-Ross, in press). When this attitudinal shift occurs with certain employees, the possibilities for social skill development will have a multifold increase.

GENERAL CONSIDERATIONS AND RECOMMENDATIONS

A wide range of approaches to social skill training have been addressed in this chapter. An emphasis was placed on formal, social skill training packages that explicitly attempt to teach interactional behaviors. The vast majority of the training programs are steeped in applied behavior analytic principles with prompting, reinforcement, and task analyzed sequences carefully defined. Historically, the pioneering work in social skill training for severely handicapped students was begun by R. Shores and his colleagues (T. Apolloni, T. Cooke, & P. Strain) at George Peabody College. This work was carried out in a controlled laboratory setting with preschoolers. Since that time, there has been a substantial expansion of social skill training efforts to include different age groups and a multiplicity of environmental domains. The authors tried to describe the ways in which social skill training can be implemented in areas like communication, leisure, community, social-sexual, and vocational domains. Some examples of task analyzed sequences were presented as well as references to other materials that the reader may use to develop his or her own social skill training programs. While an emphasis was placed on research-oriented training efforts, it was pointed out that incidental social development is likely to occur with severely handicapped students who have previously undergone social skill training as they are placed in more integrated, community-referenced settings. The possibilities multiply in normalized settings for role modeling of age-appropriate behaviors, the positive perception of the handicapped person, the development of acquaintanceships and friendships, attitudinal shifts favoring handicapped persons, and an improved self-concept in the handicapped individual. Certainly, future research investigations of social behavior development should examine these variables as well as the typical studies that identify particular behaviors and prompt and reinforce them to some criterion level of performance. While this research strategy has been quite productive, other approaches (e.g., ethnography, attitude measurement) should be used to address work climates, quality of life, social perception, and friendship patterns. In addition, almost all of the research has addressed the issue of social interactions between handicapped and nonhandicapped persons. It would also be useful to attend to handicapped–handicapped interactions. Even in well-integrated educational programs, handicapped students are still likely to have most or a substantial amount of contact with other handicapped students.

Another topic that is beyond the scope of this chapter deals with the effects of the social skills exhibited by the teacher or other special education professionals on students with handicaps. When severely handicapped students are placed for instruction in multiple settings on and off school campuses, the special education teacher must lead the way in securing placements, explaining the program to other adults, running the program smoothly, and maintaining friendly social contacts with workers at these sites. Often, the pleasant and amicable approaches of a special education professional will pave the way for acceptance of the program and ensure that the training site endures when unavoidable problems arise. Simply stated, when the special education professional is liked by workers at out-of-class training sites, it sets the stage for the acceptance of the handicapped student by these workers, and encourages social exchanges that may ensue between handicapped and nonhandicapped persons. Very little is known about the social skill training of professionals to maximize the integrative contact for severely handicapped students. One point is known, though. If the special education professional is not skillful in dealing with other educators and workers, the success of multiple site, community-referenced instruction will be seriously jeopardized.

Finally, it is important for the teacher to know how to proceed in designing social skill training programs. At present, there is no comprehensive educational approach to facilitate the social skill development of severely handicapped students. Listed below are guidelines to assist educators in promoting the social development of their students.

1. Conduct an *environmental inventory* (Brown et al., 1979) of the critical social behaviors needed to function effectively in the different domestic, school, vocational, and community settings in which the severely handicapped student will receive instruction. Undoubtedly, there are many more social behaviors that need to be trained in a given year than can be trained. Therefore, prioritize the social skills in order of importance and train the most critical skills first (short-term objectives) and designate the less important skills as long-term goals.

2. Make sure that the *social sequences* to be trained are carefully task analyzed and that effective reinforcers and prompts are used to facilitate learning.

3. Take efforts to get the trained social sequences to *generalize* to similar settings and familiar persons. Teach the student to *discriminate* the use of

social sequences so that they are not displayed in inappropriate circumstances (settings and persons).

4. Try to *incorporate* social skill training in as many instructional activities as possible. Social skill training should not be viewed as a separate activity that is done for 20 minutes each day. Rather, most instructional activities have a social component (e.g., making purchases with a cashier). Task analyses for vocational, community, and other skills should have social behaviors embedded in them. Still, it is sometimes appropriate to have an activity completely geared toward social skill development. This would be particularly true in the leisure domain.

5. Establish ongoing programs like *special friends* and *peer tutoring* (Haring, Breen, Pitts-Conway, Lee, & Gaylord-Ross, 1984) that will guarantee substantial contact between severely handicapped students and their nonhandicapped peers. This should promote both formal and incidental contact between students.

6. When selecting leisure activities for social skill training, try to pick those that will be *reinforcing* to both the handicapped and the nonhandicapped students(s).

REFERENCES

Bates, E., Benigni, L., Bretherton, I., Camaioni, L., & Volterra, V. (1979). *The emergence of symbols.* New York: Academic Press.

Bates, P. (1980). The effectiveness of interpersonal skill training on the social skill acquisition of moderately and mildly retarded adults. *Journal of Applied Behavior Analysis, 13,* 237–248.

Bradlyn, A. S., Himadi, W. G., Crimmins, D. B., Christoff, K. A., Graves, K. G., & Kelly, J. A. (1983). Conversational skills training for retarded adolescents. *Behavior Therapy, 14,* 314–325.

Breen, C., Haring, T., Pitts-Conway, V., & Gaylord-Ross, R. (1985). The training and generalization of social interaction during breaktime at two job sites in the natural environment. *Journal of The Association for Persons with Severe Handicaps.*

Brown, L., Branston, M., Hamre-Nietupski, S., Pumpian, I., Certo, N., & Gruenewald, L. (1979). A strategy for developing chronological age appropriate and functional curriculum content for severely handicapped adolescents and young adults. *Journal of Special Education, 13,* 81–90.

Brown, L., Nietupski, J., & Hamre-Nietupski, S. (1976). The criterion of ultimate functioning and public school services for the severely handicapped student. In A. Thomas (Ed.), *Hey, don't forget about me: Education's investment in the severely, profoundly, and multiply handicapped* (pp. 58–82). Reston, VA: Council for Exceptional Children.

Bruner, J. (1975). From communication to language: A psychological perspective. *Cognition, 3,* 255–289.

Certo, N., Haring, N., & York, R. (Eds.). (1984). *Public school integration of severely handicapped students: Rational issues and progressive alternatives.* Baltimore: Paul H. Brookes Publishing Co.

Certo, N., & Kohl, F. L. (1984). A strategy for developing interpersonal interaction instructional content for severely handicapped students. In N. Certo, N. Haring, & R. York (Eds.), *Public school integration of severely handicapped students: Rational issues and progressive alternatives* (pp. 221–244). Baltimore: Paul H. Brookes Publishing Co.

Dore, J. (1975). Holophrases, speech acts and language universals. *Journal of Child Language, 2,* 21–40.

Fredericks, H. D., Baldwin, V., Grove, D., Moore, W., Riggs, C., & Lyons, B. (1978). Integrating the moderately and severely handicapped preschool child into a normal day care setting. In M. Guralnick (Ed.), *Early intervention and the integration of handicapped and nonhandicapped children* (pp. 203–205). Baltimore: University Park Press.

Gaylord-Ross, C., Forte, J., & Gaylord-Ross, R. (1983). *Annual report of the technological employment project.* San Francisco: San Francisco State University.

Gaylord-Ross, C., Forte, J., & Gaylord-Ross, R. (in press). The community classroom: Technological vocational training for students with serious handicaps. *Career Development for Exceptional Individuals.*

Gaylord-Ross, R., Forte, J., Storey, K., Gaylord-Ross, C., & Jameson, D. (1984). *Community-referenced instruction in technological work settings.* Unpublished manuscript, San Francisco State University, San Francisco.

Gaylord-Ross, R. J., Haring, T. G., Breen, C., & Pitts-Conway, V. (1984). The training and generalization of social interaction skills with autistic youth. *Journal of Applied Behavior Analysis, 17,* 198–199.

Gaylord-Ross, R., & Holvoet, J. (1985). *Teaching severely handicapped children and youth.* Boston: Little, Brown & Co.

Gaylord-Ross, R., & Peck, C. A. (1985). Integration efforts for students with severe mental handicaps. In D. Bricker & J. Filla (Eds.), *Serving the severely retarded: From research to practice* (pp. 187–207). Reston, VA: The Council for Exceptional Children.

Gaylord-Ross, R., & Pitts-Conway, V. (1984). Social behavior development in integrated secondary autistic programs. In N. Certo, N. Haring, & R. York (Eds.), *Public school integration of severely handicapped students: Rational issues and progressive alternatives* (pp. 197–219). Baltimore: Paul H. Brookes Publishing Co.

Gordon, S. (1979). *Sexual rights for the people . . . who happen to be handicapped.* Syracuse, NY: Center on Human Policy.

Gottman, J., Gonso, J., & Rasmussen, B. (1975). Friendships in children. *Child Development, 46,* 709–718.

Greenspan, S., & Shoultz, B. (1981). Why mentally retarded adults lose their jobs: Social competence as a factor in work adjustment. *Applied Research in Mental Retardation, 2,* 23–38.

Greenspan, S., Shoultz, B., & Weir, M. M. (1981). Social judgment and vocational adjustment of mentally retarded adults. *Applied Research in Mental Retardation, 2,* 335–346.

Guralnick, M. (1976). The value of integrating handicapped and nonhandicapped preschool children. *American Journal of Orthopsychiatry, 42,* 236–245.

Guralnick, M. (1978). *Early intervention and the integration of handicapped and nonhandicapped children.* Baltimore: University Park Press.

Halliday, M. A. K. (1978). *Language as social semiotic.* Baltimore: University Park Press.

Halliday, M. (1975). Learning how to mean. In E. Lenneberg & E. Lenneberg (Eds.), *Foundations of language development: A multidisciplinary approach* (Vol. 1, pp. 239–265). New York: Academic Press.

Hamre-Nietupski, S., & Ford, A. (1981). Sex education and related skills: A series of programs implemented with severely handicapped students. *Sexuality and Disability, 4*, 179–193.

Hamre-Nietupski, S., Ford, A., Williams, W., & Gruenewald, L. (1978). *Sex education and related home and community functioning skill programs for severely handicapped students: Toward appropriate functioning in less restrictive environments.* Madison, WI: Madison Metropolitan School District.

Hamre-Nietupski, S., & Williams, W. (1977). Implementation of selected sex education and social skills to severely handicapped students. *Education and Training of the Mentally Retarded, 12*, 364–372.

Haring, T., Breen C., Pitts-Conway, V., Lee, M., & Gaylord-Ross, R. (1984). *The effects of peer tutoring and special friend experiences on nonhandicapped adolescents.* Unpublished manuscript, San Francisco State University, San Francisco.

Haring, T. G., Roger, B., Lee, M., Breen, C., & Gaylord-Ross, R. (1984). *Facilitating pragmatic aspects of social language use with moderate and severely handicapped children.* Unpublished manuscript, San Francisco State University, San Francisco.

Harris, D., & Vanderheiden, G. (1980). Enhancing the development of communicative interaction. In R. Schiefelbusch (Ed.), *Nonspeech language and communication: Analysis and intervention* (pp. 227–257). Baltimore: University Park Press.

Harris, S. C. (1975). Teaching language to nonverbal children —with an emphasis on problems of generalization. *Psychological Bulletin, 82*(4), 565–580.

Horner, R. H., Sprague, J., & Wilcox, B. (1982). General case programming for community activities. In B. Wilcox & G. T. Bellamy, *Design of high school programs for severely handicapped students* (pp. 61–98). Baltimore: Paul H. Brookes Publishing Co.

Johnson, W. R. (1975). *Sex education and counseling of special groups.* Springfield, IL: Charles C Thomas.

LaGreca, A. M., & Mesibou, G. B. (1979). Social skills intervention with learning disabled children: Selecting skills and implementing training. *Journal of Clinical Child Psychology, 8*, 234–241.

Mahoney, G. (1975). Ethological approach to delayed language acquisition. *American Journal of Mental Deficiency, 80*, 139–148.

McLean, J. E., & Snyder-McLean, L. K. (1978). *A transactional approach to early language training.* Columbus, OH: Charles E. Merrill Publishing Co.

Murphy, W. D., Coleman, E. M., & Abel, G. G. (1983). Human sexuality in the mentally retarded. In J. L. Matson & F. Andrasik (Eds.), *Treatment issues and innovations in mental retardation* (pp. 581–643). New York: Plenum Publishing Corp.

Peck, C. A., Apolloni, T., Cooke, J. P., & Rover, J. (1978). Teaching retarded preschool children to imitate nonhandicapped peers: Training and generalize effect. *Journal of Special Education, 12*, 195–207.

Peck, C. A., & Schuler, A. L. (1983). Classroom-based language intervention with austism: Theoretical and practical considerations for the speech and language specialist. *Seminars in Speech and Language, 4*(1), 93–103.

Peck, C. A., & Semmel, M. I. (1982). Identifying the least restrictive environment (LEA) for children with severe handicaps: Toward an empirical analysis. *The Journal of The Association for the Severely Handicapped, 7*(1), 56–63.

Perske, R. (1973). About sexual development: An attempt to be human with the mentally retarded. *Mental Retardation, 11*, 6–8.

Prutting, C. (1982). Pragmatics as social competence. *Journal of Speech and Hearing Disorders, 47*, 123–134.

Renzaglia, A. M., & Bates, P. (1983). Socially appropriate behavior. In M. E. Snell

(Ed.), *Systematic instruction of the moderately and severely handicapped* (pp. 314–356). Columbus, OH: Charles E. Merrill Publishing Co.

Rusch, F. R., & Schultz, R. P. (1981). Vocational and social work behavior: An evaluative review. In J. L. Matson & J. R. McCartney (Eds.), *Handbook of behavior modification with the mentally retarded* (pp. 247–280). New York: Plenum Publishing Corp.

Rynders, J., Johnson, R., Johnson, D., & Schmidt, B. (1980). Producing positive interaction among Down Syndrome and nonhandicapped teenagers through cooperative goal structuring. *American Journal of Mental Deficiency, 85,* 268–273.

Sailor, W., Guess, D., Goetz, L., Schuler, A., Utley, B., & Baldwin, M. (1980). Language and severely handicapped persons: Deciding what to teach to whom. In W. Sailor, B. Wilcox, & L. Brown (Eds.), *Methods of instruction for severely handicapped students* (pp. 71–105). Baltimore: Paul H. Brookes Publishing Co.

Schuler, A. L., & Goetz, L. (1981). The assessment of severe language disabilities: Communicative and cognitive considerations. *Analysis and Intervention in Developmental Disabilities, 1,* 333–346.

Schutz, R. P., Williams, W., Iverson, G. S., & Duncan, D. (1984). Social integration of severely handicapped students. In N. Certo, N. Haring, & R. York (Eds.), *Public school integration of severely handicapped students: Rational issues and progressive alternatives* (pp. 15–42). Baltimore: Paul H. Brookes Publishing Co.

Stainback, W., Stainback, S., Raschke, D., & Anderson, R. (1981). Three methods for encouraging interactions between severely handicapped and nonhandicapped students. *Education and Training of the Mentally Retarded, 16,* 188–192.

Stokes, J. R., Baer, D. M., & Jackson, R. L. (1974). Programming the generalization of a greeting response in four retarded children. *Journal of Applied Behavior Analysis, 7,* 599–610.

Stokes, T. F., & Baer, D. M. (1977). An implicit technology of generalization. *Journal of Applied Behavior Analysis, 10,* 349–367.

Storey, K., Bates, P., & Hanson, H. B. (1983). *Acquisition and generalization of coffee purchase skills by adults with severe disabilities.* Unpublished manuscript, Southern Illinois University.

Storey, K., Bates, P., & Hanson, H. B. (1984). Acquisition and generalization of coffee purchase skills by six adults with severe handicaps. *Journal of The Association for Persons with Severe Handicaps, 9*(3), 178–185.

Strain, P. S. (1981). Peer-mediated treatment of exceptional children's social withdrawal. *Exception Education Quarterly—Peer Relations of Exceptional Children and Youth, 4,* 93–105.

Strain, P. S., & Kerr, M. M. (1981). *Mainstreaming of children in schools: Research and pragmatic issues.* New York: Academic Press.

Stremel-Campbell, K., Clark-Guida, J., & Johnson-Dorn, N. (1984). *Pre-language and language communication curriculum for children/youth with severe handicaps.* Monmouth, OR: Teaching Research.

Vandervoort, H. E., & McIlvenna, T. (1979). The use of sexually explicit teaching materials. In R. Green (Ed.), *Human sexuality: A health practitioners text* (pp. 12–21). Baltimore: Williams & Wilkins.

Voeltz, L. M. (1981). Special friends in Hawaii. *Education Unlimited, 2,* 10–11.

Voeltz, L. M. (1982). Effects of structured interactions with severely handicapped peers on children's attitudes. *American Journal of Mental Deficiency, 86,* 380–390.

Voeltz, L. M. (1984). Program and curriculum innovations to prepare children for integration. In N. Certo, N. Haring, & R. York (Eds.), *Public school integration of severely handicapped students: Rational issues and progressive alternatives* (pp. 155–188). Baltimore: Paul H. Brookes Publishing Co.

Wehman, P., Abramson, M., & Norman, C. (1977). Transfer of training in behavior modification programs: An evaluative review. *Journal of Special Education, 11,* 212–231.

Wehman, P., & Hill, J. (1982). Preparing severely handicapped youth for less restrictive environments. *Journal of The Association for the Severely Handicapped, 7,* 33–39.

Williams, W., Hamre-Nietupski, S., Pumpian, I., Marks, J. D., & Wheeler, J. (1978). Teaching social skills. In M. E. Snell (Ed.), *Systematic instruction of the moderately and severely handicapped.* Columbus, OH: Charles E. Merrill Publishing Co.

Wolfensberger, W. (1972). *The principle of normalization in human services.* Downsview, Toronto, Canada: National Institute on Mental Retardation.

Chapter 7

Communication Instruction for Learners with Severe Handicaps
Some Unresolved Issues

Joe Reichle and William J. Keogh

In all likelihood, persons having more than a casual interest in the welfare and education of severely handicapped learners already know that speech, manual signing, communication board/aids, or some combination, are potential modalities for expressing wants and needs. Recent chapters, position papers, and research reports have provided useful descriptions of the options that are available (Alpert, 1980; Sailor et al., 1980; Scheuerman, Baumgart, Simpsa, & Brown, 1976; Vanderheiden & Grilley, 1976; Warren & Rogers-Warren, 1985). A consistent theme reflected in this literature is that many of the language intervention issues of the 1960s and 1970s remain unresolved; and, important new issues have emerged during the 1980s. Although the number of yet-to-be resolved issues is considerably greater than those the authors have chosen to address, three were selected for consideration because they seemed to stand out from the rest. First, there seems to be some contradiction and obscurity concerning the decision rules offered to practitioners for selecting the most appropriate communication modality for individual learners. Second, it appears as though there is a need for more thorough integration between what

This work was supported in part by Contract No. 300-82-0363 awarded to the University of Minnesota from the Division of Innovation and Development, Special Education Programs, U.S. Department of Education. The opinions expressed herein do not necessarily reflect the position or policy of the U.S. Department of Education, and no official endorsement should be inferred.

has often been referred to as "functional prerequisites" and "cognitive prerequisites" extrapolated from the study of normally developing children. Third, the intervention effort itself requires greater integration among the what, where, and how factors associated with teaching purposeful communication.

In this chapter, the authors discuss these issues as they pertain to today's communication intervention protocol for severely handicapped, "difficult-to-teach" individuals. Subsequently, the authors propose an intervention focus that they feel embraces each of the issues identified.

DECISION RULES FOR SELECTING
THE APPROPRIATE COMMUNICATION MODE(S)

One issue that has received considerable attention in the literature concerns decision rules pertaining to the selection of appropriate communication modalities for learners with severe handicaps (Alpert, 1980; Sailor et al., 1980; Schiefelbusch & Hollis, 1979; Shane, 1980). Frequently, practitioners who select strategies rely upon a straightforward dichotomous system that first separates speech potential from alternative modalities, and then, depending upon the outcome, between one alternative (i.e., gestural) or another (i.e., graphic). For example, Sailor et al. (1980) identified physiological factors such as adequate hearing, vision, and speech/sound-producing mechanisms, along with the learner's ability to learn to imitate vocally, as the primary indices for entry into speech intervention. If one or more of the factors indicated by Sailor et al. (1980) is seriously deficient (and cannot be ameliorated through prosthesis), then instruction in expressive speech is not recommended. In the Sailor et al. (1980) decision model, the learner's ability to imitate sound and speech stimuli may be considered the most promising indicator for speech training. If the learner has made little or no progress after a period of "ideal imitation training," then an alternative should be considered. Sailor et al. (1980) consider manual signing to be the preferred alternative for consideration because . . . "manual signing has the longest history and the widest social applicability, features that render it first among alternative modes for communication with and for severely handicapped persons" (p. 88). Adequate vision and manual dexterity are identified as primary factors that mitigate for or against selecting manual sign. The next alternative is to consider use of a communication board/aid.

Physiological Factors and Performance History

While Sailor et al's. (1980) decision rules are straightforward and easy to understand, there are two characteristics of the model that reflect some of the unresolved issues described above. First, the model requires physiologically intact learners to participate in vocal/verbal imitation training for a period of time without apparent concurrent instruction in a second—albeit temporary—

expressive system. It is possible that some difficulty might arise in arriving at a clinical decision to discontinue vocal imitation training primarily because of the absence of imitation acquisition data to indicate when "enough is enough." Second, the hierarchial nature of the modality selection process dictates that speech is the preferred mode for expression followed by manual sign. In addition to the physiological factors to be considered, Allaire and Miller (1983) suggested that a learner's " . . . method of communication must be understandable to many others, at least some of whom will not know sign language or how to read" (p. 302). The Sailor et al. (1980) decision rule process recognized that " . . . [I]f critical others in a child's present or future environment are unable or unwilling to become proficient in signing, selection of manual signs as a language mode is unrealistic and inappropriate if other options are available" (p. 77). The growing issue here seems to be more encompassing than a semantic distinction between "critical others" and "many others" when referring to the learners' prospective listening audience. Should the signing modality still be pursued if critical others such as parents and supervising teachers are the only ones willing to master the rudiments of manual signing? With the promising and recent development of more and more children with severe handicaps being fully integrated into regular public school programs, might not there be some utility in designing at least some aspect of a learner's expressive communication system so that he or she has the potential to converse with a majority of his or her nonhandicapped peers? Thus, environmental circumstances may and do exist for some learners where a *mixed mode system* may represent a better match with audience comprehension and override manual sign as the single mode choice even though the learner's vision and manual dexterity may accommodate gestural performance. The authors discuss the mixed modality system more fully later in this section.

Cognitive Skills

While Sailor et al. (1980) have focused upon physiological factors (e.g., vision, hearing, and motor dexterity) and a performance history (success or failure in vocal imitation training), Chapman and Miller (1980) have focused on the emergence of certain cognitive skills that predicate successful acquisition of communication, whether spoken or nonvocal. They suggested that a learner must be functioning in Stage 6 of Piaget's sensorimotor period (exhibiting intentional behavior) prior to the implementation of a communication intervention, and there must be a significant language production deficit prior to the implementation of an augmentative/alternative system such as sign or graphics. While agreeing that the failure to develop productive speech commensurate with chronological age and the failure of speech production training may be compelling reasons for instituting instruction in augmentative/alternative systems, Chapman and Miller (1980) argue that, considered alone, they are insufficient. Chapman and Miller (1980) have identified four factors that *must be present* before an individual should be considered as a candidate for a nonspeech system. They are:

1. There are no intelligible single-word utterances.
2. Cognitive development is at Piagetian sensorimotor Stage 6, at least.
3. The individual is producing performative behavior (i.e., demonstrating communicative intent).
4. The individual possesses physiological impairment to speech production mechanisms, *or* there is cognitive development at the early pre-operational stage of development, or cognitive development greater than or equal to comprehension greater than or equal to production less than or equal to communicative function.

Thus, if the individual is able to produce intelligible one- or two-word utterances, *or* demonstrates cognitive development that is equivalent to his or her ability to comprehend language, which in turn is equivalent to his or her ability to produce language, *and* his or her language production performance is equivalent to demonstrated communication functions such as requesting or describing, then the use of a nonspeech communication system would be deemed inappropriate since a production language deficit is not considered to be present. In the Chapman and Miller (1980) model, the inclusion of the alternative requirement that a deviant speech mechanism be present would appear redundant with the unintelligible speech requirement since either seems to render speech production nonfunctional.

Shane (1980) and Shane and Bashir (1980) present decision rules similar to Chapman and Miller (1980). Shane (1980), for example, supports the view that learners must exhibit a certain level of cognitive development before they will benefit significantly from instruction in an augmentative system. More specifically, the decision rules proposed by Shane (1980) and Shane and Bashir (1980) have identified Stage 5 of the Piaget's sensorimotor period (means/ends) as a critical marker. At this stage, learners demonstrate an ability to use adults as ''means/ends agents'' to procure desired objects or events. In addition, the structure of the speech production mechanism is assessed to establish the presence (or absence) of persistent oral-motor problems, and the learner's history of participation in speech production training is evaluated. Thus, like Sailor et al. (1980), Shane and Bashir (1980) consider previous training history (such as vocal imitation training) and physiological structure to be prime indicators, and, like Chapman and Miller (1980), they include a requirement that the learner be functioning at a specific cognitive level. If prior instruction in the vocal mode has been unsuccessful, and if the learner's present environment is cooperative, then implementation of an alternative to speech is initiated.

Karlan (1984) synthesized the decision rules suggested by Shane (1980) and has identified only four factors that lead directly to decision points. They include: 1) physiological factors such as the speech-producing mechanisms;

2) performance history in speech production intervention; 3) existing language repertoire, especially language production performance; and 4) level of cognitive development. Using these factors, an individual may be judged to be an appropriate candidate for augmentative communication by following any one of the three decision paths listed below:

Path 1
1. a. Cognitive development is at least a sensorimotor Stage 5 intelligence, *or*
   b. a mental age of 18 months has been attained or there is a demonstrated ability to recognize photographs, *and*
2. there are persistent oral-reflex problems; *and*
3. the family is willing to implement nonspeech systems of communication.
   or

Path 2
1. a. Cognitive development is at least at sensorimotor Stage 5 intelligence, *or*
   b. a mental age of 18 months has been attained or there is a demonstrated ability to recognize photographs; *and*
2. the individual has had trial therapy; *and*
3. the trial therapy was appropriate; *and*
4. the progress of the previous trial therapy was too slow to enable effective comunication; *and*
5. the family is willing to implement nonspeech systems of communication.
   or

Path 3
1. a. Cognitive development is at least at sensorimotor Stage 5 intelligence, *or*
   b. a mental age of 18 months has been attained or there is a demonstrated ability to recognize photographs; *and*
2. a. the individual's speech is unintelligible except to family and friends, *or*
   b. the individual's predominant mode of communication is through pointing, gesture, or facial-body affect, *or*
   c. there is a predominance of single-word utterances, *or*
   d. the individual exhibits frustration with the inability to speak; *and*
3. a. the individual cannot accurately imitate speech sounds or words, *or*
   b. the individual cannot accurately imitate gross motor or oral-motor movements; *and*
4. the family is willing to implement nonspeech systems of communication.

One factor common to each of the three paths is the level of cognitive development. If cognitive development is at or beyond Stage 5 of Piaget's sensorimotor period, then the decision process can continue. The other common factor is the willingness of the environment to implement the nonspeech systems. Following a determination of the learner's cognitive level, his or her speech production mechanism is examined for oral-motor reflex problems. If problems are found, and the environment is cooperative, instruction can begin in augmentative communication. If, however, structural impairments do not exist, then past speech production training is evaluated (Path 2). If the outcome of that evaluation indicates insufficient progress, and the learner's current environment is cooperative, augmentative instruction can begin. However, if there has been no speech production training (Path 3), the degree of existing language production is examined along with the ability to imitate speech sounds and gross motor or oral-motor movements. If deficiencies are found in these areas and the environment is cooperative, the augmentative instruction can begin.

Successive Training Strategy

Alpert (1980) identified a training/assessment procedure for determining the optimal nonspeech mode to use with autistic children once the decision has been made to consider speech alternatives. Basically, the procedure involves teaching specific language responses in two *successively* trained nonspeech modes. This strategy might be thought of as a process for generating "performance baselines" in learning alternative language skills (i.e., signing and graphics). By comparing the respective acquisition rates between the baselines, the clinician may be able to identify a single modality for a long-term intervention.

Alpert (1980) has also pointed out some of the risks in using decision rule strategies such as those proposed by Chapman and Miller (1980), Sailor et al. (1980), and Shane (1980), especially with children (such as those diagnosed as being autistic) who have normal hearing and the physiological capacity for producing speech. For such children

> . . . . alternative nonspeech intervention will be attempted only after the child has persistently failed to learn functional vocal behavior. This is unfortunate, for not only does the child remain without a means of communicating during the entire training period, but as the child gets older, the probability that he will acquire functional communication skills may be reduced. (Alpert, 1980, p. 401)

An alternative to the dichotomous approach for identifying the "best" communication mode is to consider strengthening communication exchanges in "all" modes. Whether explicitly stated or not, decision rules for identifying the most appropriate vehicle for expression seem to direct the practitioner toward the selection of a single modality. There is no empirical basis for this practice. Attempting to decide between the alternatives (i.e., speech, graphics, manual) may be viewed as a "pseudo-issue," particularly if the decision is between a graphic or manual system. An examination of the sorts of communication exchanges that are possible in the day-to-day functioning of a learner with severe handicaps often shows that, in some situations/activities, manual signing holds the most promise, and during other situations/activities that occur on the same day, a graphic system or natural gestures is judged to be more effective. By taking this view, the "potential listeners" and the "communicator-to-be" are assessed as one unit each amenable to the intervention. By utilizing recently developed assessment procedures for identifying *learner opportunities* for interaction (Brown et al., 1979; Iverson, Williams, Schutz, & Fox, 1983; Snell, 1983; Wilcox & Bellamy, 1982), a specific modality for expression (i.e., natural gestures) might be determined to be most efficient in one set of circumstances, but not in others, providing the basis for a mixed modality system.

Distinction between Mixed Mode and Total Communication

There is an important distinction between what the authors have referred to as mixed mode communication, and "total communication" or the "simultaneous method." Although Moores (1974) pointed out that there are different interpretations of total and simultaneous communication as methodologies, it is generally accepted that each is characterized by, at least, the concurrent presentation of oral and nonoral symbolic forms (Denton, 1972; Fulwiler & Fouts, 1976; Gustason, Pfetzing, & Zawolkow, 1972). The basis for advocating the simultaneous method is that a multimodal approach may maximize the probability of learning successes with low-functioning individuals (Hopper & Helmick, 1977). Thus, the operative principle in the total communication, or simultaneous, approach is the *concurrent* presentation of speech and sign, or gestures, or graphics as multisymbol equivalents.

Dual Mode Approach

Schaeffer (1980) suggested that a dual mode approach be used to establish verbal production skills among autistic learners. In his paradigm, vocal mode instruction is initiated by using imitation training procedures described by Lovaas, Berberich, Perloff, and Schaeffer (1966); concurrent with vocal imitation training, instruction is implemented in the gestural mode. Assuming that the same referents are used as vocabulary items in both the gesture and vocal modes, the learner will eventually be able to verbalize (or gesture) to produce a request or a comment specific to each referent. Schaeffer reported that the three learners who participated in the program based on the dual approach began to combine spoken words and sign approximations spontaneously. Schaeffer recommends that as these spontaneous combinations begin to occur, the practitioner should begin to require the learner to chain the sign with the verbalization; then, the practitioner is encouraged to restrain the learner from producing the gestural portion of the chained utterance.

With the exception of the final step in Schaeffer's program, it would seem as though the learner may be able to select from his or her own repertoire the most efficient mode given the context in which his or her utterance is to be produced. For example, Reichle and Ward (in press) taught a 13-year-old autistic learner to use the signing mode in the presence of those who did sign, and to use a communication board in the presence of those who did not. The learner was taught to present a message card to a prospective communication partner. The card read, "I am unable to speak, do you use sign language?" The learner's selection of an augmentative mode was based on the speaking partner's answer. Reichle and Ward reasoned that, with those who sign, a manual signing mode was quick and efficient; with those who did not, the extra time required to teach the learner the discriminative use of a communication board was worth the effort and in the child's best interest. In this study, the learner was taught two symbolically equivalent expressive modes and was able to use them interchangeably depending on the listener's answer.

Unlike a dual mode strategy, a mixed mode paradigm may elect to strengthen one mode in one context and a different mode in a different context. The mixed mode strategy attempts to identify first the comprehension requirements that exist in each component of the learner's environment, and the learner is taught the most effective and efficient means of expression while in that environment. The mixed mode strategy embraces, but does not require, concurrent presentation of multisymbol equivalents. For example, the natural gestures of shaking one's head up and down, or from side to side, or holding one's hand up to signal "stop," are universally understood actions. Gestures such as these are easy to model, may be easily embedded into a communicative exchange, and are easily physically prompted. These advantages render them more efficient than the formal manual signs even for learners who may possess all of the physiological and imitative requirements for producing the formal signs for "yes" and "no." By following this strategy, the learner, in all probability, will be understood more easily by the listening community. And, he or she is more likely to receive incidental instruction during natural daily interactions.

Natural gestures (such as nodding the head for yes and no) should be considered first when designing an intervention that uses a gestural system. If signs from a formal sign language or system are being selected, iconicity (or guessability) and relative motor difficulty should be considered. There are data (Reichle, 1984) to suggest that iconic signs are more easily acquired and maintained compared to noniconic signs. Additionally, because very few individuals with whom most learners communicate use signs, it is important that naive signers be able to surmise the meanings of signs. Most interventionists seem to agree that certain action concepts are not easily represented in the graphic mode. Actions that represent movement such as eating, drinking, running, and so on, seem to be particularly troublesome. This difficulty exists, in part, because of the inherent problems in representing movement, and also because certain object representations such as cup and drink create the potential for confusion between the object *cup* and the action *drinking*. Actions may be represented more easily in the sign mode, since movement is easier. In this example, it might be reasonable to represent "drink" in sign and "cup" in the graphic mode.

Whether the implementation of communication instruction in several modes will lead to the eventual prevalence of one mode or another represents but one potential outcome. The mixed mode system of instruction may produce two or more strong and durable communication alternatives that serve to broaden the learner's communicative repertoire.

Acquisition of a Mixed Mode

Thus far, this discussion has focused upon the logistical benefits of considering a mixed mode system. Essentially, those benefits may be summarized as: 1) increasing potential listener participation, and 2) improving message understandability. Factors associated with the acquisition—or actual learning—of a mixed mode must be addressed.

One of the fundamental objections to the use of a mixed mode communication system (especially when gestures and graphics are taught concurrently) is the belief that it will be too confusing for the learner. However, evidence exists to suggest that young normal children acquiring English engage in the use of mixed modes of communication. For example, Carter (1973) studied the progression of normal children's methods of expressing communicative intent. She indicated that the children differentially produced gestural and vocal behavior to communicate and did not begin to coordinate their gestural and vocal output systematically until around 12–13 months of age.

Recently, Allaire and Miller (1983) presented an excellent example of an intervention that embodies the essential elements of a mixed mode system. They described an intervention that included the concurrent use of line drawings, a vocal signal to request attention, and natural gestures for "stop," "give me," and "come here." The major difference between Allaire and Miller's model and the mixed mode system proposed here is that in the Allaire and Miller model, the expressive modes "may be temporary and only give . . . the instructors data about other plausible systems" (p. 304).

Summary

In summary, the authors believe that the majority of existing augmentative decision rules direct the interventionist toward the selection of a single augmentative modality. Attempting to decide between the alternatives (i.e., speech, graphics, and manual) may be viewed as a "pseudo-issue," particularly if the decision is between a graphic and a manual system. For some learners, it may be possible to implement a mixed augmentative system that enhances the advantages of gestural and graphic modes while at the same time minimizes the disavantages inherent in each system.

COGNITIVE AND FUNCTIONAL
PREREQUISITES FOR COMMUNICATION

Traditionally, language interventionists have emphasized the establishment of certain cognitive prerequisites for the implementation of language intervention procedures. Most recently, Rice (1983) stated ". . . there is a detectable sense of frustration regarding the elusiveness of cognition and its role in the language impairment and remediation process. . . " (p. 347). In part, this frustration has been fueled by a number of investigations that have compared normal children's performance on Piagetian cognitive tasks (e.g., imitation, object permanency, means/end, play) with their language repertoires (Bates, Benigni, Bretheton, Camaioni, & Volterra, 1979; Corrigan, 1978; Miller, Chapman, Branston, & Reichle, 1980). The majority of these investigators concluded that cognitive skills did not always appear to precede the language skills.

The earlier cognitive hypothesis that proposed a significant relationship between Piagetian cognitive skills and early language acquisition (Cromer, 1976) provided the impetus and theoretical framework for addressing cognitive skills in many language intervention programs (Bricker, Dennison, & Bricker, 1976; Kent, 1974; MacDonald & Horstmeier, 1978; McLean & Snyder-McLean, 1978). Since the relationship between cognition, language performance, communication, and intervention strategies seems to be somewhat elusive, a closer examination seems warranted.

The most frequently used system for operationalizing cognitive classes (in the language literature) was developed by Piaget (1929). He divided cognitive acquisition during the child's initial 2 years into six stages that comprised the sensorimotor period. The child's normal progression through the six stages is considered invariant and sequential. Within the six sensorimotor stages, investigators such as Uzgiris and Hunt (1975) have referred to cognitive classes of behavior such as imitation, means/end, causality, and object permanency. Several of these domains have been the focus of a number of investigations attempting to ascertain the relationship between cognition and language.

Imitation

Both the developmental and the learning theory approach to language point to an infant's ability to imitate as a primary factor responsible for the rapid acquisition of new vocal responses (Sherman, 1971). Failure to develop a generalized vocal imitative repertoire usually indicates an absence of functional speech. Thus, a major concern of special educators has been to identify and use instructional procedures to teach vocal imitation to nonimitative children. A number of investigators (Baer, Peterson, & Sherman, 1967; Baer, Wolf, & Risley, 1968; Hewett, 1965; Lovaas et al., 1966; Metz, 1965; Wolf, Risley, & Mees, 1964) demonstrated the use of efficient procedures to establish vocal/ verbal imitative repertoires that were based upon operant conditioning principles.

Baer et al. (1967) demonstrated that even though two severely handi- capped learners had been taught a generalized motor imitation skill, neither was able to imitate vocal demonstrations when first presented. Some time after- ward, Garcia, Baer, and Firestone (1971) attempted to experimentally examine some topographical boundaries of imitative responding, using teaching pro- cedures similar to those used by Baer et al. (1967). Results of their investigation suggested that there were subcategories of imitative behavior across which generalization does not occur. The experimental controls used in each of these studies preclude the prerequisite, or facilitation interpretation (see McCuller & Salzberg, 1982, for a recent review of imitation research).

Although most speech and language training programs emphasize the importance of teaching a generalized motor imitation repertoire prior to intervention in the vocal mode, empirical evidence does not seem to be supportive. Harris (1976) correctly pointed out that not much data exist to verify an optimum strategy for use in structuring a vocal imitation curriculum.

In summary, the reliance upon imitation as a prerequisite to language was based upon both a developmental and remedial perspective. The reliance on motor imitation as a precursor to the learning of vocal imitative behavior was born in the hope that, by establishing motor imitation, this skill would generalize to verbal topographies. Although there is no resolution to this issue, it is clear that repertoires of communicative behavior can be established in the absence of generalized imitative behavior (Reichle, Rogers, & Barrett, 1984).

Means/End

Language interventionists have placed considerable emphasis on the child's level of means/end development as a prerequisite for language intervention (particularly intervention that involves an augmentative communication sys- tem). Means/end refers to how learners obtain objects, actions, or attention. The rationale for using means/end relationships as a prerequisite for language intervention is anchored in research reporting correlations between means/end and early intentional communication production in both normal and handi- capped learners. Bates et al. (1979) reported a relationship between use of an adult as an agent and the emergence of single-word utterances among normal children.

As mentioned earlier, Shane (1980) and Shane and Bashir (1980) have suggested means/end sensorimotor Stage 5 as a precondition for communica- tion intervention using an augmentative communication system. Stage 5, means/end, equates to methods used by a normal child to seek attention, goods, and services between 12 and 18 months. However, when one considers a learner's use of an operant crying strategy during the earliest stages of life, the Stage 5 means/end period may require reconsideration. Early on, crying represents a strong signal that often produces consequences from an attentive parent. These consequences generally serve to meet a need (e.g., food, relief from discomfort). Investigators seem to be in agreement that the frequency of crying is influenced by the consequences associated with it. Obviously, the child's first cries are not emitted for the purpose of recruiting the attention of an adult, but over repeated experiences, crying for attention may take on an intentional communicative characteristic. Eventually, crying is replaced by a more socially appropriate form of attention-getting (e.g., tugging, pointing). Calling for specific consequences from the environment through the use of crying emerges early in a learner's repertoire and appears to be significantly influenced by naturalistic forms of intervention provided by the environment. Consequently, the prerequisite of Stage 5, means/end, is puzzling; other forms of behavior that can be shaped into requesting appear much earlier in development. For example, Keogh and Reichle (1985) suggested that during the initial phase of communication intervention, the learner almost always has the attention of the teacher. As a result, it might be possible to teach the use of a generalized requesting symbol (a mediator to an object or event) prior to teaching the learner to first seek out an adult's attention.

In summary, there seems to be a need to accumulate additional empirical data before the issue of treating means/end as a prerequisite to communication is resolved. As with imitation, it seems reasonable to predict that learners who already engage in a more sophisticated level of means/end behavior might be expected to engage in a greater proportion of self-initiated use of symbols that have been established in their repertoire.

Causality

Causality refers to the recognition of a relationship between some response made by the learner and the consequence that is produced. Traditionally, interventionists have attempted to link causality with both language comprehension and production. Chapman and Miller (1980) suggested that children's understanding of communicative social acts is not usually reported until intentionality has been observed. Opportunities for the production of intentional social actions occur in a number of simple games that most parents play with their children. Generally, participation in these games begins with undifferentiated but contingent response on the part of the learner. Around 6 months of age, he or she begins to anticipate the action of the adult. Around 9 months, the learner begins self-initiating the game. Even before learners are able to engage in the anticipation of social events, there is evidence that children can be taught simple cause/effect relationships. For example, Routh (1969) demonstrated that children between 5 and 7 months could be taught to produce proportionately greater frequencies of consonants or vowels based upon reinforcement history. Other examples have been reported in the motor development literature.

In summary, cause/effect relationships appear to relate to the establishment of the relationships between certain antecedants (discriminative stimuli) and their consequences, which most experts agree is an important aspect of language. There is limited empirical support demonstrating a significant relationship between the emergence of cause/effect relationships and language comprehension and production. However, it is apparent from the literature available that cause/effect relationships can be taught. If they can be taught, there seems to be no reason to exclude learners from communication intervention until cause/effect relationships emerge.

Object Permanency

Perhaps the best way to characterize object permanency is to say that when a child has this construct, he or she realizes that "out of sight does not mean out of mind." Attaining knowledge of object permanency allows infants to free themselves from the perceived environment to consider events that are not visible or immediately present. Descriptions of the development of object permanency have focused around the child's acquisition of visual pursuit and searching skills.

For some time, interventionists have assumed that object permanency is critical in the acquisition of both language comprehension and language production (Bricker & Bricker, 1974; Kent, 1974). Other investigators such as Bloom (1970) noted that children did not appear to talk about things other than those immediately present until they were nearing mastery of object permanency. In fact, Bloom (1970) expressed the belief that mastery of object permanency was a critical factor in children's acquisition of relational semantic skills (e.g., recurrence and nonexistence).

A number of investigators (Bates et al., 1979; Corrigan, 1976; Ingram, 1974; Miller et al., 1980) have searched for an empirical link between language acquisition and object permanency. The bulk of these investigations failed to find significant relationships between object permanency and initial language acquisition after chronological age had been partialed out.

The assessment of object permanency among learners with severe handicaps has received a great deal of attention (Illmer, Rynders, Sinclair, & Helfrich, 1981; Kahn, 1978; Karlan, 1980). Illmer et al. (1981) found that a child's motor abilities significantly affected performance in object permanency tasks. Filler (1973) demonstrated with a 26-month-old developmentally delayed child that preferred objects elicited a higher level of object permanence performance. Kahn (1978) attempted to teach object permanency skills to a group of severely handicapped learners. He reported differences between treatment and control groups. He did not, however, control for reinforcer preference. Consequently, it is difficult to say whether object permanency or object preference was stimulated.

Bower (1975) reported that many normal children were reluctant to remove even transparent coverings in a traditional object permanency assessment task, even though they could see the object underneath it. These results could be explained in terms of either simple reinforcement conditions or in terms of social rules. In the case of the former, it is possible that the amount of work required (i.e., moving a covering) wasn't worth performing in order to obtain the reinforcer that was available. It is also possible that many children come to understand that when an adult covers an object, it means that the object is off limits.

At present, the relationship between object permanency and language acquisition has not been satisfactorily resolved. How successful object permanency can be stimulated is another issue that remains unclear. It seems reasonably obvious that reinforcer preferences and motor skills (particularly reaching) can influence measures of object permanency. Although less clear, it appears that what the lay person refers to as curiosity, inquisitiveness, and the ability to remember are integrally linked to the domain of object permanence. Perhaps, at the level of intervention, it would be more fruitful to address those specific skills rather than a collection of observable measurable skills that are collectively referred to as object permanency.

There seems to be a lack of convincing evidence to demonstrate a causal link between particular cognitive prerequisites and the acquisition of communicative behavior. However, there does seem to be a fairly compelling logic to suggest that cognitive classes of behavior may facilitate the acquisition of communicative behavior. Perhaps the greatest negative reaction to the strong cognitive influence has been when cognitive skills have been treated as prerequisite skills, thereby "pigeon-holing" the learner into a level of intervention that might not have been necessary. A second negative reaction to a strong cognitive influence seems to be based on the lack of attention to the age-appropriateness of the intervention activity and/or the integration of the activity into the context of lifelong skills to be acquired.

Frequently, interventionists appear to overrely upon "cognitive instructional objectives" that are similar, if not identical, to items on assessment scales such as the Ordinal Scales of Psychological Development (Uzgiris & Hunt, 1975). Tasks on this scale were chosen primarily because they measure the cognitive skills that they purport to assess (they have validity) and because they are easy for an examiner to implement. Easy-to-implement tasks are not always age-appropriate and do not necessarily represent skills that can be used by the learner in his or her natural environment. Consequently, teaching a 15-year-old to uncover a pebble hidden under a washcloth, or to use a stick to rake a toy car closer tend to negatively reflect on the rationale for emphasis of a cognitive domain when, in fact, the negative reaction is to the selection of activity.

THE INITIAL CURRICULUM: WHAT SHOULD BE TAUGHT?

Major Trends in Language/Communication Intervention

Throughout its brief history, language/communication intervention has been examined from a number of theoretical perspectives (Bates et al., 1979; Bricker & Bricker, 1974; Guess, Sailor, & Baer, 1974; Miller & Yoder, 1974; Staats, 1974). During the 1960s and early 1970s, various theories about language development crystallized, and researchers who represented the different approaches began to examine language development as a process. Some examined the manner in which language emerged in normally developing infants (Brown, 1973; Lenneberg, 1967; McNeill, 1970). Others deliberately sought out language-deficient children and applied principles rooted in learning theory to modify a wide range of language-related behaviors. Each research strategy produced important data, but because their approaches and their purposes were so divergent, time was required to sort out and to synthesize the relevant findings. For example, terms such as *protoimperatives, volitional performances, mands, requests,* and even *Type I functions* were used to represent essentially the same thing. Eventually, data began to be "sorted out," and from the process, important theoretical models for language intervention began to emerge (e.g., Bricker et al., 1976; Guess et al., 1974; Kent, 1974; MacDonald & Horstmeier, 1978; Miller & Yoder, 1972; Stremel & Waryas, 1974). Thus, *language intervention* as it has come to be known today, was not considered as a serious subject for scientific investigation until the 1960s and early 1970s.

The early intervention efforts concentrated almost exclusively on designing ways to teach noncommunicating children to speak. With few exceptions (e.g., Carrier, 1976, for one), training curricula concentrated on teaching speech comprehension and expression. The emphasis on speech interventions may have resulted from: 1) the impressive vocal imitation research of the late 1960s (Baer et al., 1967), 2) the work of Lovaas and his associates (1966) in teaching modest speech skills to psychotic children, and 3) impressive accounts in applied settings of successful language intervention with language deviant children being disseminated by applied researchers (e.g., Schumaker & Sherman, 1970). Teachers and others charged with the responsibility of educating children with deviant language had available for the first time a number of language intervention curricula from which to select—all designed to give them some guidance in developing an organized *speech* communication system. Most of the early language intervention programs appeared at approximately the same time and each supported its rationale for program design by referencing data based research. It is not clear just what criteria were used by practitioners to select one program over another, but nevertheless, choices were made, and practitioners began teaching in an orderly step-by-step sequence. The typical training arrangement involved a daily 30-minute session, used a massed-trial procedure, and was conducted in a quiet location free from distractions. Early curriculum models followed a serial or vertical sequence where one class of behaviors was taught to criterion, followed by the next, and so forth. A typical curriculum training sequence included: 1) establishing attending skills; 2) achieving generalized motor imitation; 3) shaping generalized vocal/verbal imitation; 4) receptive labeling, or comprehension of object names; and 5) expressive labeling, or producing object names. Although some children began to learn as a result of "out of context" instruction, little generalization and/or spontaneity was exhibited. Other children failed to learn, particularly those who never learned to imitate vocally. A certain few could not get started because they lacked the necessary physiological "entry" or "prerequisite" skills to produce speech sounds.

In the authors' view, the first major shift away from the early curriculum model mentioned above occurred in the mid to late 1970s, and it only involved a shift away from speech as the focus of expression. Other characteristics of the model remained intact. That is, massed trials were still used to teach the same vertical skill sequences. Special educators began to enroll nonverbal learners (who were not progressing in speech training programs) in interventions that sought to develop a nonverbal mode of communication (Creedon, 1973; Richardson, 1975; Skelly, Schinsky, Smith, & Fust-Slovitz, 1974). This shift represented somewhat of a departure from the traditionally used criteria for selecting candidates for nonspeech modes of communication training. Typically, a child's ability to hear, discriminate vocally, and imitate were the primary indicators of the specific mode of language training to be used. If children were deaf, or hearing impaired, or if their speech-producing mechanisms were inhibited, a signing or communication board mode usually was recommended. Today, however, it is common practice to enroll in nonspeech systems language-deficient children who possess the usual prerequisites for speech acquisition, but for some reason have failed to learn when speech training systems were used. Typically, the speech modality is augmented through the use of signs, or some other symbol form (plastic chips, communication boards, etc.).

In a sense, nonspeech interventions represented a reversal of the manner in which speech-only language programs emerged during the late 1960s and 1970s. The majority of speech training programs were spawned from rigidly controlled laboratory experiments. Simultaneous language training with handicapped children, however, seemed to have evolved, in part, from the special education teacher's frustration with speech-only programs that did not work with some children. Searching for an alternative, the practitioner began to teach language using the multimodal approach. Thus, this possibility may account for the paucity of empirical evidence during the mid 1970s to support the hypothesis that speech could be facilitated by simultaneous language training.

A Shift to Alternative/Augmentative Communication

At least two rationales seemed to have justified the shift away from speech-only interventions. The first was that nonverbal children deserved the right to communicate in whatever mode they were capable of making the most progress. For example, if a severely handicapped child demonstrated sufficient motor control to learn simple motor imitations, or hand gestures, it was seen as possible that he or she might learn to use those gestures symbolically even though the child had not progressed in speech training curricula. Thus, this rationale attempted to identify the most expedient manner in which the nonverbal child could begin to communicate in his or her community (Carrier & Peak, 1975). Implicit in this rationale was the assumption that a manual communication system may be conceptually easier to master than speech.

The second rationale may have embraced the logic of the first, but extended it considerably. Here, an a priori judgment was made that the simultaneous training method may not only teach a manual form of communication, but may also facilitate the acquisition of receptive and productive speech. In the midst of the trend toward simultaneous training, however, Kiernan (1977) cautioned that no single study had yet set out to investigate the use of manual signs with nondeaf students and that. . . "the possibility that the learning of manual communication or other alternative systems leads to acquisition of understanding and use of speech is poorly supported" (p. 17). Today, considerable attention is being given to the issues surrounding the simultaneous approach.

As already mentioned, one of the factors that might have possibly contributed to the trend toward simultaneous communication instruction was the clinicians' frustration with speech programs that did not work with some severely and profoundly handicapped children. This statement by Richardson (1975) might best exemplify this feeling:

> . . . while progress continues in the development of techniques for educating and training severely and profoundly retarded, the area of communication development has remained one of the many difficulties and disappointments. These difficulties in teaching speech as the mode of communication were so apparent in the spring of 1973 at Southbury Training School, that several teachers, an audiologist and a psychologist jointly decided to explore an alternative approach to communication known as sign language. (p. 17)

Creedon (1973) reported the results of a simultaneous language training program used with autistic children that combined speech with manual signs. The initial rationale for using a simultaneous teaching program was based on a need for an expedient form of communication that could be shaped from existing behaviors (hand posturing). Creedon reported that all 20 children who had been exposed to the simultaneous approach began to use signs for their immediate needs and . . . "[s]ome of the children have begun to mouth words while they are signing" (p. 6). Miller and Miller (1973) also used a simultaneous method of language training with autistic children and reported that the pairing of signs with spoken words seemed to have facilitated the transfer of meaning so that the children were able to understand the speech component without the accompanying signs.

In the majority of cases, early reports concerning the improved speech performance (either expression or comprehension) of children enrolled in simultaneous training programs were presented in the form of case studies. One of the few early attempts to experimentally analyze whether sign training facilitated receptive labeling skills in low-functioning children was by Bricker (1972). In this study, Bricker developed a paradigm that involved a sequence of imitative-sign, sign-word, and sign-object training on the development of labels as discriminative stimuli for choice between objects. Bricker suggested that the results demonstrated that the training procedures facilitated the development of word-object discriminations for the experimental group.

In spite of the lack of empirical evidence during the mid 1970s to support the facilitation hypothesis, reports in the literature reinforced the belief that the simultaneous method of language training might enhance the language delayed child's ability to use speech both receptively and expressively. With such support, the trend to use the simultaneous training method with (hearing) language delayed children accelerated and, today, the facilitation hypothesis is still being studied (Carr & Dores, 1981; Remington & Clarke, 1983).

Where and How to Teach Communication Skills

The shift away from massed-trial one-to-one instruction to one that incorporated naturally occurring events and interactions stemmed largely from the lack of generalization and spontaneity so evident as a result of "out of context" instruction. Children who had learned some rudimentary speech and language skills during "therapy" were not using language in a functional manner outside of the therapy situation. Liberty, Haring, and Martin (1981) called for a shift away from what they described as "synthetic teaching and consequating procedures" (p. 5) to "strategies specifically designed to facilitate the acquisition of known skills by severely and profoundly handicapped learners" (p. 5). Holvoet, Guess, Mulligan, and Brown (1980) and Mulligan, Guess, Holvoet, and Brown (1980) offered the Individualized Curriculum Sequencing Mode (described in Chapter 8, this volume) as a strategy for teaching functional skills in a manner that facilitates optimum generalization across materials, persons, settings, and contexts (see Chapter 8). Hart and Rogers-Warren (1978) emphasized that the language learning child must learn to use language as a social communication tool, and any language use, regardless of form, should be reinforced as long as it fulfills a communication function. These observations reflect the prevailing view that speech, signing, graphics, or any combination of language skills needs to be taught within the framework of functional communicative exchanges. The authors share these observations; however, being taught within the framework of functional communication exchanges should not be interpreted to mean that one-to-one instruction is artificial, outdated, or ineffective.

For some, the issue of one-to-one versus group instructional formats has been presented as part of the dichotomy between functional and nonfunctional interventional paradigms. Hart's (1985) analysis of environmentally based or naturalistic strategies showed that these strategies primarily involved one-to-one interactions between adult and child. Hart (1985) indicated that much of the literature on mother-infant interactions emphasizes its one-to-one nature. Clearly, one-to-one instruction is not a strategy unique to remedial approaches. In fact, Hart (1985) has suggested integrating free activity periods into the instructional day so that teachers can move from learner to learner engaging in brief one-to-one teaching episodes. Consequently, those who seek to equate one-to-one instruction with a rigid out-of-context behavioral-remedial intervention strategy should consider the evidence suggesting that the majority of interactions between caregivers and young children occur during one-to-one interactions. One-to-one instruction offers the teacher a better opportunity to focus the learner's attention on criterion-related cues; small group instruction offers an opportunity to introduce naturalistic distractors that the learner must be able to overcome if he or she is to acquire a functional repertoire.

Recently, Newsom (1981) reaffirmed the advantages of one-to-one instruction by suggesting that: 1) group instruction may spread instruction thinly, thus diluting its impact on the individual student; 2) the opportunities for socialization as a result of group instruction may not be sufficient to justify the dilution of teaching that may occur; 3) social behaviors do not emerge spontaneously in many developmentally disabled persons simply through exposure to other persons without (initial) one-to-one instruction; and 4) most social exchanges require some language or cooperative skills, and instruction in these behaviors proceeds best in one-to-one and small group situations.

What Should Be Taught

Interestingly, the shift toward alternatives to speech and the shift toward a more natural training milieu began to evolve more quickly than a shift in training content. This occurred probably because attempting to define the starting point for systematic instruction in functional communication seems considerably more elusive. The present focus in language/communication intervention is on the pragmatic aspects of interactions between a "speaker" and a "listener" (Keogh & Reichle, 1985; McLean & Snyder-McLean, 1978; Shane, 1980). Specifically, curriculum models and strategies are beginning to emphasize the way that early communicative acts *function* for the language-user-to-be. And, curriculum sequences are being integrated in such a way as to ensure that they are *functional* for the learner. Thus, the content of today's language interventions reflects the efforts to teach basic communication functions that are immediately functional for the learner.

Recently, Keogh and Reichle (1985) suggested that teaching a learner to discriminate between the requesting, describing, and rejecting functions of communication may well represent the most prudent "starting point" for instruction with severely handicapped learners. The importance of mastering these discriminations transcends concern about whether a learner's expressive mode should be speech, signing, or some combination. The remainder of this section is devoted to a discussion of these three important functions.

Requesting Function   As was mentioned previously, during the first 9 months of development, normal children come to learn that their cry is a powerful communicative tool that can be used to obtain attention, goods, and services. Initially, the child is not required to use symbols to specify which particular person, good, or service is requested. The child's cry carries the implicit message, "I want something." As time passes and the child matures, his or her listeners become less willing to "carry" the conversation. Consequently, most children's cries are eventually shaped into more socially acceptable requesting forms that culminate with the child's ability to make very explicit requests (e.g., want ball, want mommy). Unfortunately, many learners displaying severe handicaps get no further than a diffuse form used to request. For these children, it should be possible to teach the production of a socially appropriate response that serves a generalized requesting function.

The rationale for the usefulness of a generalized requesting response is fairly straightforward. It allows children to have some control over access to people, objects, and events that are available in their environment. Another advantage of a generic requesting response is the large number of potential opportunities for exercising the request function. For example, assume that a specific word (e.g., "apple") is being taught. Daily routines establish that during many times of the day, apples are not available (thus limiting opportunities to use the word "apple" to request). Even if there were no limits on the availability of apples, the learner might tire quickly of apples and future request opportunities would have to wait until apples were desirable once again. Eventually, of course, children need to learn how to specify which objects, people, or activities that they want. Not only does this speed the process of communication, but it lessens the communicative demands of the learner's listener.

Describing Function   At around the age of 9 or 10 months, most children begin to play games with their parents that appear to represent the onset of communicative describing. For example, the child may be playing intently with a toy car. Without notice, he or she may pick up the car and vocalize loudly to recruit his or her parent's attention. As soon as the parent is looking, the child moves his or her hand containing the object toward the parent. The child is showing the object. Skinner (1957) would have described this event using the term "tact." A tact occurs when the child's action is intended to make contact with the outside world for interaction's sake. That is, in this example, the child was making no requests other than for the attention of another person to convey information. Other investigators have reported this describing and/or commenting function of communication (Bates et al., 1979; Dore, 1974; Halliday, 1975).

Skinner (1957) pointed out that children are taught to tact when some source of generalized reinforcement is appropriately related to the child's behavior. For example, adults comment to other adults, in a large part, because they enjoy the company of others. Like most aspects of communicative behavior, commenting or describing can occur: 1) in response to a question posed by another (e.g., "What is this?" as an object is shown, or "What are you doing?" while watching a child jump up and down), or 2) in response to some stimulus that is not directly related to the needs or state of another person (e.g., pointing to the sky in the presence of another and saying "Look at that airplane!"). This latter "self-initiated" comment and/or description seems to require that the speaker enjoy the comradery of interacting with others. If he or she does not, there appears to be no reinforcer operating, unless of course he or she likes to hear himself or herself talk. If that's the case, the comment would not necessarily be directed to another person.

Severely handicapped children can be taught to describe (Bricker & Bricker, 1974; Guess, Sailor, & Baer, 1974; Kent, 1974). Usually, intervention programs have taught learners that providing requested information results not only in social appreciation from the requester, but some other (often tangible) reinforcer as well. Unfortunately, the distinction between situations in which one requests and those in which commenting is appropriate is often confused. McLean and Synder-McLean (1978) suggested that interventionists often fail to consider the pragmatic implications of their programming. For example, a teacher may present a known reinforcer paired with the question "What's this?" When the learner responds correctly, the teacher gives him or her the reinforcer. In this instance, the teacher was requesting information. The consequence, however, more appropriately fits the request function for an object. The reciprocal pragmatic mismatch occurs when the teacher holds up an object of neutral appeal (e.g., a towel) and asks "What do you want?" When the learner says "towel," the teacher gives the learner a piece of candy. In this instance, the discriminative stimulus is consistent with a request while the consequence is consistent with providing information.

In the context of the early language acquisition, it is easy to understand how the communicative functions of requesting and commenting may be confused. Bloom (1970) observed that her child's production of the two-word utterance "Mommy sock" could mean a variety of different things depending upon the situation in which the utterance was produced. For example, "Mommy sock" produced while the mother put a sock on the child's foot represented an *agent* + *object* construction. However, the same utterance produced while the child picked up the mother's sock could be encoding *possesser* + *possession*. The ability of Bloom's child to use the same two-word construction appropriately in a variety of contexts required a general understanding of the events that set the occasion for a particular response to occur and the specific consequences produced as a result of that response.

For Bloom (1970), the importance of describing context for two-word utterances is equally, if not more critical, than the child's development of a single-word repertoire. For example, if an 11- or 12-year-old language delayed child points to a glass of milk and says ''milk,'' does he or she want it or is he or she commenting that ''there's a glass of milk over there''? It is the authors' view that learning to use the same word to encode two distinctly different classes of communicative intent may place an inordinately difficult and unnecessary burden upon the severely handicapped child's ability to process such subtleties.

For severely handicapped children, learning to match objects to one another, and, subsequently, to symbols, represents describing (tacting). For example, when shown a comb and asked ''What's this?,'' the learner may match it to another comb and subsequently to a line drawing representing a comb. The reinforcement for completing this activity is not the ''comb.'' The comb could be the reinforcer only if the child had requested it. Since, instead, he or she simply provided information (a tact), the reinforcement must be something extrinsic to a comb. There is a small body of literature (Litt & Schreibman, 1981; Rogers & Siegel, 1984) that suggests that object labels are taught more easily when the consequence exactly matches the object labeled. For example, if the child labels a cookie, the receipt of a cookie is the consequence. There are, however, two problems that the authors find in implementing this training strategy.

First, if the consequence for labeling an object is receipt of the object, has the learner been taught to describe, or, has he or she been taught to request? The consequence (reinforcement) is external to the object. It appears that strategies such as the one described may be teaching the learner the rule: ''label something if you'd like to have it.'' Since the learner would have had no experience labeling undesired objects, this conclusion seems particularly plausible. Second, use of the preceding procedures places the interventionist at the mercy of the child's likes/dislikes for the selection of all vocabulary to be acquired. Clearly, some vocabulary (e.g., size, quantity) may be important to learn even though they do not represent reinforcers. Finally, instruction may be stymied when the learner satiates on the object being used during training. If the consequence must match the objects, it seems as though training would be postponed until the object was once again desirable to the learner.

Keogh and Reichle (1985) proposed that the discrimination between requesting and describing could be established very early in a severely handicapped learner's communicative repertoire. They proposed simultaneous but separate intervention procedures to teach a generalized requesting response ''want,'' and a set of specific object labels to be used in describing. At the single-symbol level, the learner would be required to use ''want'' to request desired objects, attention, or activities. Alternatively, whenever the learner produced the name of an object or activity, the teacher would assume that the learner was simply describing some aspect of his or her environment. At the two-symbol level, "want + object label" is treated as a request, while the production of an object label would be treated as a description/comment.

Reichle and Brown (1983) taught a 23-year-old severely retarded individual to request and describe using the paradigm mentioned above. During requesting intervention, a training opportunity could be implemented anytime that the learner was near or interested in a particular reinforcer. That means that trials implemented spontaneously are more apt to occur than if requests must be tied to a specific referent such as an "apple." Request training is not as subject to satiation. For example, if "apple" is the object that the learner is taught to request, trials must cease once the learner's stomach is full. By requiring that all requests begin with the word "want," much of the communicative demand is removed from both the speaker and the listener. The listener learns that a learner's utterance does not contain the symbol "want" if it is a comment/description. Table 1 presents an example of how instruction might be designed to teach a learner to use a symbol to request. In this example, the request function is represented by the manual sign for "want." It could just as easily be a visual symbol such as the Blissymbol for "want" affixed to a communication word or a vocal approximation.

As the learner becomes proficient at signing "want," he or she may then be taught to point to a particular object immediately following his or her "want" sign. Thus, the sign sequence (*want* + [*point to "milk"*]) may be interpreted as a request for a glass of milk. Alternatively, a point directly to the milk implies a describing function to which an attending listener might respond by signing and/or saying, "Yes, that's milk!" As the learner develops some proficiency at discriminatively labeling (describing) people, objects, or activities, he or she may be taught to request by combining signs (e.g., want + milk), thus allowing him or her to request things that are not immediately within view while still retaining the fundamental distinction between a request and a comment.

Rejection Function Evidence of rejection is observed early in the normal child's development. For example, Gesell and Ilg (1937) reported that infants between 0 and 4 weeks of age are capable of withdrawing their head from a breast or bottle when full. Between 4 and 10 weeks, the same investigators reported that when attempts were made to reinsert a nipple in the baby's mouth, the lips closed tightly or the tongue actively pushed the nipple out of the mouth. If the nipple continued to be offered, the child tended to purse his or her lips and cry. By 24 weeks, the same child often refused by arching his or her back and moving his or her head to one side and then the other, or pushed the nipple away with his or her hand.

The emergence of rejecting seems to appear at approximately the same

Table 1. Strategy for teaching "want" sign

GOAL: Assuming that the environment contains things that are worth obtaining, it is possible to teach the learner to produce the sign for "want" to obtain desired objects.

LEARNER BEHAVIOR: The learner will produce the sign for "want" within 10 seconds of the question "What do you want?".

CRITERION: Twenty-four correct responses during 30 trials.

CONDITIONS: *Position of learner*—The learner and teacher should be sitting facing each other.
Materials to use—The motor model "Want."
(Traditional "want" sign: draw in toward chest.)
Locate a cafeteria-type tray and place several objects on it. Objects should represent food (drinks and edibles), toys, and any other objects judged to be reinforcing to the learner. Have a reserve of consumables nearby.

HOW TO USE MATERIALS: a) *Physical prompt*—Gain the learner's attention; place a tray of known reinforcers out of the learner's reach but clearly visible. Instruct the learner to keep his or her hands in lap. Ask "What do you want?".
As the learner reaches for the desired object, physically prompt the learner to extend both hands with arms supinated and then retract to chest (i.e., tap chest). Immediately provide the learner with the tray from which he or she may choose a desired object. Reinforce correct responses (the learner cannot fail unless he or she refuses to accept a physical prompt). Continue to train at this level until the learner is successful during 10 consecutive trials. Advance to b) *Fading physical prompt.*
   b) *Fading physical prompt*—On successive correct responses, gradually reduce the level of physical assistance needed.
      —Criteria for increasing or decreasing the level of physical assistance:
      1. If the learner responds correctly, reduce the level of physical assistance on the next trial.
      2. If the learner produced an incorrect response, *do not reinforce* and try again.
      3. If the learner fails during three consecutive trials, move back to the last successful prompting level.
The learner will have met criterion as soon as he or she produced 24 correct responses during 30 trials in the absence of any physical prompting.

SCORING: Each daily session should consist of 30 trials; however, if the learner seems disinterested, the trials may be spaced throughout the learner's day. A session is concluded as soon as 30 trials have been completed. Score in the following manner:
+ = correct response, − = incorrect response, 0 = no response.

---

time as the rudiments of requesting. The difference between the two may be somewhat unclear. Picture, for example, a very young child who has oriented his or her head and mouth to actually "seek out" a nipple in order to obtain nutriment. Now, assume that during the suckle, the nipple is removed abruptly. The cry that ensues could be interpreted as a request for more nutriment or as a rejection or protest of the removal of a bottle. At this early level, the pragmatic functions between reject and request seem to be closely related. There appears to be little interest among language interventionists in teaching rejection as an early pragmatic communication. Reichle (1984) observed three severely handicapped adolescents over a period of several months. During that time, he observed that each learner had active methods of rejecting persons or objects although they seldom were observed to attempt to obtain any objects or activities that were presented in a traditional reinforcer preference task. These observations have led to the hypothesis that a rejecting communication function may have greater salience than a requesting function for some severely handicapped learners. Particularly, this may be the case for those individuals who have developed elaborate repertoires of socially inappropriate methods of rejecting (e.g., operant vomiting, hitting, kicking, biting).

Organizing opportunities to implement rejection training would seem to be amenable to much the same strategy for teaching a symbolic form of generalized requesting. Initially, a number of instances should be selected that constitute opportunities to demonstrate rejection. Once an opportunity has been offered, the learner's behavior can either be shaped and/or prompted into a topography that more closely approximates the desired sign or symbol selected to represent rejection. To teach a learner to use a generic symbol for rejection, the goal would be to require the learner to anticipate the consequence of "yukky" taste upon seeing, for example, asparagus. Once this anticipation was made, the child could use a reject symbol to avoid the asparagus.

Just as the systematic consequence of attention is important in establishing the basis for intentional requesting, systematic withdrawal of the undesired item should strengthen the use of some appropriate behavior to signal, "I don't want that." This rejection strategy conforms to the principle of negative reinforcement.

CONCLUSION

Keogh and Reichle (1985) discussed a strategy for teaching purposeful communication to learners having severely handicapping conditions. Much of what was presented in that report represented their accumulated efforts to develop a useful curriculum while attending to most of the issues presented here. It is their view that a beginning communicator-to-be must be able to demonstrate the discriminative use of the *describing* and *requesting* functions of communication before more complex language forms can be mastered. Since "function" takes precedent over "form," a notable characteristic of the strategy is that learning the rudiments of requesting and describing need not depend on an ability to produce or even comprehend an array of graphics, complex manual signs, or speech. Thus, speech, signing, or graphics are all acceptable forms for expression, and the issue related to selection of one form over another (at least initially) may be considered a pseudo-issue. A mixed mode of expression is not an unreasonable approach and it has, in fact, been offered as part of another intervention strategy offered by Allaire and Miller (1983). Finally, deficiencies in cognitive areas as recorded by assessments such as the Ordinal Scales of Psychological Development (Uzgiris & Hunt, 1975), while important, need not force the interventionist to attend to these deficiencies as cognitive prerequisites that must be developed as separate units from functional communication. It is reasonable to assume as Rice (1983) has pointed out, that " . . . the communicative behaviors of very young children can be regarded as interactive in nature, instead of being driven solely by a child's cognitive accomplishments . . . " (p. 348).

REFERENCES

Alpert, C. (1980). Procedures for determining the optimal nonspeech mode with the autistic child. In R. Schiefelbusch (Ed.), *Nonspeech language and communication: Analysis and intervention* (pp. 389–420). Baltimore: University Park Press.

Allaire, J., & Miller, J. (1983). Nonspeech communication. In M. Snell (Ed.), *Systematic instruction of the moderately and severely handicapped* (2nd ed.) (pp. 289–313). Columbus: Charles E. Merrill Publishing Co.

Baer, D., Peterson, R., & Sherman, J. (1967). The development of imitation by reinforcing behavioral similarity to a model. *Journal of the Experimental Analysis of Behavior, 10,* 405–417.

Baer, D., Wolf, M., & Risley, T. (1968). Some current dimensions of applied behavior analysis. *Journal of Applied Behavior Analysis, 1,* 91–97.

Bates, E., Benigni, L., Bretheton, I., Camaioni, L., & Volterra, B. (1977). From gesture to first word: On cognitive and social prerequisites. In M. Lewis & L. Rosenblum (Eds.), *Interaction, conversation and the development of language* (pp. 247–308). New York: John Wiley & Sons.

Bates, E., Benigni, L., Bretheton, I., Camaioni, L., & Volterra, V. (1979). *The emergence of symbols: Cognition and communication in infancy.* New York: Academic Press.

Belmore, K., & Brown, L. (1978). A job skill inventory strategy designed for severely handicapped potential workers. In W. Haring & D. Bricker (Eds.), *Teaching the severely handicapped* (Vol. 3, pp. 223–262). Columbus, OH: Special Press.

Bloom, L. (1970). *Language development: Structure and function in emerging grammars.* Cambridge, MA: MIT Press.

Bonvillian, J., & Nelson, K. (1976). Sign language acquisition in a mute autistic boy. *Journal of Speech and Hearing Research, 41,* 339–347.

Bower, T. G. R. (1975). *Development in infancy.* San Francisco: W.H. Freeman & Co. Publishers.

Bower, T., & Wishart, J. (1972). The effects of motor skill on object permanence. *Cognition, 1,* 165–171.

Bricker, D. (1972). Imitation sign training as a facilitator of word-object association with low functioning children. *American Journal of Mental Deficiency, 76,* 509–516.

Bricker, W., & Bricker, D. (1974). An early language training strategy. In R. Schiefelbusch & L. Lloyd (Eds.), *Language perspectives—Acquisition retardation, and intervention* (pp. 431–468). Baltimore: University Park Press.

Bricker, D., Dennison, L., & Bricker, W. (1976). *A language intervention program for developmentally young children* (MCCD Monograph Series, No. 1). Miami: Mailman Center for Child Development, University of Miami.

Brown, L., Branston, M. B., Baumgart, D., Vincent, L., Falvey, M., & Schroeder, J. (1979). Using the characteristics of current and subsequent least restrictive environments as factors in the development of curricular content for severely handicapped students. *AAESPH Review, 4,* 407–424.

Brown, R. (1973). *A first language.* Cambridge, MA: Harvard University Press.

Bruner, J. (1975). The ontogenesis of speech acts. *Journal of Child Language, 2.*

Carr, E., Binkoff, J., Kologinsky, E., & Eddy, M. (1978). Acquisition of sign language by autistic children. I: Expressive labeling. *Journal of Applied Behavior Analysis, 11,* 489–501.

Carr, E. G., & Dores, P. A. (1981). Patterns of language acquisition following simultaneous communication with autistic children. *Analysis and Intervention in Developmental Disabilities, 1,* 347–361.

Carrier, J. (1976). Application of a nonspeech language system with the severely language handicapped. In L. Lloyd (Ed.), *Communication assessment and intervention strategies* (pp. 523–547). Baltimore: University Park Press.

Carrier, J., & Peak, T. (1975). *Nonspeech language imitation program.* Lawrence, KS: H & H Enterprises.

Carter, A. (1973, April). *Development of presyntactic communication system: A case study.* Paper presented at the meeting of the Society for Research in Child Development, Philadelphia, PA.

Chapman, R., & Miller, J. (1980). Analyzing language and communication in the child. In R. Schiefelbusch (Ed.), *Nonspeech language and communication: Analysis and intervention.* Baltimore: University Park Press.

Corrigan, R. (1976, April). *The relationship between object permanence and language development: How much and how strong?* Paper presented at the Stanford Child Language Research Forum, Stanford University, Palo Alto, CA.

Corrigan, R. (1978). Language development as related to the stage VI object permanence development. *Journal of Child Language, 5,* 173–189.

Creedon, M. (1973, April). *Language development in nonverbal autistic children using a simultaneous communication system.* Paper presented at the meeting of the Society for Research in Child Development, Philadelphia, PA.

Cromer, R. (1976). The cognitive hypothesis of language acquisition and its implications for child language deficiency. In D. Morehead & A. Morehead (Eds.), *Normal and deficient child language* (pp. 283–333). Baltimore: University Park Press.

Denton, D. (1972). A rationale for total communication. *American Annals for the Deaf, 51,* 53–61.

Dore, J. (1974). A pragmatic description of early development. *Journal of Psycholinguistic Research, 3,* 343–350.

Ferster, C. B., Culbertson, S., & Perrott-Baren, M. C. (1975). *Behavior principles.* Englewood Cliffs, NJ : Prentice-Hall.

Filler, J. (1973). Sensorimotor assessment performance as a function of task materials. In D. Bricker & W. Bricker (Eds.), *Infant, toddler and preschool research and intervention project report—Year III.* Nashville, TN: George Peabody College for Teachers.

Fulwiler, R., & Fouts, R. (1976). Acquisition of American Sign Language by a noncommunicating autistic child. *Journal of Autism and Childhood Schizophrenia, 6,* 43–51.

Garcia, E., Baer, D., & Firestone, I. (1971). The development of generalized imitation within experimentally determined boundaries. *Journal of Applied Behavior Analysis, 4,* 101–112.

Gesell, A., & Ilg, F. (1937). *Feeding behavior of infants.* Philadelphia: J.B. Lippincott.

Gewirtz, J., & Stingle, K. (1968). Learning of generalized imitation as a basis for identification. *Psychological Review, 75*, 374–397.

Guess, D., Sailor, W., & Baer, D. (1974). To teach language to retarded children. In R. Schiefelbusch & L. Lloyd (Eds.), *Language perspectives—Acquisition, retardation, and intervention* (pp. 529–564). Baltimore: University Park Press.

Gustason, G., Pfetzing, D., & Zawolkow, E. (1972). *Signing exact English*. Roosmoor, CA: Modern Signs Press.

Halle, J., Marshall, A., & Spradlin, J. (1979). Time delay: A technique to increase language use and facilitate generalization in retarded children. *Journal of Applied Behavior Analysis, 12*, 95–103.

Halliday, M. A. K. (1975). *Learning how to mean: Explorations in the development of language*. London: Edward Arnold.

Harris, S. (1976). Teaching language to nonverbal children with emphasis on problems of generalization. *Psychological Bulletin, 82*, 565–580.

Hart, B. (1985). Environmental techniques that may facilitate generalization and acquisition. In S. Warren & A. Warren-Rogers (Eds.), *Functional language intervention*. Baltimore: University Park Press.

Hart, B., & Rogers-Warren, A. (1978). Milieu teaching approaches. In R. Schiefelbusch (Ed.), *Language intervention strategies* (pp. 193–236). Baltimore: University Park Press.

Hewett, F. (1965). Teaching speech to an autistic child through operant conditioning. *American Journal of Orthopsychiatry, 35*, 927–936.

Holvoet, J., Guess, D., Mulligan, M., & Brown, F. (1980). The individualized curriculum sequencing model (II): A teaching strategy for severely handicapped students. *Journal of The Association for the Severely Handicapped, 5*, 337–351.

Hopper, C., & Helmick, R. (1977). Nonverbal communication for the severely handicapped: Some considerations. *AAESPH Review, 2*, 47–52.

Illmer, S., Rynders, J., Sinclair, S., & Helfrich, D. (1981). Assessment of object permanence in severely handicapped students as a function of motor and prompting variables. *Journal of The Association for the Severely Handicapped, 6*, 30–40.

Ingram, D. (1974). The relationship between comprehension and production. In R. Schiefelbusch & L. Lloyd (Eds.), *Language perspectives—Acquisition, retardation, and intervention* (pp. 313–334). Baltimore: University Park Press.

Iverson, G. S., Williams, W., Schutz, R., & Fox, T. (1983). Burlington's making special friends project: Strategies for implementing model components: Vol. IV. *Center for Developmental Disabilities Monograph Series, 3(6)*, University of Vermont.

Kahn, J. (1978). Acceleration of object permanence with severely and profoundly retarded children. *AAESPH Review, 80*, 15–22.

Karlan, G. (1980). The effects of preference for objects and repeated measures upon the assessed level of object permanence and means/end ability in severely handicapped students. *Journal of The Association for the Severely Handicapped, 5*, 174–193.

Karlan, G. (1984). *Application of criteria points in the use of decision rules used in the selection of augmentative systems*. Unpublished manuscript, Purdue University, West Lafayette, IN.

Karlan, G., & Lloyd, L. (1983, May). *Examination of recall comprehension by moderately retarded individuals responding to oral and manual cues*. Paper presented at the 107th annual meeting of the American Association on Mental Deficiency, Dallas, TX.

Kent, L. (1974). *Language acquisition program for the retarded or multiply impaired*.

Champaign, IL: Champaign Research Press.

Keogh, W., & Reichle, J. (1985). Communication intervention for the "difficult to teach" severely handicapped. In S. Warren & A. Rogers-Warren (Eds.), *Teaching functional language* (pp. 158–194). Baltimore: University Park Press.

Kiernan, C. (1977). Alternatives to speech. A review of research on manual and other alternative forms of communication in the mentally handicapped. *British Journal of Mental Subnormality, 23,* 6–28.

Lenneberg, E. (1967). *Biological foundations of language.* New York: John Wiley & Sons.

Liberty, K., Haring, N., & Martin, M. (1981). Teaching new skills to the severely handicapped. *Journal of the Association for the Severely Handicapped, 6,* 5–13.

Litt, M., & Schreibman, L. (1981). Stimulus specific reinforcement in the acquisition of receptive labels by autistic children. *Analysis and Intervention in Developmental Disabilities, 1,* 171–186.

Lovaas, O., Berberich, J., Perloff, B., & Schaeffer, B. (1966). Acquisition of imitative speech by schizophrenic children. *Science, 151,* 705–707.

MacDonald, J., & Blott, J. (1974). Environmental language intervention: A rationale for diagnostic and training strategy through rules, context and generalization. *Journal of Speech and Hearing Disorders, 39,* 395–415.

MacDonald, J., & Horstmeier, D. (1978). *Environmental language intervention program.* Columbus, OH: Charles E. Merrill Publishing Co.

McCuller, W., & Salzberg, C. (1982). The functional analysis of imitation. In N. Ellis (Ed.), *International review of research in mental retardation* (Vol. II, pp. 285–320). New York: Academic Press.

McLean, J., & Snyder-McLean, L. (1978). *A transactional approach to early language training.* Columbus, OH: Charles E. Merrill Publishing Co.

McNeill, D. (1970). *The acquisition of language. The study of developmental psycholinguistics.* New York: Harper & Row.

Metz, J. R. (1965). Conditioning generalized imitation in autistic children. *Journal of Experimental Child Psychology, 2,* 389–399.

Miller, A., & Miller, E. (1973). Cognitive-developmental training with elevated boards and sign language. *Journal of Autism and Childhood Schizophrenia, 3,* 65–85.

Miller, J., Chapman, R., Branston, M., & Reichle, J. (1980). Communicative assessment in twelve (12) to twenty-four (24) months: A reliable method. *Journal of Speech and Hearing Research, 32,* 284–311.

Miller, J., & Yoder, D. (1972). A syntax teaching program. In J. McLean, D. Yoder, & R. Schiefelbusch (Eds.), *Language intervention with the retarded: Developing strategies* (pp. 85–110). Baltimore: University Park Press.

Miller, J., & Yoder, D. (1974). An ontogenetic language teaching strategy for retarded children. In R. Schiefelbusch & L. Lloyd (Eds.), *Language perspectives— Acquisition, retardation, and intervention* (pp. 505–528). Baltimore: University Park Press.

Moores, D. (1974). Nonvocal systems of verbal behavior. In R. Schiefelbusch & L. Lloyd (Eds.), *Language perspectives—Acquisition, retardation, and intervention* (pp. 93–100). Baltimore: University Park Press.

Mulligan, M., Guess, D., Holvoet, J., & Brown, F. (1980). The individualized curriculum sequencing model (I): Implications from research on massed distributed and spaced trial learning. *Journal of The Association for the Severely Handicapped, 5,* 325–336.

Newsom, R. (1981). School. In I. O. Lovaas (Ed.), *Teaching developmentally disabled children: The me book* (pp. 223–234). Baltimore: University Park Press.

Piaget, J. (1929). *The child's conception of the world.* New York: Harcourt Brace Jovanovich.

Reichle, J. (1984). *Working paper V.* Unpublished manuscript, University of Minnesota, Minneapolis.

Reichle, J., & Brown, L. (1983). *Teaching an autistic adolescent to use a direct select multipaged communication aid.* Unpublished manuscript, University of Minnesota, Minneapolis.

Reichle, J., Rogers, N., & Barrett, C. (1984). Establishing pragmatic discrimination among the communicative functions of requesting, rejecting and commenting in an adolescent. *Journal of The Association for Persons with Severe Handicaps, 9,* 31–36.

Reichle, J., & Ward, M. (in press). Teaching discriminative use of Signed English and encoding graphic modality to an autistic adolescent. *Language Speech and Hearing Services in Schools.*

Remington, B., & Clarke, S. (1983). The acquisition of expressive signing by autistic children: An evaluation of the relative effects of simultaneous communication and sign language training. *Journal of Applied Behavior Analysis, 16,* 315–328.

Rice, M. (1983). Contemporary accounts of the cognition/language relationship: Implications for speech-language clinicians. *Journal of Speech and Hearing Disorders, 48,* 347–359.

Richardson, T. (1975). Sign language for the SMR and PMR. *Mental Retardation, 13,* 17.

Rogers, N., & Siegel, G. (1984). *Reinforcement strategies with a language disordered child.* Unpublished manuscript, University of Minnesota, Minneapolis.

Routh, D. (1969). Conditioning vocal responses differentiation in infants. *Developmental Psychology, 1,* 219–226.

Sailor, W., Guess, D., Goetz, L., Schuler, A., Utley, B., & Baldwin, M. (1980). Language and severely handicapped persons: Deciding what to teach to whom. In W. Sailor, B. Wilcox, & L. Brown (Eds.), *Methods of instruction for severely handicapped students* (pp. 71–105). Baltimore: Paul H. Brookes Publishing Co.

Schaeffer, B. (1980). Spontaneous language through signed speech. In R. Schiefelbusch (Ed.), *Nonspeech language and communication: Analysis and intervention* (pp. 421–446). Baltimore: University Park Press.

Schaeffer, B., Kollinzas, G., Musil, A., & McDowell, P. (1978). Spontaneous verbal language for autistic children through signed speech. *Sign Language Studies, 21,* 317–352.

Scheuerman, N., Baumgart, D., Simpsa, K., & Brown, T. (1976). Toward the development of a curriculum for teaching nonverbal communication skills to severely handicapped students: Teaching basic tracking scanning and selection skills. In N. Scheuerman, L. Brown, & T. Crowner (Eds.), *Toward an integrated therapy model for teaching motor, tracking, and scanning skills to severely handicapped students* (Vol. 6, Part 3, pp. 71–248). Madison, WI: Madison Metropolitan School District.

Schiefelbusch, R., & Hollis, J. (1979). *Language intervention from ape to child.* Baltimore: University Park Press.

Schumaker, J., & Sherman, J. (1970). Training generative verb usage by imitation and reinforcement procedures. *Journal of Applied Behavior Analysis, 3,* 273–287.

Shane, H. (1980). Approaches to assessing the communication of non-oral persons. In R. Schiefelbusch (Ed.), *Nonspeech language and communication: Analysis and intervention* (pp. 197–224). Baltimore: University Park Press.

Shane, H., & Bashir, A. (1980). Election criteria for the adoption of an augmentative communication system: Preliminary considerations. *Journal of Speech and Hearing Disorders, 45,* 408–414.

Sherman, J. (1971). Imitation and language development. In H. W. Reese (Ed.), *Advances in child development and behavior* (Vol. 6, pp. 239–272). New York: Academic Press.

Skelly, M., Schinsky, L., Smith, R., & Fust-Slovitz, R. (1974). American Indian Sign (Amerind) as a facilitator of verbalization for the oral verbal apraxic. *Journal of Speech and Hearing Disorders, 39,* 445–456.

Skinner, B. (1953). *Science and human behavior.* New York: Macmillan Publishing CO.

Skinner, B. F. (1957). *Verbal behavior.* New York: Appleton-Century-Crofts.

Snell, M. E. (1983). *Systematic instruction of the moderately and severely handicapped.* Columbus, OH: Charles E. Merrill Publishing Co.

Staats, A. (1974). Behaviorism and cognitive theory in the study of language: A neopsycholinguistics. In R. Schiefelbusch & L. Lloyd (Eds.), *Language perspectives—Acquisition, retardation, and intervention* (pp. 615–646). Baltimore: University Park Press.

Stremel, K., & Waryas, C. (1974). A behavioral-psycholinguistic approach to language training. In L. McReynolds (Ed.), Developing systematic procedures for training children's language. *ASHA Monographs, 18.*

Stremel-Campbell, K., Cantrell, P., & Halle, J. (1977). Manual signing as a speech initiator for the nonverbal severely handicapped student. In E. Sontag, J. Smith, & N. Certo (Eds.), *Educational programming for the severely and profoundly handicapped* (pp. 335–347). Reston, VA: CEC Division of MR.

Terrace, H. (1963). Discriminative learning with and without errors. *Journal of Experimental Analysis of Behavior, 6,* 1–27.

Uzgiris, I., & Hunt, J. McV. (1975). *Assessment in infancy: Ordinal Scales of Psychological Development.* Urbana: University of Illinois Press.

Vanderheiden, G., & Grilley, K. (1976). *Non-vocal communication techniques and aids for the severely physically handicapped.* Baltimore: University Park Press.

Warren, S., & Rogers-Warren, A., (1985). Teaching functional language: An introduction. In S. Warren & A. Rogers-Warren (Eds.), *Teaching functional language.* Baltimore: University Park Press.

Wilcox, B., & Bellamy, G. T. (1982). *Design of high school programs for severely handicapped students.* Baltimore: Paul H. Brookes Publishing Co.

Wolf, M., Risley, T., & Mees, H. (1964). Application of operant conditioning procedures to the behavior problems of an autistic child. *Behavior Research and Therapy, 1,* 305–312.

Chapter 8

Skill Cluster Instruction and the Individualized Curriculum Sequencing Model

Doug Guess and Edwin Helmstetter

Instructional procedures for educating and training learners with severely handicapping conditions have shown a gradual but progressive evolvement over the years. This evolvement has occurred, in part, because of the necessity to improve upon the efficacy of instructional programs, and also because of changing philosophical and pedagogical assumptions about which skills should be taught and how the instruction should take place. At the outset, educators were in general agreement that instructional procedures for learners with severe handicaps should not reflect a mere extension downward of procedures and curricula designed for learners who were functioning at higher developmental and cognitive levels. In retrospect, there appeared a consensus that learners with severe handicaps required a more systematic and precise instructional model in order to capitalize on the teaching of skills in small steps.

The emergence of behavioral psychology, and the instructional procedures derived from it, offered the type of exacting methodology that seemed well suited to the educational needs of learners with severe handicaps. Within that burgeoning technology existed procedures for breaking learning tasks into small and obtainable stages, available techniques to shape behavior toward the desired goals, and a wealth of related instructional operations that reflected an environmental empiricism coupled with a common reductionistic orientation.

The preparation of this chapter was supported in part by a contract through the Department of Education (No. 300 81 0357), ''A Curriculum Development Model for Deaf-Blind Youth.''

Consistent with this early educational approach was the temptation to use the animal laboratory as a model for the instructional environment. Some early educational programs for learners with severe handicaps were found to use relay racks with small candy dispensers where students were programmed to learn a variety of visual discrimination tasks. Instruction in classrooms followed a similar format that emphasized one-to-one instruction, massed-training trials, and programmed consequences often consisting of small bits of candy, sips of juice, or other salient foods. The settings for instruction were often kept purposely barren in order to remove "distracting stimuli." The educational goals for learners in classrooms were sometimes extrapolated from laboratory research studies (e.g., imitation training that stressed nonfunctional body movements, or even various academic tasks such as matching colors, placing rings on pegs). More functional skills such as communication, self-help, or vocational tasks were performed out of context, in ways that expedited the application of the instructional procedures, and almost always required the use of artificial reinforcers to both establish and maintain learning.

In the early classrooms for learners with severe handicaps, content areas were often sharply delineated. Skill training in areas such as communication, self-help, mobility, and so on were taught separately, in time, and often in specific locations that were occasionally perceived as therapy rooms.

The overall state of the art during the early years of providing education to learners with severe handicaps might best be described as a direct derivation from the experimental laboratory, where both classrooms and ongoing research reflected valiant attempts to provide empirical credibility to this new area of special education. Likely, this early beginning in the education of learners with severe handicaps was necessary. It provided a baseline from which the field could later measure its progress, and it did, indeed, precipitate the development and analysis of many instructional procedures and techniques that have continued to be refined.

AN ECOLOGICAL APPROACH

The next evolution in the education of learners with severe handicaps was two-pronged. First, in the mid 1970s, there emerged the emphasis on identifying and teaching skills that were more functional for the learner with severe handicaps. The "criterion of ultimate functioning" espoused by Brown, Nietupski, and Hamre-Nietupski (1976) provided the basis, both theoretical and practical, for this changing instructional orientation. The criterion of ultimate functioning stressed the need to provide instruction in skills that would allow learners with severe handicaps to function more productively and independently in future, integrated adult communities. Implicit in the criterion of ultimate functioning was the need to teach functional skills that were also chronologically age appropriate (Brown et al., 1978). This recommendation was made, in large part, in reaction to those instructional programs and curricula that followed a strict developmental model, where classroom materials and programs were selected on the basis of the learner's mental age, rather than chronological age (Guess & Noonan, 1982).

The identification of functional, age-appropriate skills for learners with severe handicaps was systematized through the use of ecological inventories. Procedures for using the inventories required persons to survey community living environments and identify discrete skills needed by learners with severe handicaps to function effectively in them (Brown et al., 1979). Skills, once identified, were task analyzed into smaller steps that provided the basis for instructional programs. The ecological inventory procedure has been gradually modified and refined over the years, with more recent descriptions of how to match instructional goals and objectives across environmental domains (Sailor & Guess, 1983), and with an even greater emphasis placed on providing instruction in nonschool settings (Brown et al., 1983).

Both the need to teach functional, age-appropriate skills and the use of naturally occurring environments as the location of instruction have provided a significant departure from the early years of educating learners with severe handicaps, when instructional objectives were often difficult to justify, and where the location of instruction was often confined to isolated rooms that were purposely devoid of "distracting" stimuli.

TEACHING SKILL CLUSTERS

A second, more recent evolution in the education of students with severe handicaps has centered on the instructional procedures, per se, and how content areas are organized for purposes of instruction. During the early years of providing education to learners with severe handicaps, the reductionistic orientation of behaviorism persuaded educators to follow a vertical progression of skill development within separately programmed content areas. In this orientation, education and training concentrated on the systematic expansion of skills within identified content domains; for example, self-help training was often conducted separate from communication training, which was conducted separate from leisure skill training, and so forth. This type of isolated skill training was performed, in part, to better adjust to small, task analyzed steps within a particular skill area, and to more easily accommodate a massed-trial training regime that allowed for the differential shaping (and reinforcement) of responses contained in these steps. This type of splinter skill instruction predominated the pedagogy for learners with severe handicaps for many years and, indeed, is still prevalent today in many classroom settings.

In the late 1970s, Guess et al. (1978) presented a curriculum sequencing model for learners with severe handicaps that pointed to the need to provide concurrent training across content areas in a horizontal, rather than vertical, instructional format. This model was based on the assumption that skill areas do not occur in isolation, one from the other, in naturally occurring environments. Interacting effectively in the environment requires one to use a number of skills concurrently, or in rapid succession. Teaching a learner, for example, to order food at a cafeteria requires a varied number of communication skills, gross motor responses, visual discriminations, and so forth. It followed, then, that instructional programs should, for maximum generalization, teach concurrent responses across content domains as "skill clusters."

Subsequent development of the skill cluster model pointed also to the necessity for altering, significantly, the manner in which trials were presented for training. Massed-training trials were appropriate for teaching isolated skills where the same stimulus could be presented repeatedly, and where the instructor could shape the desired response. Massed training–trial formats essentially required a program where two or more repeated trials occurred so closely together that no other behavior could be expected to occur between them. This format, however, was not consistent with the skill cluster model that emphasized the concurrent training of two or more content areas, and where the responses themselves would be expected to change from trial to trial.

The skill cluster model for concurrent training across content areas essentially dictated a distributed-trial format. In distributed-trial training, trials from another program (or content area) occur between two repeated trials from the same program. For example, in a distributed-trial program, a young child might be required to: 1) visually orient to a salient toy, 2) reach for and grasp the toy, 3) expressively describe what the toy does, and 4) demonstrate how it works. All of these responses would be included as part of an instructional sequence (or response cluster). By way of contrast, a traditional massed trial–training approach might present 10–20 trials, each, for looking at the toy, reaching for it, labeling the action, and demonstrating its function. In this example, the separate responses are trained out of context, and thus diminish the likelihood that they would be used appropriately in the natural environment.

Later development and refinement of the skill cluster approach has been described in the literature as the Individualized Curriculum Sequencing (ICS) model (Holvoet, Guess, Mulligan, & Brown, 1980; Sailor & Guess, 1983). Adaptations of the model have been described for group instruction (Brown, Holvoet, Guess, & Mulligan, 1980) as well as various age and population groupings that include preschool children (Guess, Jones, & Lyon, 1981), adolescent students (Holvoet, Mulligan, Schussler, Lacy, & Guess, 1984), and students who are deaf/blind (Helmstetter, Murphy-Herd, Guess, & Roberts, 1984). Additionally, Mulligan and Guess (1984) presented a format for emphasizing communication training as part of the ICS model.

EMPIRICAL SUPPORT FOR THE ICS MODEL

The ICS model includes both distributed-trial presentations and concurrent task sequencing (i.e., the teaching of two or more content domains within a training session). A review of literature pertaining to massed- versus distributed-trial training was conducted by Mulligan, Guess, Holvoet, and Brown (1980). This review included studies involving both nonhandicapped populations and learners who were mentally retarded. The review showed consistent findings favoring distributed-trial over massed-trial training for motor and, especially, cognitive skills.

Studies investigating concurrent task sequencing procedures (Panyan & Hall, 1978; Schroeder & Baer, 1972) have shown no differences in rate of acquisition when compared to serial-task sequencing (i.e., teaching one skill to criterion, then a second skill). These investigations did find, however, that generalization to nontrained skills within tasks was greater in the concurrent task sequencing procedures. A more recent study by Dunlap (1984), however, demonstrated that children with autism performed better on varied tasks when compared to conditions where only one task was presented per session. It was also found that optimal performance occurred in sessions where varied tasks were intermixed with tasks that had previously been learned by the children. Additional findings indicated that learner affect during training was most positive in sessions where varied tasks were mixed with previously learned tasks; positive affect was lowest in the constant task sessions.

A study by Dunlap and Koegel (1980) demonstrated that autistic children showed higher levels of not responding to cognitive tasks that were taught in a massed-trial presentation. Distributed-trial presentations produced a decrease in nonresponding. The findings of Dunlap and Koegel were substantiated by Mulligan, Lacy, and Guess (1982) who similarly found higher response rates among learners with severe handicaps who were taught in a distributed- (versus massed-) trial format.

Mild effects in favor of distributed-trial sequencing with learners who have severe handicaps have also been shown for spontaneous initiations of a response (Lacy, 1982), and for generalization of a vocational task across settings (Brewer, 1982).

On a more applied level, Guess et al. (1981) described results of using the ICS model with 16 preschoolers with severely/multiply handicaping conditions. Data over a 3-year period reflect substantial skill acquisition, even though a direct comparison was not made to other teaching strategies. Another investigation has reported considerable success using a functional, skill cluster approach in teaching students identified as autistic (Neel, Lewis-Smith, Hanashiro, McCarty, & Billingsley, no date).

In summary, the studies reported have shown varying, but consistent, findings that support the efficacy of using a curriculum strategy that is based upon the distributed-trial presentation and concurrent task sequencing assumptions of the ICS model. It is likely that subsequent investigation will show even stronger results as the strategy is further refined. A later section of this chapter addresses some of the programmatic issues involving the ICS model, including areas where future research seems to be warranted. The reader is referred also to Sailor and Guess (1983) for a more indepth rationale for the ICS model, and the use of clusters to teach skills to learners with severe handicaps.

DEVELOPING INDIVIDUALIZED CURRICULUM SEQUENCES

An Individualized Curriculum Sequence (ICS) is prepared once the skills to be taught are identified for the learner. The ICS is appropriate regardless of how the skills are derived, whether from developmentally based or task analyzed curricula, from parent or staff interviews, or from environmental inventories. It is most powerful, in any case, if skills are stated only in terms of the learner's response, without specification of materials or activities for teaching each skill. For example, the skill of "stacks three blocks" can be restated as "stacks three objects," "reaches 6 inches for a ball" becomes "reaches 6 inches," and "visually tracks cassette tape" becomes "visually tracks."

It is unlikely that such a restatement is possible for all skills targeted for a learner. It might be inappropriate, for example, to restate skills such as "pulls pants up," or "vocalizes the 'mm' sound." The point to remember is that the skill should, whenever possible, be stated in general terms.

The following pages delineate the step-by-step procedures for developing individualized curriculum sequences (complete the Activities/Skills Matrix, write the ICS, and develop instructional programs). The procedures for each step can be implemented in the classroom gradually, with one learner at a time or for part of the school day; or implemented on a larger scale, for the whole class for the entire school day.

Complete the Activities/Skills Matrix

The first step in developing an ICS involves completing the Activities/Skills Matrix (see Figure 1). The matrix, when completed, contains lists of materials and events with which to teach each skill during various daily activities. It is also useful for checking for generalization training, that is, whether skills are taught during several daily activities, with multiple materials and instructors, and in more than one environment.

Activities   To begin completing the matrix, first fill out the activities portion along its left side. These activities fall primarily into two categories: functional daily activities and school activities. Functional daily activities comprise the largest category. They consist of those natural routines that occur daily in the lives of most persons. Examples include dressing, grooming, eating, travel to/from work or school, arrival at work or school, work, toileting, and leisure/recreation. School activities are daily events necessary to the physical, social, and educational well-being of the learner. They are usually limited to daily health checks, physical education, recess, and instructional time.

Traditional classroom activities such as language sessions, fine motor group, and perceptual development time are inappropriate as activities to be listed on the matrix. These describe what is taught rather than activities that comprise a daily routine.

List activities in the matrix in the order in which they occur during the day, with the first daily activity at the top of the page. The schedule of activities may be based upon that of the learner's present or future environments for working, residing, or using community resources. If the activities cannot be based upon the schedule in present or future environments, at least naturalize the order of activities by scheduling cleanup activities after messy ones, cleanliness following toileting, and break times following work periods. Finally, toilet training schedules usually take precedence over all other activities and should, therefore, be placed strategically in the matrix before adding any other activity.

Locations The locations called for on the left side of the matrix (in parentheses under the activity) refer to the area of the environment in which the activity occurs. The location should be natural to the activity. In other words, receptive labeling of toothpaste should be taught at the bathroom sink, not at a desk. Similarly, learning to put on a shirt should be taught in the bedroom of the home or living unit, or in the shower or dressing room at the the gym or pool, not in the middle of the classroom.

Time of Activity The time referred to in the Activity/Skills Matrix is the time that an activity begins. Durations of activities should approximate what is expected in present or future environments. If the typical work schedule in potential employment settings calls, for example, for 2 hours of work followed by a 15-minute break, schedule the learner's day similarly, or at least aim at developing such a work duration and schedule. The allocation of time also provides a guide for writing skill clusters of the appropriate length.

Instructor Indicate the instructor(s) for each activity. The primary purpose for this is to ensure, once the Activities/Skills Matrix is completed, that skills are taught by more than one person.

Skills Place along the top of the matrix a brief descriptor of each skill to be taught to the learner, with one descriptor for each column. These skills will, after the ICS is written, be stated as educational objectives on the learner's individualized education program (IEP). Writing the ICS, in other words, provides additional information that is necessary in order to write comprehensive educational objectives. The ICS will indicate, for example, the materials to be used in teaching each skill, the locations of instruction, and the antecedents in the skill clusters that might serve as cues for performance of each skill.

Skills to be taught

Activity (Location)	Time / Instructor	Head up	Indicate desire for more	Segment at waist	Toilet regulation	Reach across midline	Localize to sound	Track horizontally	Drink from cup	Hands out of mouth
Arrival (Bus)	Time 8:15 Instructor Kay					To shake hands, hang coat	To name by teacher peer	Teacher, peer		X
Toileting (Bathroom)	Time 8:30 Instructor Kay	On toilet		During rolling, in sidesit	X	To sidesit	To name			X
Grooming (Bathroom)	Time 9:00 Instructor Kay	In standing table		To hang towel		For faucet, soap, towel	To name	Soap, towel		X
Group 1 (Table)	Time 9:15 Instructor Sally	In chair, in sidesit	Caps for syringe, paper for collate	During rolling, in sidesit	Pants check	For cap, paper, cereal	To name	Cap, paper, cereal		X
Group 2 (Mat)	Time 9:45 Instructor Sally	Prone on mat	Music, story	During rolling	Pants check	For sidesit, tape, book	To name, music	Cassette tape, book		X
Snack (Dining area)	Time 10:15 Instructor Nena	In chair, in sidesit	Juice, cookie	During rolling, in sidesit	Pants check	Juice, cookie, napkin, sidesit	To name	Juice, cookie	Juice for for snack	X
Toileting (Bathroom)	Time 10:30 Instructor Nena				(See 8:30 Toileting)					
Grooming (Bathroom)	Time 11:00 Instructor Nena				(See 9:00 Grooming)					

228

	Prone on mat	Caps for syringe, paper for collate	During rolling	Pants check	For cap, paper, cereal	To name	Cap, paper, cereal	Milk at lunch	
Group 3 (Mat) Time 11:15 Instructor Nena		Caps for syringe, paper for collate	During rolling	Pants check	For cap, paper, cereal	To name	Cap, paper, cereal		X
Lunch (Lunchroom) Time 11:45 Instructor Sally	In chair, in sidesit	Food, drink	During rolling, to throw away napkin	Pants check	For spoon, cup, napkin	To name	Spoon, cup	Milk at lunch	X
Toileting (Bathroom) Time 12:45 Instructor Sally					(See 8:30 Toileting)				
Grooming (Bathroom) Time 1:15 Instructor Sally					(See 9:00 Grooming)				
Group 4 (Table) Time 1:30 Instructor Kay	In chair, in sidesit	Music, story	During rolling, in sidesit	Pants check	For cassette tape, book	To name, music	Cassette tape, book		X
Departure (Bus) Time 2:15 Instructor Kay	Supine for coat on, in sidesit		During rolling	Pants check	For coat	To name	Coat		X

Figure 1. A sample Activities/Skills Matrix for a learner, Mike, who has severe handicaps.

229

Fill out the Matrix   The next step is to fill in the individual cells of the matrix. Each cell corresponds to one activity and one skill. The question asked is, "How can I teach this skill functionally during this activity?" What materials or events, for example, can be used to teach reaching across midline upon arrival on the bus? The cell completed when answering this question is shown in the matrix for Mike in Figure 1. It is the first cell under "Reach across midline," and the fifth cell in the row entitled, "Arrival." In Mike's case, the teacher will use shaking hands and hanging his coat as the events for teaching him to cross midline.

There are usually many materials and events that can be used to teach a skill during an activity. Mike, for example, could just as well have crossed midline to assist in releasing his seatbelt, unlocking the bus door, getting his gym bag to carry to the classroom, or opening the classroom door. Decide on one or a few materials or events, however, that are most appropriate for the learner's abilities and needs, and that are feasible given the teacher-student ratio and the conditions of instruction (e.g., the managing at the bus of data sheets, wheelchairs, and notebooks from home). Inventories of present and future environments, if part of the educational planning process, may provide examples of materials and events used in functional environments for similar activities. Other criteria for decision-making include selecting materials and events that: 1) are appropriate for the learner's chronological age; 2) are functional, thereby increasing the learner's independence; 3) increase the likelihood of participating with nonhandicapped peers; 4) are appropriate given the learner's motor and sensory development; 5) are enjoyed by the learner; and 6) are best for developing the skill.

One additional consideration in selecting the materials and events to use during an activity is whether choice can be incorporated into the instruction (Holvoet et al., 1984). In other words, can two or more different materials or events be presented and the learner provided the opportunity to choose the one(s) to be used during instruction? Providing the opportunity to make a choice is a valid consideration even for learners who are unable to verbalize or physically indicate their preference. Some of these students will indicate their preference in subtle ways (e.g., relaxation, visual attention), while others may require instruction in how to show it. In any case, begin incorporating choice into instruction by using more than one material or event for teaching skills.

In the example with Mike (Figure 1), choice will be incorporated into the four group sessions. During the work sessions (i.e., groups 1 and 3), Mike will choose between placing caps on veterinarian syringes and collating paper. During the leisure sessions (i.e., groups 2 and 4), he will choose between music and a book of stories.

Consider now each cell of the matrix. It is unlikely that all skills can or should be taught during every activity. Some cells will, therefore, contain no materials or events. In some cases, such as for behavioral interventions and toileting procedures, it is necessary only to indicate whether or not an intervention or other procedure will be implemented during an activity. In Mike's matrix (Figure 1), for example, an "X" indicates that the procedure for teaching him to keep his hands out of his mouth will be implemented during the activity.

After completing the Activities/Skills Matrix, examine it to determine whether each skill is taught: 1) by two or more instructors, 2) with at least two different materials or events, and 3) if appropriate, in two or more locations. Correct the matrix if generalization training is deficient in any way. This may mean changing the designated instructor, or designing a way to teach a skill in a new location. Note that incorporating generalization training into the instructional process means that skills are oftentimes taught in several different areas and by more than one instructor. This, in turn, means that training materials must be available in each area. In addition, it means that several instructors must be knowledgeable of most of the instructional procedures. No longer will teaching occur in one place only (unless this is appropriate), nor will an instructor specialize in one or a few skills.

Write the Individualized Curriculum Sequence

Arrangement of Training Trials   The second step in developing an ICS is to arrange the individual training trials for each skill. There are, as described earlier, at least two ways to do this. First, the trials can be massed together such that the same skill is taught over and over with little time between each trial. This type of instructional arrangement is appropriate when the skill typically is performed in massed repetitions under natural conditions. Certain mobility skills, for example, such as rolling, stepping, and pushing forward on a wheelchair, are usually performed in rapid succession. Also, vocational skills, such as sorting, assembling, and counting, are frequently performed one after another in a massed-trial manner. It is inappropriate, however, to repeatedly perform other behaviors. For example, a person rarely signs, "Hi," 10 times in succession. And, how often does one respond to the request, "Come," only to be placed back in order to repeat the behavior of "coming upon request"?

The second way to arrange training trials is to distribute the trials of one skill among the trials of one or more other skill(s) (i.e., distributed-trial training). Consider, for example, Mike's skills in Figure 1. One way to distribute training trials of the three skills taught during arrival is as follows: 1) visually track a peer moving across the visual plane, 2) localize to the sound of the bus door closing, and 3) reach across midline to grasp a gym bag. In this example, each skill is distributed among others that are taught.

The purpose of the ICS, though, goes beyond merely distributing training trials. Its purpose is to teach the relationship between the different skills being taught. An analogous situation is the teaching of individual steps of a task analysis such as in toothbrushing. The individual steps (e.g., remove cap, squeeze toothpaste tube, place tube down) are rarely taught in isolation. If they are taught in isolation, they must, at some point, be logically recombined into a total, meaningful task. The same is true for many individual skills. One rarely pulls to standing position, for example, just for the sake of pulling to stand, but rather to reach the cabinet, turn on the radio, sidestep to another area, or to be better able to communicate with another person.

Returning to Mike's example, the three skills during arrival might be clustered together in a related way as follows: 1) localize to his name called by a peer, 2) track the peer's movement across the visual field, and 3) reach across midline to shake the peer's hand. Skills can usually be clustered in more than one way. There is no single best cluster for a learner.

While most skills can be related to one another in a cluster, some appear unrelated to all other skills being taught. In such cases, it is unnecessary to cluster the skills. Instead, teach the skill when it naturally occurs within the activity. For example, suppose "putting in" and "drinking from a cup" are the only two skills that can be taught using a vending machine during a leisure activity. For putting in, the learner might put one coin in the vending machine, then the other coin. After carrying the refreshment to the table and being seated, instruction begins on drinking from a cup. When finished drinking, the cup is put in the trash can. The skills of putting in and drinking from a cup do not flow together in a naturally occurring sequence. In other words, putting in does not set the occasion for the immediate occurrence of drinking from a cup. A short span of time as well as other behaviors occur between the two skills (e.g., getting the refreshment, carrying it to the table, and sitting). Teaching is, however, occurring within the context of functional and age-appropriate materials (i.e., vending machine, money). So even if skills cannot be clustered, arrange them naturally within the events and with the materials being used to teach an activity. As a result, one learns not only the skill, but also the context in which to use it.

Behavior Checks Holvoet et al. (1984) suggest that checks for any behaviors targeted for reduction should be incorporated within skill clusters. These behavior checks are points of time in the cluster when the learner is observed for certain proper behavior and reinforced for its presence. The checks constitute one aspect of the procedures to lessen (decelerate) such excessive behaviors as stereotypic movements, self-injurious actions, and disruptive outbursts. All procedures for decelerating such behaviors must include a plan for strengthening an alternative and more adaptive behavior. The behavior check is a mechanism for implementing this behavior building plan. Placement of behavior checks in the daily schedule ensures that all instructors remember to reinforce proper behavior. Thus, consistent treatment is afforded throughout the day. Also, it prevents the instructors from relying exclusively on the deceleration procedures that are, oftentimes, punishing in nature.

To determine where to place the checks, first decide how often to reinforce good behavior. Next, estimate how far one will go in the cluster in this amount of time. Place the behavior check at this point. If possible, place the checks at the end of a cluster. This avoids disrupting the "flow" of instruction. As the behavior improves, reduce the frequency of reinforcers by eliminating some of the behavior checks.

Write the ICS   The ICS is comprised of a series of skill clusters, segments of massed-trial training (when appropriate), and, if necessary, isolated trials of skills that are unable to be related to other skills. When writing clusters, the best length appears to be three to six skills. Longer clusters are more difficult to remember by the instructor, and provide less of a sense of the cluster as a cohesive group of behaviors for acquiring some functional goal.

The number of clusters varies for each activity. There might be one or more clusters for each activity, and some clusters might be repeated within or across different activities. Additionally, a cluster might be repeated consecutively or interspersed with other clusters.

The process of writing the ICS requires one to combine what is known of the activity (e.g., arrival is by bus, at the front door, and with other students present), the student (e.g., gross and fine motor capabilities, sensory impairments, and cognitive abilities), the skills being taught, and the events and materials selected to teach during the activities (i.e., those in the Activities/ Skills Matrix). To begin, think through the first activity (e.g., arrival). Dertermine how to use the skills with the materials and events in the matrix, relating the skills, whenever possible, in short clusters. Using Mike's matrix (Figure 1) and the arrival activity, this process might proceed as follows:

When Mike exits from the bus in his wheelchair in the morning I'll have him cross midline in order to shake hands as a friendly greeting. I can relate this to other skills, though. So, I'll call his name from the side, then after he localizes, with help if necessary, he can track me as I walk before him, then we can shake hands. I will then reinforce him if his hands are out of his mouth. Mike's day begins, therefore, with the following cluster:

1. Localize to call of name by teacher
2. Track teacher from side to front
3. Cross midline to shake hands
4. Instructor reinforces him for hands out of mouth

I can then repeat this same three-part cluster with Mike's friend, Alice, as the instructor. During the walk from the bus to the classroom there are no materials or events that can be used for instruction. Once in the classroom, though, Mike can hang up his coat. The cluster for this, which resembles the first arrival cluster, is as follows:

1. Localize to call of name
2. Cross midline to grasp coat (for hanging it with assistance)
3. Visually track coat as he moves it across his visual field
4. Instructor reinforces for hands out of mouth

Repeat the process of clustering skills for each daily activity. Clusters for selected activities in Mike's schedule are shown in Figure 2. Toileting, for

Student: Mike

Activity: Toileting   Teacher: Kay   Time: 8:30

Teacher behavior	Student behavior	Date				
Call name	Localize	3				
"Go toilet," facilitate rolling	Segments at waist	1				
Prompt to sidesit	Cross midline	1				
—	Segments at waist	3				
—	Head up	2				
Place on toilet	Head up	1				
Behavior check	Hands out of mouth	−				

Activity: Grooming   Teacher: Kay   Time: 9:00

Place in standing table	Head up	2				
Call name	Localize	2				
"Wash," move soap horizontally	Visually tracks soap	3				
—	Cross midline for soap	1				
—	Cross midline for faucet	2				
Behavior check	Hands out of mouth	+				
—	Head up	2				
Call name	Localize	3				
"Dry," move towel horizontally	Visually tracks towel	1				
—	Cross midline for towel	2				
—	Segments to hang towel	2				
Behavior check	Hands out of mouth	+				

Figure 2.   A sample sequence for Mike that includes activities for toileting, grooming, and group work.

example, begins with localization to his name. He is then instructed to go to the toilet and assisted with rolling, measuring the amount of assistance necessary before he rotates (segments) at the hips. Upon reaching the bathroom, Mike is helped into sidesitting, teaching him to cross midline and facilitating hip rotation in order to support himself with his hands on the floor. "Head up" is prompted prior to lifting him to the toilet. While there, "head up" is recorded again, and a behavior check conducted for his hands being out of his mouth.

Student: Mike

Activity: Group 1   Teacher: Sally   Time: 9:15

Teacher behavior	Student behavior	Date				
Call name	Localize	3				
"Go to work," facilitate rolling	Segments at waist	2				
Prompt to sidesit	Cross midline	2				
—	Segments at waist	1				
—	Head up	1				
Place in chair	Head up	2				
Call name	Localize	1				
"Work," give choice of task	Cross midline cap/paper	2				
—	Cross midline cap/paper	3				
—	Requests more caps/paper	1				
Add one more cap/paper	Cross midline cap/paper	3				
Behavior check	Hands out of mouth	—				
—	Head up	3				
Call name	Localize	3				
Move cereal horizontally	Visually tracks cereal	3				
—	Cross midline for cereal	3				
Behavior check	Hands out of mouth	+				
Pants check	—	D				

(The two clusters above can be repeated alternately as needed.)

Scoring code:
W = Wet   + = Hands out of mouth   3 = Independent
S = Soiled   − = Hands in mouth   2 = Verbal prompt and modeling
D = Dry   1 = Physical prompt
                                        0 = Refusal

Figure 2. (continued)

Following toileting, two six-part clusters in which Mike washes and dries his hands comprise a grooming sequence. Note that washing and drying hands are not skills targeted for Mike to learn (i.e., they aren't IEP objectives). They are however, functional and age-appropriate events for teaching the IEP skills identified for Mike (and that are listed at the top of his Activities/Skills Matrix).

In the first grooming cluster, Mike is placed in the standing table and head up behavior is recorded. His name is then called for localization training. After he localizes with assistance, if necessary, an instructional cue is given for washing his hands, and the soap is moved horizontally across Mike's visual field to the counter top. He must then cross midline in order to retrieve the soap, and again when reaching to turn on the water. At the end of the washing cluster, a behavior check is made for having his hands out of his mouth.

A similar grooming cluster follows for drying hands. The primary difference between the washing and drying clusters is that the towel is positioned such that Mike must twist (segment) to reach it, as well as cross midline.

Mike's group activity (Figure 2) is comprised of three separate clusters. The first cluster is an entry to the activity area. The second is a work cluster in which caps are placed on sets of three veterinarian syringes, or three papers are collated. Note that Mike is given a choice of work materials. The actual work task that he performs (i.e., caps on syringes, collating) is not the focus of training. The primary emphasis is on the skills of crossing midline and requesting more materials.

The third cluster is one in which reinforcers are given for work completed. The second and third clusters may be repeated alternately as often as necessary during the activity.

Write Instructional Programs

Many educators write an instructional program describing the procedure for teaching a skill to a learner who is severely handicapped. This can still be done in conjunction with the ICS model. Program writing, however, should be delayed until after writing the ICS. The reason for this is that the development of the ICS addresses many of the factors included in instructional programs, such as the activities, schedule, locations, and materials. It may, in addition, greatly alter the cues given during instruction. In skill clusters, one behavior can serve as a natural cue for the next. This departs significantly from the more traditional model in which artificial instructional cues precede each response.

USING THE ICS WITH GROUPS

Select Skills

The most important point in writing group clusters is to be realistic in terms of how much can be taught given the learner-instructor ratio of the group and the behaviors of the learners. The first step, then, is to select for each learner two to four of his or her IEP skills to be taught in a group situation.

Select Materials or Activities

The second step in constructing group clusters is to determine the materials or events to be used during the group activity. This information is already available if an Activities/Skills Matrix has been completed for each learner. If no matrices have been completed, select materials and events using relevant criteria such as those mentioned earlier (i.e., age-appropriate, functional, facilitates integration with nonhandicapped peers).

When identifying materials and events for group instruction, use of the same materials or events for several or all of the learners in the group is one of the best ways to facilitate cohesive and smooth flowing group instruction. This is true primarily because there is no need to set up different materials or a different event for each learner. In addition, peer interaction is easier to facilitate in such situations.

Write the Group Cluster

The two primary types of clusters for groups are those with and those without interaction among the learners in the group (Brown et al., 1980). In non-interactional clusters, two to four of each learner's skills are grouped with no planned interaction between the learners. In this approach, the instructor teaches the first learner with his or her brief cluster, then teaches the next learner with his or her cluster, then goes to the next learner's cluster, and so forth. Learners do not interact in any way (e.g., they do not pass materials to the next person at the table, or greet one another).

The following is an example of a noninteractional cluster for a group of three learners:

Alicia	Eli	Nancy
1. Select ball or puzzle.	1. Scan cup and cookie.	1. Localize to name.
2. Say "ba" or "pa."	2. Receptively label cup.	2. Track radio.
3. Roll ball or play with puzzle.	3. Drink from cup.	3. Activate radio with touch panel.

In this example, the instructor begins by teaching Alicia using her three-part cluster. Next, Eli is taught using his cluster, then Nancy's cluster is taught.

Noninteractional clusters are written primarily when the learners' objectives differ so greatly that one is unable to identify functional materials or events that are useful for teaching skills to two or more learners. These clusters have the advantage of being easier to write than interactional clusters. For, without interaction, the clusters are just like those written for an individual learner, except shortened to accommodate the learner-instructor ratio of the group.

The major disadvantage of noninteractional clusters is that when different materials and events are used to teach each learner (as in the example above), teaching becomes less efficient. This happens because so much time is spent arranging instructional materials and events that less time is available for teaching, and the transition from instructing one learner to another is poor. Frequently, the result is loss of instructional or behavioral control over the group. In addition, with different materials and events for each learner, there is little to unite the group—nothing upon which to base each learner's presence there.

To avoid these disadvantages, use the same materials and events to train some or all of the learners in a group. This results in a cohesive and smoothly flowing group, with more time to devote to teaching.

The second type of cluster for groups utilizes interactions between the group members. Interaction might occur, for example, as learners provide antecedents such as passing materials, greeting one another, and holding out training items to be selected; or as they consequate one another's performance by providing feedback such as reinforcing correct responses (with assistance, if necessary) and passing materials requested by another learner.

In the following interactional group cluster, Mark provides the antecedent by greeting Beth with, "Hello." Beth consequates the response by returning the greeting. Interaction is once again initiated by Mark's antecedent request, "Cup." Beth receptively labels cup by selecting it from other stimuli, then follows the teacher's request to pass it to Mark. Passing the cup to Mark is the antecedent that signals him to pour pop.

Mark	Beth
1. Sign "Hello."	
	2. Sign "Hello."
3. Sign "Cup."	
	4. Receptively label cup.
6. Pour pop into cup.	5. Pass cup.

In this cluster, instruction follows the flow of the interaction. Mark is taught to sign, "Hello," Beth is taught to sign, "Hello," Mark is instructed on the sign for cup, Beth is taught to receptively label the cup, then to respond to the sign, "Pass," then Mark is instructed in pouring from a bottle into a cup.

Although interactional clusters are written primarily to teach peers to interact with one another, there are additional advantages. They provide more opportunities to program for generalization, since the learner must respond to other persons. Also, when the same training materials and events are utilized, it is an extremely efficient and easy-to-use instructional arrangement. The major disadvantage of interactional clusters is that they are difficult to write whenever the same materials and events cannot be used for two or more learners in the group.

During group instruction, it is often necessary to attend more frequently to some learners in the group than to others. This can be done either with behavior checks or with more frequent instruction. In the following leisure cluster, for example, Linda is attended to frequently in order to reinforce sitting with her hands down (instead of hitting others):

Tony	Linda	Roy

| | 1. Behavior check. | |

2. From a box, selects
   item that matches
   picture card.
3. Passes item to Roy.

4. Signs the name of the
   item.

5. Behavior check.

6. Selects item that
   matches second
   picture card.
7. Passes to Linda.

8. Signs the name of the
   item.

9. Uses item appropri-
   ately.

10. Behavior check.
11. Uses item appropri-
    ately.

FUTURE PROGRAM DIRECTIONS OF THE ICS MODEL

The curriculum sequencing strategy described in the previous section was developed, in part, to provide a more natural instructional format for teachers of learners with severe handicaps. In some respects, the conceptualization of the ICS model was a reaction to instructional regimes in the early and mid 1970s when classroom environments resembled all too closely research laboratories. In these cases, educational practices for learners with severe handicaps were following a progressively narrower path of reductionism, and its accompaning tendency to unrealistically compartmentalize human behavior into a fragmented array of unrelated (and often nonfunctional) responses. Efforts by Lou Brown and his colleagues to emphasize the teaching of functional skills in natural environments provided a major impetus for the movement by educators and researchers toward the principle of normalization. The authors' efforts at the University of Kansas were similarly designed to provide a more normalizing approach to classroom instruction by placing a greater emphasis on the interrelationship between behaviors, and the necessity to educate more completely the whole child.

Only partial success toward this goal has been achieved, and there exists the continuing need to more fully develop the ICS model in a direction that better involves the learner in the educational process. The success of the model is partially realized in the encouraging results that have been observed in research studies reported earlier. A much less quantified, but likely more important, success of the model has been the feedback from teachers who enjoy using this instructional approach, even in spite of its greater complexity when compared to more traditional approaches. Anecdotally, teachers at the University of Kansas who have been trained with the ICS model report that it is challenging to implement, and that it removes them from the boredom often associated with massed-trial training (for both the learner and the teacher).

There are, nevertheless, several important areas where refinement and further development of the ICS model are warranted. These relate to the issues of identifying more natural and normalizing sequences, the development and enhancement of learner-initiated behavior during training, and the teaching of choice as a desired educational objective among learners with severe handicaps. All three of these areas are interrelated and must be considered as important new directions in the development of the ICS model—directions that will require a more sophisticated and complex level of empirical analysis.

Identification of Normalizing Sequences

During the past few years, there has been a tremendous growth in the development of a technology for surveying and analyzing the types of skills needed by learners with severe handicaps to function in a variety of community settings. Indeed, this ecological approach has given new meaning to functional skill development, and it has moved the field more closely to the basic assumptions that underlie the normalization principle.

The ICS model, as described in the previous section, is heavily oriented to the ecological approach where content domains are identified, and later inserted into training sequences. The identification of skills to be taught in sequence are derived from environmental inventories, interviews with parents and other service providers, and the use of traditional assessment instruments. Certainly, attempts to survey student preferences for environmental conditions and activities is an important addition to the process of determining skills to be taught, and to the compilation of IEP goals and objectives.

There still exists, however, a large vacuum of knowledge that pertains to the interrelationship between skills that are used by everyone in interactions with their environments. The fact that responses are not always emitted in exactly the same way, or in the same situation, points both to the tremendous complexity of human behavior, and the more practical problem of promoting generalized behavior among learners with severe handicaps. Ignorance in identifying interrelationships between skill areas (and co-variations in skill development) is not unexpected given the fact that most assessment instruments and developmental scales also are divided into content domains and specific skill areas. Indeed, most textbooks on educating learners with severe handicaps follow similar formats where chapters are divided into content domains.

When using the ICS model, or any approach that advocates the teaching of skill clusters, there exists the problem of exactly what should be included in the training sequence. Conducting environmental inventories to determine what interrelated series of skills is needed to perform a task provides only a partial answer to the problem. This is because skill sequences (or single skills, themselves) are derived from persons who already know how to complete the task. For the nonhandicapped person, performing a task in its proper sequence involves a combination (or recombination of skills) that have already been learned. The ability to perform the sequence, then, is evidence that the interrelated series of skills included in the sequence has already been mastered.

For learners with severe handicaps, skill clustering involves not only teaching a sequence of responses, but often the development of individual responses that are included as part of the sequence. Thus, performance on the sequence could be affected, adversely, by failure to learn an important skill within the sequence. For more traditional approaches where skills were taught in isolation, and often in massed-trial presentation, this was not such a problem since one could merely select another training objective without having to revise a complete program.

The solution to this problem is not an easy one in the absence of significant normative data, handicapped or nonhandicapped, showing the relationship, longitudinally, between and among various types of skills. At best, the authors' recommendation is to include in sequences those skills that are not too far beyond the developmental level of the learner for each content area that is included in the sequence. This increases the likelihood that each skill in a cluster will be acquired to some level of proficiency. Their second recommendation, and one that is not of immediate practical value to the teacher, is the need to conduct research on the interrelationship between skills as they develop in nonhandicapped persons, as well as in learners with handicapping conditions. If the teaching of skill clusters is to be advanced, it is essential to gather more empirical data on just how behaviors interrelate in the acquisition of critical skill development.

Developing Learner-Initiated Behavior

The use of the ICS model, or any skill cluster approach, assumes that behaviors are interrelated, such that the learner with severe handicaps must acquire the ability to connect, in a functional manner, diverse responses from two or more skill areas (i.e., content domains). This assumes, at least implicitly, that behavior is more than a collection of individual parts (or responses); that there exists an organizing dimension, whether developmentally regulated or learned, that brings a cohesiveness and meaning to the particular situation where the responses are to be emitted. In the past, the assumption has been made that it is merely sufficient to teach a repertoire of skills, and the learner will demonstrate competence in naturally occurring situations, and with repeated consistency once the original training cues have been withdrawn.

Unfortunately, this has not always occurred, as attested by the continued problems associated with the maintenance of skills taught to learners with severe handicaps. One aspect of this dilemma is that the educational objectives chosen for the learner with severe handicaps might not always be perceived as important to the learner. As pointed out by Guess and Siegel-Causey (1985), the learner with severe handicaps is too often perceived as a passive agent of the environment, resulting in program objectives and goals that are determined by well-meaning adults, but that may not always reflect attempts by the learner to express his or her own *existing abilities and needs*. The expression of existing or emerging abilities relates to the development of learner-initiated behavior; the expression of needs or desires leads to the issue of choice.

The ICS model was intended, in part, to move away from the tightly structured training regimes that preoccupied the field during the 1970s. By alerting teachers to the interrelationship between skills, it was hoped that more attention could be brought to the learner as an active participant in the educational process. Unfortunately, this has not always happened in instructional settings, where "getting through the sequence" has often engendered the same rigidity as previous massed-trial training procedures; and where inflexible adherence to the written program sequence has sometimes made teachers intolerant of learner-initiated behavior that deviated from the IEP objectives. Indeed, the ICS model can be susceptible in actual implementation to the same insensitivity to the self-initiated behavior of the learner that has characterized previous programming efforts.

The ICS model, like any training effort with learners who have severe handicaps, attempts to teach a relatively small number of skills needed to interact effectively with the environment. And, while attempts are made to identify and teach critical skills, the fact remains that neither time nor the present level of technology will allow for the teaching of all those skills that might be chosen for the learner with severe handicaps. This situation was recognized earlier by Baumgart et al. (1982), who advocated for at least partial participation of learners with severe handicaps in community leisure skill activities.

Another tactic, and one that is easily incorporated into the ICS model, is the development and refinement of self-initiated, emerging skills that are displayed by learners with severe handicaps during training sessions. *Learner-initiated* behaviors are not typically included as part of the prepared program, or might not even be identified as an IEP objective. These are behaviors that, for whatever their cause, are attempts by the learner to interact with the environment and that all too frequently are either ignored or not observed by the teacher. The following example from Guess and Siegel-Causey (1985) serves to illustrate this point.

As Rachel is rolled to her wheelchair, her feet brush across a pillow; she extends her legs and pushes against the soft foam. This motor action deters Rachel from the task-analyzed sequence, and the supine to right side rolling pattern is marked incorrect (-) on the data sheet. Her well-trained teacher quickly pulls Rachel away from the pillow and continues the *correct* rolling sequence. Could this teacher attend to Rachel's initiated movement by moving her legs toward the pillow and helping develop further movements to foster Rachel's spontaneous exploration? The appropriateness of such diversion from the task-analyzed sequence is dependent on the knowledge of Rachel's overall functioning level and the relationship of this behavior to her repertoire of skills. Our contention is that such "off task" behavior can be explored and integrated within Rachel's objective at that moment. Then within that natural occurrence it could be easily worked into the desired rolling pattern. Thus, behavioral technology becomes a tool utilized within the identified sequences of both the student's spontaneous and elicited behaviors. (p. 240)

As shown in the above example, the ICS becomes more than a written, inflexible instructional regime. It now becomes a more dynamic interchange between the learner and student and, significantly, an interaction that allows the learner to become a more active participant in determining the instructional outcome. This, the authors believe, will produce behaviors that are more durable over time, simply because they already existed or were already emerging in the learner's repertoire and, with further instruction, can be more fully developed.

Future directions in the use of the ICS model might well include a better orientation to prepare teachers to observe spontaneously emitted behaviors during training, and to systematically utilize these observations in continually modifying the content of skills in the sequences as well as the manner in which the skill clusters are organized. For more discussion on this issue, the reader is referred to Bricker and Schiefelbusch (1984) and Guess and Siegel-Causey (1985).

Programming for Choice

In the section on the application of the ICS model, reference was made to procedures for providing opportunities for choice-making in the skill sequence. Including choice as a component of the ICS model is a relatively new addition, and one that has not been described in earlier presentations of it. This, in retrospect, is a major oversight, and one that can hopefully be corrected in further development of the model. Unfortunately, the teaching of choice to learners with severe handicaps, and the designing of programs to allow them the options of choice during training, are not prominent considerations in the field (at least as evidenced in the published literature; cf. Holvoet et al., 1981).

The ability and opportunity to make choices is an important and cherished component of each person's life, reflecting favorably on his or her perceived independence and self-worth. The options to make choices are carefully protected and valued. For learners with severe handicaps, however, choice-making has not been a frequent instructional objective, nor has it been a widely discussed topic in the literature (or at conferences). One might have concluded that persons with severe handicaps either could not learn to make choices or, if so, their choices might not have reflected what attending adults and other care providers thought to be in their best interests. Indeed, the general orientation of the field has been to program *for* learners with severe handicaps, rather than to program *with* them in the instructional process (cf. Guess & Siegel-Causey, 1985, for further discussion of this issue).

At the University of Kansas, there are several areas of investigation underway that pertain to choice-making among learners with severe handicaps. The first is a federally funded project to incorporate choices in the IEP objectives of secondary level students. The strategies will include choices for training that reflect future preferences for postschool living, such as leisure and vocational skill development. The rationale underlying this endeavor is based upon the assumption that chosen activities by the learner will result in better acquisition during training, and a more durable maintenance of the skills once they have been learned.

A second area of investigation pertains to the more basic question of how choice-making affects acquisition during training with younger learners with severe handicaps. These investigations will involve dependent variables such as the choice of materials, settings for training, persons who conduct the training, and so on. All of these will, hopefully, provide information on how choice-making can be most effectively, and practically, incorporated into the ICS model.

The ICS model offers a potentially valuable vehicle for teaching choice, and for measuring the outcome of choice-making or skill acquisition. The arrangement of multiple, diverse responses across and within content areas contained in a sequence provides the opportunity to teach choice-making during programmed instruction. For the young learner who is severely handicapped, the sequence might, for example, reflect choices in objects to play with, foods or drinks to consume, or places to go. For the older learner, choices might be included in the sequences for types of clothing to dress with, vocational activities to learn, persons to be with, and so forth. For the creative teacher, the options for teaching choice to learners with severe handicaps are virtually limitless. What is needed is an orientation that values choice-making as an important skill area in itself, and the willingness to perceive the learner with severe handicaps as capable of making choices that reflect his or her own personal needs and desires.

In the absence of data it is only speculation, but choice-making among learners with severe handicaps might well be a skill that needs to be taught (and acquired) over many years. Certainly, choice-making should be started at an early age with learners who are severely handicapped, and extended and expanded throughout the school years. The combination of teaching choice-making and of developing spontaneous behavior during training are perceived as important additions to the ICS model—additions that hopefully will move the field yet another step closer to a naturalized instructional process that results in learners with severe handicaps who can lead more productive and satisfying lives.

FUTURE RESEARCH DIRECTIONS OF THE ICS MODEL

Numerous research questions exist pertaining to skill cluster training and, specifically, the ICS model as it has evolved over the past 5 years. First, there are research areas that relate to the original conceptual bases for the model, as well as application of this approach to educational settings. Second, new program directions discussed in the previous section provide additional, and even more complex questions that need empirical analyses.

Investigations into the educational efficacy of skill cluster training (including distributed-trial training) have generally supported the conceptual basis of the model, as discussed in an earlier section of this chapter. The need exists now for investigations to assess the effectiveness of the ICS model in comparison to other educational approaches, including especially those curriculum approaches that teach skills predominately within (as opposed to across) content areas. Specific areas of comparative analysis would include initial rate of acquisition, durability over time, generalization, and the ability to combine into functional responses skills from different content areas.

Additional research on the ICS model should address issues of educational efficiency in teacher training programs. This would include ability of teachers to learn and use appropriately the more complex and demanding procedures of the model, as compared to more traditional approaches that use massed-trial training formats. Related to this is the question of teacher enthusiasm for the ICS model, based upon anecdotal reports that it is a more enjoyable instructional procedure. This latter issue is especially relevant to reducing teacher burnout with learners who have severe handicaps. Given indications that learner enthusiasm and interest are higher when instructional tasks are varied (Dunlap, 1984), the possibility exists that teachers would also exhibit higher positive affect ratings when they use these procedures.

Newer directions in the ICS model such as increased attention to learner-initiated behavior and teaching choice open up additional areas of needed research. The programmatic recommendation to prepare teachers to better observe and enhance learner-initiated behavior during scheduled instructional sessions will require a somewhat significant departure from most existing educational practices with learners who have severe handicaps. Empirical data are needed on both the quantitative and qualitative dimensions of learner-initiated behavior. How are they to be measured? What guidelines are to be used in the decision by teachers to attend to and enhance those behaviors that deviate from the specified instructional objectives? How should teachers, and others, be trained to be more sensitive to learner-initiated behavior? What effects might this have, if any, on the more general issue of teaching spontaneity and self-direction?

The programmatic recommendation to teach choice-making as an integral component of the ICS model provides an equally challenging direction for future research. Basic questions need to be answered on the extent to which learners with severe handicaps have the opportunity to express choice during instruction, whether they even know, conceptually, what choice is and, if not, how choice-making can be taught. It is, indeed, an embarrassment to the field that choice-making among learners with severe handicaps has received so little attention (cf. Guess & Siegel-Causey, 1985). With respect to the skill cluster approach using the ICS model, research is needed on how choice-making can best be inserted into the instructional process; that is, how can it be most efficiently taught to learners with severe handicaps within the guidelines and components of the model. Importantly, what are long-term benefits to the learners in helping them achieve more independent lifestyles in future environments, and how does choice-making affect, positively, their perceptions of self-worth and personal dignity as adults?

SUMMARY

Skill cluster instruction, as encompassed in the ICS model, is a relatively new approach to the education and training of learners with severe handicaps. This approach, based upon the combining and teaching of skills across content areas, is consistent with current values associated with the need to provide instructional methods that are more similar to occurrences in the natural environment and that emphasize functional skill training for optimal generalization. The conceptual basis of the model is supported by several areas of systematic research pertaining to distributed- versus massed-trial training formats. Preliminary anecdotal feedback suggests that both teachers and learners like the instructional procedures used in the model.

Suggestions for extending the model involve teaching choice-making in the instructional sequences, and preparing teachers to better observe and enhance learner-initiated behavior during instructional sessions. Directions for further research into the ICS model include a comparative analysis to more traditional approaches that use massed-trial training formats, studies involving teacher training with the model, and new investigations into the areas of learner-initiated behavior and teaching choice-making.

REFERENCES

Baumgart, D., Brown, L., Pumpian, I., Nisbet, J., Ford, A., Sweet, M., Messina, R., & Schroeder, J. (1982). Principle of partial participation and individualized adaptations in education programs for severely handicapped students. *Journal of The Association for the Severely Handicapped, 7*, 17–27.

Brewer, M. (1982). *The efficacy of distributed practice training on the facilitation of generalization skills of the severely retarded.* Unpublished master's thesis, Department of Special Education, University of Kansas, Lawrence, KS.

Bricker, D., & Schiefelbusch, R. L. (1984). Infants at risk. In L. McCormick & R. L. Schiefelbusch (Eds.), *Language intervention.* Columbus, OH: Charles E. Merrill Publishing Co.

Brown, F., Holvoet, J., Guess, D., & Mulligan, M. (1980). The individualized curriculum sequencing model (III): Small group instruction. *Journal of The Association for the Severely Handicapped, 5,* 352–367.

Brown, L., Branston, M., Hamre-Nietupski, S., Pumpian, I., Certo, N., & Gruenewald, L. (1978). A strategy for developing chronologically age-appropriate and functional curricular content for severely handicapped adolescents and young adults. *The Journal of Special Education, 13,* 80–90.

Brown, L., Branston-McClean, M. B., Baumgart, D., Vincent, L., Falvey, M., & Schroeder, J. (1979). Using the characteristics of current and subsequent least restrictive environment as factors in the development of curricular content for severely handicapped students. *Journal of The Association for the Severely Handicapped, 4,* 407–424.

Brown, L., Nietupski, J., & Hamre-Nietupski, S. (1976). The criterion of ultimate functioning. In M. A. Thomas (Ed.), *Hey, don't forget about me.* Reston, VA: Council for Exceptional Children.

Brown, L., Nisbet, J., Ford, A., Sweet, M., Shiraga, B., York, J., & Loomis, R. (1983). The critical need for nonschool instruction in educational programs for severely handicapped students. *Journal of The Association for the Severely Handicapped, 8,* 71–77.

Dunlap, G. (1984). The influence of task variation and maintenance tasks on the learning and affect of autistic children. *Journal of Experimental Child Psychology, 37,* 41–64.

Dunlap, G., & Koegel, R. L. (1980). Motivating autistic children through stimulus variation. *Journal of Applied Behavior Analysis, 13,* 619–627.

Guess, D., Horner, D., Utley, B., Holvoet, J., Maxon, D., Tucker, D., & Warren, S. (1978). A functional curriculum sequencing model for teaching the severely handicapped. *AAESPH Review, 3,* 202–215.

Guess, D., Jones, C., & Lyon, S. (1981). *Combining a transdisciplinary team approach with an individualized curriculum sequencing model for severely/multiply handicapped children.* Lawrence: University of Kansas.

Guess, D., & Noonan, M. J. (1982). Curricula and instructional procedures for severely handicapped students. *Focus on Exceptional Children, 14,* 1–12.

Guess, D., & Siegel-Causey, E. (1985). Behavioral control and education of severely handicapped students: Who's doing what to whom? and why? In D. Bricker & J. Filler (Eds.), *Severe mental retardation: From theory to practice.* Reston, VA: The Council for Exceptional Children.

Helmstetter, E., Murphy-Herd, M., Guess, D., & Roberts, S. (1984). *Individualized curriculum sequence and extended classroom models for learners who are deaf and blind.* Unpublished manuscript, University of Kansas, Lawrence.

Holvoet, J., Brewer, M., Mulligan, M., Guess, D., Helmstetter, E., & Riggs, P. (1981). *Influence of activity choice on learning among adolescent severely, multiply handicapped students.* Unpublished manuscript, University of Kansas, Lawrence.

Holvoet, J., Guess, D., Mulligan, M., & Brown, F. (1980). The individualized curriculum sequencing model (I): A teaching strategy for severely handicapped students. *Journal of The Association for the Severely Handicapped, 5,* 337–351.

Holvoet, J., Mulligan, M., Schussler, N., Lacy, L., & Guess, D. (1984). *The Kansas Individualized Curriculum Sequencing model: Sequencing learning experiences for severely handicapped children and youth.* Portland, OR: A. S. I. E. P. Education Co.

Lacy, L. (1982). *The effect of functional scheduling on the initiation and latency responses of severely handicapped students.* Unpublished master's thesis, Department of Special Education, University of Kansas, Lawrence, KS.

Mulligan, M., & Guess, D. (1984). Using an individualized curriculum sequencing model. In L. McCormick & R. L. Schiefelbusch (Eds.), *Language intervention.* Columbus, OH: Charles E. Merrill Publishing Co.

Mulligan, M., Guess, D., Holvoet, J., & Brown, F. (1980). The individualized curriculum sequencing model (I): Implications from research on massed, distributed, or spaced trial learning. *Journal of The Association for the Severely Handicapped, 5,* 325–336.

Mulligan, M., Lacy, L., & Guess, D. (1982). The effects of massed, distributed, and spaced trial sequencing on severely handicapped students' performance. *Journal of The Association for the Severely Handicapped, 7,* 48–61.

Neel, R., Lewis-Smith N., Hanashiro R., McCarty F., & Billingsley, F. (no date). *Validation of a functional curriculum: The IMPACT project.* Unpublished manuscript, University of Washington.

Panyan, M., & Hall, V. (1978). Effects of serial versus concurrent task sequencing on acquisition, maintenance, and generalization. *Journal of Applied Behavior Analysis, 11,* 67–74.

Sailor, W., & Guess, D., (1983). *Severely handicapped students: An instructional design.* Boston: Houghton Mifflin Co.

Schroeder, G., & Baer, D. M. (1972). Effects of concurrent versus serial training on generalized vocal imitation in retarded children. *Developmental Psychology, 6,* 293–301.

INSTRUCTIONAL PROCEDURES AND TECHNOLOGY

Chapter 9

Community Intensive Instruction

Wayne Sailor, Ann Halvorsen,
Jacki Anderson, Lori Goetz,
Kathy Gee, Kathy Doering,
and Pam Hunt

Students with severe disabilities have experienced a transition over the past decade in terms of their education, moving from institutions and church basements to segregated schools for disabled individuals only, and, most recently, to special classes in regular public schools. While these placements have not been characteristic of every program or community's history, the sequence does describe a clear trend in service delivery over the past 10 years. The purpose of this chapter is to discuss the most recent link in the service delivery chain—a movement from the regular public school to direct instruction in the community at large.

This chapter presents the structure of the "community intensive" model and the considerations involving implementation of that model, followed by examples of the system in its current stage of development in the San Francisco Bay Area together with some research related to the model development process. This model effort, which is underway for students of preschool, elementary, middle school, high school, and postsecondary age with extensive

This work was partially supported by U.S. Office of Education Contract No. 300-82-0365 and Grant No. G0008301356 to San Francisco State University. The content, however, does not necessarily reflect the position or policy of the U.S.O.E., and no official endorsement of these materials is implied.

The authors wish to extend their appreciation to the following Bay Area teachers who assisted in the preparation of this chapter: Blair Cassani-Hodgkin, Nan Graham, Deb Jager, Jill Mooney, Debra Moore, Gail Oshima, Blair Roger, and Karen Yoshioka.

special needs, operates out of regular public educational facilities, is age appropriate, includes both school and nonschool instruction, and is completely integrated (including regular and sustained interactions with nondisabled peers). The school-age components of the model are the focus of this chapter. The reader interested in preschool services under this system is referred to Hanson (1984), and Sailor and Guess (1983, pp. 319–340) for a more detailed description of both the infant and the postsecondary aspects of the community intensive model. For further information, see the following articles and chapters: Baumgart et al. (1982); Falvey, Brown, Lyon, Baumgart, & Schroeder (1980); Hanson (1981); Holvoet, Mulligan, Schussler, Lacy, and Guess (1982); and Vincent et al. (1980).

STRUCTURE OF A COMMUNITY INTENSIVE INSTRUCTIONAL MODEL

The field of education for persons with severe disabilities has now reached phase six of the historical sequence described by Brown et al. (1983): "[c]hronological age-appropriate regular schools in accordance with the natural proportion and instruction in nonschool environments" (p. 72). The argument for "nonschool" instruction is put succinctly:

> . . . envision someone who can learn, but who cannot learn as much as 99% of his or her age peers; who needs more time and trials to learn and to relearn than almost all other persons; who remembers some things but forgets more than almost all other persons; who has difficulty transferring that learned in one environment to another; and who rarely synthesizes skills acquired from several different experiences so as to function effectively in a novel situation. Then, ask the question: How much instructional time should be spent in the physical space of a school, and how much should be spent providing direct, individualized, longitudinal, comprehensive, and systematic instruction in the actual nonschool environments in which that someone currently functions and those in which s/he is likely to function upon graduation? (p. 74)

Figure 1 presents a schematicized conceptual model for community intensive instruction developed by Sailor and Guess (1983), and that has been extended to preschool-age students. The model suggests that an appropriate education for severely disabled students really occurs in three different environmental domains to provide a functional life skills curriculum: 1) *classroom* (in a regular public school or integrated private school, never in a segregated, isolated facility; 2) *the school, or nonclassroom areas,* including the playground, hallways, restroom, gym, locker rooms, cafeteria, and partial mainstream situations such as art or music classes, the library, adaptive P.E., and so on; and 3) *the community at large, or nonschool areas* including parks, playgrounds, pools, stores, restaurants, work environments, residential environments, and other age-appropriate community environments.

Education of students with severe disabilities has, in many ways, "inherited" the classroom instructional model. Because education is traditionally imparted in classrooms within schools, the application of this physical service

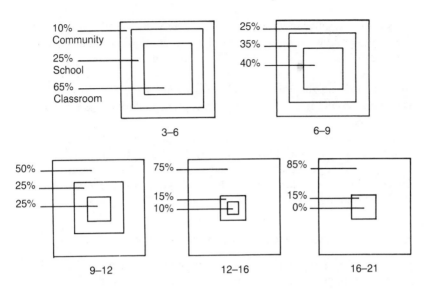

Chronological Age Groups

Figure 1. Percentages of optimal educational time spent in these areas: classroom, other school, and nonschool community, all as a function of chronological age grouping regardless of severity of handicapping conditions.

model to students with severe disabilities following their "enfranchisement" for education in 1974 was to be expected. When curriculum consisted of an adaptation of preschool "cognitive-developmental" instructional tactics, the classroom served instructors well. Students could learn to sort colors, stack blocks, identify shapes, do massed-trial language tasks, take off and put on articles of clothing, and so on, in classrooms as well as anywhere. The shift in the 1980s to a functional, life skills curriculum model, however, strongly raises the issue of the relevance of the traditional classroom for instruction. Extensive research in generalization of skill acquisition to other similar situations and exemplars has shown that students with severe disabilities do not readily generalize skills to new environments (e.g., Coon, Vogelsberg, & Williams, 1981; Hill, Wehman, & Horst, 1982). For example, teaching a student to dress himself or herself in the classroom is less likely to generalize to environments where dressing *appropriately* takes place, such as in a bedroom at a nearby group home or in the locker room at a neighborhood swimming pool. In addition, removing one's clothes in the midst of a classroom at an integrated school site is an extremely inappropriate activity that would be stigmatizing to the severely disabled student.

Objectives for severely disabled students are shaped by the environments in which education is conducted. Confinement to a classroom or even to a school campus for the entire instructional day might well comprise an unnecessarily restrictive environment for a severely disabled 10-year-old child, even if the program is on a regular school campus, where interactions with nondisabled peers are structured and encouraged. Elementary-age students need to acquire street-crossing skills, use public recreational facilities and stores in their neighborhoods, and, in general, maximize their ability for functioning in multiple, normal, age-appropriate environments (cf. Sailor & Guess, 1983).

Figure 1 thus illustrates how the relative proportion of time in different environments changes as a student with severe disabilities moves through the school years. The postsecondary component of the model (not discussed in this chapter) reflects the pattern of the high school application and would ideally be based at a community college campus (Sailor & Guess, 1983).

CONSIDERATIONS IN MODEL IMPLEMENTATION

As the direction of exemplary educational programs for students of all ages with severe disabilities moves increasingly toward a focus on the instruction of functional skills across a multiplicity of nonclassroom environments, a critical need for synthesis and extension of available information on best practices is beginning to be identified by educators in the field (e.g., Hamre-Nietupski, Nietupski, Bates, & Maurer, 1982). Teachers of recently integrated classes of severely handicapped students in the San Francisco Unified School District are struggling with questions related to balancing the amount of time spent in nonschool instruction of community, leisure, vocational, and domestic skills with the amount of time spent in school-based integrated activities with nondisabled peers. Teachers are seeking direction in determining the relative weight that should be given to, for example, "horizontal" (peer-to-peer) interaction within the school versus generalization of skills across nonschool natural environments. The percentages provided in Figure 1 represent the best estimates of optimum time in different environments as judged from applications of the model to date. Projected future applications of the model with students who have participated in community intensive instruction throughout their school lives will lead to increased expectations of higher percentages out-of-class for younger groups of students. Finally, the individualized program plan for each student, taking into consideration the full range of each student's needs, becomes the final criterion against which the proportion of time in different environments is weighed. The model in Figure 1 is intended to convey a sense of relative proportions in a general approach to the initiation of community intensive instruction.

Issues related to the transfer of instructional technology from classrooms to nonschool environments have been addressed only recently in the literature (e.g., Ford & Mirenda, 1984; Hill et al., 1982; Liberty, Haring & Martin, 1981). Kazdin (1977), Peck and Semmel (1982), and Wolf (1978) have all pointed out the need for an empirical data base to validate both the effectiveness and *acceptability* of specific interventions across nonschool environments. Falvey et al. (1980) and Liberty et al. (1981) raised the issue of a need for information related to the effect of added natural stimuli present in community environments. Data are needed regarding the use or facility of transfer of various types of materials and adaptive devices, as well as cueing, prompting, and reinforcement strategies. Stainback and Stainback (1981) identified the need for research on interventions that will be effective in promoting social interaction between severely disabled students and nondisabled persons in the community. Portable, functional, and efficient data collection systems for off-site instruction need to developed as well.

Policy and procedures regarding community intensive instruction also require delineation and clarification across different types of district structures (i.e., single district versus multidistrict consortium). To date, only a few reports have addressed these issues in the literature (cf. Freagon et al., 1983; Hamre-Nietupski et al., 1982; Taylor, 1982). Areas that require attention include staffing ratios for nonschool instruction, legal policies regarding off-campus training, parent permissions, insurance liability, paraprofessional job descriptions, transportation, and the transfer of monies to support instructional programs off-site. Cohesive and district-wide policies are required for full implementation of a community intensive model.

The ease with which a community-based model is implemented will differ across types of communities. For example, in an urban environment, domestic and vocational training sites may be readily accessible to the school site, whereas a suburban or rural community may have few resources in close proximity to the public school. However, the urban environment may have other constraints related to safety or population congestion. Menchetti, Rusch, and Lamson (1981) have pointed out that community norms may also vary in terms of acceptability of educational interventions. Rusch, Schutz, and Agran (1982) identified the need for social validation of interventions across locales. For example, programs such as those established in Illinois, Iowa, and Wisconsin have not needed to address the issue of community ethnic diversity to the same extent as has been required in Hawaii and in the metropolitan area of San Francisco, to cite but two examples of ethnically diverse communities. Determination of future environments for instruction in these areas must take into consideration the impact of the multiethnic and multilingual nature of the community and, specifically, the families of the students with severe disabilities. In San Francisco, 24% of 85 families involved in the integration of the district's students with severe disabilities were non–English speaking. Seven languages were represented among these families (Halvorsen, 1983a).

Recent reports (cf. Ford et al., 1983; Hamre-Nietupski et al., 1982) and the authors' own experiences in the Bay Area indicate that regardless of the chronological ages, district structure, or categorical disability of the students for whom community intensive instruction is being developed, most constraints to model implementation fall within one of the following four basic factors: 1) administrative-logistical factors, 2) parent factors, 3) student factors, and 4) teacher factors.

Administrative-Logistical Factors

Liability and Insurance   Bay Area programs have handled the issue of liability and insurance in a variety of ways, ranging from board of education district-wide policy development to school-specific agreements often based on an individual student's IEPs. In the case of San Francisco's Presidio Middle School, the teacher and program specialist requested a policy statement from the district's legal department regarding the utilization of unaccompanied classroom paraprofessionals as primary staff persons for some of the planned off-campus sites. This staffing arrangement was approved by the district as long as the program was both teacher-designed and monitored. In other words, the classroom aide was permitted to implement off-campus instruction, given joint planning and periodic teacher supervision. This same position statement permitted secondary-age nondisabled students working as peer tutors to accompany teaching staff with students off-campus for instructional purposes.

In addition, university practicum students and student teachers working with all San Francisco Unified School District (SFUSD) classes for severely disabled students have received approval to conduct community intensive instruction. These students are required to register with the San Francisco School Volunteers for insurance coverage, and are supervised periodically at community sites by the master teacher and the San Francisco State University supervisor.

Of course, *permission* for community intensive instruction involves much more than basic staffing issues. A district may require that the teacher obtain specific parent permission forms for each nonschool environment in which instruction will occur, or it may simply require a yearly ''blanket'' off-campus permission form. In contrast, one Bay Area district utilizes the IEP as the vehicle for signed parent permission. If a student's goals state that, within the general community domain, he or she will be shopping weekly in a grocery store and traveling there with his or her group on public transportation, this statement and the parental approval of the goal are considered to be sufficient. IEP goals can also be used as permission for increasing levels of student independence in performance of the skill, as in the case where a student may require minimal and eventually no supervision to walk to his or her after-school job from his or her high school.

Clearly, the safety of the students is the major issue in district liability and insurance concerns. In moving to an integrated model of service delivery in San Francisco, this emerged as the primary concern of school site administrators, especially those who had had minimal previous experience with severely disabled pupils. With instruction occurring in additional off-site environments, teachers, administrators, and parents have worked cooperatively to develop emergency procedures, such as: 1) having all students carry identification including emergency phone numbers and any medical alert information at all times, 2) considering the proximity of nonschool sites to medical facilities and/or personnel in the site selection process, 3) training those students who have effective communication systems in specific procedures if they become separated from their group, and 4) where necessary, ensuring that teachers, aides, and relevant community persons are trained in first aid and cardiopulmonary resuscitation (CPR) techniques.

Unions Teacher and paraprofessional unions may need to become involved with administration in consideration of liability issues when a community intensive program is developed. Paraprofessional job descriptions may require alteration for the inclusion of instructional responsibilities off-campus. Bay Area teachers have found it advantageous to arrange for meetings that include site administrators, paraprofessionals, and union representatives for the purpose of cooperative development of these guidelines. At the same time, the teacher's union may wish to participate in policy development related to the teachers' and/or aides' use of their own cars for transportation of students to community sites. Hamre-Nietupski et al. (1982) point out that most systems in their experience have either reimbursed staff for additional personal liability coverage or have covered staff vehicles within district insurance policies. Resolution of this issue will be a key factor in getting a community intensive program off the ground, especially in suburban and rural areas where the school may not be in proximity to commercial areas or neighborhoods that afford a variety of instructional environments.

Transportation to Community Environments While it would be ideal to have integrated classes for severely disabled students, particularly younger age groups, located in close proximity to shops, stores, and other commerce, this is not always the case. Jose Ortega Elementary School in the San Francisco Unified School District, which houses both an infant-toddler and an early elementary class, is located on top of one of San Francisco's higher hills, a least a mile from any concentrated commercial area. Four of suburban San Mateo County's integrated classes for severely disabled pupils are located in a residential area similarly removed from most environments where community instruction could be implemented. Few public transportation lines are accessible within these two neighborhoods (accessible means both near the school and wheelchair lift equipped). In addition, neither of these sites is the "neighborhood school" for the majority of the students for two reasons: 1) because the boundary areas for each San Francisco school are broadly defined, and 2) because San Mateo is a county-administered program housed within one of its two dozen or so participating districts.

Therefore, transportation is often viewed as a roadblock to nonschool instruction for these preschool and elementary-age students. However, several solutions do exist and have been pursued by these and other classes. As mentioned above, teachers and/or classroom aides may be able to transport small groups of students in their own vehicles to bring them in proximity to commercial areas. Second, parent volunteers may be recruited for this same purpose. Teachers may be able to arrange for district school buses to transport pupils directly to a community environment in the morning and pick them up at the same or a different environment at the end of the school day. This would be most appropriate, for example, where a domestic training site is available for self-care and necessary caregiving at the start and close of the day. Since many districts currently bus students to related services and/or to after-school programs instead of to their homes, this possibility is not unrealistic.

In a recent survey conducted by Falvey, Smithey, and Zivolich (1984) in southern California, teachers reported several additional solutions to transportation problems, including: 1) use of bus passes earned through vocational training activities in bus stations, 2) use of district Driver's Education vehicles and Career Education buses, 3) bicycling to commercial areas, and 4) purchasing a vehicle for use by several classes through a CalTrans (California Transportation Department) grant.

Other alternatives to public transportation often exist. In San Mateo County, free bus services are available to disabled persons if reserved in advance. In San Francisco, the state university has lift-equipped vans that can be used by staff and faculty personnel who meet specific driver's education requirements. Finally, since many students still may not be able to receive instruction in their own neighborhoods, the authors suggest that sites be selected according to the similarity of these environments to those generally found near students' homes. Environmental inventories and parent interviews could be used, for example, to show that students' families frequent certain playgrounds, parks, grocery stores, or laundromats, and so on, and efforts could be made to locate placement in schools that have similar potential training environments within reasonable proximity.

Staff Ratios   The utilization of paraprofessionals, university practicum students, and student teachers for community instruction, as well as nondisabled middle and high school peer tutors, has been mentioned elsewhere. Since ratios of 1:4 or less are generally considered necessary for effective nonclassroom and nonschool instruction, additional resources should be explored. Ancillary staff such as physical, speech, and occupational therapists are integral to the planning process. If an integrated therapy model is in place within the school (cf. Nietupski, Scheutz, & Ockwood, 1980; Sternat, Messina, Nietupski, Lyon, & Brown, 1977), the rationale for nonschool service delivery is a logical extension of this model. For example, an occupational therapist will be extremely helpful in developing the adaptations necessary for students' eating programs in restaurants, or for equipment that will facilitate a student's participation in a specific community work station. Speech clinicians will be integral to the development of portable communication systems for use in shopping, restaurant, travel, and work training environments. Brown et al. (1982) and others have discussed the lack of skill transfer and generalization across environments by severely disabled students. For this reason, it is imperative that related service delivery occur within the actual environments where skills will be utilized (e.g., physical therapy during mobility training on bus route). Although the logistics of working this out may appear insurmountable at first, the process is likely to be similar to that which occurred with school integration of severely disabled pupils. Again, it will involve elements of "role release," or the mechanism by which a professional trained in one discipline (e.g., physical therapy) trains another (e.g., teacher) to implement specific procedures that were traditionally the sole responsibility of that particular discipline (cf. Hutchison, 1974; Lyon & Lyon, 1980). The process may also involve alterations in existing interagency agreements and/or job descriptions, as well as creative scheduling efforts.

Other sources of staff support include parent volunteer and foster grandparent programs. The primary consideration here, as well as with paraprofessionals, peer tutors, and university students, will be the provision of ongoing training by teachers to these individuals so that they are capable of effective off-campus instruction. While this may mean brief periods of "down time" or increased amounts of large-group instruction at the outset, it will be balanced out by the improved quality of instruction that this "extra staff" delivers.

Finally, an effective vehicle for increasing staff ratios and amounts of community instruction, particularly in the vocational domain, has been successfully implemented in the San Diego area with assistance from Dr. Ian Pumpian of San Diego State University (personal communication, May 18, 1984). Heterogeneous grouping (across disability groups) has proved effective in both reducing staff-student ratios for moderately disabled students and in providing for sustained individualized attention to more severely, multiply disabled students in the same instructional group. Similarly, Freagon et al. (1983) have utilized heterogeneous groupings to facilitate community-based instruction in rural areas of Illinois.

Cost Factors District commitment to the implementation of community intensive instruction, in the form of monetary support, is integral to ongoing programming. However, in the authors' experience, systems change is a gradual process (Piuma, Halvorsen, Murray, & Porter Beckstead, 1983). Commitment of funds to the model has occurred as community-based objectives become more clearly delineated on students' IEPs, as documentation of student achievement progresses, and as parents advocate for district support of the program. Frequently, this commitment may simply involve a transfer of funds from one budget category to another. For example, an elementary school may have a per-pupil allotment for book purchases. Since the students with severe disabilities may not need to use these funds for textbooks, this money can be moved into a petty cash fund for community instructional purposes.

Grossmont Union High School District in Southern California has developed an extensive procedural handbook for its teachers of severely disabled students, entitled *Natural Based Educational Programming* (Grossmont Union High School District, 1983). The handbook's guidelines permit, for example, expenditure of school funds for food if the student will be actively involved in meal preparation, but do not permit school funds to be utilized for students' restaurant meal purchases. The administrative unit has published several recommended alternatives that staff may use to obtain funding for community educational programming. Both informal surveys of Bay Area teachers and the Falvey et al. (1984) survey yield similar suggestions for initial and ongoing sources of monetary support, including: 1) use of the classroom instructional supplies budget; 2) use of district career education monies; 3) use of funds allotted per class by the student government of the school; 4) requests for funds from school or area PTA; 5) establishing open purchase order accounts between the school and local merchants; 6) writing for grants from local, state, or federal agencies/governments; 7) performance of services by students, for example, laundry and cleaning for faculty and/or families, or in group homes, in return for use of the training site; 8) reduced-fare bus passes for students; 9) running a school restaurant that serves the dual purpose of domestic/vocational training and generating funds; 10) structuring shopping around students' making regular purchases for their families, who supply the list and necessary funds; and 11) opening a bank account at the outset of the school year to which parents contribute a set amount for uncovered expenses (such as meals).

In conclusion, while alternate funding sources are not presented as substitutions for full district support, the authors have found them to be viable interim alternatives to the expenditure of teachers' personal funds during the initial stages of program development.

Parent Factors

Many parent concerns, such as safety-liability, staff ratios, provision of related services, and costs of the program, will be similar to those of the school administration at the outset of community intensive program development. For this reason, the importance of providing accurate information regarding the program's goals and rationale, as well as involving parents in the planning process, cannot be overemphasized. Parent preferences for current and future environments in which instruction will occur need to be included in the environmental inventory process and resulting IEP goals. Processes for "significant other" or caregiver interviews regarding parental priorities for instruction have been designed and effectively implemented in Bay Area community intensive programs. These processes are described in detail elsewhere (cf. Doering & Hunt, 1983; Halvorsen, 1983b; Savage, 1983); however, several additional key practices merit description here.

Halvorsen (1983b) found school-site parent groups to be an effective vehicle for initiation of parent-designed collaboration and interaction with the integrated, community-based education program. These groups served multiple purposes for parents, including: 1) parent-to-parent support; 2) provision of information based on families' stated needs; 3) networking across school sites and programs; 4) interaction with existing district and community parent-based organizations, for example, state-mandated Community Advisory Councils on Special Education (CACs), PTAs, local Associations for Retarded Citizens (ARC), and neighborhood groups such as the Coallisión de los Padres (Latino parents of disabled children); and 5) formation of parent trainer-of-trainer programs to increase school/community awareness and promote positive attitudes toward students with severe disabilities.

A generative parent trainer model has proved particularly effective in familiarizing parents with the rationale for, benefits, and feasibility of the integrated, community intensive instructional model. Piuma et al. (1983) found that attitude change and communication about new practices were facilitated by peer-peer or horizontal interactions; an administrator is more interested in hearing from another administrator than from a teacher, and a teacher will be more open to advice from other teachers. Similarly, parents are likely to have more credibility with other parents than are teachers, administrators, or university personnel. For this reason, during the integration process in San Francisco, Project REACH (Contract No. 300-800-0745) designed a specific series of trainings with interested parent volunteers, the goal of which was provision of accurate information and disability awareness education techniques to parent, school, and community persons and agencies. Both content on integrated community intensive best practices, and processes for promoting community awareness (Murray & Porter Beckstead, 1983) comprised the trainings. Two core groups of parents—one available for daytime and one for evening presentations—were established, and included bilingual parents, parents representing elementary- and secondary-age students, and parents serving on the ARC, local CAC, and the San Francisco School Volunteers, thus ensuring continuity of the model program. During the first 6 months, approximately 1,000 regular education students and staff, parents of regular and special education students, and community members were recipients of trainings provided by the volunteer parent trainers (Halvorsen, 1983b).

This type of early involvement of parents in the planning process—as trainers and as members of equal status on community intensive task forces or advisory groups—guarantees greater parent investment and collaboration in the child's education. In an evaluation of a community-based instructional model in DeKalb, Illinois, Freagon et al. (1983) found strong parent support for the program; 80% of parents responding reported that their sons and daughters were more interested in attending school since the initiation of community instruction, and 83% reported that their children had acquired greater access to the community at large. Two-thirds of the parents felt more comfortable taking their children into the community as a result of the integrated program. Additionally, parents perceived greater independence of their children across most recreational, vocational, and social activities.

In conclusion, evidence of this type indicates that while there may be initial parental resistance to a curriculum shift toward community intensive instruction, procedures such as those described above can facilitate support and parent advocacy for the model.

Student Factors

Type and Degree of Disability The kind and severity of a student's disability(ies) becomes an important factor in determining environments for instruction, for what may be the opposite reason of what many would expect. Specifically, as discussed by Ford et al. (1983), the *more* disabled a student is and the less he or she is able to transfer skills or adapt to a variety of situations, the *more* that student needs to receive instruction in nonclassroom environments. It can be assumed that the more disabled student will need greater amounts of instruction to acquire skills, and that the more complex the skill, the sooner instruction should begin and the more frequently it needs to occur. Therefore, rather than *excluding* the more disabled pupils because they are "not yet ready" for community environments, off-campus efforts should be concentrated to a greater extent on these students than with less disabled students who may demonstrate some transfer of skills from simulated to natural settings (Ford et al., 1983).

The type and severity of the students' disabilities also relate to the principle of partial participation, or the value of a student's involvement in the sequence/skill/activity to the greatest of his or her ability to participate. For example, students whose physical disabilities preclude them from standing up to remove clothes from a top-loading washer in the laundromat should not be excluded from partially participating, which might involve them in transferring wet clothing from a basket placed in front of them into a front-loading clothes dryer. These same students, having acquired one or more components of a clothes-washing sequence, will now be able to assist in a family household task.

Severely multiply disabled students may require several adaptations of materials in order to function effectively in the full range of nonclassroom and nonschool environments. In addition to the active involvement of therapists toward this end, teachers conducting inventories of potential sites will need to evaluate architectural barriers in terms of the probability of their providing or preventing a learning experience. Accessibility of entrances, exits, bathrooms, and all program areas must be evaluated, and features such as table and cabinet heights should be considered.

Portability of and easy access to communication systems should be considered in adaptation development. A student carrying packages or pushing a shopping cart is unlikely to be able to manipulate an unwieldy notebook as well. The same will be true for a student in line in a cafeteria. Pocket-size communication cards or flip books specific to the activity facilitate communication and are less obtrusive and more appropriate to the task. Pictorial adaptations may also be necessary for students who utilize manual sign systems in order to facilitate their communication with the general public in nonclassroom and community environments.

Transfer of Technology and Social Validity   The area of necessary adaptations to school materials and instructional programs raises the question of transferability and acceptability of various systematic instructional practices within community settings. During the site selection process, teachers can interview a sample of key community persons who are consistently present in domestic, vocational, recreational, and general community sites, in order to socially validate (determine the acceptability of) various interventions and develop alternatives when necessary (cf. Rusch et al., 1982).

Ford et al. (1983) have discussed additional student factors such as chronological age, postschool projections, performance history, and unique learning or performance characteristics that require consideration in community intensive program design and implementation. Table 1 illustrates the matrix format provided by these authors for identifying how each factor might influence the locations, amount of time, length, and frequency of community intensive sessions. Similar matrices are provided for the evaluation of activity and logistical factors. Ford and Mirenda (1984) also describe a natural cues and consequences model developed for community intensive instruction. These guidelines for selecting corrective procedures, relevant natural cues, appropriate teaching procedures, and methods of data collection are particularly helpful for program design.

The importance of program continuity cannot be overemphasized. Teachers and parents need to continue to review the program in light of all of the student factors discussed. The question of "what is normalized" for each particular age group must be continually reevaluated. For younger elementary-age pupils, the community intensive approach must ensure that integration opportunities with nondisabled peers are not restricted, by taking full advantage of nonclassroom training environments within the school campus.

Teacher Factors

Recency of Training   The teacher's commitment to or support of the rationale for the community intensive instructional model is perhaps the single most important factor to its success. It should be noted that even those teachers of severely disabled pupils who completed their training as recently as 3–5 years ago did not experience a concentration on curriculum program development in nonclassroom and nonschool environments. Although their training focused on a functional life skills curriculum and school integration, the

Table 1. A matrix of the "student factors" that influence the arrangements made for instruction in community environments (Ford et al., 1983)

Identify student: How might this factor influence:	Chronological age	Postschool projections	Student factors: motoric, sensorial, health-related and behavioral difficulties	Performance history	Parent/guardian information	Unique learning and performance characteristics
a) The exact locations in which instruction will occur?						
b) The amount of time allocated to instruction in community environments?						
c) The length of instructional sessions, the frequency at which the sessions should occur, and the time between sessions?						

From Ford, Mirenda, Sweet, Shiraga, Zanella, Nisbet, and Loomis (1983), reprinted with permission.

community component received less emphasis, except in terms of generalization across home settings, parent participation, and vocational-community training for high school–age students with severe disabilities. It is now known that the community intensive emphasis must begin early, increase with the student's chronological age and/or the complexity of the skill, and comprise objectives in critical functions across all domains.

However, this information and current research needs further communication to preservice and present teachers in the field. State personnel development units, as well as local inservice efforts, need to ensure teacher participation in workshops dealing with the rationale, supporting research, and current practices in community intensive instruction. More specific workshops are required on processes such as site inventory and acquisition, public relations skills with nonclassroom and community personnel, unobtrusive data collection methods, creative scheduling and staffing, and the integration or infusion of multiple objectives or critical skills within a variety of environments.

Teachers who are reticent to "buy into" the idea of nonschool instruction for their students because of factors such as chronological age or severity of disability must become aware of the parallel between the rationale for an integrated public school education and the rationale for this extension of the model into additional "LREs" (least restrictive environments). "Prerequisite skills," multiple disabilities, medical fragility, student age, or administrative convenience were not legitimate reasons to delay the integration process (cf. Brown et al., 1979). Today's teachers need to be persuaded that these are also not legitimate reasons to exclude these same students from participation in all community environments.

COMMUNITY INTENSIVE MODEL IMPLEMENTATION

Elementary (6–12 Years)

Students between the ages of 6 and 12, attending Bay Area integrated public schools are receiving instruction within the classroom in environments such as the snack area, play area, and at the sink; in a variety of nonclassroom environments, such as the playground, lunchroom, gym, bathroom, hallways, library, and auditorium; and at community facilities similar to those that the student and his or her family patronize.

Setting and Program Structure   At the setting and program structure level, instruction is directed toward performance of many basic skills and functional activites in each of the daily living domains. Basic skills (e.g., eye contact, reach/grasp) are trained within and across functional activities (e.g., eating a snack, playing a game with a nondisabled peer, brushing teeth). These chronologically age-appropriate skills and functional activities are selected through the inventory processes discussed above by parents, teacher, and ancillary staff. All instruction is designed to prepare the severely disabled student for, and enable him or her to function in, environments appropriate for nondisabled peers of the same age or even for somewhat older students. Once the skills and activities are determined, they are then trained at the time that the activity would naturally occur.

A particular area of importance is that of socialization with nondisabled peers. One initial approach is to implement a "special friends" program (cf. Voeltz, 1984). Teachers of severely disabled students throughout the San Francisco Bay Area recruit nondisabled students who are interested in participating in structured interactions. Frequently, a slide show about the students is used for initial preparation of nondisabled students and staff. Once peers are selected for a special friends or tutoring program, they are assigned to activities (e.g., washing a table, preparing a drink, playing a game with a severely disabled student) that are intended to motivate communication and social interaction. These functional activities are performed in the classroom and/or in nonclassroom environments.

As severely disabled primary students reach approximately age 9, they make a transition to the next stage of their elementary educational program, the "intermediate" level. During the next 3–4 years, the student continues to receive individualized instruction in a variety of curricular areas in the classroom, nonclassroom locations, and community sites; however, the amount of time spent in each environment changes substantially at this new level. Instruction now occurs in many more natural environments where opportunities for training of functional skills and interactions with nondisabled persons are available. Up to 50% of the school week is spent on instruction in community environments.

Nonclassroom Instruction Integrating the severely disabled student within the school building remains a priority at this age. For approximately 2 hours each day, the schedule provides for interaction with nondisabled peers. The classroom teacher ensures that his or her severely disabled students are participating in the same daily activities and environments as general education students, including all of those discussed earlier. Visibility of the students within the school is highly important. As the student moves to this intermediate level, instruction on preparing a drink or a snack occurs in the kitchen and/or at a nonclassroom domestic environment rather than at a classroom table.

Specific vocational training sites within the school building are developed based on the identification of jobs that nondisabled age peers perform. After these jobs are pinpointed, the teacher of severely disabled students works on integrating his or her students into those environments to guarantee the severely disabled students opportunities to perform meaningful work in natural environments, and exposure to nondisabled peers who model appropriate social and work behavior. Some activities that are performed by intermediate level severely disabled students include passing out milk, emptying trash in the office, delivering speech cards, passing out cookies after lunch, and taking attendance. Data from the May 1984 external evaluation of community intensive classrooms in development indicated that 58% of instructional time was spent in nonclassroom environments within the elementary school, with 28% of time spent in classroom instruction, and the remaining approximately 14% of instruction occurring in community settings (Anderson, Filler, & Falvey, 1984).

Community/Nonschool Instruction At the intermediate elementary level, community intensive programming occurs at least twice a week, and is again directed at delivering instruction on relevant basic skills by incorporating them into functional community activities. The skill of reach/grasp is meaningful and motivating when performed within the activity of selecting a snack from a store shelf or picking up a can of soda, activities that have an important function in the student's daily life. Skills that will provide students with greater access to the total community are emphasized.

The most frequented community sites for students of elementary age, based on parental preference and student need, are usually the community streets, grocery stores, and fast food restaurants. Additionally, residential environments such as apartments, private homes, or group-care homes and public transportation services such as bus lines are used where possible to begin early training of a greater proportion of those skills that cannot be simulated within the school environment (e.g., bed-making, bathing, mobility, travel).

Middle School (12–16 Years) and High School (16–21 Years)

Setting and Program Structure Ideally, the only use of a classroom, particularly at the high school level, is for purposes of a "home base" and for storage of materials. However, at the beginning of the school year, it is probable that severely disabled students will spend a small portion of time in their assigned classroom until the teacher is able to complete detailed inventories of potential nonschool environments, conduct parent interviews, secure appropriate sites, determine which students would benefit from instruction at each location, and create a workable community-based schedule. Instruction in the classroom is phased out as soon as possible. Systematic training is implemented in those environments that have been demonstrated to be of high priority in each student's life. For middle school–age students, May 1984 program evaluation data indicated that Bay Area model classrooms had 31% of their instruction occurring in the class, 27% in other school environments, and 42% off-campus in community settings. High school–age students spent approximately 16% of their day in the classroom, 34% in nonclassroom environments within the school, and 50% of instructional time in community settings (Anderson et al., 1984).

Prioritization of the student's needs is determined by looking at: 1) the number of "school" years left, 2) the living and working environments that the student is currently participating in and those that he or she will use following graduation, and 3) the skills that the student has acquired and those additional skills that are needed in order to maximize his or her participation in current and subsequent community environments.

As severely disabled students become adults, work becomes a significant part of life. Therefore, it is necessary to develop independence and productivity related to work, and to promote those work-related behaviors required at community vocational sites.

Nonclassroom Instruction Within the school building, severely disabled students continue to participate in integrated activities with their non-disabled peers. Since the majority of their "school" day (75%–85%) is spent in the community, the remaining inschool time (roughly 1 hour a day) is focused on meeting social, leisure, domestic, and vocational needs. Severely disabled students participate in nonclassroom environments such as the bus area, bathroom, lunchroom, gym, yard, hallways, locker room, home economics room, and vocational sites such as the office, kitchen, faculty room, library, or school grounds. A variety of dressing, grooming, hygiene, clothing care, meal preparation, housekeeping, and social skills can be effectively programmed and trained on school grounds. In addition, there is increasing emphasis on extracurricular activities (e.g., clubs, school dances, evening concerts) that will increase opportunities for age-appropriate social interaction with non-disabled age peers at the school site.

Community/Nonschool Instruction Severely disabled middle and high school students are provided numerous opportunities to participate in natural community environments. In addition to leisure (e.g., bowling alley, video arcade), domestic (kitchen in nearby church, private apartment), and general community environments (mass transit system), secondary-age students in Bay Area programs are receiving training in a variety of vocational settings. Among those training options that have been secured are sorting, shelving, and hanging clothes at a department store; maintaining the grounds at a local park and at a private home; washing station wagons used by Red Cross personnel; setting/busing tables at a sit-down restaurant; assembling intravenous kits at a local hospital; and purchasing kitchen supplies for a nearby church program. Additional job sites are in development (Sailor, Anderson, & Doering, 1983).

Training is provided on integral, related work skills such as mobility (getting to and from community sites), communication (money management/exchange), interacting with the supervisor and other nondisabled co-workers, using break time productively (vending machines, communication and leisure skills), and dressing appropriately (to age of student and job activity).

Teachers coordinate training activities with adult service agencies, particularly during the last few years of the student's high school experience. Parents, educators, and adult service providers design individualized *transition plans* related to the student's participation in postschool environments (cf. Wehman, 1981).

Figure 2 illustrates the current instructional unit schedule for a community intensive secondary level class in San Francisco. The number in the small square at the right of each box indicates the number of half-hours per week in which instruction occurs in that domain. Domestic skills such as cooking and household chores are occurring in residential environments where kitchens are similar to home. Dressing and personal care programs are practiced in real bedrooms as well as in the locker room at school. Peer tutors accompany students off-campus in addition to continuing their on-campus involvement with the program. Nondisabled peers are considered to be indispensable to social and leisure skill training for students with severe disabilities. For this reason and in order to take advantage of the presence of nondisabled peers (as depicted in Figure 2), a number of innovative approaches to scheduling have been explored. For example, some peers are accompanying students to the laundromat on Wednesdays, and to physical education class on Thursdays during the same time period.

As is illustrated by Figure 2, the community intensive model for this age group involves a complex flow of varied environments and programs. The number of nonschool environments increases as well as the amount of time spent in these environments. School time is still maintained but decreased, and there is a substantial drop in classroom time. By the time the students reach age 16, they are spending approximately 10% of their time in the classroom, 15% in the school at large, and 75% of their time in the community, as shown in Figure 1.

While the number of environments is increasing, so is the time spent in the vocational domain of instruction. Within the San Francisco Unified School District, several classes of 10- to 13-year-old students are participating in off-campus work and have been trained on school jobs systematically. In the same district, many 12- to 16-year-old students receive most of their vocational instruction off-campus (with all instruction occurring off-campus for 15- and 16-year-old students). With this heavier emphasis on vocational training and job sampling, the teacher following this model seeks out nonschool placements for students to spend approximately 10 hours a week practicing a specific job skill. Partial or full participation occurs depending on the students' disabilities. Work skills, work behavior difficulties, ease or complexity of job types, and job preferences are identified. Recognizing that students with severe disabilities do not transfer skills easily from one environment to the next, and that it is impossible to simulate all of the details of a natural workplace and all of its personnel within a classroom, the model again stresses the natural context for training. This is age appropriate and similar to the experiences of nondisabled teenagers who work at part-time jobs within their community.

Domestic instruction, recreation, and leisure programs take place more in community facilities than on campus, which again is similar to what occurs in nondisabled students' typical daily lives. Further inspection of one section of the schedule in Figure 2 gives additional information about the specific programs that a teacher might organize within the instructional sessions. At

Morning		Environments, students, and their general program descriptions		
Time	Staff	Total % = 10% Classroom	Total % = 15% Nonclassroom	Total % = 75% Nonschool
8:20 to 8:45	All	Drop off/pick up materials	Bus arrival, use lockers, use bathroom, etc.	Transition to sites
8:45	Teacher			Vocational site, four students Domestic site 80
to	Full-time paraprofessional			Domestic site, four students Vocational site 80
10:45	Part-time paraprofessional			Vocational site, three students 60
10:45 to 11:00	All			Transition 22.5
11:00	Teacher, peers, and extra staff (Tu, Th)		*M W F* Use cafeteria, recreation/leisure, six students 36	*Tu Th* Eat in community 24
to	Full-time paraprofessional, peers, and extra staff (Tu, Th)		*M W F* Use cafeteria, recreation/leisure, five students 30	*Tu Th* Eat in community 20
12:00			Cafeteria line training ─ ─ ─ ─ ─ ─ 11:30 stop	Assist transition ─ ─ ─ ─ ─ ─

Figure 2. Secondary level community intensive classroom schedule.

Afternoon		Environments, students, and their general program descriptions		
Time	Staff	Classroom	Nonclassroom	Nonschool
12 to 12:20	Teacher/ paraprofessional		go to classroom, mobility to bathrooms	
12:20 to 1:00	Teacher (extra staff) (Tu, Th)	Domestic/voca- tional, commu- nity preparation, independent leisure 66		
	Full-time paraprofessional		Break	
1:00 to 1:50	Teacher peer tutors (extra staff MWF)		*Tu Th* Dressing (locker room) — — — — — — P.E.—Recreation, six students — — — — — Dressing (locker room) 21	*M W F* Community domestic: -Laundromat -Restaurant -Stores -Recreation 36
	Full-time paraprofessional and peer tutors (extra staff) Tu, Th)		*Tu Th* Dressing (locker room) — — — — — — P.E.— Recreation — — — — — Dressing (locker room), five students 18	*M W F* Domestic: Hygiene Dressing 30
1:55 to 2:45	Teacher peer tutors (extra staff Tu, Th)			*M W F* Continue as above 36 *Tu Th* Domestic recreation/leisure 24
	Full-time paraprofessional (extra staff (Tu, Th)			*M W F* Same site recreation/leisure 30 *Tu Th* Community 20
2:45 to 3:05	All	Pick up materials	Use lockers, load buses	

Figure 2. *(continued).*

1:00 P.M. on Mondays, Wednesdays, and Fridays, the teacher, peer tutors, and extra staff membes are off-campus with six students in various locations. They continue with these small groups until it is time to go home, at 2:45 P.M. Figure 3 presents a closer examination of their activities.

The students represented in Figure 3 have a wide variety of abilities and disabilities. Some are working on long concurrent chains of behaviors related to community skills. Others are working on partially participating in community activities while practicing parts of the tasks or basic skills. In all instances, each student *participates* to his or her fullest extent at the present time.

Note that there are several skills worked on within each session. While at first glance this may seem cumbersome and too complicated to carry out, further inspection of the total schedule helps to put into perspective the large amount of time allowed for the session. By carrying out small numbers of trials at the appropriate time in natural contexts (cf. individualized curriculum sequences), rather than massed trials of each skill separately, generalization of skills is facilitated (Sailor & Guess, 1983). In Figure 3, Carey uses her electric wheelchair to travel in the community. She is working on more independent mobility skills. She may practice these skills on this community trip, but she also practices within the school building, on the way to her vocational placement, and on the way to other community facilities. Her teacher measures progress on her mobility skills across several environments.

The physical therapist and other ancillary staff using a community intensive model also increase their activities across multiple environments. Despite some logistical problems with related service delivery, several Bay Area school districts have been successful in expanding the integrated model to include community contexts. Rather than providing only direct, "hands-on" service to students for objectives listed under "therapy," the therapist also provides training to the teachers so that specific techniques can be applied to a range of functional life skills (i.e., eating, mobility, stair climbing, transfers). In turn, the teacher provides training to the therapist on the additional skills that the student needs to work on during that activity period (i.e., communication, social programs, shopping, money exchange). For example, instead of working on mobility skills up and down the halls of the school with no purposeful destination, the therapist trains the staff to run the mobility programs *en route* to community locations and then monitors progress once a week or more. Rather than working on eating skills only in the school lunchroom, the therapist also trains these skills in a nearby restaurant. The classroom staff further extends the contexts in which these skills are taught. Note that in Figure 3, the therapist meets the teacher at the laundromat to exchange students and return to the school building while working on different mobility skills with another pair of students. Innovative schedule plans such as these make it easier for the therapist to use the time allotted for each particular class to the best advantage.

Having therapists, graduate students, peer tutors, and volunteers function as ancillary staff is a key component of providing community intensive instruction. Larger instructional groups do not approximate natural proportions in the community and often prevent the instructor from systematically carrying out programs. Flexibility in the use of staff time is necessary if the model is going to work, especially when class sizes are very large. As mentioned earlier, heterogeneous (rather than categorical) groupings of students may also facilitate innovative staffing arrangements.

Parents continue to be closely involved with the implementation of all aspects of community programming at this age level. In the domestic area, students make regular purchases for their families during shopping activities. Examples of other responsibilities performed for the family include mailing letters, and dropping off or picking up clothes at the cleaners, or shoes at the shoe repair shop. In the vocational area, parents provide information about neighborhood businesses for potential training sites. Most important, as mentioned above, parents provide information on their son's or daughter's expected subsequent environments, as well as the family's preferences for postschool work and residential placement.

RESEARCH: INSTRUCTIONAL TECHNOLOGY IN COMMUNITY CONTEXTS

Successful applications of community-based instruction that document acquisition of new skills as a function of instruction in the natural environment have been reported with increasing frequency. Individual students have learned such skills as shopping in supermarkets (Ford, 1983; Wheeler, Ford, Nietupski, Loomis, & Brown, 1980); performing appropriate pedestrian skills (Vogelsberg & Rusch, 1979); riding a city bus (Coon et al., 1981; Sowers, Rusch, & Hudson, 1979); eating appropriately in public restaurants (van den Pol et al., 1981); playing a pool game in public recreation facilities (Hill et al., 1982); and carrying out specific self-care routines in a group-home setting (Freagon & Rotatori, 1982).

Numerous questions are raised by this body of research. Some authors have provided evidence that skills taught in the classroom generalize to natural community settings (Page, Iwata, & Neef, 1976), while others have failed to replicate this finding (Coon et al., 1981). The relative efficacy of natural environments versus artificial (classroom) training contexts also remains to be established, with conflicting data reported in the literature (Page et al., 1976; Freagon & Rotatori, 1982). In addition to comparative evaluations of the time and place of instruction, the selection of appropriate teaching strategies for use in the community remains an empirical question (cf. Peck & Semmel, 1982). Vogelsberg and Rusch (1979) found, for example, that three severely disabled

Time	Teacher	Physical therapist	Graduate student
1:00	Activity: With peer tutor walk to laundromat Systematic programs: —Tan—1) Street crossing, 2) walking on sidewalks without eating garbage, 3) walking by peer tutor —David—1) Use walker on sidewalks, 2) step off curbs with assistance	—Meet students in class Activity: Walk to nearby restaurant Systematic programs: —Carey—Using electric wheelchair in the community —Janet—Assist by grasping purse as P.T. pushes her	Activity: Take city bus to business district with peer tutors Systematic programs: —Felicia—1) Bus riding sequence with assistance, 2) socially acceptable behavior (no self-abusive behavior) —Lamonte—1) Climb stairs of bus, take transfer with assistance, 2) sit down with assistance, 3) no rocking behavior on bus, 4) give piece of gum to peer tutor
1:10	Activity: Use of laundromat and stores Systematic programs: —Tan—1) Laundry sequence—partial participation on money and sorting, 2) coin-operated soap machine programs, 3) money changer, 4) video game play with peer tutor, 5) shop for items at produce market nearby using precounted money, uses picture list with assistance to communicate in store, 6) maintain (no screaming or climbing) socially appropriate behavior, 7) folding clothes	Activity: Use restaurant Systematic programs: —Carey—1) Use communications board to indicate choice, use order card; 2) smile at waitress, listen; 3) open purse, get money out, hand precounted money to hostess when leaving; 4) use wheelchair in restaurant —Janet—1) chew food with assistance, 2) swallow liquids through straw, 3) use communication card to give order to waitress by grasping it and looking up when she arrives, 4) keep glasses on while in restaurant	Activity: Play cards and basketball in nearby park —Felicia—1) Throw, catch, and shoot with partial assistance (with peer tutor), 2) behavior (same) —Lamonte—1) Play modified card game with peer tutor with assistance, 2) same behavior program —Felicia—1) Do part of shopping sequence independently with supervision and assistance with money handling, 2) choose drink using communication booklet, remember to find same drink in store, 3) walk with peer tutor. —Lamonte—1) Carry drink to store counter, give money, put change in bag, 2) offer cookies out of backpack to peers with prompt from teacher, 3) eat with moderate speed

2:15	—*David*—1) Open washer, put soap and clothes in and out with assistance; open dryer and put in and out with assistance, 2) push money changer in and vending machine selector button in, 3) keep hearing aids in while in laundromat, 4) use walker to enter corner market to buy juice for tomorrow's lunch, 5) hand store clerk money and receive change, place in pocket, 6) fold clothes with assistance *Activity:* Greet friends when they arrive; —Tan—smile, wave; Carey—smile, sounds (switch with P.T.) *Activity:* Return to school *Systematic programs:* —*Carey*—use electric wheelchair —*Janet*—hold purse	*Activity:* Walk to nearby laundromat, meet teacher and other students, switch for the return to school *Systematic programs:* Same mobility programs, and: —*Carey*—1) greet friends using communication board and answer questions using known pictures —*Janet*—smile at friends and look at them while talking (switch with teacher)
2:30	*Activity:* Return to school *Systematic programs:* —*Tan*—Street crossing —*David*—Use walker	*Activity:* Return on bus to school—same as above

Figure 3. Nonclassroom instruction for M-W-F, 1:00–2:45 P.M. (names are fictional).

students instructed in the natural environment acquired specific components of a "street crossing" behavior chain only after they were presented as two-behavior (versus four-behavior) chains. Ford (1983) compared antecedent and consequential teaching strategies used in a community training program and found both to be effective in producing skill acquisition, generalization, and maintenance in eight moderately and severely disabled adolescents. However, post hoc analysis between groups (moderate and severe) indicated that the severely disabled students did make significantly greater performance gains under the antecedent condition than under the consequential condition. This suggests that antecedent teaching procedures may be more effective for the more severely disabled students, and Ford recommends this possibility as an area for further investigation.

Despite these unanswered questions, what characterizes this literature as a whole is the empirical documentation that severely disabled persons can learn when instructed in integrated, natural community contexts. A second feature that characterizes this literature is the direct transfer of established teaching technologies for learners with severe disabilities (cf. Sailor & Guess, 1983; Snell, 1983) from classroom to nonschool settings. Such transfer of "old" training technologies to new environments is supported on both theoretical and empirical grounds; it represents a logical extension of principles known to be effective in teaching new skills to disabled students. However, the transition to an integrated, community intensive model of instruction also offers an opportunity to adapt this "old" instructional technology to facilitate skill acquisition in ways that utilize the unique features of naturally occurring, socially integrated settings. Both recent theoretical analyses and recent data from the California Research Institute on the Integration of Students with Severe Disabilities (CRI) (Sailor, 1982) suggest some possible directions that such innovations in instructional technology might take.

The Nature of Integrated Environments

Gaylord-Ross and Peck (1985) have proposed a model of social skill development in severely disabled students that stresses the interaction between environment and person in assessing the individual's potential for learning. According to their model, which derives its logic from the historical "nature-nurture" controversy (Hirsch, 1975), integrated, normalized settings are crucial to accurate assessment of the severely disabled students' functioning because they provide opportunities for skill development that are, by definition, not available in segregated settings. Only through this interaction of person and environmental opportunity is an accurate picture of the individual's potential possible:

> . . . Integrated settings present a wide range of situational stimuli. The important point is that these represent opportunities for the individual to develop a rich repertoire of responses. . . . The highly differentiated environment induces the

development of skills and behaviors that never would have been observed in less differentiated settings. (Gaylord-Ross & Peck, 1985, p. 197)

Empirical validation of this model requires, of course, both accurate description of the dimensions along which integrated community environments differ from segregated, self-contained settings, and demonstration of functional relationships between these dimensions and actual behavior.

A recently completed study at the California Research Institute on the Integration of Students with Severe Disabilities (Contract No. 300-82-0365) (Sailor, 1982) has provided evidence that the nature of the opportunities for social interaction experienced by severely disabled children does in fact differ as a function of an integrated versus a segregated school setting (Anderson & Goetz, 1983).

In order to examine the nature of social interactions available in segregated versus integrated settings, Anderson and Goetz (1983) conducted a directed observational study (Holm, 1978) of "vertical" (nondisabled peer/severely disabled student) interactions during recess in both settings. The number and type of interactions experienced by severely disabled students during 10 minutes of free play at recess were measured using the EASI (Educational Assessment of Social Interaction) (Goetz, Haring, & Anderson, 1983). The EASI is an observational checklist developed specifically to evaluate social interactions between nondisabled (ND) and severely disabled (SD) persons, indicating the role of ND or SD persons in the interaction (initiate/ acknowledge), the purpose of the interaction (teaching, helping, social), and the topography of SD student behavior (isolate, inappropriate to self or others, appropriate).

The independent variable was placement at an integrated site. Integration was defined as an elementary site containing one SD classroom in which the "best practices" of inservice for ND students, staff and families, special friends, and peer tutoring programs were employed. Control was available for teacher differences across settings as the teachers of the experimental group moved from the segregated to the integrated sites with their students. A matched group design was utilized with seven severely disabled students in each group. Students were matched informally on the basis of teacher consensus along the dimensions of motoric, communicative, and social abilities and disabilities. (Subsequent statistical analysis of premeasure scores indicated no differences between the groups.) Pre- and postmeasures were taken at intervals of 8 months, with both measures taken at segregated sites for the control group and the postmeasure for the experimental group taken at the integrated site. Reliability measures were taken on 60% of the observations with an interobserver agreement of 84%.

The results indicated that there are differences in the opportunities for and the nature of social interactions experienced by severely disabled students in integrated settings. Defining an opportunity for interaction by SD students as an initiation by a ND person, there were significantly more opportunities for interaction between SD and ND persons in the integrated setting. (All statistical analyses were conducted using the Wilcoxon Matched-Pairs Signed-Ranks for small *n* research.) There were more than twice as many ND initiations toward SD students in the integrated setting as there were in the segregated setting. While a finding of increased opportunities for interaction in an integrated environment may seem self-evident, the data further indicated qualitative differences in the *nature* of these increased opportunities for social interaction in integrated versus segregated settings. One hundred percent of the inter-actions in the segregated settings were vertical (between an ND adult and an SD student) in nature. Only 11% of the interactions in the integrated setting were vertical. Thus, in the integrated settings, 89% of the social initiations directed toward the SD students were generated by ND peers. This leads to the question of whether SD students participated in more interactions in integrated settings as a function of increased opportunities. In fact, the SD students acknowledged significantly more ND initiations in the integrated settings than in the seg-regated settings. (Results presented here are part of a larger data set described in detail in Anderson and Goetz, 1983.)

It appears that students with severe disabilities increase the rate of their participation in interactions with nondisabled persons as a function of increased opportunities for interaction. This indicates that students with severe dis-abilities are not only able to take advantage of the increased opportunities in the natural environment of an integrated playground, but are also equally effective as participants in social interaction in integrated settings as in segregated settings and with ND peers as with adult educators.

Preliminary data indicate, then, that the nature of the social environment experienced by severely disabled students is different in integrated settings, and that a higher percentage of horizontal (peer-peer) interactions is one charac-teristic of this difference. A logical next step is to investigate the outcomes of this changed social environment. Do severely disabled students learn more quickly when instructed by a peer than when instructed by a teacher? What are the outcomes correlated with different forms of social interaction (i.e., struc-tured versus unstructured)? Is there evidence of correlated social skill and/or affect changes?

Instructional Factors in Integrated Settings

The range of opportunities for social experiences by severely disabled students is but one area of difference between segregated and integrated school envi-ronments. The range of opportunities for instruction by the special education teacher is also greater in integrated community intensive settings. This is particularly true in relation to the number and type of persons for whom instruction is provided. As was mentioned in the study described above, "integration" included an entire package of interventions for educators, families, and nondisabled students in the areas of disability awareness, specific inservice regarding individual severely disabled students, and instruction in teaching and social behavior for peer tutors and special friends. This has the potential for a tremendous increase in the caseload of the special class teacher. However, the need for specific intervention to facilitate horizontal interaction between nondisabled and disabled peers has been well documented (Guralnick, 1976; Peck, Apolloni, Cooke, & Raver, 1978; Voeltz, 1982, 1984). It is therefore incumbent on educational researchers to explore the comparative efficiency and impact of various interventions upon the social interaction of nondisabled and severely disabled students.

In order to determine whether anything less than the full package of integration intervention described above would facilitate horizontal interactions, Anderson (1984) measured the impact of general and specific inservice upon nondisabled students participating in interaction with severely disabled students in an unstructured recess setting. The subjects included seven elementary-age severely multiply disabled students with little or no formal communicative skills, and 12 randomly selected nondisabled third grade students. Intervention consisted of: 1) general or disability awareness inservice, 2) specific inservice that provided information regarding motor abilities and communicative abilities (including nonvocal means), and 3) preferred social activities or games for each severely disabled student. The dependent measures included a cumulative duration of SD/ND interaction during a 10-minute sample at recess and the occurrence of quality indicators (that included use of the SD students' names, invitation to participate in an activity), indication of termination of the activity, and the use of alternative modes of communication. Data were collected on the above variables on three occasions (baseline, postgeneral inservice, postspecific inservice) for each of the 12 nondisabled students. Reliability measures, which were taken on 30% of the 10-minute sessions, resulted in an average in interobserver agreement of 98%.

Baseline data support the available literature on the need for specific intervention in order for cross-group (ND/SD) horizontal interactions to occur. The nondisabled students had been going to the same school as the severely disabled students for 2 years, but ND students had not participated in any structured interactions such as peer tutoring or special friends. During baseline, the 12 ND students participated in interactions with the severely disabled students for a total of 48 seconds during 120 minutes of observation, or an average of .13 minutes for 10 minutes of recess. Postgeneral inservice data indicated an increase to an average of 1.6 minutes per 10 minutes of recess. Postspecific inservice data indicated the largest increase to a mean of 3.8 minutes per 10 minutes of recess. (These data are displayed in Figure 4.) Quality indicators followed a similar trend.

These data indicate that general and specific inservice do result in an increase in both the amount and quality of horizontal interaction between

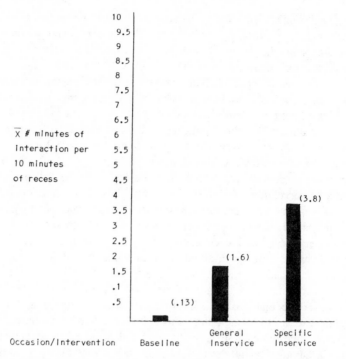

Figure 4. Mean duration (in minutes of nondisabled/severely disabled interaction during 10 minutes of recess on three occasions).

nondisabled and severely disabled students. The majority of regular education schools in California house from 300 to 3,000 nondisabled students. As it is not possible for all nondisabled students at a given school to participate in structured interventions such as peer tutoring or special friends programs, it is encouraging that there may be effective forms of intervention that can be administered to groups of students in relatively small amounts of time.

These inservice data have implications not only for the proportion of nondisabled students who can receive intervention, but also for the amount of special class teacher time required for this intervention. Also, general inservice can be provided by someone other than the special class teacher. As mentioned earlier, there are two volunteer groups of parents of severely disabled students who have provided general disability awareness inservice to more than 700 elementary, middle and high school–age nondisabled students at integrated sites throughout the San Francisco Unified School District.

However, the results of this study (Anderson, 1984) must be considered with caution as there are no data to indicate longitudinal impact of the intervention, nor can conclusions be drawn as to the effectiveness of either general or specific inservice in isolation. Further research is needed that compares the impact of various types of intervention upon the social behavior of both nondisabled and severely disabled students.

Murata (1982), for example, evaluated the effects of a peer training procedure for nondisabled (ND) peers upon the social interaction behaviors of severely disabled elementary school students. This study was designed to evaluate the effects of a training package to teach ND students four cooperative games (e.g., velcro darts, bean bag throw) to play with the SD student using role play and modeling procedures. Murata's dependent measure, however, was not skill acquisition of the games by the severely disabled students. Rather, she measured changes in the severely disabled students' social interaction behaviors as a function of peer-delivered instruction in specific game skills. Using a multiple baseline design across three students, she demonstrated that during intervention phases, all three SD students showed immediate and marked increases in social interaction behaviors ($\overline{X}$ = 67.8 interactions per 10-minute observation interval) in comparison to baseline conditions ($\overline{X}$ = 3.9 interactions per 10-minute observation interval).

The infusion of chronologically age-appropriate nondisabled peers into the severely disabled student's learning environment is clearly one dimension that holds promise for future and ongoing research. The preliminary evidence available to date suggests that this may be one dimension of a community intensive model, the outcomes of which are both dramatic and supported by newly emerging research.

Innovative Teaching Strategies

Use of peer tutors for instruction reflects one innovative teaching practice that is made possible by a community intensive model. As Ford and Mirenda (1984) have discussed, community-based instruction also requires that educators pay particular attention to the use of naturally occurring cues and consequences (Falvey et al., 1980) in developing instructional programs. Many characteristics of instruction in a controlled classroom setting would be both unnecessarily stigmatizing and logistically impractical if applied to instruction occurring in natural contexts. The use of massed practice, for example, in which one instructional trial is repeated several times, translates poorly to a community setting. Not only would it appear abnormal to the community at large to "practice" buying a grocery store item 10 times in a row, but it would also be vastly impractical in terms of what Ford and Mirenda (1984) have termed "logistical factors": staff-to-student ratios, transportation, and cost. Staff time, the technical details of getting to the store 10 times (or even five times) in one day, and the cost of buying 10 cans of juice would be prohibitive.

Similarly, standard positive reinforcement practices may also be unnecessarily stigmatizing and/or largely impractical. As Ford et al. (1983) observe, ". . . [b]ecause of the complex and public nature of community environments, reinforcement procedures, such as tokens, food rewards, lavish praise, and some types of physical affection may be inappropriate'' (p. 172). Naturally occurring reinforcers are clearly preferable, yet educators working with students with severe disabilities are often faced with the dilemma of trying to establish motivation in students who are unresponsive to conventional reinforcement practices (Devany & Rincover, 1982).

Goetz, Schuler, and Sailor (1983) have recently proposed an alternative model of motivation that specifically addresses the problem of ''unresponsive'' (i.e., lack of response to conventional instructional practices) students, and that results in an instructional model that appears uniquely suited to community intensive instruction. They have hypothesized that the opportunity to reinstate an ongoing behavior sequence after it has been interrupted is a major source of motivation that can result in acquisition of new skills.

Goetz, Gee, and Sailor (1983) worked with two severely disabled adolescents, both of whom were learning to use a pictorial communication system through systematic, data based instruction in the classroom. Joe had acquired a vocabulary of six to eight pictures, but the learning time for each new picture was several months. Chip had failed to learn his first picture despite 5 months of systematic instruction.

To evaluate the hypothesis that interrupting an established behavior sequence would result in acquisition of communication responses, three behavior sequences were selected for each student. Criteria for selection of a sequence included a series of at least three behaviors that the student anticipated (i.e., tried to do, even if performance was not totally independent), and that the sequence occurred naturally at least once a day. The three sequences for each student were as follows:

Joe	Chip
1. Washing dishes in classroom after lunch	1. Making toast in the local church kitchen
2. Brushing teeth in the locker room	2. Getting a pivot pool game from the closet to play with peers
3. Going outside the classroom to dump garbage	3. Collecting attendance slips in school hallway

Following a baseline phase to determine that the pictures for these events were in fact unknown, two different instructional procedures were compared. In the ''traditional sequence'' phase of instruction, a communication trial was inserted at the beginning of the sequence. The student was asked, ''What do you want?'' and was required to point to the correct picture. If correct, he was allowed to start the sequence. If incorrect, he was shown the correct response, and the trial was repeated once. Consequences for the correction trial included the opportunity to start the task if correct, and the termination of the trial if incorrect. Due to the nature of the sequences, which occurred naturally only once a day, a session consisted of two trials, with a maximum of four trials possible per day (two initial trials and two correction trials.)

With one exception, procedures were identical in the "interrupted sequence" phase. The communication trial was inserted into the middle of the ongoing sequence. The exact location of the trial in the sequence had been pretested to ensure that the interruption did not cause a high degree of frustration that might have interfered with learning. During the pretesting, the student's teacher and a classroom aide interrupted the student at several places within a given sequence and scored the student's distress on a three-point scale, with a score of "one" indicating indifference or no distress, and "three" indicating high distress expressed as aggressive or self-abusive behaviors. The places selected for interruption were those consistently scored as "two," or moderate distress.

Figure 5 presents representative data from two of the sequences for Chip. (Reliability checks on these data were taken on the average of once every 3 days, with mean reliability at 100%.) As is evident from these data, use of a traditional sequence strategy resulted in essentially flat data trends for both pictures. However, each time the instructional strategy was switched to an interrupted sequence strategy, the result was a dramatic increase in correct responding. Chip met the criterion of five consecutive correct responses on the initial presentation of each trial for both pictures within 12 sessions of interrupted sequence training. Joe's data replicated these trends within the context of an internally valid experimental design, as reported in detail in Goetz, Gee, and Sailor (1983).

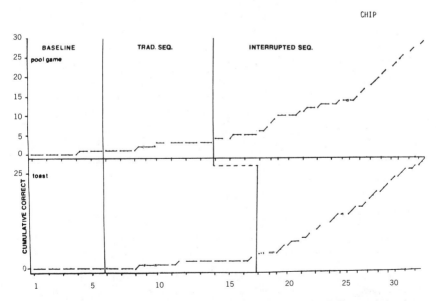

Figure 5. Cumulative trial-by-trial data from two pictures for Chip. ( ) Indicates missing data points due to absence from school.

In terms of implications for community training, several aspects of the interrupted sequence training merit comment. The first aspect has to do with the relative number of training trials per session. A strategy that requires massed repetition of instructional trials for success is clearly less well suited for community intensive instruction than one that requires only one or two presentations of a trial within an instructional session. The procedures used in the above investigation utilized a minimum of two trials (if the student was correct on the initial presentation of each trial) and a maximum of four trials (initial trial plus a correction trial), yet learning still occurred relatively rapidly. Additionally, the reinforcement was entirely naturally occurring; the opportunity to reinstate the ongoing behavior chain contingent upon correct responses appeared to be sufficient motivation to result in learning.

Much more information about the interrupted sequence strategy is needed before it is recommended as a successful strategy for use in the community, including topics such as its extension to skills other than communication, the criteria by which optimal chains for instruction are selected (i.e., making toast is possibly more reinforcing than playing pivot pool), the role of anticipated outcomes in establishing sequences, and so forth. Nevertheless, it serves as a successful example of how the unique demands of community intensive instruction can be met through innovations in "old" instructional technology.

Future Research Directions

Building an instructional technology that utilizes both the unique features of integrated community settings and that can be readily applied in diverse, complex environments presents a major research challenge. While major administrative and policy concerns (cf. Hamre-Nietupski et al., 1982) may shape the implementation of community intensive models on a systems level, one of the ultimate outcome measures will be what students with severe disabilities actually experience when given the opportunity for full participation in a heterogeneous society. Although the data discussed here are limited, they do provide educators with the beginnings of empirical support for integrated, community-based instruction, and with grounds for optimism concerning the outcome of community intensive programs for their students.

REFERENCES

Anderson, J. (1984). *The effects of two strategies for increasing regular education students' awareness about their severely disabled peers.* Unpublished manuscript, San Francisco State University, Department of Special Education, San Francisco.

Anderson, J., Filler, J., & Falvey, M. (1984). *Year 1 evaluation report. Nonschool personnel project* (Grant G0008301356). Washington, DC: U.S. Department of Education, Office of Special Education.

Anderson, J., & Goetz, L. (1983, November). *Opportunities for social interaction between severely disabled and nondisabled students in segregated and integrated educational settings*. Paper presented at the 10th Annual Conference of the Association for Persons with Severe Handicaps, San Francisco, CA.

Baumgart, D., Brown, L., Pumpian, I., Nisbet, J., Ford, A., Sweet, M., Messina, R., & Schroeder, J. (1982). Principle of partial participation and individualized adaptations in educational programs for severely handicapped students. *Journal of The Association for the Severely Handicapped, 7*(2), 17–28.

Brown, L., Branston, M. B., Baumgart, D., Vincent, L., Falvey, M., & Schroeder, J. (1979). Utilizing the characteristics of a variety of current and subsequent least restrictive environments as factors in the development of curricular content for severely handicapped students. *AAESPH Review, 4*(4), 407–424.

Brown, L., Nisbet, J., Ford, A., Sweet, M., Shiraga, B., & Gruenewald, L. (1982). *Education programs for severely handicapped students* (Vol. XII). Madison: University of Wisconsin-Madison and Madison Metropolitan School District, and Department of Specialized Education Services, Madison Public Schools.

Brown, L., Nisbet, J., Ford, A., Sweet, M., Shiraga, B., York, J., & Loomis, R. (1983). The critical need for nonschool instruction in education programs for severely handicapped students. *Journal of The Association for the Severely Handicapped, 8*(3), 71–77.

Coon, M., Vogelsberg, T., & Williams, W. (1981). Effects of classroom public transportation instruction on generalization to the natural environment. *Journal of The Association for the Severely Handicapped, 6*, 46–53.

Devany, J., & Rincover, J. (1982). Self-stimulatory behavior and sensory reinforcement. In R. Koegel, A. Rincover, & A. Egel (Eds.), *Educating and understanding autistic children* (pp. 127–141). San Diego: College-Hill Press.

Doering, K. F., & Hunt, P. C. (1983). *Inventory processes for social interaction*. San Francisco: San Francisco State University; San Francisco Unified School District. (ERIC Document Reproduction Service No. ED 242 181).

Falvey, M., Brown, L., Lyon, S., Baumgart, D., & Schroeder, J. (1980). Strategies for using cues and correction procedures. In W. Sailor, B. Wilcox, & L. Brown (Eds.), *Methods of instruction for severely handicapped students* (pp. 109–133). Baltimore: Paul H. Brookes Publishing Co.

Falvey, M., Smithey, L., & Zivolich, S. (1984) *Development and implementation of community based programs*. Unpublished manuscript, California State University, Los Angeles.

Ford, A. (1983). *The performance of moderately and severely handicapped students in community environments as a function of the cues available and the antecedent versus consequential teaching procedures used*. Unpublished doctoral dissertation, University of Wisconsin, Department of Behavioral Disabilities, Madison.

Ford, A., & Mirenda, P. (1984) Community instruction: A natural cues and corrections decision model. *Journal of The Association for Persons with Severe Handicaps, 9*, 79–88.

Ford, A., Mirenda, P., Sweet, M., Shiraga, B., Zanella, K., Nisbet, J., & Loomis, R. (1983). Teaching strategies for use in community environments. In L. Brown, A. Ford, J. Nisbet, M. Sweet, B. Shiraga, J. York, R. Loomis, & P. Vandeventer (Eds.), *Educational programs for severely handicapped students* (Vol. XIII, pp. 147–186). Madison, WI: Madison Metropolitan School District.

Freagon, S., & Rotatori, A. F. (1982). Comparing natural and artificial environments in training self-care skills to group home residents. *Journal of The Association for Persons with Severe Handicaps, 7*(3), 73–86.

Freagon, S., Wheeler, J., Brankin, G., McDaniel, K., Costello, D., & Peters, W. M. (1983). *Curricular processes for the school and community: Integration of severely handicapped students aged 6–21. Project replication guide*. Dekalb: Northern Illinois University.

Fredericks, B., Anderson, R., & Baldwin, V. (1979). The identification of competency indicators of teachers of the severely handicapped. *AAESPH Review, 4,* 81–95.

Gaylord-Ross, R., & Peck, C. A. (1985). Integration efforts for students with severe mental handicaps. In D. Bricker & J. Filler (Eds.), *Serving the severely retarded: From research to practice* (pp. 185–207). Reston, VA: The Council for Exceptional Children.

Goetz, L., Gee, K., & Sailor, W. (1983, November). *Using interrupted sequences to establish pictoral communication skills.* Paper presented at the 10th Annual Conference of The Association for Persons with Severe Handicaps, San Francisco, CA.

Goetz, L., Haring, T., & Anderson, J. (1983). *Educational assessment of social interaction (EASI): An observational checklist for measuring social interactions between nondisabled and severely disabled students in integrated settings.* San Francisco: San Francisco State University, San Francisco Unified School District. (ERIC Document Reproduction No. ED 242 184).

Goetz, L., Schuler, A., & Sailor, W. (1983). Teaching communication skills to severely handicapped students: Motivational considerations. In M. Hersen, V. Van Hasselt, & J. Matson (Eds.), *Behavior therapy for the developmentally and physically disabled* (pp. 57–77). New York: Academic Press.

Grossmont Union High School District. (1983). *Procedural handbook for implementation of natural-based educational programming.* La Mesa, CA: Author.

Guralnick, M. J. (1976). The value of integrating handicapped and non-handicapped preschool children. *American Journal of Orthopsychiatry, 46,* 236–245.

Halvorsen, A. T. (1983a). *Models of parent involvement in the educational process of their severely handicapped child: Past assumptions and future directions.* San Francisco: San Francisco State University, Department of Special Education. (ERIC Document Reproduction Service No. ED 232 354).

Halvorsen, A. T. (1983b). *Parents and community together (PACT).* San Francisco: San Francisco State University, San Francisco Unified School District. (ERIC Document Reproduction Service No. ED 242 183).

Hamre-Nietupski, S., Nietupski, J., Bates, P., & Maurer, S. (1982). Implementing a community-based educational model for moderately/severely handicapped students: Common problems and suggested solutions. *Journal of The Association for the Severely Handicapped, 7*(4), 38–43.

Hanson, M. J. (1981). A model for early intervention with culturally diverse single and multiparent families. *Topics in Early Childhood Special Education, 1*(3), 37–44.

Hanson, M. (1984). *Atypical infant development.* Austin, TX: PRO-ED.

Hill, J., Wehman, P., & Horst, G. (1982). Toward generalization of appropriate leisure and social behavior in severely handicapped youth: Pinball machine use. *Journal of The Association for the Severely Handicapped, 6*(4), 38–44.

Hirsch, J. (1975). Jensenism: The bankruptcy of "science" without scholarship. *Educational Theory, 25,* 3–27.

Holm, R. A. (1978). Techniques of recording observational data. In G. Sackett (Ed.), *Observing behavior: Vol. 2. Data collection and analytic methods* (pp. 99–108). Baltimore: University Park Press.

Holvoet, J., Mulligan, M., Schussler, N., Lacy, L., & Guess, D., (1982). *The KICS Project: Sequencing learning experiences for severely handicapped children and youth.* Lawrence: The Kansas Individualized Curriculum Project, University of Kansas, Department of Special Education.

Hutchison, D. J. (1974). *A model for transdisciplinary staff development.* New York: United Cerebral Palsy Association.

Kazdin, A. (1977). Assessing the clinical or applied importance of behavior change through social validation. *Behavior Modification, 1,* 427–452.

Liberty, K. A., Haring, N. G., & Martin, M. M. (1981). Teaching new skills to the severely handicapped. *Journal of The Association for the Severely Handicapped, 6,* 5–13.

Lyon, S., & Lyon, G. (1980). Team functioning and staff development: A role release approach to providing integrated educational services to severely handicapped students. *Journal of The Association for the Severely Handicapped, 5,* 250–263.

Menchetti, B. M., Rusch, F. R., & Lamson, D. S. (1981). Social validation of behavioral training techniques: Assessing the normalizing qualities of competitive employment training procedures. *Journal of The Association for the Severely Handicapped, 6,* 6–16.

Murata, C. (1982). *The effects of an indirect training procedure for nonhandicapped peers on interaction response class behaviors of autistic children.* Unpublished master's thesis, Department of Special Education, San Francisco State University, San Francisco.

Murray, C., & Porter Beckstead, S. (1983). *Awareness and inservice manual (AIM).* San Francisco: San Francisco State University, San Francisco Unified School District. (ERIC Document Reproduction Service No. ED 242 182).

Nietupski, J., Scheutz, G., & Ockwood, L. (1980). The delivery of communication therapy services to severely handicapped students: A plan for change. *Journal of The Association for the Severely Handicapped, 5,* 13–23.

Page, T., Iwata, B., & Neef, N. (1976). Teaching pedestrian skills to retarded persons: Generalization from the classroom to the natural environment. *Journal of Applied Behavior Analysis, 9,* 433–444.

Peck, C., Apolloni, T., Cooke, T., & Raver, S. (1978). Teaching retarded preschool children to imitate nonhandicapped peers: Training and generalization effects. *Journal of Special Education, 12,* 195–207.

Peck, C., & Semmel, M. (1982). Identifying the least restrictive environment for children with severe handicaps: Toward an empirical analysis. *Journal of The Association for the Severely Handicapped,7*(1), 56–62.

Piuma, M. F., Halvorsen, A. T., Murray, C., & Porter Beckstead, S., (1983). *Project REACH administrator's manual (PRAM).* San Francisco: San Francisco State University, San Francisco Unified School District. (ERIC Document Reproduction Service No. ED 242-185).

Rusch, R., Schutz, R., & Agran, M. (1982). Validating entry level survival skills for service occupations. *Journal of The Association for the Severely Handicapped, 8*(3), 32–41.

Sailor, W. (1982). *California Research Institute on the Integration of Students with Severe Disabilities (CRI).* (Contract No. 300-82-0365). Washington, DC: U.S. Department of Education, Office of Special Education.

Sailor, W., Anderson, J. L., & Doering, K. (1983). *Personnel preparation in a nonschool instructional model for severely handicapped students.* (Grant #G0008301356). Washington, DC: U.S. Department of Education, Office of Special Education.

Sailor, W., & Guess, D. (1983) *Severely handicapped students: An instructional design.* Boston: Houghton Mifflin Co.

Savage, S. (Ed.). (1983). *Individualized critical skills model (ICSM).* Alameda, CA: Training and Resource Group, California Department of Education, Personnel Development Unit.

Snell, M. (1983). *Systematic instruction of the moderately and severely handicapped.* Columbus, OH: Charles E. Merrill Publishing Co.

Sowers, J., Rusch, F., & Hudson, C. (1979). Training a severely retarded young adult to ride the city bus to and from work. *AAESPH Review, 4,* 15–22.

Stainback, W., & Stainback, S. (1981). A review of research on interactions between severely handicapped and nonhandicapped students. *Journal of The Association for the Severely Handicapped, 6,* 23–29.

Sternat, J., Messina, R., Nietupski, J., Lyon, S., & Brown, L. (1977). Occupational and physical therapy services for severely handicapped students. In E. Sontag (Ed.), *Educational programming for the severely and profoundly handicapped* (pp. 263–278). Reston, VA: The Council for Exceptional Children.

Taylor, S. (1982). From segregation to integration: Strategies for integrating severely handicapped students in normal school and community settings. *Journal of The Association for the Severely Handicapped, 8,* 42–49.

van den Pol, R., Iwata, B., Ivancic, I., Page, T., Neef, N., & Whitley, F. (1981). Teaching the handicapped to eat in public places. *Journal of Applied Behavioral Analysis, 14,* 61–69.

Vincent, L. J., Salisbury, C., Walter, G., Brown, P., Gruenewald, L. J., & Powers, M. (1980). Program evaluation and curriculum development in early childhood/special education: Criteria of the next environment. In W. Sailor, B. Wilcox, & L. Brown (Eds.), *Methods of instruction for severely handicapped students* (pp. 303–328). Baltimore: Paul H. Brookes Publishing Co.

Voeltz, L. M. (1982). Effects of structured interactions with severely handicapped peers on children's attitudes. *Ameican Journal of Mental Deficiency, 86,* 380–390.

Voeltz, L. M. (1984). Program and curriculum innovations to prepare children for integration. In N. Certo, N. Haring, & R. York (Eds.), *Public school integraion of severely handicapped students: Rational issues and progressive alternatives* (pp. 155–183.) Baltimore: Paul H. Brookes Publishing Co.

Vogelsberg, R. T., & Rusch, F. R. (1979). Training severely handicapped students to cross partially controlled intersections. *AAESPH Review, 4,* 24–273.

Wehman, P. (1981). *Competitive employment: New horizons for severely disabled individuals.* Baltimore: Paul H. Brookes Publishing Co.

Wheeler, J., Ford, A., Nietupski, J., Loomis, R., & Brown, L. (1980). Teaching moderately and severely handicapped adolescents to shop in supermarkets using pocket calculators. *Education and Training of the Mentally Retarded, 15,* 105–112.

Wolf, M. (1978). Social validity: The case for subjective measurement or how applied behavior analysis is finding its heart. *Journal of Applied Behavior Analysis, 11,* 203–214.

Chapter 10

Teaching Generalized Skills
General Case Instruction in Simulation and Community Settings

Robert H. Horner,
John J. McDonnell, and G. Thomas Bellamy

A fundamental assumption in American education is that skills learned by students in the classroom will generalize to home and community situations. For the majority of students in the educational system, this assumption is valid. For students with severe mental handicaps, this assumption is tenuous at best. This chapter explores recent research on procedures for teaching generalized skills to students with severe handicaps. The emerging strategies for general case instruction are described, and the theoretical foundation provided by general case instruction is applied to the problem of inclass simulated instruction. A critique of current simulation research and practice is followed by an alternative approach to simulation that may provide an important supplement to popular community-based training approaches.

TEACHING GENERALIZED SKILLS

Education for students with severe handicaps is relevant only to the extent that the knowledge and behaviors that the students acquire become part of their daily routine. This simple concept is being increasingly evoked in an effort to

The activity that is the subject of this report was supported in whole or in part by the U.S. Department of Education, Contract No. 300-82-0362. However, the opinions expressed herein do not necessarily reflect the position or policy of the U.S. Department of Education, and no official endorsement by the Department should be inferred.

focus education on functional, age-appropriate, community-referenced skills (Brown, Nietupski, & Hamre-Nietupski, 1976; Wilcox & Bellamy, 1982). Functional behaviors are those behaviors that students can use immediately to perform self-help, leisure, work, and social activities. Functional behaviors have the greatest effect on a student's life-style when they are taught as "generalized responses," that is, responses that are performed reliably across the range of natural environments and situations that the student encounters in his or her day-to-day activity.

The Challenge Facing Teachers

The educational challenge facing teachers today is to teach adaptive behaviors that: 1) are performed across the full range of appropriate stimulus conditions encountered by the student, 2) are not performed in those stimulus conditions where it is inappropriate, and 3) endure over time.

A "stimulus condition" refers to everything that a student is exposed to at a single point in time. All the sounds, colors, movements, tastes, tactile events, and smells present at one time combine to form a stimulus condition. When functional behaviors such as street crossing, purchasing, and toothbrushing are taught, the teacher can identify many situations or stimulus conditions where the behavior will be appropriate. These appropriate stimulus conditions form the class of events that should control (or cue) the new behavior. Becker, Engelmann, and Thomas (1975) have labeled this class of appropriate stimulus conditions an "instructional universe." A teacher will have taught a general-ized skill when, after instruction with some examples of appropriate stimulus conditions, the learner performs correctly across the entire universe of appro-priate stimulus conditions.

Consider the student who is learning to cross streets. Each street is a unique stimulus condition. The instructional universe may be all streets in the city where the student lives, or all streets in the area of the city where the student is located. The teacher has the task of instructing the student in the waiting, orienting, and walking behaviors necessary for correct performance. If this instruction results in a functional life-style change, it will leave the student with the ability to cross all streets in the instructional universe (i.e., all appropriate stimulus conditions), not just those streets used as part of his or her training.

Of equal importance, the student will not emit "street crossing" in inappropriate stimulus conditions. This means that the student will not attempt to cross a street at inappropriate times, and that she or he will not engage in "street crossing" in situations such as the school hallway. Students must know when *not* to perform adaptive behaviors as well as when to perform them. It is insufficient to teach behaviors that "generalize" to all nontrained situations (both appropriate *and* inappropriate situations). Quality instruction will pro-duce generalized responses that occur across the full range of appropriate stimulus conditions. and do not occur in inappropriate stimulus situations. The "trick" is teaching the student what makes a stimulus condition "appropriate" or "inappropriate" for performing the target behavior. Achieving this end is a major focus of the rapidly developing technology of general case instruction.

General Case Instruction

General case instruction is a process for teaching generalized skills. Originally developed for teaching functional math, reading, and language skills (Becker et al., 1975), the technology of general case instruction has also been used successfully to teach generalized behaviors to students with severe handicaps (Colvin & Horner, 1983; Horner, Bellamy, & Colvin, 1984; Sprague & Horner, 1984). General case instruction emphasizes the importance of selecting and sequencing teaching examples so students learn skills that are performed across all appropriate stimulus conditions, and are not performed in inappropriate stimulus conditions. This discussion provides a brief overview of general case programming. The serious reader is referred to Engelmann and Carnine (1982) and Horner, Sprague, and Wilcox (1982) for a more indepth analysis of general case programming and its application to students with severe handicaps.

General case instruction stresses specific procedures for selecting and sequencing teaching examples. These procedures are especially important for teachers of students with severe handicaps because these teachers often must develop their own curricula. Teachers facing the challenge of building general case programs should attend to five steps:

1. Defining the instruction universe
2. Selecting teaching and test examples
3. Sequencing teaching examples
4. Teaching
5. Testing

Defining the Instructional Universe   The first step to teaching generalized skills is operationally defining the set of stimulus conditions across which the skills should be performed. This set of conditions may vary depending on the behavior under analysis, the existing competencies of the learner, and the characteristics of the performance environment. A student being trained to purchase groceries, for example, may have an instructional universe that includes "all food items in all stores in town" or "any food item in the one store close to home," or "any dairy item in the store by his or her home." Each of these instructional universes defines a set of stimulus conditions within which the student should perform "grocery purchasing." Each instructional universe defines conditions that are functional for the student, yet differs greatly in the range of variation with which the student must learn to deal. By defining the instructional universe, the teacher has specified the functional outcome of the program and provided the critical detail needed for selecting training examples.

Select Teaching and Testing Examples   General case instruction always involves teaching with multiple examples that sample the range of relevant stimulus variation. A major disservice done to students with severe handicaps is to expect generalization of complex skills to a wide range of nontrained situations after teaching with only one or two examples. The student often fails to make this "leap" and as such fails to use his or her skill in any but the most restricted situations. General case instruction avoids this problem by teaching with multiple examples. The objective is to select a logistically feasible set of examples that sample the relevant stimulus variation in situations that the student will encounter after training.

When selecting teaching examples, begin by looking at each response that the student is to learn. For each response, define the stimulus that should exert control. Then examine how that controlling stimulus changes across the different stimulus conditions within the predefined instructional universe. An example of this process can be seen in the procedures used by McDonnell, Horner, and Williams (1984) to teach purchasing of grocery items. One response in this task was to count out the correct number of $1 bills. The controlling stimulus was the "charge amount" on the cash register. The instructional universe included all dollar amounts between $1.00 and $10.00 on all cash registers in the city. During training, the authors presented 20 slides of four different cash registers that sampled each of the whole dollar amounts between 1 and 10 (i.e., $1.10, $2.25, $3.46 . . .). While all cash registers and all dollar values were not presented, the *range* of variation was sampled.

When faced with the task of selecting multiple teaching examples that sample the range of stimulus variation, teachers may be dismayed at the image of managing a large number of examples. This concern is unnecessary. The skill of generalized street crossing was taught with 20 teaching examples to students with moderate and severe retardation (Horner, Jones, & Williams, in press). Generalized vending machine use and the crimp/cutting of biaxle circuit board components were both trained with only four well-selected teaching examples (Horner & McDonald, 1982; Sprague & Horner, 1984). Students with severe handicaps in a public high school were taught generalized telephone use with 10 teaching examples (Horner, Williams, & Steveley, 1984). The teacher does not need to select a large number of examples, but the examples selected should conform to the following criteria provided by Engelmann and Carnine (1982, p. 8):

1. The set of positive examples should be similar only with respect to relevant stimuli. Irrelevant stimuli should be as different as possible across examples.

2. The set of positive examples should sample the range of stimulus variation across which the learner is expected to respond (i.e., across the instructional universe).

3. A range of negative examples should be included (where appropriate) that are maximally similar to positive examples (e.g., when teaching the generalized skill of busing cafeteria and restaurant tables, the set of teaching examples should include tables that should *not* be bused [Horner, Eberhard, & Sheehan, 1983]).

In addition to these criteria, Horner et al. (1982) have added two more that are of particular relevance for teachers focusing on community-referenced behaviors:

4. Select a set of positive examples that includes significant exceptions (e.g., for generalized street crossing, cars that pull away from curbs or out of driveways are "exceptions" that need to be taught).
5. Select training examples that are logistically feasible in terms of cost, time, and location. As much as possible, keep community teaching examples near the school or training site.

Once teaching examples have been selected, the teacher should repeat the process to define a set of examples to test for generalization to the natural setting. Testing examples should be different from teaching examples but share the five criteria noted above. Testing examples are used at the end of training to determine if the student responds successfully to totally novel examples of the skill or activity being taught.

Sequence Teaching Examples   The sequence in which teaching examples are presented affects the generalizability of the skill acquired and the efficiency of instruction. The research base for guidelines on how examples should be sequenced is much less developed than that for how teaching examples should be selected. The studies that have addressed the issue of sequencing, however, support the following five suggestions (Carnine, 1980; Engelmann & Carnine, 1982; Gersten, White, Falco, & Carnine, in press; Panyan & Hall, 1978; Schroeder & Baer, 1972):

1. Teach multiple components of an activity or skill within each training session. With simple skills (e.g., toothbrushing), teach all the behaviors within each session; with more complex skills, such as assembling circuit boards, teach portions of the skill that include multiple components rather than teaching a single component.
2. When the whole skill or activity is taught, use multiple examples within individual training sessions. *Do not train one example at a time in an easy-to-hard sequence.* While the learner experiences more success with an easy-to-hard sequence, she or he also learns generalization errors that decrease the efficiency of instruction and limit the utility of the acquired behavior. When presenting multiple examples of varying difficulty, however, it is reasonable to present a mix of 60% easy examples, 20% intermediate examples, and 20% hard examples within a session. This

allows the student the opportunity to succeed with easy examples yet experience the full range of variation needed to prevent generalization errors.

3. Present maximally similar positive and negative examples one right after the other. This is especially important for behaviors in which learning when (or where) not to perform the behavior is as important as learning when (or where) to perform the behavior. This sequencing technique teaches the learner the specific stimuli that define the limits within which the target behavior is appropriate.

4. Review examples learned during previous sessions. A basic tenant of general case instruction is that anything worth teaching is worth reviewing (Becker et al., 1975). When many examples are being taught, instructional sequences should include some new and some "old" examples during each training session.

5. Teach the general case before teaching exceptions. "Exceptions" are those examples that do not fit the basic rule being taught with the teaching examples. If exceptions are taught with the regular teaching examples, the number of trials to criterion and the number of student errors increase. For example, when teaching generalized street crossing, teach the learner how to respond to intersections with lights and oncoming cars before adding instruction on how to cope with bicyclists, turning cars, and cars pulling out of driveways. Initially, the teacher should intervene to minimize exposure to these "exception" stimuli or provide prompts that preclude learner errors. After the student has mastered the general skills associated with street crossing, the exceptions are taught.

Teaching   Once the instructional universe has been defined, and teaching examples have been selected and sequenced, the next step is to use this new "curriculum" during teaching sessions. Here the teacher should apply the impressive array of techniques related to prompting, fading, shaping, reinforcing, and pacing that are the foundation of quality instruction (Sailor, Wilcox, & Brown, 1980; Snell, 1983; Wilcox, & Bellamy, 1982).

Testing   The final step to general case instruction involves testing the student with a new set of examples to ensure that a generalized skill has been learned. A student's competent performance during training sessions in no way assures his or her competent performance in novel, generalization situations. After the student has met the training criterion, the teacher should "probe" for generalized performance with "test" examples. This bit of extra effort is often the key to teaching the student a truly functional behavior. The test may, and often does, show some situations in which the student is not yet skillful. Additional training with one or two new training examples is typically sufficient to overcome this problem. Without conducting generalization tests, however, the teacher is left to assume that training has produced generalized responding. With students who experience severe handicaps, this is not an acceptable assumption. Success in instructional situations should always be followed by tests under natural performance conditions.

The brief description provided above outlines the major elements of general case instruction. It is an approach that builds on the applied behavior analysis techniques so essential for successful instruction, and extends these existing procedures into strategies for teaching generalized, functional activities.

RESEARCH ON GENERAL CASE INSTRUCTION WITH SEVERELY HANDICAPPED LEARNERS

The general case approach has been researched extensively with mildly handicapped and disadvantaged learners (Becker & Engelmann, 1976, 1978; Carnine, 1980; Engelmann & Carnine, 1982; Gersten, 1981a, 1981b; Gersten et al., in press). Only recently, however, has the general case approach been used to teach students with severe handicaps (Bates & Cuvo, 1984; Engelmann & Colvin, 1983; Horner et al., 1982; Pancsofar, Schafer, Blackwell, & Gavron, in press; Singer, Close, Colvin, & Engelmann, 1983). A summary of this research indicates the following outcomes that should be of interest to teachers.

The general case approach is both effective and efficient for teaching generalized skills. Effectiveness refers to the ability of the teaching procedure to reliably produce generalized responding. The general case approach has been used with severely and profoundly retarded individuals to teach such generalized community behaviors as street crossing (Horner, Jones, & Williams, in press), restaurant use (Storey, Bates, & Hansen, 1984), vending machine use (Sprague & Horner, 1984), dressing (Day & Horner, in press), telephone use (Horner, Williams, & Steveley, 1984), soap dispenser use (Pancsofar & Bates, in press), and grocery item purchasing (McDonnell & Horner, in press); and to teach such generalized vocational skills as table busing (Horner, Eberhard, & Sheenan, 1983), tool use (Colvin & Horner, 1983), zip code sorting (Woolcock & Lengel, 1984), and crimp/cutting biaxle circuit board component (Horner & McDonald, 1982). In each of these studies, general case procedures were shown to result in students performing correctly across a functional array of nontrained stimulus situations. The general case approach works. Students acquire important skills without developing generalization error patterns.

The efficiency of a teaching procedure refers to the resources required to reach the training criterion. A careful assessment of efficiency should include measurement of: 1) the number of training trails to criterion, 2) the average amount of teacher time per student for students to reach criterion, 3) the average amount of student time requried to reach criterion, and 4) the actual dollar cost of materials, supplies, and staff time to reach criterion. Together these measures provide a broad picture of instructional costs. Efficiency is assessed by comparing these costs against the value of the learned behavior(s), and the costs (in dollars, teacher time, and student time) of alternative teaching procedures that produce the same outcome (Gilbert, 1978).

At present, there are insufficient data to assess all the variables listed above for all teaching techniques that focus on generalized behavior. In the general case studies noted earlier, however, most students acquired the target behavior within 2–6 weeks of training, where instruction occurred 30–45 minutes a day, 4–5 days a week. This is not an excessive investment of time given the value of the skills learned. Student time to reach criterion was never more than 12 hours of training, with teacher time requirements being approximately the same plus an additional 1–5 hours spent in pre-instruction preparation. The dollar costs associated with instruction varied dramatically depending on the skill being taught. No materials or supply costs were consumed to teach generalized street crossing, while an average of $25 per student was consumed when generalized vending machine use was taught. Until similar data are available for alternative teaching procedures, comparative assessment of efficiency must be delayed. However, from the general case studies completed thus far, the resources used during instruction have been judged by teachers to be an efficient expenditure given the value of the generalized skills acquired.

The general case approach produces functional, socially valid life-style changes. Generalized skills are desirable because they give students the ability to perform across the range of situations that they normally encounter on a day-to-day basis. The social validity of any approach claiming to teach generalized skills, therefore, rests on whether the learner is able to incorporate the new skill as part of his or her life-style. Recent research efforts to evaluate general case instruction have added social validity data to the regular experimental system. Horner, Jones, and Williams (in press) taught generalized street crossing and documented that the learners were not only competent on an array of experimentally selected nontrained streets, but were also able to cross a second group of nontrained streets selected by their family members as most important for that learners' community integration. Horner, Williams, and Steveley (1984) taught generalized telephone use and then documented that students were using their new skills on a regular basis at home. These results support the utility of general case instruction for teaching behaviors that have a socially valid impact on student life-style.

To teach generalized skills, use multiple teaching examples; a single teaching example will not be sufficient. In the past, teachers have used single teaching examples when building programs to teach community, home, and work behaviors with severely handicapped learners. Recent research with students who exhibit severe handicaps supports previous results from disadvantaged (Becker & Engelmann, 1976) and infrahuman (i.e., nonhuman analogue research using rats, mice, birds) (Reynolds, 1961) learners showing that generalized behaviors are not learned with single teaching examples. Horner and McDonald (1982) taught the generalized crimp/cutting of circuit board components to youth with severe retardation using both a single teaching example strategy and a set of examples that followed the general case guidelines. To determine if a generalized skill had been learned, students were "probed" with a group of 20 components that sampled the range of different components that they would be expected to work with in normal production settings. The results from this study are presented in Figures 1 and 2. After

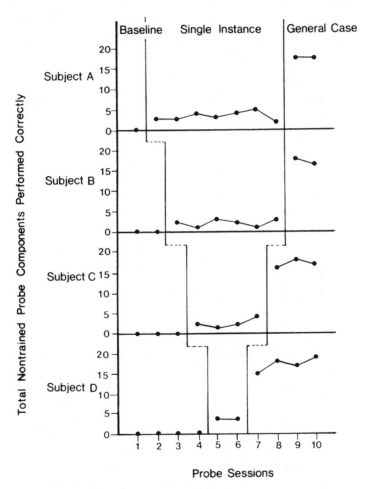

Figure 1. The total number of nontrained probe capacitors performed correctly across phases. (Reprinted with permission from Horner, R. H. & McDonald, R. [1982]. Comparison of single instance and general case instruction in teaching a generalized vocational skill. *Journal of The Association for the Severely Handicapped, 8,* 7–20.)

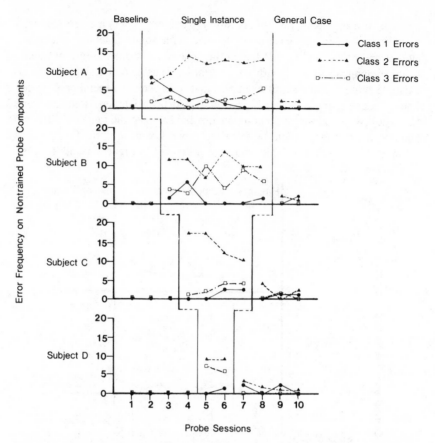

Figure 2. The frequency of errors performed during probe sessions by error class. (Reprinted with permission from Horner, R. & McDonald, R. [1982]. Comparison of single instance and general case instruction in teaching a generalized vocational skill. *Journal of the Association for The Severely Handicapped, 8,* 7–20.)

being trained with the single teaching example, students not only failed to succeed with nontrained examples, but (as can be seen in Figure 2) actually became more likely to perform certain generalization errors. When instruction was done via the general case approach, these same students performed with consistent success across the entire range of nontrained components.

Teaching generalized skills requires the use of training examples that sample the range of relevant stimulus variation. The general case approach is not unique in advocating that multiple training examples are needed. Many authors have argued for the use of multiple teaching examples (Baer, 1981; Sanders & James, 1983; Stokes & Baer, 1977). The general case approach, however, adds that these multiple teaching examples should sample the range of relevant stimulus variation found in the instructional universe. If multiple examples are used that do not provide this variation, a generalized skill is less likely to be learned.

Sprague and Horner (1984) examined this variable when testing generalized vending machine use. Six students labeled moderately or severely retarded were taught to purchase items from vending machines. They were tested using a group of 10 nontrained "probe" machines that sampled the range of machines in the students' home town. Following a baseline phase, three of the students were trained first with a single machine and then with three "general case" machines that provided the range of variation needed for generalized responding. Students 4, 5, and 6 were also trained first with a single machine and then with three "multiple instance" machines. The multiple instance machines were similar to each other, but they did *not* sample the range of relevant stimulus variation. Eventually, Students 4, 5, and 6 were also trained with the "general case" machines. The results from this study are provided in Figure 3. Training with the single machine did not result in generalized responding. Training with "multiple instance" machines that did *not* sample the range of relevant stimulus variation (i.e., multiple instance) was also ineffective for teaching generalized skills. Only when students were trained with multiple machines that sampled the range of relevant stimulus variation (i.e., the general case machines) did they perform successfully across the 10 nontrained, probe machines. Results consistent with these findings were found by Colvin and Horner (1983) when generalized screwdriver use was taught to secondary students with moderate and severe retardation.

In summary, the general case approach offers a functional alternative to teachers interested in developing generalized skills with learners who exhibit severe handicaps. While a great deal needs yet to be determined, existing results indicate that the general case approach is effective, efficient, and functional. One area of instruction that logically should benefit from the general case approach is the use of "inclass simulations." All simulations are constructed to teach responding in nontrained (generalization) situations. Extension of the general case approach to instruction via simulations has not occurred to date. This chapter provides an initial step toward applying general case analysis to simulation training.

IMPLICATIONS OF GENERAL CASE
INSTRUCTION FOR INCLASS SIMULATION

Simulations have been used extensively as a method of teaching community skills; however, no empirically validated guidelines are available to assist teachers in determining when to use or how to build effective simulations. Examination of simulation as an instructional strategy is especially relevant given its widespread use, and the increasing expectation from parents and professionals that students with severe handicaps should function competently

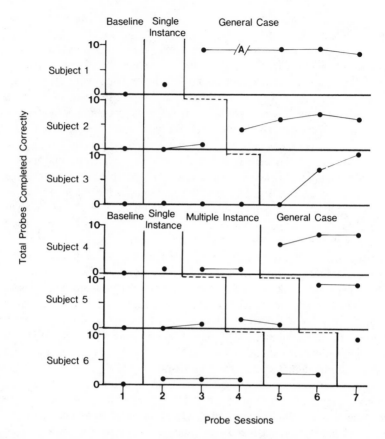

Figure 3. The number of nontrained probe machines completed correctly by students across phases and probe sessions. (Reprinted with permission from Sprague, J. & Horner, R. H. [1984]. The effects of single instance, multiple instance, and general case training on generalized vending machine use by moderately and severely handicapped students. *Journal of Applied Behavior Analysis, 17*, 273–278.)

in community settings (Brown et al., 1976; Wilcox & Bellamy, 1982). The following discussion: 1) describes the traditional approach for using simulations, 2) suggests an alternative definition of simulation using a general case perspective, 3) describes why simulations can be useful, 4) outlines a method for using simulations to teach generalized skills, and 5) addresses issues of "values" and needed research related to using simulations.

The Traditional Approach to Simulation

The term "simulation" has been used to describe a wide variety of instructional materials, settings, and formats. Page, Iwata, and Neef (1976) used a tabletop model of city intersections to teach street crossing; Williams, Brown, and Certo (1975) used cardboard replicas of city buses to teach bus riding; Bates (1980) used inclass role playing to teach social skills; Thompson, Braam, and Fuqua (1982) used a simulated apartment ot teach laundry skills; and Potter, Biacchi, and Richardson (1977) used a modular room to teach such skills as using a light switch. The inherent logic of all simulations is to re-create demands of actual performance environments in the classroom in order to teach responses required under natural conditions.

Proponents of simulations argue that they are a logical response to the increasing pressure to teach functional community skills that would otherwise be inaccessible because of transportation, logistical, or financial constraints. The result has been the widespread practice of equipping classrooms and schools with a full range of simulated residential and community paraphernalia that attempt to approximate situations found in the student's community (i.e., inclass "stores," bedrooms, kitchens, and laundry facilities).

While the use of simulation is ubiquitous, the effectiveness of simulations to produce generalized responding in community settings enjoys mixed empirical support. A group of studies have been reported that support the use of simulation as an efficient strategy for improving community performance with some students, under some conditions (Giangreco, 1983; Page et al., 1976; Sarber & Cuvo, 1983; Sarber, Halaxz, Messmer, Beckett, & Lutzker, 1983; Thompson et al., 1982; van den Pol et al., 1981). An equally impressive data base, however, documents situations where simulations have proven an ineffective (or less effective) strategy (Coon, Vogelsberg, & Williams, 1981; Marchetti, McCartney, Drain, Hooper, & Dix, 1983; Matson, 1980; McDonnell & Horner, in press). Additionally, studies conducted to date report that simulation strategies have been less successful in teaching adaptive skills to learners who are more severely mentally handicapped.

The absence of a clear empicical base for the effectiveness of simulation has contributed to concerns raised by advocates that simulations are age inappropriate (Brown et al., 1983). The materials and tasks sometimes used in simulation training can create a preschool atmosphere that reinforces the view of individuals with severe handicaps as eternal children. Equally distressing is the tendency to use simulations as prerequisites to community participation. De facto segregation is often created by requiring students to perform successfully in simulations before they have access to training in normal performance environments.

The current controversy over the effectiveness and appropriateness of simulation emphasizes the need for a more indepth analysis of its utility in teaching generalized community skills. The remainder of this chapter addresses the issue of simulation from the perspective of general case instruction. The research conducted to date on general case instruction provides a theoretical perspective for getting beyond simple questions about whether simulations work and into identification of those features within simulations that may account for current differences in research results.

A Functional Definition of Simulation

Simulations are always constructed to approximate some other set of stimulus conditions in which the learner is ultimately expected to perform. To be of value as an instructional strategy, therefore, simulations must produce generalized responding to natural situations. Any definition of simulation should include the relationship between the simulation and the ultimate performance environment. The definition provided below meets this test.

A simulation is a stimulus condition used during training that includes: 1) relevant stimuli that are the same as (or close approximations to) stimuli in natural performance setting, and 2) irrelevant stimuli (i.e., a stimulus context) *not* found in natural situations where the target response should occur. This definition expands the conventional notion of a simulation as a simple recreation of an environmental or social context. It emphasizes the similarities and differences between relevant and irrelevant stimuli used during training, and the relevant and irrelevant stimuli experienced in performance settings. This emphasis highlights the functions of simulation as a method to achieve performance in natural settings.

Why Use Simulations?

Current research results suggest that when a range of examples can be presented in the natural setting, training in the natural setting is the most effective method of teaching generalized responding (Coon et al., 1981; Marchetti et al., 1983; Matson, 1980; McDonnell et al., 1984). Simulations require that staff, instructional time, and other resources be redeployed away from training in the community for use in inclass instruction. Given the risks related to generalization and segregation inherent in this decision, it is not surprising that some authors have argued against simulations.

Why, indeed, use simulations? There are several potential benefits. First, simulations allow teachers to adapt to restricted training options in community settings. The effectiveness of any instructional program in the community is threatened whenever the natural environment does not allow for massed practice on difficult behaviors and when the range of relevant stimuli cannot be presented. When training exclusively in natural environments is not feasible, simulations provide an important supplement to available community instruction. For a few tasks, natural performance environments may be totally unavailable, with the result that any instruction must involve simulations. In these circumstances, it is important to ensure that the range of relevant stimulus and response variation can be presented during instruction, and that the response topographies required during training match the response topographies required in performance settings. The final consideration in determining the feasibility of isolated simulation is whether the same stimuli found in natural situations can be presented during training. Stimuli used during simulation that are significantly different in shape, color, size, form, texture, and so on, from those found in actual environments significantly reduce the likelihood that students will generalize to actual stimuli under normal performance conditions (Hundert, 1981; Welch & Pear, 1980).

The second potential benefit of simulation is the savings in both time and dollars required to learn an adaptive community skill. Training in the community can be costly. Community-based training often involves considerable time in transporting the student to and from a training site. In addition, when a community activity requires the purchase of goods or services, training can lead to nontrivial cash expenses. Simulations have been viewed as one option for increasing the efficiency and cost effectiveness of training. The number of training trials that a student receives per training hour or per training session can be increased via simulations. The total amount of teacher and student time to reach criterion often can be decreased, and dollar costs can be minimized.

The efficiency of simulations is especially alluring to teachers faced with minimal staff support. A danger, however, lies behind the seductive lure of improved efficiency. A simulation may end up as a cost-effective method of teaching irrelevant skills if careful attention is not paid to generalization. Too often, simulations have allowed learners to be successful during training but have had no impact on learner performance in real community situations (Coon et al., 1981). There is little doubt that simulations are easier to coordinate, reduce total teacher time, and allow for reduced dollar costs. This improved efficiency is a major boon for teachers, only if the simulation is *effective* at teaching a functional, generalized skill.

A third potential benefit of simulation is the ability to present the student with a greater range of stimuli during training. While presentation of multiple training examples is a programmatically sound technique, it can be extremely cumbersome to implement in community settings. Generalized grocery purchasing, for example, would require a teacher to do training in multiple grocery stores that systematically sample such relevant stimuli as location of items, configuration of shelving, and type of cash register. Many teachers do not have the time, money, or transportation to deliver such training. They can, however, use inclass simulations that present a range of products, situations, and contents that no one store could provide. A major advantage of using simulation is that the teacher can often control the characteristics of training stimuli to ensure that an appropriate range of teaching examples are delivered.

The fourth potential benefit of simulation is the increased control that the teacher has over the sequencing of teaching examples. Simulations allow the teacher to select the sequence in which training examples are presented. Teaching complex discriminations to learners with severe handicaps often requires the juxtaposition of similar training examples that demand different responses. This juxtaposition increases the likelihood that the student will learn to identify those critical stimulus characteristics that make the two examples different (Engelmann & Carnine, 1982). The general case approach relies on teachers using this level of sequencing flexibility to avoid generalization errors (Horner, Bellamy, & Colvin, 1984). Events in the community seldom afford a teacher such powerful control. It can be extremely frustrating, for example, to sequence the order that buses arrive at the bus stop while teaching general case bus riding. In situations where the natural environment prevents appropriate sequencing of teaching examples, simulation can be used in conjunction with natural setting training to improve the generalization of acquired skills.

The fifth potential benefit of simulation is that it avoids potential dangers associated with the community. Simulations have been defended on the grounds that they offer a "safer" mode of instruction (Page et al., 1976). There is no question that the community offers more hazards than the classroom. To the extent that a short time of inclass simulation substantially reduces a student's level of risk, it is a defensible solution. As Brown et al. (1983) point out, however, the logic of "protection" is unsubstantial when compared with the need of severely handicapped students for structured community participation. In a very small number of instances, a simulation may be appropriate because of the major safety benefits it affords. In most cases, however, the use of simulation is difficult to defend if the sole purpose is to avoid dangers in the community.

Both the natural constraints on instruction in the community and the potential benefits of simulation argue for continued investigation of the use of simulation in instruction of persons with severe handicaps. Simulations are developed and defended for multiple reasons. With different students, different behaviors, and different situations, the functions of a simulation will vary. Any time that a simulation is used, however, the teacher should be able to identify the specific benefits that are expected. Unless the simulation leads to performance under natural stimulus conditions, it is dysfunctional.

How to Build Simulations that Teach Generalized Behaviors

The greatest dangers in building simulations are that they will teach a skill only useful in the constrained context of simulation settings, or that the simulation will lead to extended training sessions that teach little, and functionally exclude the student from more adaptive, integrated contacts. These dangers are avoided by building simulation training sessions that teach the "general case," and by ensuring that all simulations include some instruction with real community situations.

When simulation strategies are incorporated into the general case instruction strategy, new options are created in the selecting and sequencing of teaching examples. Since simulations essentially involve construction of new teaching instances, other aspects of the general case instruction model are unchanged: the instructional universe must be defined prior to instruction, delineating the range of circumstances in which the target behavior is expected as a result of training. Once training examples are selected, instruction should progress just as it does with other programs. And, like other programs, testing with nontaught examples from the instructional universe provides the critical measure of instructional success.

When simulations are used within the context of general case programs for students with severe handicaps, a few additional guidelines may help implement the suggestions for selecting and sequencing teaching examples that were described above:

1. Select simulation teaching examples that have the same, or nearly the same, relevant stimuli found in natural settings. While less handicapped persons often generalize from abstract stimuli (i.e., cardboard cut-outs, pictures) to real situations, existing research suggests that students with severe retardation are more likely to learn generalized skills when the simulation example includes the *same* relevant stimuli found in the natural environment. Hill, Wehman, and Horst (1980) taught generalized pinball use to three students with severe mental retardation by bringing a pinball machine into the classroom. This technique allowed students to perform with the same relevant stimuli found in the community, but without the distracting irrelevant stimuli. Sedlak, Doyle, and Schloss (1982) used a similar strategy to teach generalized video game use to severely handicapped students. Horner, Williams, and Steveley (1984) taught generalized telephone use to high school students with moderate and severe retardation using an inclass simulation that involved several types of real telephones hooked to a ''teletrainer.'' The ''teletrainer'' allowed the teacher to make the telephones ring, and allowed conversations to be transmitted between the telephones. This simulation included the presentation of a wide variety of different telephones and telephone situations in a short amount of time without the logistical constraints, cost, and irrelevant stimuli that would have occurred with telephone training in the community. Results indicate that as a function of this general case simulation training, students learned to use telephones successfully in nontrained, natural situations. The simulation was effective in teaching a generalized skill.

Simulation training that has not included the same relevant stimuli found in natural settings has proven less effective with severely handicapped learners. Studies using approximations of relevant stimuli that have claimed to teach generalized skills often have worked only with less handicapped students. van den Pol et al. (1981) used a simulation made with laminated cardboard cut-outs of relevant fast food restaurant stimuli to teach three moderately retarded students to use a variety of community fast food establishments. Page et al. (1976) and Neef, Iwata, and Page (1978) taught generalized street crossing and bus riding behaviors to moderately retarded adults via inclass simulations with a posterboard model of streets, street signs, slides of relevant bus riding stimuli, and a set of chairs for bus seats. When these simulations were replicated with students exhibiting more severe retardation, training did not lead to success in generalization situations (Coon et al., 1981; Marchetti et al., 1983). A conservative assessment of these results suggests that teachers of students with severe handicaps should avoid simulations when the relevant natural setting stimuli cannot be presented during simulation training trials.

This conservative assessment is supported by three recent studies with severely handicapped subjects that have compared simulations using "approximations" of relevant stimuli with training in the natural setting. In each case, the simulation training was ineffective at teaching a generalized skill, yet training in the real setting proved more functional. Coon et al. (1981) taught generalized bus riding skills to a woman who did not generalize after inclass simulation training by giving her access to real buses in the community situation. Marchetti et al. (1983) demonstrated in a group design that adults with moderate to severe retardation learned more functional street-crossing skills when training was done in the community rather than with a cardboard simulation.

Recently, McDonnell et al. (1984) trained high school students with moderate and severe mental retardation to purchase grocery items. Initially, training was done in the classroom with slides of grocery items and cash registers. This simulation provided a close approximation of the relevant cash register stimuli associated with natural settings, but proved ineffective in teaching generalized purchasing. Students mastered the inclass training trials, but did not succeed in real stores. Only after training included instruction in one real store did generalized responding occur in nontrained stores.

Together, these studies suggest that simulation training alone may be a useful method for teaching generalized skills only under certain conditions, and with learners who enter training with certain skills. For teachers of students with severe handicaps, the advantages of simulation training appear most likely if the teacher selects inclass teaching examples that present a range of the exact same relevant stimuli that the student will encounter under natural conditions. The authors recognize, however, that many community-referenced skills do not allow classroom presentation of the exact relevant stimuli found in the natural setting. In these situations, a simulation with stimuli that closely approximate natural stimuli can be supplemented with training in one natural situation.

2. *When relevant stimuli from the natural environment cannot be presented in simulation training trials, conduct training in one natural training setting combined with inclass simulation training.* When faced with teaching generalized behavior that should be performed in nontrained, home, community, work, and school settings, teachers should select teaching examples that meet the basic criteria for general case instruction. When possible, these training examples should be drawn from real community situations. When this is not feasible, inclass simulation training examples should be selected so that a range of the same relevant stimuli in natural situations is presented by the simulation training examples. When neither of these can occur, the teacher

should select at least one natural setting training example and supplement this example with simulation training trials that maximally "approximate" relevant stimuli in the natural setting.

Avoid training formats in which one natural setting condition is used alone in hopes that success with this one training example will produce generalized responding. This is the "train and hope" strategy that Stokes and Baer (1977) have described, and that subsequent articles have documented as an ineffective approach for teaching generalized behavior (McDonnell & Horner, in press). Also, avoid building inclass simulations that do not present the full range of relevant stimuli for each behavior required for a community activity. These simulations will be easy to use and produce rapid inclass success, but have little or no effect on the student's behavior in natural situations.

3. Sequence training examples to teach difficult discriminations. One of the great advantages of simulation training is the increased teacher control over the sequences in which training examples are presented. This variable alone can account for dramatic improvements in the acquisition of generalized behaviors (Engelmann & Carnine, 1982). The general case guidelines for sequencing apply to teaching with simulations: 1) teach multiple examples of the target activity in each training session; 2) use the opportunity to juxtapose maximally similar positive and negative examples as a way to teach precise "boundaries" within which the behavior should occur; 3) once a training example is learned, present it as a "review" in later training sessions; and 4) sequence training trials so trials that include exceptions are presented after acquisition of trials that do not include exceptions (Engelmann & Carnine, 1982).

An additional guideline for sequencing examples relates to instruction of difficult teaching examples. It is not uncommon for severely handicapped students to find a particular teaching example, or one part of an example, very difficult. Simulation training provides an opportunity to remove that step or trial and conduct massed practice in the classroom. This difficult step can be presented in several repetitions, with increased teacher assistance (Bellamy, Horner, & Inman, 1979). If necessary, the step or trial can be modified to allow initial success; and over several repetitions, the modification is faded. When the student is performing correctly in the massed trials, the step can be reincorporated into the activity and sequencing of teaching examples can continue as planned. The use of massed trials with difficult behaviors has been advocated by several authors (Bellamy et al., 1979; Engelmann & Colvin, 1983; Engelmann, Colvin, & Singer, in preparation), and is a teaching technique that is often difficult to use in the community.

Beyond Technology: The Values Affecting Simulation

Educational technology is "value-free" only as long as it is not applied. When procedures, techniques, and programs are used with students, the values associated with defining who, what, when, where, and why they are used become an integral part of the technology itself. Simulation is a part of the technology available to teachers and services providers. As such, the use of simulation should be guided by the values that affect all services to people with severe handicaps.

Simulation and Integration Integration is a major value affecting educational, vocational, and residential services for persons with handicaps. Students with severe handicaps should spend at least part of each school day in nonsegregated settings with nonhandicapped peers. Students should also have access to the most effective and efficient education possible. The easy decision is to focus on the content of instruction; clearly the skills and activities targeted for instruction should meet the "functional," "age-appropriate," "community-referenced" standards that facilitate physical and social integration (Wilcox & Bellamy, 1982). The more difficult decision arises when considering *how* instruction will occur. If the student can learn the target behaviors as quickly in the community as she or he could with an inclass simulation, then the added value of the intra-instruction integration argues in favor of teaching in the community. If, however, inclass simulations are a more efficient and effective method of teaching, they may actually provide students with the skills that lead to a much greater integration in a shorter time period. Given the existing ambiguity about how best to use simulations, a teacher would err not to have some part of each student's day involved in integrated events. Similarly, the potential value of simulations make their unilateral rejection unwise.

Simulation Should Be Age Appropriate Since simulation will occur most often in school settings, it is critical that the materials, assistance, techniques, and reinforcers used during training are appropriate to the chronological age of the student. The use of such materials as dolls, primary worksheets, and Play Skool grocery carts are inappropriate for adolescents or adults. Business and industry have used simulation as a method of training employees and executives for years, while maintaining dignity and professionalism for the trainees (Mallory, 1981). Simulation used in educational settings (especially with older students) should be no less age appropriate.

Simulation Should Be Balanced with Community Training Simulation provides an effective means of addressing difficult responses in controlled instructional situations. However, it can also be used as an inadvertent method for preventing community integration. If a student's performance on a simulation exercise is a prerequisite for community training, the student may be retained unnecessarily in an overly segregated training setting. Whenever possible, simulation training should be balanced with instructional time in those environments where the student will be expected to perform. Simulations should never function as a prerequisite to community participation.

Research on the Use of Simulation Training: Current Needs

Simulation training is an approach that has been much used and much abused in classrooms across the nation. It is an approach that is now receiving increasing criticism because it can be used to limit access to integrated events (Brown et al., 1983). At present, however, there is insufficient research data to answer important questions that are critical for teachers. As the discussion surrounding simulation training becomes more heated, research in the following areas will be needed.

Effectiveness and Efficiency of Simulation Training Earlier in this chapter, results were presented to support the effectiveness and efficiency of the general case approach. Similar data are needed across an array of behaviors, settings, and people to determine the usefulness of simulation training. At present, there is evidence that with some students, and some behaviors, simulation is an effective and efficient procedure. More studies are needed that define specific guidelines for the use of simulation. Studies that address effectiveness and efficiency should use dependent variables that are relevant for teachers and students. "Effectiveness" should be measured by a student's ability to perform across an array of "natural," nontrained situations that adequately sample a targeted instructional universe. To say that a training technique is effective at teaching a generalized skill by showing that the student was successful in one or two nontrained settings is inadequate.

Similarly, efficiency should be assessed by standards useful to teachers. The number of training trials to criterion, total amount of teacher time to criterion, total amount of student training time to criterion, and dollar costs to reach criterion will serve as a useful set of dependent variables.

Comparisons of Simulation Trainings, Natural Setting Trainings, and Combinations A critical research area is analysis of the comparative effects of simulation training, natural setting training, and combinations of simulation plus natural setting training. Teachers are faced today with a limited set of options. The few studies that have compared simulation training and natural setting training to date have been restricted by methodological flaws (McDonnell & Horner, in press), and none have addressed the feasibility of combining simulation and natural setting approaches. It may be possible, for example, to enhance natural setting training by conducting simulations with only one part of the activity being taught. Until more information is available on the variables that make a simulation effective, and how these interact with natural setting training, teachers will need to rely on the broad guidelines provided earlier in this chapter.

Generalized Control of Maladaptive Behavior Thus far, the focus has been on the generalization of newly acquired behaviors. The general case approach has important implications, however, for developing generalized control of inappropriate behaviors as well (Dunlap & Johnson, 1984; Engelmann & Colvin, 1983; Horner & Budd, 1985). At present, very little information is available to the teacher interested in reducing maladaptive behavior so that the reduction "generalizes" across situations. Simulation training may be one alternative for building the breadth of stimulus control needed to achieve generalized suppression of maladaptive behaviors.

Methodological Issues in Generalization and Simulation Research A variety of authors have questioned the adequacy of current research methodology addressing generalization (Horner, Bellamy, & Colvin, 1984; Kendall, 1981; Sanders & James, 1983). These concerns apply directly to research focused on the use of simulations. Four methodological recommendations appear most relevant for researchers: 1) the primary dependent variable should be responding across a set of nontrained examples in actual performance settings sampling the range of relevant stimulus variations in the instructional universe; 2) to ensure that readers can compare the stimuli used as teaching examples with generalized performance, researchers should provide detailed descriptions of their teaching examples (Peterson, Horner, & Wonderlich, 1982); 3) the research designs used in generalization and simulation studies should document experimental control over generalized responding (all too often, research designs show that teaching procedures were effective at changing behavior during teaching sessions, but provide no experimental control for changes in behavior in generalization situations); and 4) research on generalization and simulation should include data that document the "social validity" of the skills learned (Horner, Bellamy, & Colvin, 1984; Kazdin, 1980; Voeltz & Evans, 1983). Even if the social validity data do not meet the rigorous standards necessary for experimental control, they can show that the targeted skill was associated with meaningful life-style changes.

SUMMARY

Teaching students with severe handicaps has its greatest rewards when students acquire behaviors that result in immediate, generalized changes in adaptive behavior. Teachers, service providers, advocates, parents, and educators need to maintain critical and unswerving attention to the life-style changes expected from educational and behavioral interventions. Significant changes that affect a student's life-style and result in functional behavior patterns in school, work, home, and community setting require careful attention to variables that affect generalization. One approach that provides this attention is general case instruction. Results from research in using the general case approach with severely handicapped learners offer major cause for optimism.

One area where the general case approach has important implications is in the use of inclass simulations to teach generalized behaviors. There is a growing concern that inclass instruction is ineffective and irrelevant for teaching the skills needed by severely handicapped students. There is equal concern, however, that community-based instruction will prove an ineffective and inefficient method of teaching generalized skills. This chapter provides a set of guidelines for using simulations that are consistent with both the current research and the major reservations of simulation critics. It is clear that poor simulations produce poor results, just as poor natural setting training produces poor results. What is needed is better documentation of the variables that make simulations effective, and development of specific guidelines that can direct teacher construction and use of simulations.

REFERENCES

Baer, D. M. (1981). *How to plan for generalization*. Lawrence, KS: H & H Enterprises.

Bates, P. (1980). The effectiveness of interpersonal skills training in the social skill acquisition of moderately and severely retarded adults. *Journal of Applied Behavior Analysis, 13,* 237–248.

Bates, P. E., & Cuvo, A. J. (1984). Simulated and naturalistic instruction of community functioning skills with mentally retarded learners. *Direct Instruction News, 4*(2).

Becker, W. C., & Engelmann, S. E. (1976). *Analysis of achievement data on six cohorts of low-income children from 20 school districts in the University of Oregon direct instruction follow through model: Appendix B: Formative Research Studies.* Eugene: University of Oregon, College of Education, Follow Through Project.

Becker, W. C., & Engelmann, S. E. (1978). Systems for basic instruction: Theory and applications. In A. Catania & T. Brigham (Eds.), *Handbook of applied behavior analysis: Social and instructional processes* (pp. 325–378). New York: Irvington Publishers.

Becker, W., Engelmann, S., & Thomas, D. (1975). *Teaching 2: Cognitive learning and instruction.* Chicago: Science Research Associates.

Bellamy, G. T., Horner, R. H., & Inman, D. (1979). *Vocational habilitation of severely retarded adults: A direct service technology.* Baltimore: University Park Press.

Brown, L, Nietupski, J., & Hamre-Nietupski, S. (1976). The criterion of ultimate functioning. In M.A. Thomas (Ed.), *Hey, don't forget about me!* (pp. 2–15). Reston, VA: CEC Information Center.

Brown, L., Nisbet, J., Ford, A., Sweet, M., Shiraga, B., York, J., & Loomis, R. (1983). The critical need for nonschool instruction in educational programs for severely handicapped students. *Journal of The Association for the Severely Handicapped, 8,* 71–77.

Carnine, D. (1980). Relationships between stimulus variation and the formation of misconceptions. *Journal of Educational Research, 74,* 106–110.

Colvin, G. T., & Horner, R. H. (1983). Experimental analysis of generalization: An evaluation of a general case program for teaching motor skills to severely handicapped learners. In D. Hogg & P. Mittler (Eds.), *Advances in mental handicap research: Vol. 2. Aspects of competence in mentally handicapped people* (pp. 309–345). Chichester, England: John Wiley & Sons.

Coon, M. E., Vogelsberg, R. T., & Williams, W. (1981). Effects of classroom public transportation instruction on generalization to the natural environment. *Journal of The Association for the Severely Handicapped, 6,* 46–53.

Day, H. M., & Horner, R. H. (in press). *A comparison of single instance and general case instruction of generalized dressing skill.*

Dunlap, G., & Johnson, J. (1984). *Teaching generalized behaviors: General case instruction in simulation and community settings.* Unpublished manuscript, University of California at Santa Barbara.

Engelmann, S., & Carnine, D. (1982). *Theory of instruction: Principles and applications.* New York: Irvington Publishers.

Engelmann, S., & Colvin, G. T. (1983). *Generalized compliance training.* Austin: Pro-Ed.

Engelmann, S., Colvin, S., & Singer, G. (in preparation). *Direct instruction for very low performers.*

Gersten, R. (1981a). *The San Diego Direct Instruction Follow Through Program.* Final report submitted to Joint Dissemination Review Panel, U.S. Department of Education.

Gersten, R. (1981b). *The Uvalde Direct Instruction Follow Through Program.* Final report submitted to Joint Dissemination Review Panel, U.S. Department of Education.

Gersten, R., White, W., Falco, R., & Carnine, D. W. (in press). Enhancing attention of handicapped and nonhandicapped students through a dynamic presentation of instructional stimuli. *Analysis and Intervention in Developmental Disabilities.*

Giangreco, M. F. (1983). Teaching basic photography skills to a severely handicapped young adult using simulated materials. *Journal of The Association for the Severely Handicapped, 8,* 48–50.

Gilbert, T. F. (1978). *Human competence: Engineering worthy performance.* New York: McGraw-Hill Book Co.

Hill, J. W., Wehman, P., & Horst, G. (1980). Acquisition and generalization of leisure skills in severely and profoundly handicapped youth: Use of an electronic pinball machine. In P. Wehman & J. W. Hill (Eds.), *Instructional programming for severely handicapped youth: A community integration approach* (pp. 43–62). Richmond: Virginia Commonwealth University School of Education.

Horner, R. H., Bellamy, G. T., & Colvin, G. T. (1984). Responding in the presence of nontrained stimuli: Implications of generalization error patterns. *Journal of The Association for Persons with Severe Handicaps, 9,* 287–295.

Horner, R. H., & Budd, C. M. (1985). Teaching manual sign language to a nonverbal student: Generalization of sign use and collateral reduction of maladaptive behavior. *Education and Training for the Mentally Retarded, 20,* 39–47.

Horner, R. H., Eberhard, J., & Sheehan, M. R. (1983). *Generalization of table bussing skills with moderately and severely retarded adolescents.* Unpublished manuscript, University of Oregon, Eugene.

Horner, R. H., Jones, D., & Williams, J.A. (in press). Teaching generalized street crossing to individuals with moderate and severe mental retardation. *Journal of The Association for Persons with Severe Handicaps.*

Horner, R. H., & McDonald, R. S. (1982). A comparison of single instance and general case instruction in teaching a generalized vocational skill. *Journal of The Association for the Severely Handicapped, 7,* 7–20.

Horner, R. H., Sprague, J., & Wilcox, B. (1982). General case programming for community activities. In B. Wilcox & G. T. Bellamy, *Design of high school programs for severely handicapped students* (pp. 61–98). Baltimore: Paul H. Brookes Publishing Co.

Horner, R. H., Williams, J. A., & Steveley, J. D. (1984). *Acquisition of generalized telephone use by students with severe mental retardation.* Manuscript submitted for publication.

Hundert, J. (1981). Stimulus generalization after training an autistic boy in manual signs. *Education and Treatment of Children, 4,* 329–337.

Kazdin, A. E. (1980). Acceptability of alternative treatment for deviant child behavior. *Journal of Applied Behavior Analysis, 13*(2), 259–275.

Kendall, P. C. (1981). Assessing generalization and the single-subject strategies. *Behavior Modification, 5*(3), 307–319.

Mallory, W. J. (1981, September). Simulation for task practice in technical training. *Training and Development Journal,* 13–20.

Marchetti, A. G., McCartney, J. R., Drain, S., Hooper, M., & Dix, J. (1983). Pedestrian skills training for mentally retarded adults: Comparison of training in two settings. *Mental Retardation, 21,* 107–110.

Matson, J. L. (1980). A controlled group study of pedestrian-skill training for the mentally retarded. *Behavior Research and Therapy, 18,* 99/106.

McDonnell, J. J., & Horner, R. H. (in press). Effects of in vivo and simulation-plus-in vivo training on the acquisition and generalization of a grocery item search strategy by high school students with severe handicaps. *Analysis and Intervention in Developmental Disabilities.*

McDonnell, J. J., Horner, R. H., & Williams, J. A. (1984). A comparison of three strategies for teaching generalized grocery purchasing to high school students with severe handicaps. *Journal of The Association for Persons with Severe Handicaps, 9,* 123–133.

Neef, N. A., Iwata, B. A., & Page, T. J. (1978). Public transportation training: In vivo versus classroom instruction. *Journal of Applied Behavior Analysis, 11,* 331–344.

Page, T. J., Iwata, B. A., & Neef, N. A. (1976). Teaching pedestrian skills to retarded persons: Generalization from the classroom to the natural environment. *Journal of Applied Behavior Analysis, 9,* 433–444.

Pancsofar, E. L., & Bates, P. (in press). The impact of the acquisition of successive training exemplars on generalization by students with severe handicaps. *Journal of The Association for the Severely Handicapped.*

Pancsofar, E. L., Schafer, S., Blackwell, R., & Gavron, S. (in press). Utilization of general case programming for teaching health education behaviors to students with severe handicaps. *Journal of School Health.*

Panyan, M., & Hall, R. V. (1978). Effects of serial versus concurrent task sequencing on acquisition, maintenance and generalization. *dddddd of Applied Behavior Analysis, 11,* 67–74.

Peterson, L., Homer, A. L., & Wonderlich, S. (1982). The integrity of independent variables in behavior analysis. *Journal of Applied Behavior Analysis, 15,* 477–492.

Potter, J. T., Biacchi, A. J., & Richardson, E. A. (1977). Simulating real-life situations in a classroom setting: The Montgomery County training module. In E. Sontag, J. Smith, & N. Certo (Eds.), *Educational programming for the severely and profoundly handicapped* (pp. 142–149). Reston, VA: Council for Exceptional Children.

Reynolds, G. S. (1961). Attention in the pigeon. *Journal of the Experimental Analysis of Behavior, 4,* 203–208.

Sailor, W., Wilcox, B., & Brown, L. (Eds.). (1980). *Methods of instruction for severely handicapped students.* Baltimore: Paul H. Brookes Publishing Co.

Sanders, M. R., & James, J. E. (1983). The modification of parent behavior: A review of generalization and maintenance. *Behavior Modification, 7,* 3–28.

Sarber, R. E., & Cuvo, A. J. (1983). Teaching nutritional meal planning to developmental disabled clients. *Behavior Modification, 7,* 503–530.

Sarber, R. E., Halasz, M. M., Messmer, M. C., Beckett, A. D., & Lutzker, J. R. (1983). Teaching menu planning and grocery shopping skills to a retarded mother. *Mental Retardation, 21,* 101–106.

Schroeder, G. L., & Baer, D. M. (1972). Effects of concurrent and serial training on generalized vocal imitation in retarded children. *Developmental Psychology, 6,* 293–301.

Sedlak, R. A., Doyle, M., & Schloss, P. (1982). Video games: A training and generalization demonstration with severely retarded adolescents. *Education Training for the Mentally Retarded, 17,* 332–336.

Singer, G., Close, D., Colvin, G., & Engelmann, S. (1983). Direct instruction for severely handicapped learners. *Direct Instruction News, 2,* 3–4.

Snell, M. E. (1983). *Systematic instruction of the moderately and severely handicapped* (2nd ed.). Columbus, OH: Charles E. Merrill Publishing Co.

Sprague, J. R., & Horner, R. H. (1984). The effects of single instance, multiple instance and general case training on generalized vending machine use by moderately and severely handicapped students. *Journal of Applied Behavior Analysis, 17,* 273–278.

Stokes, T. F., & Baer, D. M. (1977). An implicit technology of generalization. *Journal of Applied Behavior Analysis, 10,* 349–367.

Storey, K., Bates, P., & Hansen. (1984). Acquisition and generalization of coffee purchase skills by adults with severe disabilities. *Journal of The Association for the Severely Handicapped, 9,* 178–185.

Thompson, T. J., Braam, S. J., & Fuqua, R. W. (1982). Training and generalization of laundry skills: A multiple probe evaluation with handicapped persons. *Journal of Applied Behavior Analysis, 15,* 177–182.

van den Pol, K. A., Iwata, B. A., Ivancic, M. T., Page, T. J., Neef, N. A., & Whitley, F. P. (1981). Teaching the handicapped to eat in public places: Acquisition, generalization, and maintnenance of restaurant skills. *Journal of Applied Behavior Analysis, 1,* 61–70.

Voeltz, L. M., & Evans, I. M. (1983). Educational validity: Procedures to evaluate outcomes in programs for severely handicapped learners. *Journal of The Association for the Severely Handicapped, 8*(1), 3–15.

Vogelsberg, R. T., Williams, W., & Bellamy, G. T. (1982). Preparation for independent living. In B. Wilcox & G. T. Bellamy, *Design of high school programs for severely handicapped students* (pp. 153–175). Baltimore: Paul H. Brookes Publishing Co.

Welch, S. J., & Pear, J. S. (1980). Generalization of naming responses to objects in the natural environment as a function of training stimulus modality with retarded children. *Journal of Applied Behavior Analysis, 13,* 629–643.

Wilcox, B., & Bellamy, G. T. (1982). *Design of high school programs for severely handicapped students.* Baltimore: Paul H. Brookes Publishing Co.

Williams, W., Brown, L., & Certo, N. (1975). Basic components of instructional programs for severely handicapped students. *AAESPH Review, 1,* 1–39.

Woolcock, W., & Lengel, M. (1984, November). *A general case simulation of national zip code sorting by first and second digits: Acquisition, maintenance and extension.* Paper presented at the national meeting of The Association for Persons with Severe Handicaps, Chicago, IL.

Chapter 11

Modification of Excess Behavior
An Adaptive and Functional Approach for Educational and Community Contexts

Luanna H. Meyer and Ian M. Evans

Behavior problems present a special challenge to those concerned with the implementation of habilitative, community-based programs for learners with severe disabilities. Aberrant or excess behaviors, such as self-injurious behavior, stereotyped behavior, disruptive and aggressive behavior, and failure to respond to social stimuli and verbal instruction, clearly interfere with efforts to teach new skills, as well as with the learner's ability to interact positively with others in various environments. Such excess behaviors are considered to be so characteristic of persons with severe disabilities that they are included in the federal definition of severe handicapping conditions (*Federal Register*, 1975). There is evidence, however, that such behavior problems are typically most prevalent among institutional residents in comparison to those living in any other kind of facility (Borthwick, Meyers, & Eyman, 1981). It would be expected, then, that as more normalized living and educational environments become available, the prevalence of behavior problems should decline accordingly. Yet, even with the provision of community-based opportunities, behavior problems continue to occur in a percentage of this population (Evans & Voeltz, 1982). And though the occurrence may be less than previously reported for institutional settings, such problems present major obstacles to the imple-

Preparation of portions of this chapter was supported in part by Contract No. 300-82-0363 awarded to the University of Minnesota with a subcontract to Syracuse University from the Division of Innovation and Development, Special Education Programs, U. S. Department of Education. The opinions expressed herein do not necessariy reflect the position or policy of the U.S. Department of Education, and no official endorsement should be inferred.

mentation of the recommended least restrictive program options. Learners who display severe behavior problems are generally the last to be included in a community-based training program, and, when they do participate, are often the first to be returned to a restrictive setting when their behaviors clash with community training efforts (Mayeda & Sutter, 1981; Singer, Close, Irvin, Gersten, & Sailor, 1984).

The well-trained practitioner can refer to the extensive intervention literature in remediating such problems, and there are several exemplary demonstrations of maintaining learners with severe behavior problems in community settings (Donnellan, LaVigna, Zambito, & Thvedt, 1985; Singer et al., 1984). But with rare exception, this literature is derived from program models involving intervention strategies designed for implemention in highly controlled environments. Such environments artificially restrict stimuli and consequences and often assume one-to-one staffing conditions. Until recently, practitioners have been hard pressed to identify behavior management procedures that are both ecologically valid and known to be effective in normalized educational and other everyday environments. Unless such practices are developed and validated, the learner with severe disabilities who also exhibits serious excess behavior is at risk for continuing to be an exception in efforts to integrate all persons into normalized community opportunities (Hill & Bruininks, 1984).

This chapter provides an overview of adaptive and functional approaches to the remediation of behavior problems in persons with severe disabilities, along with a summary of the empirical evidence supporting their effectiveness. These approaches could be described as reflecting a "second generation" of applied behavior analysis and modification. In what might be called "traditional" behavior modification, the emphasis has been upon the derivation of effective intervention techniques from the careful analysis of learning principles. This previous phase of behavior modification has been instrumental in demonstrating that persons with severe disabilities could learn meaningful new skills, and that severe behavior problems could be remediated. The importance of this contribution to the subsequent and long overdue development of educational and other habilitative services can in no way be understated. But improvements in the daily and longitudinal life experiences of the individual child have tended to be secondary to the demands of the scientific experiment; emphasis has been upon the demonstration of effective intervention techniques, regardless of the nature of the technique or the changes in environment that would be required to maintain the behavioral improvements.

Thus, once the effectiveness of aversive punishment strategies had been demonstrated, such punishments were considered to be a viable treatment option. Objections to the use of aversives, and documentaion of negative side effects, have led to the development of procedural and legal/ethical guidelines for their use, such as those proposed by the Association for the Advancement of

Behavior Therapy (Favell, Azrin, et al., 1982). But these guidelines do not represent a fundamental principle regarding the nature of habilitative services and the need to be consistent with basic quality of life issues that imply a moratorium on the use of such aversives. The resolution on Intrusive Interventions passed by The Association for Persons with Severe Handicaps (1981) represents this principle (see Table 1). Implementation of the spirit of this resolution would require the systematic application and adaptation of learning principles and instructional strategies to the context of normalized, habilitative, and integrated learning environments (what the authors refer to as "second generation" behavior modification). This next phase demands that caregivers and interventionists focus on far more than individual behavior problems in individual children, and move beyond the design of isolated behavioral interventions that "work" in highly controlled (and restrictive) settings. The acceptance of principles such as normalization and integration precludes the manipulation of contingencies at the expense of certain fundamental rights of individuals. Certain restrictive and aversive options are simply no longer

Table 1. Resolution on Intrusive Interventions adopted by The Association for Persons with Severe Handicaps

Resolution on Intrusive Interventions
(Passed, October 1981)

WHEREAS, in order to realize the goals and objectives of The Association for Persons with Severe Handicaps, including the right of each severely handicapped person to grow, develop, and enjoy life in integrated and normalized community environments, the following resolution is adopted;

WHEREAS, educational and other habilitative services must employ instructional and management strategies which are consistent with the right of each individual with severe handicaps to an effective treatment which does not compromise the equally important right to freedom from harm. This requires educational and habilitative procedures free from indiscriminant use of drugs, aversive stimuli, environmental deprivation, or exclusion from services; and

WHEREAS, TASH supports a cessation of the use of any treatment option which exhibits some or all of the following characteristics: (1) obvious signs of physical pain experienced by the individual; (2) potential or actual physical side effects, including tissue damage, physical illness, severe stress, and/or death, that would properly require the involvement of medical personnel; (3) dehumanization of persons with severe handicaps because the procedures are normally unacceptable for nonhandicapped persons in community environment; (4) extreme ambivalence and discomfort by family, staff, and/or caregivers regarding the necessity of such extreme strategies or their own involvement in such interventions; and (5) obvious repulsion and/or stress felt by nonhandicapped peers and community members who cannot reconcile extreme procedures with acceptable standard practice;

RESOLVED, that The Association for Persons with Severe Handicaps' resources and expertise be dedicated to the development, implementation, evaluation, dissemination, and advocacy of educational and management practices which are appropriate for use in integrated environments and which are consistent with the commitment to a high quality of life for individuals with severe handicaps.

available for use by caregivers and intervention agents. Just as an institution is no longer viewed as an acceptable "treatment environment" for any individual, the use of aversive contingencies and the placement of children and adults into separate and homogeneous behavior management centers, programs, and/or classrooms are neither desirable nor appropriate for use as means for solving behavior problems.

These are fine-sounding principles, but, as anyone reading this chapter surely knows, putting them into practice requires administrative, fiscal, and clinical flexibility in addition to professional commitment and the availability of effective interventions. The present service delivery system is organized along a continuum of services model whereby increasing resources to deal with increases in children's needs involves movement of the child to places where such resources are located. For children who exhibit severe behavior problems, additional services are invariably tied to more restrictive and separate settings such as behavior management classrooms, units, and even special schools. One might logically ask why a continuum of services cannot be provided to a child in the context of community environments. That is, can systems be redesigned to allow for the "movement" of staff, resources, and specialized intervention options to the child? This model would add services as they are needed to maintain that child in the community, and fade them as crises are resolved and needs are met (Warren & Juhrs, 1984).

The evidence presented in this chapter provides support for the assumption that technological knowledge is adequate to deal with behavior problems within the context of integrated educational and community environments. There is an impressive, growing data base regarding the effectiveness of adaptive and functional approaches (Evans & Meyer, 1985; LaVigna & Donnellan, in press). The major purpose of this chapter is to present an overview of these recent developments organized according to the steps that can be taken by practitioners in educational settings to remediate severe behavior problems in children (and adults) with severe disabilities. Each of these strategies is workable without moving the child to a specialized, separate environment. Most can be implemented by existing staff in the child's current setting where difficulties are occurring. But some do imply the provision of additional services. These additional services may involve staff, resources, and program options; where such services are generally not made available to children without movement of those children to another setting, a certain level of advocacy will be needed to change this situation. In the interim, however, much information is available for use for practitioners committed to delivering effective, quality programs to children in integrated school and community environments. This information relates to two major classes of decisions that must be made to deal effectively with excessive behavior. These are assessment decisions, involving the selection and interpretation of excess behavior, and intervention decisions that follow logically from the assessment information. Thus, assessment considerations are discussed first in an effort to place excess behavior in the context of the child's total repertoire and ecology.

ASSESSMENT

Assessment to plan interventions with excess behavior has typically included attention to two general categories of concern. First, decisions must be made regarding which of a particular child's various excess behaviors are intervention priorities. Just as it is not practical to implement simultaneous instruction on all skill objectives that could be considered program needs, it is unlikely that every excess behavior that a child exhibits would be an immediate intervention target. This "limitation" is also appropriate in many ways, as not all excess behaviors are of equal priority. Some are more critical than others, and will thus require immediate attention. Others are relatively trivial or minor in nature, and can be tolerated indefinitely while being monitored informally (Voeltz, Evans, Derer, & Hanashiro, 1983). This selection and decision-making proces should occur in a systematic way, such that critical criteria are applied that provide justification for the choices made by intervention agents.

Second, once priority target behaviors have been identified, a functional analysis of the excess behavior is conducted. The functional analysis involves formulating hypotheses regarding why the behavior occurs, and under what conditions the child is most likely to exhibit or fail to exhibit the excess behavior. This analysis may provide evidence regarding the actual cause of the behavior, or may simply reveal those contingencies that appear to be maintaining the behavior at the present time, regardless of the original cause. The information generated by a functional analysis will typically suggest experimental conditions that can be applied to test the hypothesis and, if results support it, implement a relevant intervention program to bring the excess behavior under rapid instructional control. Once the intervention program is implemented, dramatic decreases in the occurrence of the excess behavior can generally be documented. Intervention research represents this process of hypothesis testing and demonstration of experimental control over excess behavior.

As the authors have argued elsewhere, assessment (and intervention) must also attend to two additional issues (Evans & Meyer, 1985). Third, if the intervention agent is concerned with more than a demonstration of experimental control and instead wishes to produce meaningful and lasting change in the child's repertoire, assessment must include an analysis of the function of the specific excess behavior, *for that child*. This is a different concept than that of the functional analysis of behavior. An assessment of the behavior's function implies that children's excess behaviors are not random negative responses that may have been superstitiously reinforced in the past and thus are amenable to modification through a more thoughtful application of contingencies. While this contingency management process may well bring the behavior under instructional control, if the behavior performs some function for the child (accomplishes a purpose) it can be anticipated that it will reoccur whenever the contingencies are not in effect. Or, it can be hypothesized that some alternative (perhaps equally or even more undesirable) behavior will be used by the child to achieve the original purpose. Thus, if the excess behavior is not random but is purposeful in that its occurrence results in the attainment of something the child wants, any lasting change in that behavior would have to involve establishing a more appropriate, functional alternative that is equally or more powerful from the child's point of view.

Finally, educational validity criteria must be applied to both the design of the educational intervention and to judgments regarding the success of intervention outcomes. This "last" step in measurement (which should not actually occur last!) requires knowledge of the learner's personal ecology. The intervention strategy used must be consistent with socially acceptable, normalized, and ecologically feasible practices for integrated community environments. Well-documented difficulties in generalization or transfer of behavior change from environment to environment provided empirical support for the need to implement intervention efforts directly in the criterion environment. While interventions are obviously easier to implement in highly controlled and artificial "treatment" settings that are purposely designed for dealing with such behavior problems, eventually the child must be returned to the environment in which the problem originally occurred and may well occur again. In addition, of course, current "most promising practices" principles supporting integration and normalization of the life experiences of persons with disabilities bring social validity criteria to bear as further support for efforts to develop and validate strategies reflecting these principles. Equally important is the crucial need to document not simply that a behavior can be controlled when the teacher is present or under certain conditions, but that the behavioral outcome involves changes independent of the presence of the original intervention components. That is, assessment (and evaluation) must include a description of the various natural conditions and situations in which the learner needs to display a functional alternative to the excess behavior.

The next section describes strategies for accomplishing the first three assessment steps outlined above; relevant educational validity issues are noted in the summary section of the chapter.

Selecting Excess Behavior Intervention Priorities

Through the written IEP, the instructional team is to work with the parents to identify priority instructional objectives for a given school year (i.e., those particular skill needs that will be given highest priority for attainment by the child). As students with severe disabilities need to acquire many more skills than could feasibly be part of the IEP each year, it is important that this process of identifying priorities be carefully done so that it ultimately leads to maximum participation by that child in integrated community environments when she or he leaves school upon graduation. Voeltz, Evans, Freedland, and Donellon (1982) found that when students exhibited serious excess behavior, experienced teachers included behavior management (deceleration) goals on the IEP regardless of the level of functioning of the child, but that they were most likely to do so when the child had severe rather than moderate intellectual delay. Thus, it would seem that the child most in need of the acquisition of new skills was also most at risk for an IEP that is dominated by goals for reducing or eliminating behavior, to the exclusion of those that would involve learning new skills. The authors have argued elsewhere that the IEP is an educational program, and that skill acquisition goals cannot be sacrificed to behavior management goals unless this is unavoidable, as in the case of health- and life-threatening behavior (Evans & Meyer, 1985). All other excess behavior intervention plans should be designed *after* a comprehensive educational plan has been formulated. While this educational plan may well be altered in response to the information generated by the student's excess behavior repertoire, skill acquisition goals should never be replaced by goals to reduce or eliminate behavior.

How, then, does one identify those excess behaviors that are of sufficient priority that intervention should occur? In which cases should the modification of those excess behaviors be reflected in the formulation of the IEP? The task is not simply to list in order of importance a series of obvious behavior problems. Judgments regarding which behaviors require immediate attention must be related to the functions that those behaviors play in the child's total repertoire (Evans, 1985; Voeltz & Evans, 1982). Intervention decisions should also be guided by whether or not there are social and educational consequences for the child who exhibits the behavior (Voeltz & Evans, 1983). Elsewhere, the authors have detailed a formalized decision model that can be used to select intervention priorities from among many possible target behaviors that a child might exhibit. Briefly, there are three levels of seriousness, with different implications for the extent to which a behavior is reflected in the IEP. Intervention decisions are not based only upon the topography of the behavior, but also upon its relationship to other behaviors, program resources, and various critical social and empirical criteria that can ultimately affect the child's adjustment to his or her environment. Table 2 provides a summary of this three-level decision model and consequent intervention decisions.

Clearly, the questions that must be asked as part of this decision process involve clinical judgments more than they involve factual or empirical data. For example, one of the questions to be answered is ''Does the excess interfere with learning?'' In spite of rather widespread acceptance of the notion that stereo-

Table 2. Three levels of excess behavior intervention decisions[a]

Level	Characteristics of the excess behavior	Example	Intervention implications	Specific intervention decision
I. Urgent behaviors requiring immediate attention	—Behavior is health- or life-threatening	—Self-biting that results in tissue damage	Behavior is serious enough to be reflected directly on the IEP through the identification of a deceleration goal and alternating skill acquisition goal.	Always intervene, monitor formally
II. Serious behaviors requiring formal consideration	—Behavior interferes with learning —Behavior is likely to become serious in near future if not modified —Behavior is dangerous to others —Behavior is of great concern to caregivers	—Screaming and crying that interferes with attention to activity task —Self-biting that does not involve tissue damage —Hitting peers —Tantrumming in public places	Behavior is serious enough to be reflected indirectly on the IEP through the identification of alternative skill acquisition goals. In addition, separate (from the IEP) behavior deceleration objectives may be needed and appropriate, provided that an equally or more serious excess behavior or critical skill need would not be adversely affected.	Most typically intervene; monitor formally along with any equally/more serious behavior that might be related

| III. Excess behavior reflecting "normal deviance" | —Behavior is not improving or is getting worse
—Behavior has been a problem for some time
—Behavior damages materials
—Behavior interferes with community acceptance
—An improvement in the behavior would generate another behavior improvement | —Screaming and crying during non-instructional times
—Thumbsucking
—Throwing toys onto the floor
—Echolalia in public places
—Teasing peers (which interferes with positive peer play) | Behavior is not serious enough to be reflected on the IEP. If consistent with skill acquisition needs already reflected on the IEP, alternative skill acquisition goals may be evident. Separate (from the IEP) behavior deceleration objectives may be needed and appropriate, provided that an equally or more serious excess behavior or critical skill need would not be adversely affected and the program resources are adequate to conduct the intervention. | Most typically would intervene only if all other needs being met (i.e., not very often!); monitor informally if no intervention; monitor formally (along with other more serious behavior if intervention) |

[a]Adapted from Voeltz, Evans, Derer, and Hanashiro (1983).

typed behavior interferes with learning (as opposed to interfering with teaching), an early study by Koegel and Covert (1972) is generally the only empirical report cited as support for this presumed relationship. In contrast, Hung (1978) reported increased appropriate language use by two autistic children as a function of allowing them brief periods of stereotyped behavior as a contingent reward. While intervention agents might not be inclined to use stereotyped behavior as a reinforcer in this way, the second study does suggest that its relationship to learning can vary considerably. Until clear empirical evidence exists to support definite answers to questions in the decision model, practitioners will need to employ their own familiarity with how each individual learner responds under different conditions to answer such questions.

In fact, it is critical that professionals and parents utilize clinical judgments regarding how a child's behaviors might be interrelated, such that a change in one excess behavior could have a dramatic impact (either an improvement or a serious setback) on another. Behaviors may co-occur or be inversely related, such that if one behavior does not occur, another almost certainly will. There is ample evidence that these behavioral chains and clusters are both common and idiosyncratic. Although behavioral co-variation is a widespread phenomenon, available research data reveal that the individual patterns of the interrelationships vary a great deal from child to child (Voeltz & Evans, 1982). This means that the person making intervention decisions must know the specific child quite well in order to formulate an "individualized hypothesis" regarding how the child's various behaviors interrelate to form a system, and how this system might be affected by changes in any component behavior (Evans, 1985; Evans & Nelson, in press). Consequently, whenever two equally serious behaviors are evident in a child's repertoire and appear to be interrelated with one another, it is critical to monitor both. This would be so even though the intervention plan intends to modify only one of those behaviors at a time (Evans & Meyer, 1985).

Conducting a Functional Analysis of an Intervention Target

Once an excess behavior has been identified as an intervention priority, hypotheses need to be specified and tested regarding the conditions under which the behavior occurs. Causality in science is a complex issue. If a child engages in body rocking while he or she is alone, is this caused by boredom, lack of alternative solitary play skills, imitation of peers who body rock in an institutional setting, or is it a "purposeless" continuance of a behavior that began because he or she was understimulated as a young child? Each of these "causes" may have contributed to the present form of the excess behavior, but some are of more immediate relevance than others when planning an intervention to change the behavior. It is thus accepted in the behavior modification literature to think of casuality in terms of Skinner's concept (Skinner, 1953) of the functional analysis (i.e., what are the current factors that affect the onset, duration, persistence, or general occurrence of the behavior?). If it is determined that the student rocks when alone but not when others are present, then the rocking is a function of being alone, even though it might be inferred that what is really happening is that he or she has no alternative behavioral responses with which to occupy his or her time when alone but does have alternative behaviors for use in the presence of others.

Functional analyses can vary in formality. Iwata, Dorsey, Slifer, Bauman, and Richman (1982) have described a formal assessment process for determining the functional relationship between self-injury and specific environmental events. Children in their study were exposed to a series of analogue test conditions: 1) play materials were either present or absent; 2) instructor demands were high or low; and 3) social attention was absent, noncontingently present, or contingently present. They reported that for six of the nine children, higher levels of self-injury were consistently associated with specific stimulus conditions. However, the patterns differed across children, so that their results support Carr's (1977) contention that self-injury may be a function of different sources of reinforcement for different children. For the three children for whom no consistent pattern could be identified, Iwata and his colleagues suggest that further work might reveal that the same behavior served different functions for the same child, depending upon situational circumstances (see also Carr & Durand, 1985a). This would indicate the need for different treatments for the same individual and behavior, implemented depending upon the specific situation.

One advantage of this formal testing procedure is that it allows for the identification of variables that affect self-injury prior to the implementation of lengthy intervention efforts based upon "best guesses." Iwata and his colleagues also note that their procedure is a necessary alternative to clinical research practices that involve collecting baseline data in a "single invariant situation" (p. 18). A disadvantage of the procedure is that even though the test conditions involve variables that exist in the natural environment and could be manipulated for an intervention, the actual test environment does not closely resemble naturalistic situations. Thus, it is possible that other environmental stimuli not present in the analogue test conditions relate to the frequency of the self-injurious behavior. This pattern could not be properly identified in the analogue situation assessments. It is also likely that the formal test situation cannot entirely substitute for obtaining further supporting evidence from naturalistic observations, before and/or after formal testing. Incident reports by parents and staff can be used as a source of clues as to which variable might be tested in the formal situations. This would reduce the amount of time required for a formal baseline assessment (the sample in the Iwata et al. study spent an average of 8 days in the assessment, ranging from 4 to 11 days). Finally, a more careful delineation of such situational variables in the child's current environments could allow for the identification of behavioral interrelationships without a formal assessment. Evans and Meyer (1985) have suggested that clinicians generate several "intervention hypotheses" for any excess behavior, and list corresponding, naturally occurring environmental situation tests for each hypothesis. Table 3 provides three behavioral examples of how this process might occur. This would require a careful record of incidents, including information on the setting, activity, who was present, and what the child was doing at the time. These records could be used to generate such hypotheses, and corresponding "function tests" conducted in the naturalistic setting over a period of days to gather information that could support a particular intervention plan. Such informal incident records would not be a substitute for a formal evaluation of the effectiveness of the intervention. But, at the very least, before the results of formal testing are used to design interventions, support for such plans should be obtained from information on occurrences of the excess behavior in naturalistic situations where the behavior is a problem.

In many situations, the functional analysis may also conveniently suggest the appropriate intervention strategy. If, for example, an excess behavior increases when social attention is present, and decreases when it is withheld, the teacher can be reasonably certain that the behavior is being maintained at least partially by social reinforcement (regardless of its original, historical cause). In this instance, it would be possible (even desirable) to insure that social attention does not occur following an occurrence of the excess behavior and, alternatively, that it does occur when the student engages in more positive behaviors, which may need to be taught. However, in other cases, the functional analysis will not be as conveniently related to treatment plans. For example, Colman, Frankel, Ritvo, and Freeman (1976) were able to show that a stereotyped behavior increased with fluorescent lighting and decreased with incandescent lighting. Such an experiment provides a possible ecological modification of short-term usefulness only. Incandescent lighting can be used to obtain immediate behavioral improvement, but eventually the learner must adjust to fluorescent lighting if he or she is to enjoy maximum participation in everyday community environments. In the second example, even though the functional analysis provides a demonstration of a clear relationship between an environmental contingency and the behavior, it has not provided an easy guideline for intervention. Even in the first example, the simple manipulation of social reinforcement contingencies will not adequately address the student's intervention needs if the excess behavior is his or her only strategy to obtain caregiver attention. If the student has no alternative positive behaviors in his or her repertoire for gaining caregiver attention, it is likely that, outside the training situation, he or she will continue to use that excess behavior for this purpose.

The important point is that the functional analysis of behavior will reveal information about contingencies that can be manipulated in order to bring the excess behavior under experimental or behavioral control. It is possible that if those behavioral control conditions last long enough and are employed consistently enough by every person in the child's environment, he or she will "forget" the excess behavior over time. But more often than not, contingency management will be a temporary solution; additional information is needed to plan for long-term improvement. Specifically, it is necessary to know not only what is maintaining the behavior, but what alternative strategies could be taught to the student to accomplish the same purpose in a more positive, socially appropriate way. This is discussed in the next section.

Determining the Function of an Excess Behavior

There is a subtle difference between the concept of the functional analysis and the idea that every behavior has a *function* (a purpose) for the child. White (1980) articulated the distinction between the *form* of a behavior and its *function,* or the critical effect that the child hopes to attain by using a particular behavioral form. Although this concept of form versus function has most typically been applied to skill acquisition issues (such as developing an alternative form to accomplish the function of mobility for a child who has severe cerebral palsy), it is a useful distinction to consider with respect to excess behavior as well. Essentially, a particular excess behavior may be viewed as a socially inappropriate form (e.g., tantrums) to achieve a particular function (e.g., escape or social attention). Children may utilize various forms of excess behavior for individually idiosyncratically determined purposes. Depending upon the reactions of his or her environment, he or she may or may not be successful in obtaining desired critical effects. And, consistent with efforts to manage contingencies to avoid reinforcing excess behavior, it is possible that eventually an excess behavior that was intended to attract caregiver attention will extinguish if ignored. But unless interventionists attend to the child's need to attract caregiver attention, they cannot predict that the excess behavior will not be used for this purpose whenever contingencies change.

There are, of course, those behaviors that appear to serve no purpose and may be unrelated to environmental contingencies, such as laughing or shrieking for no apparent reason. But the evidence is accumulating to suggest that many excess behaviors serve at least three functions in children with severe disabilities (different ones at different times and in different children):

1. Some behaviors function as "simple" *social-communication* mechanisms, letting others know that the child wishes social attention, wants to be left alone, wants to get away, cannot do the task, and so forth. These behaviors would be clearly related to social interaction situations and contingencies.
2. Certain behaviors may be *self-regulatory* in nature, allowing the child to adjust arousal level, selectively attend to a particular (preferred or required) activity, and so forth. These behaviors would presumably vary as a

Table 3. Assessing the function of an excess behavior in natural contexts

Description of excess behavior	Alternative explanations		Corresponding function test—will excess decrease if:
After approximately 15 minutes of one-to-one instruction, child tantrums, including crying, screaming, throwing objects, and slipping out of chair onto floor.	1.	Child dislikes one-to-one instructional situations, a particular teacher, or the task itself.	1.1 Demands are alternated with low-demand interactions? 1.2 Teacher or task is changed?
	2.	Child tires quickly, and loses control after a short period of instructional demands.	2.1 Instructional sessions are shortened, then increased gradually to longer periods? 2.2 Instructional sessions are alternated with "easy" and enjoyable activities?
	3.	Task is too difficult, and child is unable to cope with stress, errors, and so forth.	3.1 Task is broken down into smaller steps? 3.2 Errorless learning strategies are used? 3.3 Another equally important task is substituted that is less difficult?
When walking in the room (or indoor environment), child "makes the rounds," pushing objects off table and shelf surfaces onto the floor.	1.	Child enjoys (is reinforced by) attention from peers and/or teacher that results from behavior.	1.1 Teacher ignores behavior? 1.2 Teacher says "No"? 1.3 Peers are not present in the room?
	2.	Child enjoys watching and hearing objects fall onto the floor (and may be otherwise bored).	2.1 Floor is carpeted or objects themselves are soft? 2.2 Child is busy with a novel or preferred activity?

After approximately 10–20 minutes in community training experience, teenager hits a peer and/or begins to shout at others.	3. Child needs physical activity and exercise.	3.1 Walking across room occurs after recess versus after a sedentary activity?
		3.2 Child is tired?
	1. Teenager cannot tolerate relatively unstructured settings (with multiple stimuli, etc.) for more than a short time.	1.1 Community experience is initially shortened to 10–15 minutes?
		1.2 Supervision and structure is increased?
	2. A specific peer is making him or her angry.	2.1 Peer is absent, or another peer is closer, interacting more, and so forth?
		2.2 Any aversive behavior by specific peer is interrupted in some way?
	3. When peer or another person does not respond as she or he wishes, teenager is attempting to "get his or her way."	3.1 Peer is taught to respond positively when possible, and
		3.2 Peer taught to move away when she or he cannot respond?
	4. Teenager is attempting to communicate with others, but is not understood or is ignored unless she or he tantrums.	4.1 Attention is provided on a consistent schedule?
		4.2 Any request or initiative is responded to versus ignored?

Reprinted with permission, with some revisions, from Evans and Meyer (1985).

function of different stimulus conditions as well as the child's physiological state.

3. Other behaviors appear to serve as *play* or serve a self-entertainment purpose, giving the child something to do during unstructured time whether alone or with others. These behaviors appear to be self-reinforcing (i.e., they are not under the control of social contingencies).

It can also be the case that the same behavior (topographically) can serve different functions in different children, or even in the same child at different times and in different contexts. Carr and Durand (1985a) describe children for whom particular topographies of self-injurious behavior clearly serve an escape versus an attention-getting function across and within the same children.

If a behavior is being used by the child to accomplish a purpose, the intervention implication is clear. Alternative strategies that are socially more appropriate must be acquired by the child to achieve those desired critical effects. In addition, those alternative strategies must be acquired along with a behavior shaping process to "normalize" the child's access to those desired critical effects. Neel (1983) notes that an analysis of function (for those cases where it can be determined what the child wants) can reveal two quite different situations: 1) the caregivers know what the child wants and are willing to provide access, but the child needs to learn a more acceptable form to use for that purpose; and 2) the caregivers know what the child wants, but prefer not to give in to his or her request (or give in less frequently than the child wishes) because his or her purpose is contrary to his or her best interests. For example, a child may tantrum because he or she finds a task too difficult and has no functional communicative repertoire that he or she can use to tell the teacher that he or she cannot perform the task. In this case, the intervention plan could involve teaching the child a positive communication signal that he or she can use to indicate when a task is too difficult or when he or she needs a break, and so forth. If, however, the child typically tantrums during instruction on any new task and the teacher judges that the child wishes to avoid all tasks regardless of difficulty, the situation is more complicated. It may still be essential for the child to acquire a positive communication skill to ask for a break or for help, but he or she must also learn to use this new strategy far less frequently than the rate at which tantrumming is occurring. The problem cannot be solved simply by allowing the child to use another, socially acceptable form to achieve a critical effect that itself is at an unacceptable level for the child.

Several studies conducted by Carr and his colleagues support the position that various excess behaviors serve communicative functions for persons who lack appropriate verbal communicative repertoires to meet their needs (Carr & Durand, 1985a; Carr & Newsom, in press; Carr, Newsom, & Binkoff, 1980). Carr and Durand (1985b) argued in particular that behavior problems such as aggression, tantrums, and self-injury can be determined to be performing one of two major social-communicative functions: 1) an escape strategy, controlled by negative reinforcement processes, and 2) attention-seeking behavior, controlled by positive reinforcement. In order to establish which intent was responsible for an excess behavior in a specific child, they devised an assessment procedure that combined two levels of task difficulty (easy vs. difficult) and adult attention (100% of the time vs. 33% of the time) to produce three test conditions: Easy 100, Easy 33, and Difficult 100. Easy 100 was compared with Easy 33 to identify behavior intended by the child to attract adult attention, and Easy 100 compared with Difficult 100 to discriminate behavior serving an avoidance function. For the four children in their study, three distinct patterns of disruptive behavior emerged. Two of the children exhibited excess behavior primarily during the Difficult 100 condition, indicating that they were attempting to terminate a difficult task regardless of instructor attention. One child was disruptive primarily during the Easy 33 condition, supporting an attention-getting function regardless of task difficulty. The fourth child was disruptive in both the Easy 33 and Difficult 100 conditions, indicating that her behaviors, under different conditions, were being used for both purposes. Their results clearly support the usefulness of such an assessment in providing information needed to plan an intervention in each case. Equally important, the very different intents established across behaviors for even this small sample of children emphasizes how critical it is to individualize these interventions, as opposed to attempting to propose specific intervention techniques that would work for a particular behavior form across children.

Schuler (1981) maintained that excess behavior could serve numerous communicative functions, and proposed a communication interview to gather information regarding a student's verbal and nonverbal communication means (including excess behavior) to accomplish a broad range of functions. These could include requests for objects of assistance, protests, and statements about things (declarations). Based upon this model, two similar assessment protocols and structured behavioral checklists have been developed to assist practitioners in formulating hypotheses regarding what the student does and why he or she does it (Donnellan, Mirenda, Mesaros, & Fassbender, 1984; Peck et al., 1984). For each individual student, these hypotheses would form the basis for designing curricular interventions to teach the child more socially appropriate strategies to accomplish apparent communicative purposes.

In contrast to excess behavior that appears to have social and communicative intent, other behaviors are not as clearly related to social contingencies (Baumeister, 1978; Schroeder, Mulick, & Rojahn, 1980). Excess behavior may occur when the child is alone or, if others are present, may appear to ''preoccupy'' the child so that he or she is unresponsive to ongoing events. This phenomenon is typical of various forms of stereotyped behavior such as body rocking, finger flicking, repetitive vocalizations and laughing, head weaving, and so forth. There is also evidence that some occasions of self-injurious behavior are not socially motivated (i.e., they do not appear to be serving an attention-getting or escape function), but occur regardless of social consequences (Rojahn, 1984). As these behaviors do produce obvious visual, auditory, kinesthetic, tactile, gustatory, vestibular, and/or olfactory consequences for the child, they may be self-reinforcing such that the child deliberately engages in the behavior in order to obtain this sensory feedback (Rincover & Devany, 1982). In fact, stereotyped behavior is often referred to as "self-stimulation" based upon the assumption that it generates its own reinforcement. In these cases, excess behavior might be analogous to play or self-entertainment for a person with few skills or who is, at the time, deprived of needed resources to occupy himself or herself more appropriately.

As noted earlier, excess behavior can also be self-regulatory, that is, used by the child to regulate his or her homeostatic state (body temperature, etc.) or to reduce or increase his or her arousal level (cf. Zentall & Zentall, 1983). Where behavior might reflect efforts to regulate arousal, the excess behavior would occur both when the child is alone and in social situations, depending upon the various multiple stimuli present under different circumstances. An example of this might be a child who momentarily "bursts" into stereotyped hand flapping after a correct response during instruction (for which he or she is being praised or rewarded by the teacher). This response may last for only a few seconds, after which the child seems to become calm and ready for instruction once again. It seems logical to consider this to be a behavior that is performing a self-regulatory function for the child, such as reducing excitement or anxiety. Nonhandicapped persons who are intensely engaged in difficult or demanding tasks (or boring ones) may similarly engage in behaviors like leg swinging, pencil tapping, and cigarette smoking.

Intervention implications for behaviors that serve as play would differ somewhat from behaviors that are self-regulatory. In the latter case, if the child remains involved in the instructional situation while he or she is engaged in periodic or low intensity excess behavior, it might be concluded that: 1) the excess behavior could be his or her coping mechanism to remain engaged, and 2) if the behavior is at a level that can be tolerated, allowing him or her to continue using it in this way might be, temporarily, a positive alternative to attempts to have him or her "sit quietly." There are virtually no data on this issue. Hence, if a Level III behavior is involved (see Table 2), practitioners would make different intervention decisions based upon predicted and actual costs and benefits to both the child and the program. For behavior that typically occurs in the absence of alternative positive activities, however, the obvious intervention decision would be to teach the child alternative positive leisure skills. In any case, a careful examination of the probable sensory feedback characteristics of the excess behavior would facilitate the selection of alternative skills that will ultimately be equally reinforcing to the child. Thus, Favell,

McGimsey, and Schell (1982) were able to show a significant decrease in eye poking by a young child by substituting play with prisms, presumably because the prisms provided equally powerful visual stimulation for the child.

INTERVENTION

There are three broad categories of procedural approaches to intervening with excess behavior (see also Gaylord-Ross, 1980):

1. *Ecological*   An ecological intervention involves rearranging the environment so that the behavior is prevented from occurring. This can be done either by removing/reducing strong stimuli that are reliably associated with the excess behavior, or by physically interfering with the child's ability to engage in the behavior.
2. *Curricular*   The curricular approach involves teaching the child an alternative positive behavior (a behavior that will substitute for the excess) that he or she can then use as an equally effective strategy to obtain desired critical effects (i.e., accomplish the same purpose).
3. *Negative Consequence*   This intervention procedure requires rearranging contingencies such that negative stimuli (i.e., those that reliably predict a future decrease in the occurrence of the behavior they follow) are imposed as negative consequences contingent upon the occurrence of the excess behavior.

The information derived from the assessment procedures outlined in the previous section should suggest which of these approaches is most likely to be effective in both the immediate and long-term reduction of an excess behavior. If, for example, there is no apparent purpose for the occurrence of an excess behavior, it is difficult to conceptualize how one can utilize a curricular approach. If the behavior is not being used to accomplish some purpose, teaching an alternative skill that is equally "powerful" makes little sense. Often, however, behaviors that fall into this category (where a meaningful function for the behavior cannot be determined) can be most effectively modified through an ecological intervention that involves removing or reducing certain situational events that set the stage for the excess. If these situational events are in fact nonhabilitative as well, sound educational practices add further support for an ecological intervention that would change this situation so that the child is no longer at risk for exhibiting the excess behavior. Before using a negative consequence to modify an excess behavior for which no curricular alternative seems logical, one should first make some decisions about the desirability of the stimulus events associated with the excess behavior. Where these stimuli are representative of poor practices and/or negative environments, an improvement in these antecedent circumstances may have a dramatic positive effect upon behavior (Horner, 1980).

A successful intervention with an excess behavior is most likely to represent some combination of these procedural categories. In any event, a curricular approach is essential to achieve *behavior change,* as opposed to *behavioral control,* as an outcome. The only exceptions to this general guideline are those instances in which a nonhabilitative environment is directly responsible for eliciting or failing to inhibit an excess behavior that would simply not occur under different circumstances. But whenever an excess behavior is clearly associated with attempts to accomplish some purpose, the ultimate criterion of effectiveness requires that the child has learned another, more positive and socially acceptable strategy to meet those particular needs. Both ecological and negative consequence approaches involve behavioral control, and should be viewed as temporary measures that ultimately must be superceded by a more enduring outcome.

The distinction between behavioral control and behavior change is a crucial one for interventions with excess behavior. An intervention that utilizes behavioral control to effect improvements in behavior involves some re-arrangement of contingencies around the occurrence of that behavior (i.e., either an ecological or negative consequence approach). In some cases, these interventions utilize extinction, or the removal of positive social consequences following the occurrence of a nonpreferred or excess behavior. In other cases, the intervention involves the contingent occurrence of a negative consequence for that child (a punishment) following instances of the excess. While these interventions can be "effective" in producing an immediate and often dramatic decrease in the frequency or duration of the excess behavior, such behavioral improvements often fail to maintain across time and/or to generalize to other environments and under different stimulus conditions. The extensive follow-up by Lovaas and his colleagues of students with autism who had received intensive intervention in his program reported that once-documented improve-ments had maintained only if the parents had continued to implement the various contingency management intervention techniques with their children at follow-up. Those children whose parents did not consistently utilize the procedures and whose school programs also failed to maintain the con-tingencies had regressed (Lovaas, Koegel, Simmons, & Long, 1973).

Finally, the appearance of various negative "side effects" has been frequently reported in the literature on punishment interventions (Voeltz & Evans, 1982). These negative side effects include both the occurrence of various highly negative protest behaviors exhibited by the child during the intervention itself, and the subsequent appearance of alternative and equally negative excess behavior that increased in frequency and/or duration as the original target behavior was decreased. Thus, the authors have argued else-where that behavioral control interventions are of limited benefit to the child and the environment as a strategy to remediate excess behavior in a meaningful way (Evans & Meyer, 1985).

The alternative approach to interventions with excess behavior is to design behavior change programs that involve teaching the child a socially acceptable skill behavior that will replace the excess behavior. Theoretical support for this approach derives from those hypotheses that excess behavior is functional for the child, as was discussed in the previous section. Even when the purpose of the excess behavior is difficult to ascertain, that behavior nevertheless occupies a place in the child's behavioral repertoire. It "fills time" for a young person (or older person) who has few constructive strategies to deal with time and context in the absence of structure and control. Thus, in any event, an educational program that is directed toward producing lasting and meaningful behavior change must emphasize curricular strategies to intervene with excess behavior just as curricular strategies are utilized to address the child's needs in each environmental skill domain (Evans & Meyer, 1985). The next section summarizes available evidence on effective interventions with excess behavior using each of three approaches.

Ecological Approaches

Ecological interventions can focus specifically upon preventing the occurrence of an excess behavior either by removing items associated with it or by physically and/or verbally interrupting the child as the behavior is initiated, thus preventing the child from completing the behavior. Other ecological interventions can be broad-based, involving changes in general circumstances affecting the child, such as rearrangements of the physical environment and/or the nature of the child's program. Informal interventions like removing or taking away objects (which might otherwise be thrown, etc.) or rearranging seating (which prevents one student from provoking another, etc.) are commonly used by parents and teachers whenever such antecedent stimuli are reliably associated with a behavior problem. In this section, the authors discuss three categories of ecological interventions. As indicated earlier in this chapter, however, the reader should keep in mind that such interventions are generally most appropriate in conjunction with curricular strategies (see the next section) to ensure that when naturally occurring environmental events are present, the student can maintain improved behavior patterns.

Setting Factors   Wahler and Fox (1981) called for efforts to increase the range of environmental phenomena that could be manipulated to achieve a meaningful change in children's behavior. They noted that *setting factors,* as opposed to specific stimulus events (which might sometimes be difficult to isolate or control), are the general set of circumstances characteristic of the context of the problem behavior. These setting factors are associated with the specific stimulus-response relationships that one might attempt to identify through a functional analysis of behavior. Using this perspective, Lazar and

Rucker (1984) recently maintained that traditional contingency management interventions, which are *microenvironmental*, are likely to lose their effectiveness whenever inconsistencies occur during intervention, as is often the case in natural environments. In contrast, *macroenvironmental* setting factor manipulations should be easier to use effectively because immediacy and consistency in response to child behavior (which can be difficult to predict and thus respond to when it does occur) are not an issue. In their study, Lazar and Rucker manipulated a number of variables associated with rumination by an 11-year-old boy with profound retardation (who had chronically vomited since approximately age 7), and successfully reduced the behavior to 6% of baseline levels. Variables that were manipulated in their intervention included reducing liquid intake with meals and for an hour afterward, changing from strained to chopped food, extending the duration of the meal itself, and ensuring that the child moved from the lunch area to his next class activity within 5 minutes of meal completion.

Barton and Barton (in press) reported success in using a "simple and effective program" for the significant reduction or elimination of ruminative behavior in four children with multiple disabilities. Their intervention was somewhat similar to the Lazar and Rucker technique. Small portions of peanut butter were given to the child (in the context of snacks and in a positive way) along with reducing liquid consumption at meals (increasing it at other times to compensate). These two intervention components were faded systematically as the behavior improved. They hypothesized that the peanut butter was simply difficult to ruminate, and noted apparent confusion by the children as they unsuccessfully attempted to ruminate after eating it. Given that medical consultation occurs to insure that the peanut butter consumption and reduced fluid intake would not be health-threatening for a particular child, *and* information that the child likes the peanut butter, they argue that their strategy offers a benign, effective, and normalized treatment for this severe behavior problem.

Looking at the results from the two studies, we cannot clearly isolate which components might have been responsible (such as reduced fluid intake along with peanut butter, or food that differed in consistency with food that the student generally ate), or if *any* changes would have produced a positive behavior change. In both cases, the affective context of meal time clearly shifted to one in which considerable social reinforcement was now made available to the children in the absence of the ruminative behavior. Thus, it may be that the critical component was to somehow interrupt the behavior for a period of time long enough to allow caregivers to provide the desired social attention and preferred activities for alternative positive behaviors that the children would exhibit once the rumination was interrupted (Evans & Meyer, 1985). Interventionists might follow similar procedures to remove or reduce any circumstances that seem to serve as antecedents to excess behavior. In most cases, however, such antecedent or setting event manipulations provide only a temporary solution to the difficulty (see discussion below).

Task Structure Several studies have reported improvements in affect and behavior as a function of changes in *task structure*. Although this is covered in more detail in the curricular section below, Carr and Durand (1985a) were able to show that self-injury increased when the task itself was difficult for the child, and that exposure to performance demands with an easier task, for some children, resulted in dramatic improvements in behavior. Weeks and Gaylord-Ross (1981) also demonstrated that the frequency of self-injury and other excess behaviors was associated with the level of task difficulty. Carr and Durand (1985b) suggest that even when the excess behavior is associated with task difficulty, in some cases the task may nevertheless be appropriate. But since the child apparently lacks problem-solving skills, he or she must be taught a functional response to, for example, ask for help from the teacher when he or she does not understand what to do. But whenever task difficulty is suspect (i.e., it exceeds the child's ability to learn a particular skill form at that time), an ecological alteration is indicated. A less complex form of that skill could be targeted for instruction, the skill could be broken down into smaller steps for instruction, and/or errorless learning techniques might be tried during the initial phases of acquisition.

In other cases, the child's excess behavior seems to occur whenever any instruction takes place, regardless of task difficulty. Whenever the task itself and/or the way in which it is taught are highly artificial and not meaningful for the child, protest behavior may occur because the child is not motivated to participate, is bored, irritated, and so forth. The traditional, massed-trial instructional model for teaching new responses to children with disabilities obviously reflects a continuous demand situation for the child, where artificial reinforcers must be carefully selected and contingently delivered on rich schedules. Motivating children who have severe disabilities to engage in repetitive and boring tasks on a demand schedule is a challenge, not unlike that of motivating nonhandicapped children who do not do well in school nor enjoy it to stay there and continue to perform in academic coursework year after year. Where the skills are clearly important and functional, and the instructional strategies well motivated and reflective of the individual child's needs, changes in instructional design may not be necessary. But where tasks are intrinsically aversive, the teacher-pupil interaction produces little social reinforcement, or the method of instruction is repetitive and/or boring, change might be both overdue and the most effective means for generating positive behavior in the child.

Several studies have reported improvements in affect and behavior as a function of changing task structure. Dunlap and Koegel (1980) compared the effects of massed- and distributed-trial training across five discrimination tasks for two children with autism, and reported a declining trend of correct responding during massed training along with an increased and stable level of correct responding during the distributed condition. One of the children exhibited a high rate of ''no responses'' to initial trial presentation during massed training, but responded consistently during the distributed-trial condition. Finally, trained observers rated the children's interest, happiness, enthusiasm, and cooperativeness more positively under the varied-trial condition. Dunlap and Koegel attribute the overall poor performance during massed-trial training to boredom.

Similar results were reported by Mulligan, Lacy, and Guess (1982) who compared massed-, distributed-, and spaced-trial training of cognitive and motor skills for 11 students with severe disabilities. In comparison to massed training, the distributed condition resulted in increased correct responding and decreased refusals to respond. Dunlap (1984) compared training in massed, varied-acquisition (a distributed-trial condition), and a third condition that he termed varied-maintenance (which included acquisition and maintenance trials on different tasks in distributed-trial format). Five academically oriented discrimination task sets were developed for each of five students with autism. Learning was significantly more efficient under the varied-maintenance condition, which was also associated with the most positive judgments regarding the children's affect during instruction. Similarly, Evans and Voeltz (1982) reported considerable difference in the behavior of a 10-year-old boy with profound retardation under two instructional conditions. While this student displayed relatively high rates of object spinning, object dropping, and bolting, and was on task an average of only 33% of the time during massed-trial instruction, a shift to use of a distributed-trial, functional routine instructional format was associated with significant reductions in these excess behaviors and on-task behavior increasing to 64% of the observed intervals (Evans & Voeltz, 1982).

It is relevant to ask how appropriate highly structured, one-to-one massed-trial instruction *is* as a major instructional mode for children with severe disabilities (see also Donnellan & Neel, Chapter 4, and Guess & Helmstetter, Chapter 8, this volume). Intuitively, it is evident that this is not the major instructional mode for nonhandicapped children, and that children may have physical difficulties complying with long periods of inactivity and direct demand situations. Highly structured programs also do not necessarily ensure high levels of social reinforcement. In the authors' 3-year study of teacher-pupil interactions in classrooms serving students with severe disabilities in public school settings throughout the state of Hawaii, they found that even very young children 8 years of age and under were experiencing teacher approval only 18% of the time during one-to-one instruction, and 10% of the time during group instruction. These were averages based upon multiple observations of 32 children (Evans & Voeltz, 1982). The authors are not implying that programs for children should not be data based, structured, and consistent. Rather, strategies need to be developed to ensure that instructional design includes program features associated with increased learning of meaningful skills in personally motivating circumstances.

Response Interruption Response interruption involves the use of a prosthesis or protective clothing (arm or hand restraints, Velcro straps, mittens, a soft helmet, etc.), manual restraint (blocking the child's movement to hit himself or herself, holding his or her hands down briefly, etc.), and/or verbal cueing ("Put your hands down, please.") prior to or during instruction. When such techniques interrupt the child's ability to engage in the excess behavior, they are conceptually similar to adaptive equipment or supported postitioning techniques that allow a child with a motor disability to participate fully in various activities. However, it is important to distinguish response interruption procedures from contingent brief restraint, which is intended as a negative consequence to decrease the excess behavior that it follows. In response interruption, the emphasis is upon preventing the behavior from occurring, and/or helping the child to prevent it from occurring, while other meaningful tasks and activities are ongoing (Evans & Meyer, 1985).

There is considerable evidence that restraint procedures may take on positive reinforcement features as a function of continued use (Favell, McGimsey, & Jones, 1978). In fact, some individuals who exhibit self-injurious behavior seem to develop their own "self-restraint" procedures, such as wrapping their own hands and arms in clothing or a towel, placing them under other parts of their bodies, and so on (Favell, McGimsey, Jones, & Cannon, 1981; Sommers, 1982). Use of such self-restraint behaviors could be regarded as an adaptive self-control strategy that the child uses during periods when self-injury would otherwise occur. Assuming that such strategies can be somewhat "normalized" and can be faded to acceptable levels and forms later, there are reports of effective interventions with very severe excess behaviors of long-standing duration by using brief physical restraint as a reinforcer (Foxx & Dufrense, 1984). Protective clothing has been used effectively to reduce self-injurious behavior (Dorsey, Iwata, Reid, & Davis, 1982). Rincover and Devany (1982) maintained that protective clothing works to the extent that it eliminates that desired sensory feedback through barriers, padding, and so on that would otherwise occur from the excess behavior. Other authors have argued that protective clothing simply provides the individual with a prosthetic device that he or she can temporarily use while engaged in learning activities. Once alternative positive behaviors have been acquired and have increased, the protective devices can be faded because of the corresponding decrease in self-injury and self-restraint (Silverman, Watanabe, Marshall, & Baer, 1984).

Because restraints inhibit a range of behavior (and thus potentially interfere with the acquisition of various curricular goals and participation in various activities), *and* because students do become dependent upon restraints, their use is controversial and must always involve close monitoring and eventual fading procedures so that they can be eliminated. Most recently, two studies successfully utilized brief response interruption procedures in combination with differential reinforcement of other, more appropriate behaviors to reduce stereotyped behavior (Fellner, Laroche, & Sulzer-Azaroff, 1984) and eye gouging (Slifer, Iwata, & Dorsey, 1984). Each study reported corresponding increases in positive alternative behavior such as toy play. In both cases, response interruption was used in conjunction with simultaneous programming to increase the positive alternative behaviors. Again, these techniques should best be thought of as ecological interventions that can be used along with curricular interventions rather than as a substitute for teaching new skills.

Curricular Approaches

Peck et al. (1984) emphasize that it is not only important to teach students skills that are immediately useful in their current environments, but that priority should be given to selecting useful or functional skills for instruction *from the student's point of view*. Rather than relying upon ecological inventory processes and caregiver/teacher judgments to identify the most critical environmental performance needs, an analysis of "real social situations in which the student is already trying to accomplish something (e.g., obtain objects, initiate or terminate social interaction, request assistance) . . . is the best motivation strategy for assuring acquistion and maintenance of basic social and communication skills" (p. 109). Whenever excess behavior can be related to social-communicative intent, *a curricular goal that is immediately functional in current environments has been empirically identified*. As the child is highly motivated to meet this particular need (funtion), he or she can presumably learn an alternative, more socially appropriate strategy (form) to do so. Thus, rather than simply detracting from instructional goals, in many cases, excess behavior can provide certain evidence of a priority skill acquisition need. Peck and his colleagues propose a core of communication and social decision guidelines, with accompanying activity sequences to facilitate the acquisition of positive forms for each of their lists of critical social-communicative functions.

In contrast to the widely held notion of cognitive readiness, which has only recently been called into question (see Reichle & Karlan, in press, for a review), it is interesting that excess behavior that does appear to have communicative intent has not been emphasized as one clear sign of motivational readiness for language acquisition. Carr and Durand (1985a) maintain that communication training should be implemented as an effective treatment for excess behavior. The authors would go one step further; where excess behavior can be shown to indicate social-communicative intent, appropriate social and communication skill acquisition goals are overdue. Excess behavior may not be caused by deficits in educational programming, but its presence can be a nonambiguous sign of important skill acquisition needs.

Excess behavior can also provide useful additional clues regarding individualized instructional strategies. The actual behavioral and topographical characteristics of the excess behavior can provide information regarding a child's preferences, feedback on the child's reactions to apparently well-designed instructional and other activities, and an indication of what specific kinds of behavioral forms are already under control by that child. For example, if a child's self-stimulatory behavior involves visual stimuli (e.g., poking or pushing on his or her own eye surface or flicking his or fingers in front of a light source), this could indicate that he or she would be highly motivated to acquire a play skill that produced visual stimuli. If a child's tantrum behaviors were most frequent in one particular instructional activity (e.g., during a vocational object sorting task standing at a work bench), this might be clear information that the activity, no matter how well it seems to "match" available job opportunities, caregivers' ideas of what persons with severe disabilities can do, and/or the level of functioning and skill repertoire of this individual learner, will simply not be a meaningful occupational goal for that person. The point is that while indeed interventionists may be able to successfully replace finger flicking with an alternative play skill that involves similar sensory feedback, and that they can decrease the occurrence of tantrums by modifying a task in some way, the excess behavior should also provide them with ideas as to how best to teach that particular child in general. This includes information on what might be the most desired educational outcomes for that child from his or her perspective.

Compliance Training Jensen et al. (1983) were specifically interested in the effectiveness of various efforts to provide institutional staff with training and feedback on less intrusive management strategies to deal with severe behavior problems. In particular, they reported that focusing on training staff to primarily reinforce residents for various compliance behaviors (praising residents for following instructions, etc.) resulted in an 80% reduction in the use of soft-tie restraint, which they described as "a common means of controlling the assaultive behavior of mentally retarded residents in institutions" (Jensen et al., 1983, p. 155). They note that their results are consistent with those of Russo, Cataldo, and Cushing (1981), who reported a decrease in nontargeted behavior problems as a result of compliance training.

Singer et al. (1984) also used compliance training to successfully maintain several youth described as "at risk for institutionalization," because of their severe maladaptive behaviors, in a group home. Singer and his colleagues indicate that their procedures followed Engelmann and Colvin's (1983) guidelines, which include a multi-element procedure of requiring that directions be followed across settings, materials, and persons. To the extent that these young people learned positive responses to environmental demands that replaced the excess behavior that they initially exhibited, this intervention could be considered curricular in orientation. However, their procedures apparently also included overcorrection (a punishment procedure) whenever noncompliance occurred. Thus, it is not clear which component of the program is responsible for the noted behavioral improvements. And, of course, teaching persons with disabilities generalized "compliance" with staff instructions is not quite the same as developing a competency such as "follows rule and routines" (see Meyer et al., 1983). As a social competence, learning to follow rules and routines would involve compliance to verbal and posted instructions in some situations, but in other situations would involve adherence to rules that are no longer stated, making personal choices, and advocating for changes in rules and routines.

Toy Play   Leisure skill instruction has received increased emphasis as a critical curriculum need for persons with severe disabilities (Voeltz, Wuerch, & Wilcox, 1982). Having a varied leisure repertoire is considered essential to one's quality of life, and the absence of constructive leisure skills in persons with disabilities has been cited as a major concern expressed by caregivers (Katz & Yekutiel, 1974). Where leisure or play skills are absent and activities are not provided, free time is likely to be associated with high levels of stereotyped behavior in comparison to environments in which activities are made available (Horner, 1980). Recently, a number of studies have demonstrated a negative correlation between stereotyped behaviors and the acquisition of preferred leisure time activity skills, supporting the argument that leisure activity training is an effective intervention for certain excess behaviors (Meyer, Evans, Wuerch, & Brennan, 1985). A more constructive statement of this relationship, however, would be that whenever a child does not evidence a varied repertoire of preferred and appropriate leisure time skills and activities, he or she may be at risk for engaging in maladaptive behaviors during unstructured times. An obvious intervention is to provide leisure skill instruction. It is disappointing that so little systematic research has occurred regarding the substitutability of appropriate leisure activities for excess behavior since Favell's (1973) now classic study.

It would be equally interesting to document the incidence of excess behavior as a function of whether or not work training opportunities match learner needs and preferences and result in desired outcomes for the learner. It is clear that much research needs to be done in investigating the effects of providing meaningful work and leisure experiences upon the excess behavior repertoires of persons with severe disabilities.

Social-Communicative Interventions   As has been emphasized throughout this chapter, many excess behaviors appear to have social-communicative intent and there are promising reports of significant reductions in excess behavior as a function of acquiring contextually meaningful communication skills. Horner and Budd (in press), for example, reported a dramatic reduction in grabbing and yelling by an 11-year-old nonverbal boy with autism as a function of acquiring manual signs to communicate wants and needs in a natural setting. In their elegant, two-phase study, Carr and Durand (1985a) first documented functional relationships between certain excess behaviors and social reinforcement or task difficulty situations in four children. Corresponding hypotheses as to the function of the excess behaviors for each of the children were then formulated, and the children were taught socially appropriate communication strategies to either solicit help on difficult tasks (by saying "I don't understand") or solicit teacher attention (by saying "Am I doing good work?"). By contrasting the effects of using the appropriate functional verbalization with an irrelevant response phrase that the children were also taught, these investigators were able to validate the relationship between the acquisition of a relevant communication skill and a corresponding decrease in maladaptive behaviors.

Meyer et al. (1983) have proposed an assessment of 11 social competence functions, each of which is hierarchically organized into increasingly complex forms of a particular function. Within the measure, various excess behaviors are listed where they may serve as possible forms of, particularly, lower levels of given social competence functions. Validation of this measure is now ongoing. Implicit in the model is the assumption that acquisition of the more appropriate (and generally more complex) forms of each function may require intervention, but the presence of any form for each response category provides a starting point for curriculum planning.

Again, efforts to teach alternative social-communicative skills to replace various forms of excess behavior are rare in comparison to the extensive literature on contingency management interventions. Much work is needed to take advantage of these promising new directions.

Programming Negative Consequences

In learning theory, the term "punishment" means a planned negative contingency that reduces the future probability of a response. The colloquial use of the word, however, gives it an everyday meaning that is very close to the types of intrusive interventions addressed by the TASH Resolution (Table 1). The more neutral term "negative consequences" is used to make clear that only those natural events that provide feedback to a student that a response is unacceptable and that have none of the five characteristics mentioned in the resolution should be employed in programs for children with severe disabilities. The distinction between natural and intrusive is not difficult to make (see also Donnellan, 1984). Deliberately ignoring a child who is interrupting is a widely used parental strategy (followed by giving him or her the desired attention at an appropriate break point). In contrast, time out, while conceptually a similar extinction contingency, involves uncommon physical structures unavailable in community environments, eliminates all learning opportunities for fairly long time periods, and cannot be easily managed so as to differentially reinforce appropriate behavior (removal from timeout is contingent upon being quiet only in the artificial timeout room).

Verbal reprimands, brief physical interruption and redirection, explanation of rules, loss of privileges, extra duties and chores, or being sent to one's own room are all fairly commonly used negative consequences for nonhandicapped children (Salend, Esquivel, & Pine, 1984). Some intervention techniques that have been reported in the literature seem to resemble these strategies, but the manner in which they are applied often violates the principle of positive and natural behavioral control. For example, restitutional over-correction (Foxx & Azrin, 1972) contains one natural element (the idea of "putting to right" some damage or disruption), but is often carried out in an unnatural way, such as requiring *repeated* restitution, or even such extremes as cleaning up a far larger area than the one disturbed by the student.

It is somewhat ironic that, in certain settings, specific negative conse-quences must be artificially arranged because opportunities for natural conse-quences are no longer available—social ones in particular. For example, when children with severe disabilities are in social situations with nonhandicapped peers, the latter are quite effective in providing age-appropriate negative consequences for inappropriate behavior. Peers give simple direct verbal reprimands, physically discourage some excess behaviors such as mouthing and avoid or move away from students who are either overly aggressive or overly friendly. Adults, on the other hand, often tolerate immature behavior in students with severe disabilities. Employers and other adults in the community may be reluctant to implement standard policies with handicapped individuals that they would utilize for a nonhandicapped person's inappropriate behavior, consequences such as brief suspension, loss of pay, or assignment to less enjoyable tasks. In the absence of properly habilitative programs (including the absence of a job or meaningful activity from which the student could be suspended!), unusual and punitive procedures are presumed to be acceptable options. And although one can perhaps be relieved that highly intrusive techniques are generally seen as less acceptable (e.g., Kazdin, 1980; Witt & Elliott, in press), such criteria are largely irrelevant compared to professional standards defining educative procedures.

There are various ways in which intrusive interventions reduce edu-cational opportunities. One is to make another functional situation aversive. An example of this would be the "overcorrection" technique of making a student brush his or her teeth with a foul-tasting substance such as mouthwash or diluted tabasco sauce. This may well reduce learning of spontaneous tooth brushing, an adaptive skill. Another deleterious impact is when the intervention produces a variety of additional excess behaviors, such as emotional outbursts, struggling, or collateral negative behaviors that have often been reported (Voeltz & Evans, 1982). Such side effects have resulted in the addition of a second punishment procedure to suppress the negative reactions to over-correction, with reports that even those efforts are unsuccessful (Holburn & Dougher, 1985). To improve learning potential, negative consequences must be delivered so that the student's task performance and teacher instructional behaviors are not interrupted. This also implies that negative consequences would be delivered at a far slower rate than specific positive consequences. If the excess behavior occurs frequently, for instance, verbal reprimands would soon outweigh praise, and the instructional atmosphere would no longer be positive and effectively structured (cf. Clark & Rutter, 1981). Thus, ecological conditions may need to be rearranged and tasks selected to ensure low rates of failure and/or excess behavior. Therefore, one technique that has been used successfully with high-rate or otherwise dangerous excess behavior during instruction has been brief physical restraint (e.g., Bitgood, Crowe, Suarez, & Peters, 1980). DRO schedules alone may not be effective without the addition of such a simple physical interruption of a high frequency excess behavior (Azrin, Besalel, & Wisotzek, 1982; Slifer et al., 1984). In all cases, it is obviously important that any contingent physical restraint procedure be brief, applicable without a struggle, and can be faded systematically (see also pages 339–340).

There may be emergencies when some degree of forceful restraining is needed to prevent a student from injuring himself or herself and/or others. Proper techniques for physically limiting a student who has become uncontrollable through verbal means can be necessary. However, these emergency procedures are not learning trials. They do not produce significant permanent reduction in behavior, and, if any mechanical restraint is used (splints, straps, ties, etc.), they are rapidly incorporated into the inappropriate behavior pattern. Restraints that are natural sources of self-control or protection used by non-handicapped students are appropriate (see the section on ecological manipulations). The important point is that effective negative consequences are oriented toward enhancing self-control and clarifying social rules and expectancies. Environments that support and demand age-appropriate behaviors are the only ones in which negative feedback could be effective. And it would be difficult to conceptualize any situation in which negative consequences would be the only program strategy used. They would only be appropriate when used in conjunction with the functional curricular and ecologically oriented educational program arrangements already described.

A SUMMARY STATEMENT: EVALUATING OUTCOMES

As has been emphasized repeatedly throughout this volume, it is no longer sufficient to document changes in behavior in the classroom alone, in the context of relatively artificial instructional situations, only in the presence of the teacher. Charting decreases in the frequency or duration of behavior problems is of limited usefulness as a demonstration of behavioral change that is educationally or socially significant. Similarly, it is no longer acceptable to simply demonstrate that the child has acquired an alternative positive skill to replace the excess behavior that he or she uses while in his or her program. Claims of improvements in behavior that can be considered significant must include documentation that those improvements are evident in the child's behavior in all relevant naturalistic situations, outside of the classroom, and have maintained across time. In many cases, this will require direct programming to ensure that the learner realizes that the new skills are useful outside the instructional situation. Persons other than professionals and parents in the child's daily environments must also learn to provide the child with opportunities to use those new behaviors in responsive interactions. Teaching a play skill to replace finger flicking will have little value in the long run if the child seldom has access to enjoyable and appropriate leisure materials and activities in his or her daily life. Similarly, learning to ask for help rather than tantrum will only be effective if persons in the child's environment have acquired the skills to interact appropriately with and provide assistance in a nonextraordinary way to someone who has severe disabilities. Again, as is the case with programs designed to teach new skills, efforts to remediate excess behavior cannot be meaningful unless they reflect the conditions, circumstances, and demands of naturalistic environments.

REFERENCES

Azrin, N. H., Besalel, V. A., & Wisotzek, I. E. (1982). Treatment of self-injury by a reinforcement plus interruption procedure. *Analysis and Intervention in Developmental Disabilities, 2,* 105–113.

Barton, L. E., & Barton, C. L. (in press). An effective and benign treatment of rumination. *Journal of The Association for Persons with Severe Handicaps.*

Baumeister, A. A. (1978). Origins and control of stereotyped movements. In C. E. Meyers (Ed.), *Quality of life in severely and profoundly mentally retarded people: Research foundations for improvement* (pp. 353–384). Washington, DC: American Association on Mental Deficiency.

Bitgood, S. C., Crowe, M. J., Suarez, Y., & Peters, R. D. (1980). Immobilization: Effects and side effects on stereotyped behavior in children. *Behavior Modification, 4,* 187–208.

Borthwick, S. A., Meyers, C. E., & Eyman, R. K. (1981). Comparative adaptive and maladaptive behavior of mentally retarded clients of five residential settings in Western states. In R. H. Bruininks, C. E. Meyers, B. B. Sigford, & K. C. Lakin (Eds.), *Deinstitutionalization and community adjustment of mentally retarded people* (pp. 351–359). Washington, DC: American Association on Mental Deficiency.

Carr, E. G. (1977). The motivation of self-injurious behavior: A review of some hypotheses. *Psychological Bulletin, 84,* 800–816.

Carr, E. G., & Durand, V. M. (1985a). Reducing behavior problems through functional communication training. *Journal of Applied Behavior Analysis, 18,* 111–126.

Carr, E. G., & Durand, V. M. (1985b). The social-communicative basis of severe behavior problems in children. In S. Reiss & R. Bootzin (Eds.), *Theoretical issues in behavior therapy* (pp. 219–254). New York: Academic Press.

Carr, E. G., & Newsom, C. D. (in press). Demand-related tantrums: Conceptualization and treatment. *Behavior Modification.*

Carr, E. G., Newsom, C. D., & Binkoff, J. A. (1980). Escape as a factor in the aggressive behavior of two retarded children. *Journal of Applied Behavior Analysis, 13,* 101–117.

Clark, P., & Rutter, M. (1981). Autistic children's responses to structure and to interpersonal demands. *Journal of Autism and Developmental Disorders, 11,* 201–217.

Colman, R., Frankel, F., Ritvo, E., & Freeman, B. J. (1976). The effects of fluorescent and incandescent illumination upon repetitive behavior in autistic children. *Journal of Autism and Childhood Schizophrenia, 6,* 157–162.

Donnellan, A. M. (1984). The criterion of the least dangerous assumption. *Behavioral Disorders, 9,* 141–150.

Donnellan, A. M., LaVigna, G. W., Zambito, J., & Thvedt, J. (1985). A time limited intensive intervention program model to support community placement for persons with severe behavior problems. *Journal of The Association for Persons with Severe Handicaps, 10*(3)

Donnellan, A. M., Mirenda, P. L., Mesaros, R. A., & Fassbender, L. L. (1984). Analyzing the communicative functions of aberrant behavior. *Journal of The Association for Persons with Severe Handicaps, 9,* 201–212.

Dorsey, M. F., Iwata, B. A., Reid, D. H., & Davis, P. A. (1982). Protective equipment: Continuous and contingent application in the treatment of self-injurious behavior. *Journal of Applied Behavior Analysis, 15,* 217–230.

Dunlap, G. (1984). The influence of task variation and maintenance tasks on the learning and affect of autistic children. *Journal of Experimental Child Psychology, 37,* 41–64.

Dunlap, G., & Koegel, R. L. (1980). Motivating autistic children through stimulus variation. *Journal of Applied Behavior Analysis, 13,* 619–627.

Engelmann, S., & Colvin, G. (1983). *Generalized compliance training.* Austin: Pro-Ed.

Evans, I. M. (1985). Building systems models as a strategy for target behavior selection in clinical assessment. *Behavioral Assessment, 7,* 21–32.

Evans, I. M., & Meyer, L. H. (1985). *An educative approach to behavior problems: A practical decision model for interventions with severely handicapped learners.* Baltimore: Paul H. Brookes Publishing Co.

Evans, I. M., & Nelson, R. O. (in press). The behavioral assessment of children. In A. R. Ciminero, K. S. Calhourn, & H. E. Adams (Eds.), *Handbook of behavioral assessment* (2nd ed.). New York: John Wiley & Sons.

Evans, I. M., & Voeltz, L. M. (1982). *The selection of intervention priorities in educational programming of severely handicapped preschool children with multiple behavior problems.* (Final report, Grant No. G00-790-1960). Honolulu: University of Hawaii Departments of Psychology and Special Education. ERIC Report # ED 240 765.

Favell, J. E. (1973). Reduction of stereotypes by reinforcement of toy play. *Mental Retardation, 11,* 21–23.

Favell, J. E., Azrin, N. H., Baumeister, A. A., Carr, E. G., Dorsey, M. F., Forehand, R., Foxx, R. M., Lovaas, O. I., Rincover, A., Risley, T. R., Romanczyk, R. G., Russo, D. C., Schroeder, S. R., & Solnick, J. V. (1982). The treatment of self-injurious behavior (AABT Task Force Report: Winter, 1982). *Behavior Therapy, 13,* 529–554.

Favell, J. E., McGimsey, J. F., & Jones, M. L. (1978). The use of physical restraint in the treatment of self-injury and as positive reinforcement. *Journal of Applied Behavior Analysis, 11,* 225–241.

Favell, J. E., McGimsey, J. F., Jones, M. L., & Cannon, P. R. (1981). Physical restraint as positive reinforcement. *American Journal of Mental Deficiency, 85,* 425–432.

Favell, J. E., McGimsey, J. F., & Schell, R. M. (1982). Treatment of self-injury by providing alternate sensory activities. *Analysis and Intervention in Developmental Disabilities, 2,* 83–104.

Federal Register (1975), *4* (35), 7412.

Fellner, D. J., Laroche, M., & Sulzer-Azaroff, B. (1984). The effects of adding interruption to differential reinforcement on targeted and novel self-stimulatory behaviors. *Journal of Behavior Therapy and Experimental Psychiatry, 15,* 315–321.

Foxx, R. M., & Azrin, N. H. (1972). Restitution: A method of eliminating aggressive-disruptive behavior of retarded and brain damaged patients. *Behaviour Research and Therapy, 10,* 15–27.

Foxx, R. M., & Dufrense, D. (1984). "Harry": The use of physical restraint as a reinforcer, timeout from restraint, and fading restraint in treating a self-injurious man. *Analysis and Intervention in Developmental Disabilities, 4,* 1–13.

Gaylord-Ross, R. (1980). A decision model for the treatment of aberrant behavior in applied settings. In W. Sailor, B. Wilcox, & L. Brown (Eds.). *Methods of instruction for severely handicapped students* (pp. 135–158). Baltimore: Paul H. Brookes Publishing Co.

Hill, B. K., & Bruininks, R. H. (1984). Maladaptive behavior of mentally retarded individuals in residential facilities. *American Journal of Mental Deficiency, 88,* 380–387.

Holburn, C. A., & Dougher, M. J. (1985). Behavioral attempts to eliminate air-swallowing in two profoundly retarded clients. *American Journal of Mental Deficiency, 89,* 524–536.

Horner, R. H. (1980). The effects of an environmental "enrichment" program on the behavior of institutionalized profoundly retarded children. *Journal of Applied Behavior Analysis, 13,* 473–491.

Horner, R. H., & Budd, C. M. (in press). Acquisition of manual sign use: Collateral reduction of maladaptive behavior, and factors limiting generalization. *Education and Training of the Mentally Retarded.*

Hung, D. W. (1978). Using self-stimulation as reinforcement for autistic children. *Journal of Autism and Childhood Schizophrenia, 8,* 355–366.

Iwata, B. A., Dorsey, M. F., Slifer, K. J., Bauman, K. E., & Richman, G. S. (1982). Toward a functional analysis of self-injury. *Analysis and Intervention in Developmental Disabilities, 2,* 3–20.

Jensen, C. C., Morgan, P., Orduno, R., Self, M. A., Zarate, R. G., Meunch, G., Peck, D., Reguera, R. A., & Shanley, B. (1983). Changing patterns of residential care: A case study of administrative and program changes. *Journal of Organizational Behavior Management, 5,* 155–174.

Katz, S., & Yekutiel, E. (1974). Leisure time problems of mentally retarded graduates of training programs. *Mental Retardation, 12,* 54–57.

Kazdin, A. E. (1980). Acceptability of alternative treatments for deviant child behavior. *Journal of Applied Behavior Analysis, 13,* 259–273.

Koegel, R. L., & Covert, L. (1972). The relationship of self-stimulation to learning in autistic children. *Journal of Applied Behavior Analysis, 5,* 381–387.

LaVigna, G. W., & Donnellan, A. M. (in press). *Alternatives to punishment: Non-aversive strategies for solving behavior problems.* New York: Irvington Press.

Lazar, J. B., & Rucker, W. L. (1984, November). *The effectiveness of manipulating setting factors on the ruminative behavior of a boy with profound retardation.* Paper presented at the annual conference of the Association for Persons with Severe Handicaps, Chicago, IL.

Lovaas, O. I., Koegel, R. L., Simmons, J. Q., & Long, J. S. (1973). Some generalization and follow-up measures on autistic children in behavior therapy. *Journal of Applied Behavior Analysis, 6*, 131–166.

Mayeda, T., & Sutter P. (1981). Deinstitutionalization: Phase II. In R. H. Bruininks, C. E. Meyers, B. B. Sigford, & K. C. Lakin (Eds.), *Deinstitutionalization and community adjustment of mentally retarded people* (pp. 375–381). Washington, DC: American Association on Mental Deficiency.

Meyer, L. H., Evans, I. M., Wuerch, B. B., & Brennan, J. M. (1985). Monitoring the collateral effects of leisure skill instruction: A case study in multiple-baseline methodology. *Behaviour Research and Therapy, 23*, 127–138.

Meyer, L. H., Reichle, J., McQuarter, R. J., Evans, I. M., Neel, R. S., & Kishi, G. S. (1983). *Assessment of social competence (ASC): A scale of social competence functions.* Minneapolis: University of Minnesota Consortium Institute.

Mulligan, M., Lacy, L., & Guess, D. (1982). Effects of massed, distributed and spaced trial training on severely handicapped students' performance. *Journal of The Association for the Severely Handicapped, 7*, 48–61.

Neel, R. S. (1983, November). *Assessment of communication form and function in children with autism.* Paper presented at the annual meeting of The Association for Persons with Severe Handicaps, San Francisco, CA.

Peck, C. A., Schuler, A. L., Tomlinson, C., Theimer, R. K., Haring, T., & Semmel, M. I. (1984). *The social competence curriculum project: A guide to instructional programming for social and communicative interactions.* Santa Barbara: University of California Special Education Research Institute.

Reichle, J., & Karlan, G. (in press). The selection of an augmentative system in communication intervention: A critique of decision rules. *Journal of The Association for Persons with Severe Handicaps.*

Rincover, A., & Devany, J. (1982). The application of sensory extinction procedures to self-injury. *Analysis and Intervention in Developmental Disabilities, 2*, 67–81.

Rojahn, J. (1984). Self-injurious behavior in institutionalized, severely/profoundly retarded adults—prevalence data and staff agreement. *Journal of Behavioral Assessment, 6*, 13–27.

Russo, D. C., Cataldo, M. F., & Cushing, P. J. (1981). Compliance training and behavioral covariation in the treatment of multiple behavior problems. *Journal of Applied Behavior Analysis, 14*, 209–222.

Salend, S. J., Esquivel, L., & Pine, P. B. (1984). Regular and special education teachers' estimates of use of aversive contingencies. *Behavioral Disorders, 9*, 89–104.

Schroeder, S. R., Mulick, J. A., & Rojahn, J. (1980). The definition, taxonomy, epidemiology, and ecology of self-injurious behavior. *Journal of Autism and Developmental Disorders, 10*, 417–432.

Schuler, A. L. (1981, November). *The relationship between disruptive behaviors and communicative deficiencies.* Paper presented at the annual meeting of the American Speech and Hearing Association, Los Angeles, CA.

Silverman, K., Watanabe, K., Marshall, A. M., & Baer, D. M. (1984). Reducing self-injury and corresponding self-restraint through the strategic use of protective clothing. *Journal of Applied Behavior Analysis, 17*, 545–552.

Singer, G. H. S., Close, D. W., Irvin, L. K., Gersten, R., & Sailor, W. (1984). An alternative to the institution for young people with severely handicapping conditions in a rural community. *Journal of The Association for Persons with Severe Handicaps, 9*, 251–261.

Skinner, B. F. (1953). *Science and human behavior.* New York: Macmillan Publishing Co.

Slifer, K. J., Iwata, B. A., & Dorsey, M. F. (1984). Reduction of eye gouging using a response interruption procedure. *Journal of Behavior Therapy and Experimental Psychiatry, 15,* 369–375.

Sommers, D. (1982). Self-injurious behavior and self-restraint. *the Behavior Therapist, 5,* 4.

The Association for Persons with Severe Handicaps. (1981, November). Resolution on intrusive interventions. *TASH Newsletter, 7* (11), 1–2.

Voeltz, L. M., & Evans, I. M. (1982). The assessment of behavioral interrelationships in child behavior therapy. *Behavioral Assessment, 4,* 131–165.

Voeltz, L. M., & Evans, I. M. (1983). Educational validity: Procedures to evaluate outcomes in programs for severely handicapped learners. *Journal of The Association for the Severely Handicapped, 8*(1), 3–15.

Voeltz, L. M., Evans, I. M., Derer, K. R., & Hanashiro, R. (1983). Targeting excess behavior for change: A clinical decision model for selecting priority goals in educational contexts. *Child & Family Behavior Therapy, 5,* 17–35.

Voeltz, L. M., Evans, I. M., Freedland, K., & Donellon, S. (1982). Teacher decision making in the selection of educational priorities for severely handicapped children. *Journal of Special Education, 16,* 179–198.

Voeltz, L. M., Wuerch, B. B., & Wilcox, B. (1982). Leisure and recreation: Preparation for independence, integration, and self-fulfillment. In B. Wilcox & G. T. Bellamy (Eds.), *Design of high school programs for severely handicapped students* (pp. 175–209). Baltimore: Paul H. Brookes Publishing Co.

Wahler, R. G., & Fox, J. J. (1981). Setting events in applied behavior analysis: Toward a conceptual and methodological expansion. *Journal of Applied Behavior Analysis, 14,* 327–338.

Warren, F., & Juhrs, P. (1984). Community philosophy: Continuum of services. *Community News, 1*(1), 1–2.

Weeks, M., & Gaylord-Ross, R. (1981). Task difficulty and aberrant behavior in severely handicapped students. *Journal of Applied Behavior Analysis, 14,* 449–463.

White, O. R. (1980). Adaptive performance objectives: Form versus function. In W. Sailor, B. Wilcox, & L. Brown (Eds.), *Methods of instruction for severely handicapped students* (pp. 47–69). Baltimore: Paul H. Brookes Publishing Co.

Witt, J. C., & Elliott, S. N. (in press). Acceptability of classroom management strategies. In T. R. Kratochwill (Ed.), *Advances in school psychology.* Hillsdale, NJ: Lawrence Erlbaum Associates.

Zentall, S. S., & Zentall, T. R. (1983). Optimal stimulation: A model of disordered activity and performance in normal and deviant children. *Psychological Bulletin, 94,* 446–471.

Chapter 12

The Application of Technology to the Education of Persons with Severe Handicaps

Alan M. Hofmeister and Susan G. Friedman

During the last decade, computers have appeared in almost every aspect of society. This emergence has fostered the common classification of developing technologies as components of the computer age; however, they are really part of a much larger phenomenon. The content of society's knowledge base is rapidly changing, and an overexpanding number of technological tools are needed to process, access, and apply this knowledge. This phenomenon—much larger in scope than the increased visibility of computers—is known as the information age.

The field of special education is a part of the current information age. As evidenced by the passage of Public Law 94-142, progress has far exceeded simple maintenance of persons with handicaps. Great strides have been made in the quantity and quality of educational services demanded and provided. Parallel to society at large, the content of special education's knowledge base is rapidly changing. Determining the extent to which the technological tools of the information age can assist in processing, accessing, and applying special education services is one of the most interesting challenges facing special educators today.

Exploration of the applicability of technology to education is in its infancy. To date, there have been few technological innovations directed specifically toward persons with severe handicaps. As a result, a discussion of the applicability of technology to this population of learners is necessarily limited more to description of the potential than evaluation of the role of technology.

Although there are presently far more questions than answers, and far more possibilities than examples, the potential for technological assistance is promising and covers a wide range of possible functions. The computer is the major technological tool involved in this potential, but it is not the only tool; nor is direct instruction the only goal in need of technological assistance. Much creativity and a strong commitment to research will be needed before technology applied to persons with severe handicaps "comes of age."

It is also important to recognize that the application of technology to education will continue to be an ongoing process. The very presence of technology in an educational environment will change the environment in ways that cannot yet be determined. This means that discussion of the applicability of technology to education will always be, to some degree, a matter of endless possibilities.

The purpose of this chapter is to describe several technological tools currently available in this stage of the information age and the varied roles that these tools can potentially play in improving direct and indirect services to persons with severe handicaps.

AVAILABLE TECHNOLOGIES POTENTIALLY APPLICABLE TO PERSONS WITH SEVERE HANDICAPS

Computer Technology

As mentioned above, computers are the major information age tool. With the development of the microcomputer, educational applications of the computer were expanded beyond business functions to include instructional applications as well. As with general education, there are presently three ways in which computer technology can potentially assist in the provision of services to persons with severe handicaps: computer-assisted instruction (CAI), computer-managed instruction (CMI), and computer-based communication systems for the individual and the service providers. The reader will notice that these categories of computer use are not mutually exclusive. There is much overlap among them.

Computer-Assisted Instruction (CAI) CAI involves the use of the computer for direct contact with the learner. In this capacity, the computer can be used for the practice of recently acquired skills and the teaching of new skills.

There are several characteristics of CAI that account for much of the widespread interest in its application to education, but current research suggests that an unquestioning emphasis on CAI should be tempered with caution (Alderman, Swinton, & Braswell, 1978; Deaton, 1983; Fisher, 1983; Hartley, 1977). Some CAI characteristics do not contribute significantly to improved educational service. For example, CAI is often lauded for its ability to allow learners to "learn at their own rate" by student-controlled presentation of instruction. However, there are other instructional sources, such as a textbook, that also offer this capability with considerable ease and at a modest cost. Alternatively, the capacity of the computer, rather than the student, to adjust the rate of instruction based on learner responses is indeed one of the major and relatively unique characteristics of CAI. The number of repetitions of a particular unit of instruction can be varied, as can be the speed with which material is presented and the amount of material covered. During an instructional interaction, then, the computer can record, analyze, and modify the instructional sequence presented to the learner based on the ongoing analysis of student responses.

Another characteristic of CAI is the ability of the computer to provide a range of feedback to a learner's response. This capability is, clearly, of major importance to effective instruction. However, the notion of feedback is too often confused with the notion of reinforcement, especially where computers are concerned. Feedback refers to only the provision of information. Whether or not receiving that information serves a reinforcing capacity (i.e., that is, serves to increase the frequency of a certain behavior) is highly subject to individual variation. Capitalizing on the feedback capability in such a way as to make CAI reinforcing has been a formidable challenge to software developers.

The capability of the computer to faithfully replicate instruction is also an important characteristic of CAI. Programs of varied structure and sequence can be developed based on specific behavioral objectives that reflect known skill hierarchies relevant to many different types of subject matter and students. These programs can be delivered specifically as intended over and over again. With the computer's ability to collect information on the strengths and weaknesses of instructional interactions, these programs can be systematically improved. The technology's capabilities to faithfully replicate instruction and provide detailed information needed for program improvement may be two of the most important CAI characteristics.

There are presently four basic approaches to CAI. The first is the programmed instruction approach that makes use of both drill and practice programs designed to help consolidate a specific skill, and tutorials designed to introduce and consolidate a skill area. The second approach is artificial intelligence–based CAI designed to emulate the human thinking process, such as the problem-solving stages and procedures that a tutor uses to identify the type of error a child might make in a subtraction problem. The third approach is simulation-based CAI. The classic example of simulation CAI is the flight simulators used in pilot training programs. The last approach to CAI is tool application. Word processing and calculation software are examples of instructional tools.

Determining the extent to which these CAI approaches can be applied to persons with severe handicaps should include consideration of their service providers as well. CAI holds much promise for teacher and parent training. Given its present level of development, CAI may have its greatest impact when applied to the training and support of professional and paraprofessional staff.

The approaches and characteristics described above are used to help exemplify the possibilities. To date, the degree of CAI effectiveness has been highly variable, depending on its role (total or supplemental), the subject area (math is generally more effective than language arts), and student population. However, it must be stressed that, given the rapid and diverse nature of technological developments, the limitations that may be uncovered in the present attempts to apply CAI are not likely to be lasting.

Computer-Managed Instruction (CMI)   CMI is one of the oldest and most extensive applications of the computer to education. It is concerned with the diagnosis of pupil's strengths and weaknesses, the prescription of learning activities based on this diagnosis, and the monitoring of these learning activities. Defined by Burke (1982) as "[t]he systematic control of instruction by the computer . . . characterized by testing, diagnosis, learning prescriptions, and thorough record keeping" (p. 188), CMI refers to essentially the same program activities required under Public Law 94-142. These tasks are critical to the effective conduct of instructional programs for persons with severe handicaps.

There are three basic approaches to the computer software used for CMI activities: 1) large comprehensive systems, 2) programs prepared from general-purpose data based management programs, and 3) small systems developed from word processing software. Depending on the size and sophistication of the CMI system being used, the educator can request a range of computer-generated reports. The greatest breadth of information can be obtained from the large comprehensive systems that offer the following variety of data based information.

Individual Pupil Progress Reports   Individual pupil progress reports show the progress that a learner is making in his or her individual program of study. The report usually identifies which skills have been mastered and the date on which they were mastered. This computer-generated information can be of enormous assistance to the development, monitoring, and modification of individual programs, and for teacher accountability to learners, parents, and administrators as well.

Class Reports   Class reports group the individual information on one chart. This information can be particularly useful for identifying problematic curricular areas and is also helpful in planning and preparing for future instructional activities. Class grouping reports can identify those curricular objectives that several children may be working on at the same time. This type of report can generate useful information for the planning and evaluation of small group instruction.

Instructional Resource Reports   Instructional resource reports specify instructional objectives cross-referenced with instructional materials relevant to the objective. In addition, many CMI programs can provide curricular and instructional analysis reports that identify specific objectives that are being mastered and those that represent problems to significant numbers of pupils. These reports generally combine pupil data at the school or district level and can be invaluable for curriculum supervisors or principals who systematically evaluate program effectiveness.

Because of the similarity between CMI activities and the inventory problems of small businesses, data based management programs originally intended for small business are highly applicable for developing partial or comprehensive programs for education. In the case of an individual classroom, there is a constantly changing inventory of the skill mastery levels of all pupils. Several of these CMI systems have been developed for microcomputers, and a major strength of this data based management software is that it allows the individual teacher with no computer programming experience to develop very powerful, flexible record keeping systems at a modest cost.

Some record keeping can be done with word processing software. This application can be especially useful for the individual teacher, although it does not have the power or flexibility of the systems previously described.

The value of CMI for the education of persons with severe handicaps appears to be based on the fact that it stresses the same variables listed by Briggs (1968) and Rosenshine and Berliner (1978) as most relevant to effective instruction. That is, CMI required that subject matter be analyzed and sequenced, that pupils be assessed for entering competencies and carefully monitored, and that the focus be on specific objectives. Whitney and Hofmeister (1983), describing the impact of a CMI system designed to monitor the progress of special education pupils (many classified as "severely emotionally disturbed") noted three benefits. The first benefit, and major purpose, was the elimination of errors of omission where students simply "fall through the cracks." The second benefit was the rather painless introduction to computers and the associated observation that teachers and administrators began exploring other applications of the computer. The third benefit was "an artifact of development." Users were forced to look at their existing practices and revise them to ensure that there were logical and meaningful relationships among the different instructional and administrative activities that comprise the total educational effort. It is an understatement to say that these benefits are relevant to the provision of services to persons with severe handicaps.

In light of the important contributions that CMI can offer, it is essential to realize that CMI will be effective only when educators commit to using the information it generates for improvement. At present it is, unfortunately, all too common for special educators to view the record keeping associated with Public Law 94-142 as just an end product. As with all data, then, if the data generated by CMI are not used to systematically improve program practices, their use will likely perpetuate meaningless information. Using a computer to perform inappropriate tasks faster is a possibility that definitely exists, but it is a possibility that must be diligently guarded against.

Computer-Based Communication and the Service Provider Many of the current advances in the education of persons with severe handicaps have depended on the extensive collaboration of a wide range of expert personnel. Interdisciplinary service teams often include medical specialists, speech and language specialists, vocational specialists, and a host of paraprofessionals such as parents and aides. Persons with handicaps requiring services from these experts, and the experts themselves, are often dispersed across wide geographic areas. The availability of the information that these personnel can provide is often critical to the ability to effectively maintain persons with severe handicaps within the community. Additionally, when one examines the components of a community-based instructional program, with its large numbers of diverse instructional objectives, its multitude of environments, and its needs for continuity across environments, there can be little doubt that communication is central to maintaining program quality. Accessing, processing, and applying this information is a serious problem currently faced by educators of persons with severe handicaps. With the existing and developing technologies of the information age, there is enormous potential for increasing the accessibility of a wider range of resources rapidly, at a modest cost, and regardless of distance. By capitalizing on this potential, the problems of time and distance can be minimized, thus increasing the quality and quantity of services provided.

Videotex "Videotex" is the term used to describe any system that makes computer-stored information available via computer screens or a printing terminal. Videotex exists in two forms: interactive and noninteractive. Either form can provide a multitude of information dissemination functions as well as CAI and CMI applications.

Interactive videotex information usually moves via telephone lines. The user may interact through a personal computer, a terminal with a screen and keyboard, an adapted television set, or a printing terminal. Most interactive videotex systems are designed to allow the individual to conduct indepth searches through large amounts of information. The individual can work in either a search mode or an interactive mode in which the individual adds information to the system as well as retrieves information.

With interactive videotex technology, it would be possible for a parent to access a demonstration of a specific instructional sequence on a videodisc stored at a remote site, receive suggestions for teaching a specific self-care skill, or treat a problem behavior. The parent could then leave a message for a professional requesting help on a problem not covered by the packaged instructional program. The professional could then reply in person, by phone, or by electronic mail.

"Electronic mail" is the term for the electronic distribution of messages. While most forms of telecommunications are "realtime" communications, electronic mail is not. Messages are sent and stored until the recipient wishes to read them. This facility has some of the advantages of normal postage, which allows the individual to choose when to read or respond, but with the speed of electronic communications.

Electronic mail systems usually include electronic bulletin boards, where messages of general and specific interest can be "posted." A number of states have developed statewide videotex systems that include bulletin boards for special educators, curricular specialists such as the math and language arts teachers, employment counselors, and information for school administrators. It will only be a matter of time before well-developed bulletin boards will exist for professionals and paraprofessionals working with persons with severe handicaps.

Noninteractive videotex is usually transmitted in association with television signals. A television signal that is received in the home is capable of carrying more information than is usually used. If a modification is made to the television set, additional information can be accessed. One example of this capacity for extra information transmission is the captioning service available for the deaf—a noninteractive videotex service. Noninteractive videotex information bases are usually limited to a few hundred pages of information, and while individuals with modified televisions can select from among the several hundred available pages of information, they cannot enter information into the system. These noninteractive videotex services often duplicate some of the offerings of the daily newspaper and carry information that can be updated daily.

The pages of information offered by these noninteractive videotex services are available for purchase in a manner similar to that in which advertising space is sold on television. This means that it is possible for schools to obtain command of a number of the available videotex information pages to keep the community informed on school events and educational offerings.

It would be logical to expect the school district to maintain information pages in a noninteractive videotex system for parents with particular needs, such as the parents of persons with severe handicaps.

Practical Uses of Computer Technology in Communication

Almost every human sensory facility used for communication can be augmented by computer technology. Because many who are severely handicapped have some type of sensory impairment, computer technology is important in providing access to the world of nonhandicapped individuals. Considerable progress has been made in using technology to enhance visual, auditory, and tactile input and output.

While the contribution of rehabilitation engineering has been extensive (Perlman & Austin, 1984; Vanderheiden, 1982), much remains to be done. Using a computerized language board with a single-switch scanner will provide access to most computer software as well as facilitate communication via speech synthesis or visual displays with other individuals. However, if the person has an intellectual handicap, then access to most existing software may not be that meaningful. Also, providing "communication" is not the same as providing "conversation." The common assumption that technological advances have provided the necessary "communication" aids is not correct.

The response time in normal conversation is 3 seconds. If response time exceeds 10 seconds, communication is labored. With technological assistance, it may take a communicatively disabled person several minutes to communicate a single thought. Baker (1982) summed it up as follows:

> The source of the difficulty seems to lie outside the realm of technology. The very nature of the alphabet is at the heart of the problem. The quantity of information borne by a single letter is quite small. Information transfers conducted in such small units will necessarily require many units. Biomedical engineering cannot change this. Perhaps a semantic approach can. (p. 187)

It is obvious, then, that hardware needs "intelligent" software and informed application if the potential is to be achieved. Informed application will require that the priorities of the individual be considered.

For the person with severe handicaps, extensive leisure time is one of the realities (Cheseldine & Jeffree, 1981; Schleien, Kiernan, & Wehman, 1981). Given that the recreational computer market exceeds the education market in size, one would hope that the adaptation of the technology to meet the recreational needs of those who are severely handicapped would be more advanced than its present state.

There is research evidence to support the use of computer-based video games for persons with severe handicaps. Sedlack, Doyle, and Schloss (1982) were successful in teaching video game playing to three youths with severe handicaps. These researchers also took the necessary steps to facilitate generalization to a community setting and concluded that such recreation skills helped "bridge the gap between retarded and nonretarded individuals when integrated into community settings" (p. 336).

Powers and Ball (1983) demonstrated that persons with severe handicaps could be effectively involved in video games. The persons involved in the Powers and Ball study were in a living unit for adolescents and young men who were nonambulatory and profoundly retarded. Powers and Ball justified such involvement as follows:

> Video games enable developmentally disabled people to manipulate their environment and receive immediate auditory and visual feedback. They provide an opportunity for cooperation, competition, social interaction and cognitive and sensorimotor development. And also, they are age-appropriate. Poor initial performance challenges the players to improve. Repetition develops physical agility, directionality, strategy and sequence-learning. The graphics, color, sound and fast pace capture and increase the attention span of the players and decreases inappropriate behaviors. (p. 49)

Videodisc Technology

A recent development in the exploration of media combinations with the computer is videodisc technology. Videodisc technology consists of the videodisc, videodisc player, and the equipment necessary to produce the videodisc. Videodiscs are produced by "pressing" video and audio information onto a disc that looks like a silver phonograph album. A major advantage of the videodisc over other computer technologies is that it is an omnibus medium; motion picture film, slides, graphs, and very high quality audio can be pressed on the videodisc. Each side of a videodisc is capable of storing 54,000 individual frames of information. When single frames are played at 30 frames per second, each side of the disc contains 30 minutes of motion. Associated with each video track are two audio tracks. The two audio tracks enable applications such as the presentation of information in two different languages.

The videodisc can be played at regular speed, in single frame stop motion, and at various speeds of slow motion. The videodisc also has rapid random access capabilities. It can search all 54,000 frames in less than 3 seconds.

Videodiscs can be designed to play in a linear fashion, that is, straight through from beginning to end like home entertainment movie videodiscs. The technology becomes significantly more powerful for educational uses when interfaced with a microcomputer. Microcomputer-interfaced videodiscs are referred to as interactive videodiscs. Possessing the capabilities of both the microcomputer and the videodisc, these systems can be programmed to present a segment of instruction that requires a response from the learner and, depending on that response, can present appropriate feedback, remediation, or subsequent instruction.

Of major importance to educational applications is the capability of the interactive videodisc to maintain data on student progress. Data, such as the number of correct and incorrect responses and the amount of time it took to respond to each question, can assist in individualizing instruction and in improving the instructional format and specific content.

One disadvantage of the videodisc is that it is currently a read-only medium; once the information is pressed on the videodisc, it cannot be changed; however, "read/write" discs are being developed.

Interactive videodiscs have been designed for a variety of students and content areas. There are videodiscs to support the study of biology, geography, economics, art, history, physics, law, and astronomy. The applicability of videodisc technology to special education, currently being researched at Utah State University, is described in the next section.

EXAMPLES OF CURRENT APPLICATIONS OF TECHNOLOGY

Two examples of current research and practice of technological applications in education can be illustrated by describing the Interactive Videodisc in Special

Education (IVSET) project (Thorkildsen, 1982; Thorkildsen, Allard, & Reid, 1983), and the Goal-Based Education Management System (GEMS) (Stevenson, Edwards, & Bianchi, 1978). Both examples are highly relevant to the exploration of technology and persons with severe handicaps.

IVSET

The IVSET project at Utah State University has developed seven instructional videodiscs and one assessment videodisc intended for persons with intellectual handicaps. The first, "Matching," teaches students to identify and group objects of different sizes, shapes, and colors. "Time Telling" teaches students to tell time with both clockface and digital formats. "Identification of Coins" teaches students to identify pennies, nickels, dimes, quarters, and half-dollars. "Functional Words" teaches students to sight-read survival words such as "exit" and "restroom." "Sight-Reading" teaches students to read a beginning sight vocabulary. "Directional Prepositions" teaches students the concepts of prepositions such as "on" and "under." "Social Skills" teaches skills required for appropriate adaptive behavior with peers and adults. The assessment videodisc, "Math Assessment," is a criterion-referenced math assessment instrument intended to assess the math skills of students in grades 1–3.

One unique feature of the IVSET system is the touch panel device attached to the television monitor. The touch panel consists of a light interrupt system that allows the student to interact with the videodisc by directly touching the screen. Thus, students do not have to possess the reading or fine motor skills typically needed to use a computer terminal. These reading and fine motor skills have, in the past, limited the applicability of more traditional CAI to persons with severe handicaps. When students touch their answer choice on the screen, two light beams transmitted from each axis of the touch panel are interrupted, and the point of interruption is read by the computer in x/y coordinates. These coordinates are matched to the coordinates stored in the computer to score the correct answer. Thus, the following instructional interaction can be executed:

1. The computer directs the videodisc to present an instructional segment on the television screen.
2. The instructional segment ends with a question or test sequence. The student responds to the question by touching one of the answer choices presented on the screen.
3. The computer reads the coordinates where the light beams were interrupted by the student's touch and matches those coordinates to the computer-stored coordinates for the correct answer.
4. If the answer is correct (i.e., the coordinates match), the computer directs the videodisc to play the next instructional segment.

5.   If the answer is incorrect (or the test is not passed), the computer directs the videodisc to branch to a remediation segment; or, if the same answer is incorrect several times, the system signals the teacher for assistance with a beeping sound.

In addition to presenting instruction, the IVSET software maintains data on student progress. These data include the starting and ending question number, the number and percent of correct and incorrect items, the number of times the student did not respond to a question, the number and length of the instructional session, and the number of times that the program signaled for teacher assistance. This information can be viewed on the television screen, or a hard copy can be obtained from the printer in either graphic or summary form.

A number of field tests have been conducted with the IVSET videodiscs listed above. These tests were conducted with different populations of handicapped learners to determine the extent to which the programs could be considered effective (Thorkildsen, 1982; Thorkildsen et al., 1983). In general, the IVSET videodiscs with academic skill content were most effective with learners with mild intellectual handicaps, but were not as effective with young (4–13-year-old) learners with moderate and severe intellectual handicaps. The disc designed to teach selected social interaction skills has been shown to be effective with persons with moderate handicaps and has yet to be evaluated with persons with severe handicaps. The lack of success of some of the discs may relate to the content level. Also, the ability of videodisc technology to supply the needed physical prompts may be reducing the system's effectiveness. Those children whose handicaps included motor involvement had a difficult time steadying their hands to touch the screen. Other human interface alternatives using single-switch devices would reduce problems related to motor involvement.

Given the comparative lack of success with the learners with severe handicaps, two directions are suggested. The setting or the approach to content and presentation could be modified. To change the setting, the goal of teacher-independent videodisc instruction could be modified for persons with severe handicaps. The integration of videodisc technology with teacher-delivered instruction needs to be explored with the goal of developing a cohesive instructional program that can be richer than what a teacher alone can provide.

Given the similarity in technology (to the participant) between interactive videodisc instruction and video games, then the success of video game instruction (Powers & Ball, 1983; Sedlack et al., 1982) suggests a direction for content modification. This approach would study those elements of video games that make them successful, and apply them to instructional presentations. If any of the social consequences supplied by an effective human tutor are to be deleted, a powerful attention-commanding alternative will be needed. The attention-commanding elements of video games may provide such a source. The identification of such elements has been conducted by Malone (1980) using nonhandicapped individuals. Malone grouped the elements in three areas: challenge, fantasy, and curiosity. Included in the challenge area were such elements as variable difficulty levels, multiple level goals, hidden information, and randomness. A review of these few elements suggests that video games represent a potential source of techniques to increase the interest values of instructional programs for students with severe handicaps.

GEMS

The GEMS program was developed and validated for students in regular classrooms and for some mildly handicapped populations. The program exemplifies the major characteristics of an appropriately implemented CMI system and is worthy of research for application to students with severe handicaps.

In the GEMS project, the data on student behavior was used as "the essential research base" for program improvement. By analyzing the progress of students through the specific curricular units, staff at the school and district levels were able to identify areas of program weakness. The information was then used to remediate these weaknesses. Alternative teaching strategies were developed, curricular sequences were revised, instructional materials were changed, and inservice training programs were developed. The effects of these changes were monitored by using the computer to analyze the achievement gains of pupils. Ineffective practices and materials were replaced. What resulted was a continuous process of intervention, evaluation, and program revision. In the GEMS project, the effect of this process was substantial. Within a 2-year period, the average reading comprehension scores of the 6,000 pupils involved in the program jumped 10 percentile points, from 45 to 55, and the average vocabulary score jumped 21 percentile points, from 45 to 66.

In describing the elements of the CMI program that were important in producing change, the GEMS staff included the following characteristics:

1. The system provided a program and continuum that allowed for the integration of all curricular levels.
2. A formative evaluation system was implemented that allowed teachers to evaluate their teaching effectiveness as well as student mastery.
3. The system provided a rational basis for inservice training.
4. The system clarified the curriculum and allowed for the evaluation of all strategies and materials, commercial or teacher-made, including new computer-related technologies.
5. The system supported the teachers as decision-makers and provided opportunities for teachers to apply their innovativeness, expertise, and creativity to operate in the classroom.

6. The system provided the continuity and accountability needed to support competency-based instructional progammming.

Again, the presence of computerized banks of data on pupil achievement is of little value by itself. There must be a commitment by teachers and administrators to use the data to help direct improvements. This commitment to self-evaluation and professional accountability was present in the GEMS project and was *the* major factor responsible for the success of GEMS. The computer was a tool—a tool that was used with skill and sensitivity to make a significant improvement in the achievement levels of thousands of pupils.

Although the GEMS project was not focused on learners with severe handicaps, the model is essentially an IEP process carried out for program improvement and not just for outward compliance with federal law.

For the future, a high priority must be placed on the adaptation and validation of existing CAI and CMI procedures to the needs of persons with severe handicaps. Programs such as the GEMS project must be explored in that such a system would allow a range of interventions to be evaluated and improved in a field setting.

Preparing for the Future

In planning for the future, the primary objective should be to meet valid needs and not just implement technology. Improvement in the quality of life of persons with severe handicaps will not necessarily be achieved by the implementation of technology. It must be certain that technology does not supplant an important service. For example, the replacement of a human tutor by a computer may be no great achievement if the only reason that a student looks forward to instruction is the social contact with the tutor.

To effectively capitalize on the new technologies, the developing technologies must be monitored while still trying to enhance proven practices. With this approach in mind, the following section examines a new technology—artificial intelligence—and a proven characteristic of many successful programs for persons with severe handicaps—the use of paraprofessionals to ensure cost-effective instructional engagement.

ARTIFICIAL INTELLIGENCE

It has been called the "fifth generation" or "second computer age," and it is characterized, not so much by increases in the power of hardware, but by dramatic increases in the sophistication of software. In discussing this second computer age, Feigenbaum and McCorduck (1983) observed:

> We view it as the important computer revolution, the transition from information processing to knowledge processing, from computers that calculate and store data to computers that reason and inform. Artificial intelligence is emerging from the laboratory and is beginning to take its place in human affairs. (p. 1)

The early years of artificial intelligence (AI) research were characterized by a belief that it was possible to identify a few basic laws of reasoning, couple those laws with the speed and memory of powerful computers, and produce practical "intelligent" applications. In reality, these general-purpose, problem-solving approaches proved to be too weak when applied to specific problems. In reaction, a number of researchers de-emphasized computer information processing. For them, the structure and nature of knowledge itself became the area of interest. The terms "knowledge engineering" and "knowledge programming" reflect their thinking. Expert systems are a result of their work.

Stefik et al. (1983) describe this area of AI as follows:

> Expert systems are problem-solving programs that solve difficult problems requiring expertise. They are termed knowledge based because their performance depends critically on utilizing facts and heuristics used by experts. Expert systems have been used as vehicles for AI research with the rationale that they provide a forcing function for research issues in problem solving and a reality test for their workability. (pp. 59–60)

Expert systems are already making contributions in medicine, geology, mathematics, chemistry, and computer science. The potential exists for expert system technology to make a considerable contribution to special education. This can be demonstrated by studying the categories of application where the technology has been successful. These generic categories include: interpretation, prediction, diagnosis, design, planning, monitoring, debugging, repair, instruction, and control (Hayes-Roth, Waterman, & Lenat, 1983). When expert system technology is applied to instruction, it is often known as an intelligent tutoring system (ITS).

A review of the above listed generic categories indicates the potential that exists to match "knowledge engineering" approaches with problem areas in special education. The categories of diagnosis, planning, and instruction are highly related to important special education activities. Applications of expert systems technology to special education are under development (Colbourn & McLeod, 1983). Researchers have developed a system to provide computer-guided diagnosis of learning problems with learning disabled students. After comparing computer-guided diagnoses with those of human evaluators on 22 files, the researchers concluded:

> In general, the results of the evaluation were encouraging; the expert system's diagnoses were accurate. Furthermore, because of the system's speed at analyzing error patterns, its diagnostic reports included more information than those of the human diagnosticians. This was particularly noticeable with regards to the analysis of phonics skills. (p. 37)

If it is possible to use expert systems to capture and replicate the problem-solving processes of expert diagnosticians and instructors in special education, then artificial intelligence can make a major contribution. The research community should be searching for ways to increase the quality and availability of such core special education services.

In addition to increasing the availability of high quality, direct services, AI research could improve thinking about teaching and learning. This point was made by Sleeman and Brown (1982) when describing the development of intelligent tutoring systems. They stated that:

Much of what constitutes domain-specific problem solving has never been articulated. It resides in the heads of tutors, getting there through experience, abstracted but not necessarily accessible in an articulatable form. Since a computer-based coach has limited opportunities to learn experientially, at least in the foreseeable future, its designers must make this knowledge explicit. Likewise in an area of tutorial strategies, much remains to be discovered and made explicit. We hope that educational theorists will find the explicit formulation of tutoring, explanation and diagnostic processes inherent in intelligent tutoring systems a test bed for developing more precise theories of teaching and learning. (p. 9)

APPLICATION OF TECHNOLOGY TO
PROFESSIONAL AND PARAPROFESSIONAL SUPPORT

Hofmeister (1982) has noted that:

When we work with the nonhandicapped and the mildly handicapped, we tend to view the teacher as the primary instructional agent. When we start applying the new technologies to the needs of the severely handicapped, we should remember that the paraprofessional, and the parent in particular, have a major instructional role. It may be that the new technologies will have their greatest impact initially when applied to the training and support of the paraprofessionals that have the most contact with the severely handicapped child. (p. 53)

Reference has already been made to the need for programs for learners with severe handicaps to focus on the communication tools of the information age. These communication tools may well increase the ability to effectively maintain persons with severe handicaps in the community.

CONCLUSION

A motivation driving many of the early researchers investigating teaching machines, programmed learning, and computer-assisted instruction was the notion of universal excellence. As far back as 1966, in congressional hearings, advocates of computer-assisted instruction discussed the potential of this new tool to "do for every child what once could be done for only a few" (Hofmeister, 1983).

Given the needs of persons with severe handicaps, it is unlikely that present approaches to using CAI will offer much in the way of attaining universal excellence. It is, however, very likely that existing and developing technologies can contribute significantly to reaching this goal by decreasing many of the information communication problems related to the education of those who are severely handicapped. The technological tools of the information age can significantly increase efficient access to information that directly supports instruction such as training, planning, and ongoing assistance to professionals and paraprofessionals.

There are several issues that must be considered. First, availability of technological tools does not guarantee their use. Many administrators, teachers, and teacher trainers appear reticent to embrace the potential of technological applications to education. Second, limited fiscal resources may hinder the wide-scale adoption of available tools regardless of their capabilities. Third, electronic information cannot and should not replace all other forms of communication. Even if we were to become highly committed to technological information exchange, we would need to determine the extent to which we want and need direct personal contact.

For technology to assist in reaching the goal of universal excellence, continued creativity, research, and serious commitment will be needed. The impact of the information age on the education of learners with severe handicaps will also depend on the abilities of professionals in the field to capitalize on the advantages and avoid the problems associated with the new technologies.

REFERENCES

Alderman, D. L. Swinton, S. S., & Braswell, J. S. (1978). *Assessing basic arithmetic skills across curricula. Computer assisted instruction and compensatory education: The ETA/LAUSD study*. Princeton, NJ: Educational Testing Service.
Baker, B. (1982). Minspeak, *Byte, 7*(9), 186–202.
Briggs, L. J. (1968). *Sequencing of instruction in relation to hierarchies of competence*. A final report prepared by the Instructional Methods Program of the Center for Research and Evaluation in Applications of Technology in Education (CREATE), American Institutes for Research.
Burke, R. L. (1982). *CAI sourcebook*. Englewood Cliffs, NJ: Prentice-Hall.
Cheseldine, S. E., & Jeffree, D. M. (1981). Mentally handicapped adolescents: Their use of leisure. *Journal of Mental Deficiency Research, 25,* 49–59.
Colboum, M., & McLeod, J. (1983). Computer guided educational diagnosis: A prototype expert system. *Journal of Special Education Technology, 6*(1), 30–37.
Deaton, W. J. (1983, April). *Computer assisted instruction: No effects and unexpected relationships*. Paper presented at annual meeting of the American Educational Research Association, Montreal, Canada.
Feigenbaum, E. A., & McCorduck, P. (1983). *The fifth generation*. Reading, MA: Addison-Wesley Publishing Co.
Fisher, G. (1983). Where CAI is effective: A summary of the research. *Electronic Learning, 3*(3), 82–84.
Hartley, S. S. (1977). Meta-analysis of the effects of individually paced instruction in mathematics (Doctoral dissertation, University of Colorado at Boulder). (University Microfilms International No. 77–29, 926).

Hayes-Roth, F., Waterman, D. A., & Lenat, D. B. (1983). An overview of expert systems. In F. Hayes-Roth, D. A. Waterman, & D. B. Lenat (Eds.), *Building expert systems*. Reading, MA: Addison-Wesley Publishing Co.

Hofmeister, A. M. (1982). Microcomputers and the special education teacher: New technologies. *Journal of Special Education Technology, 5*(4), 53.

Hofmeister, A. M. (1983). *Computer applications in the classroom*. New York: Holt, Rinehart & Winston.

Malone, M. (1980). *What makes things fun to learn? A study of intrinsically motivating computer games*. Palo Alto, CA: Cognitive and Instructional Sciences Group, Palo Alto Research Center.

Perlman, L. G., & Austin, F. G. (1984). *Technology and rehabilitation of disabled persons in the information age*. Alexandria, VA: National Rehabilitation Center.

Powers, J., & Ball, T. S. (1983). Video games to augment leisure programming in a state hospital residence for developmentally disabled clients. *Journal of Special Eduation Technology, 6*(1), 48–57.

Rosenshine, B. V., & Berliner, D. C. (1978). Academic engaged time. *British Journal of Teacher Education, 4*, 3–16.

Schleien, S. J., Kiernan, J., & Wehman, P. (1981). Evaluation of age-appropriate leisure skills program for moderately retarded adults. *Education and Training of the Mentally Retarded, 16*, 13–19.

Sedlack, R. A., Doyle, M., & Schloss, P. (1982). Video games: A training and generalization demonstration with severely retarded adolescents. *Education and Training of the Mentally Retarded*, 332–336.

Sleeman, D., & Brown, J. S. (1982). *Intelligent tutoring systems*. London: Academic Press.

Stefik, M., Aikins, J., Balzer, R., Benoit, J., Birnbaum, L., Hayes-Roth, F., & Sacerdoti, J. (1983). The architecture of expert systems. In F. Hayes-Roth, D. A. Waterman, & D. B. Lenat (Eds.), *Building expert systems*. Reading, MA: Addison-Wesley Publishing Co.

Stevenson, G., Edwards, P., & Bianchi, E. (1978). *Program statement: GEMS*. Report submitted to the Office of Educational Dissemination Review Panel.

Thorkildsen, R. J. (1982). *Interactive videodisc for special education technology*. (Final Report, ED 230187). Logan: Utah State University.

Thorkildsen, R. J., Allard, K., & Reid, R. (1983). The interactive videodisc for special education project: Providing CAI for the mentally retarded. *The Computing Teacher, 7*(2), 73–76.

Vanderheiden, G. (1982). *Computers can play a dual role for disabled individuals. Byte, 7*(9), 136–162.

Whitney, R. A., & Hofmeister, A. M. (1983). Management of special education compliance information: The MONITOR system. *AEDS Monitor, 21*(9), 12–18.

Index

Excess behavior—*continued*
in natural contexts, 329
selecting excess behavior intervention priorities in, 320–324
self-regulatory function of excess
behavior in, 327
social-communication function of
excess behavior in, 327
three levels of excess behavior
intervention decisions in, 322
aversive punishment strategies and,
316
exemplary demonstrations of, 316
intervention and, 333–345
curricular approaches to, 340–343
distinction between behavioral control and change in, 334
ecological approaches to, 335–340
programming negative consequences in, 343–345
three broad categories of, 333
resolution on intrusive interventions
for, 317
special challenge of, 315
summary statement of evaluating outcomes of, 345–346

Families, 127–157
overview of history and current policy on, 127–130
cultural deficit model and,
128–129
intervenor role and, 129
movement toward more humanitarian view in, 128
Public Law 94-142 and, 128
parents in
attitudes about, 127
roles of, 128, 130–137
research about, 130–137, 151–152
service delivery in, 147–151
assessment guide for family systems approach and, 150–151
gathering information for, 148
model programs for, 148
Family systems theory, 137–147
assessment guide for family systems
approach in, 150–151
family functioning and, 144–145
family interaction in, 142–144

family life cycle in, 146–147
family structure in, 137–142
Functional curriculum, 99–104
see also Community intensive
instruction

GEMS, 362–363
General case programming, 291–295
see also Generalized skills
Generalized skills, teaching, 289–314
challenge facing teachers in, 290–291
common assumptions regarding, 289
general case instruction, 291–295
defining instructional universe for,
291
five steps of, 291
selecting teaching examples for,
292
selecting testing examples for, 292
sequencing teaching examples for,
293–294
teaching and, 294
testing and, 294–295
implications of inclass simulation,
299–310
age-appropriate simulation and,
308
building simulations to teach generalized behavior and, 304–307
community training and, 308
comparisons of trainings and, 309
effectiveness of simulation training, 309
efficiency of simulation training,
309
functional definition of simulation
and, 302
generalized control of maladaptive
behavior, 309
integration and, 308
methodological issues in generalization and simulation research,
310
reasons for simulations and,
302–304
research on use of simulation training and current needs, 308–310
traditional approach to simulation
and, 300–301
values affecting simulation and,
307–308